ENGLISH SNUFF-BOXES

ENGLISH
SNUFF-BOXES

—

G. Bernard Hughes

MacGibbon & Kee   London

Granada Publishing Limited
First published in Great Britain 1971 by MacGibbon & Kee Ltd
3 Upper James Street London WIR 4BP

ISBN 0 261 63227 2
Printed in Great Britain by Ebenezer Baylis & Son Ltd
The Trinity Press, Worcester, and London

For My Good Friend
GWENOCH TALBOT

CONTENTS

ILLUSTRATIONS

CHAPTER I

Introduction

ELEGANT Englishmen of Tudor and Stuart days seldom stirred from home without pomander or perfumed pouncet box. From these they could inhale aromatic perfumes to counteract the community's unsavoury odours. Until early in the reign of James I (1603–25) men carried them attached to black cord or in the pocket. Fashion evolved a prescribed procedure for handling these jewels and this eventually became virtually a ceremonial ritual. Perfume was superseded in the pouncet box from the 1590s by coarsely ground tobacco leaves.

This powder, snuffed up the nostrils, had quickly established itself as a pungent protection against various maladies. The word *snuff* is an inflexion of the old northern verb *sniff* – a term that described strong inhalation through the nostrils or expressing angry impatience long before the introduction of powdered tobacco leaves.

The story that Sir Walter Raleigh (1552–1618) introduced tobacco into England has no basis in fact. In 1584, the very year in which Ralegh founded the colony of Virginia, Queen Elizabeth issued a decree, still preserved in the Public Record Office, condemning the use and abuse of tobacco. The smoking of tobacco appears to have been customary in England twenty years earlier, for in 1563 the Statute of Labourers laid down that no man or woman should be employed in making clay tobacco pipes without serving a five-year apprenticeship in the craft. The inference may be drawn that tobacco-smoking in England dates from late in the reign of Henry VIII. When Ralegh, at the age of eighteen, was appointed a gentleman volunteer in the army, tobacco was actually being grown in England. Its culture was recorded by Matthias de l'Obel and

Petrus Pena in their book published in London during 1570: l'Obel later became chief botanist to James I.

By the end of the 16th century the powdered snuff was carried in a small box with a tightly fitting hinged lid. Such boxes were elegant trifles for the well-to-do and were successors of the gold pouncet box. More modestly they were made in pewter, horn and latten. Harrison's *Chronicle* in 1580 described snuff-taking as 'the taking-in of the finely pulverised Indian herbe called Tabaco by an instrument formed like a little ladell.' Dekker in his *Gulls Horne-booke*, 1609, confirmed the use of the ladle or snuff-spoon: 'the gallant must draw out his tobacco-box, the ladle for the cold snuff into the nostril. . . . '

In his *Counterblaste to tobacco*, 1604, James I complained that peers and rich merchants were spending several hundred pounds a year on tobacco and snuff. In an effort to discourage this luxury the king placed tobacco under a royal monopoly and increased excise duty from twopence to 6s 10d per lb, its shop price then being about 3s 4d per oz – almost as much as a labourer's weekly wage. Even so, ten years later nearly 7,000 London shops, vintners and alehouses were retailing tobacco. This naturally encouraged the production of tax-free native-grown tobacco and in 1615 a pamphlet was published: 'An Advise how to plant Tobacco in England: and how to bring it to colour and perfection, to whom it may be profitable and to whom harmful.'

In the same year Joshua Sylvester, court poet to James I, was denouncing snuff as 'hell-dust, England's shame, a madness, a frenzy, that by the devil's agency has been brought from the savages to England'. Tobacco was eventually cultivated in about forty English and Scottish counties. Charles II, however, condemned native tobacco-growing as a penal offence in the 1660s.

At this time snuff became known colloquially as 'snush', a term continued into the Georgian period. An advertisement in the *London Gazette* in 1682 announced the loss of 'a Round Gold Snush-Box'. Ned Ward in *The London Spy* a few years later, invariably used the term snush when commenting upon the use of

snuff-boxes in London coffee-houses. Of one eminent but un-
named establishment he wrote: 'We squeezed thro' the Fluttering Assembly of Snuffing Peripateticks . . . the Clashing of their
Snush-Box Lids, in opening and shutting made more noise than
their Tongues: and sounded as Terrible in my Ears as the
Melancholy Ticks of so many Death Watches.' Later he noticed
the demand for 'perfumed snushes'.

So far snuff had always been rasped by the purchaser of the
carotte of tobacco leaves or else bought ready-powdered from
foreign hawkers. Charles Lillie, a perfumer and tobacconist of
the Strand, London, in 1702 recorded the capture of about fifty
tons of milled snuff from Spanish ships at anchor in Vigo Bay
and at Port St Mary. Lillie wrote: 'This sort of bale snuff had
never been seen or known in England before, except through
the Spanish Jews who in the present case, bought up almost the
whole quantity at a considerable advantage. From the quantity
of snuff thus distributed throughout the kingdom, novelty being
quickly embraced by us in England, arose the custom and
fashion of snuff-taking.' Lillie described snuff-taking as being
'chiefly a luxurious habit among foreigners residing here, and
the English gentry who have travelled abroad. Amongst these
the mode of taking the snuff is with pipes of the size of quills out
of small spring boxes. These pipes let out a very small quantity
of snuff upon the back of the hand, and this is snuffed up the
Nostrils with the intention of producing sneezing, which I need
not say forms now no part of the design or rather fashion of
snuff-taking.'

During the next decade snuffing became an important social
accomplishment. Schools were established for teaching the now
fashionable art of snuff-taking. An advertisement inserted by
Charles Lillie in No. 138 of *The Spectator*, 1711, outlines the
curriculum of his school: 'The exercise of the snuff-box according to the most fashionable airs and motions, in opposition to the
exercise of the fan, will be taught with the best plain or perfumed snuff, at Lillie's, perfumer in the Strand, and attendance
given for the benefit of young merchants about the Exchange,

for two hours every day at noon, at a toy shop near Garraway's Coffee-house. There will be taught the ceremony of the snuff-box, rules for offering snuff to a stranger, a friend, or a mistress, with an explanation of the careless, the scornful, the politic and the surly pinch, and the gestures proper to each of them.'

Horace Walpole's collection of snuff-boxes in the mid-century included an oval and 'a square-shaped snuff-box of lapis lazuli mounted in gold; a circular gold snuff-box, engine-turned, with the image in wax of Madame la Marquise du Deffand's dog Tonton' which she bequeathed to Walpole.

The approved method of taking snuff evolved at this time continued until its decline in the 1860s. The snuff-box was carried in the left hand waistcoat pocket from which it was withdrawn with the right hand and passed to the left hand. The user gave the lid three smart taps near the hinge, opened the box and inspected the contents. A pinch of snuff was then taken and held for a second or two between thumb and first finger of the right hand while the box was closed and put away, so that the pinch of powder could be placed on the back of the left hand or on the thumb-nail and inhaled by both nostrils simultaneously without any grimace. Less elegantly but more commonly, however, the snuff was carried directly to the nose and snuffed with each nostril in turn. By this method the final gesture could be to close the box with a flourish. Sneezing formed no part of fashionable snuff-taking. The preliminary tapping of the snuff-box was to attract the powder away from the opening of the essentially tight-fitting lid and so avoid an undignified cloud of dust. The complete ritual was outlined in an anonymous pamphlet of 1750.

The fashionable Georgian snuff-taker selected his snuff from a wide range of ready-made snuff rather than rasping his own: sweet, strong or salt; fine, medium or coarse; dry, semi-moist or moist; and scented with lemon, jasmine, orange flowers, rose, verbena, bergamot or cloves. Many snuffers enriched the character of their snuff by adding such ingredients as mustard, ginger, ambergris or green tea. More commonly inexpensive snuff was perfumed by carrying a fragrant tonka bean in the snuff-box. Sold as 'snuff-beans' these were black almond-shaped seeds from the *dipterix odurata* tree of Guiana.

The most popular of the finer snuffs was macouba, dispensed by snuffmen who ground and sifted together 40 parts of French or St Omer tobacco leaves with 20 parts of powdered fermented Virginian stalks. To this was added 2½ parts of finely powdered rose petals. The whole was then moistened with salt and water and thoroughly incorporated. After being worked up with salts of tartar it was packed in lead foil to preserve its delicate aroma.

A bill from Fribourg & Treyer, who have operated at No. 34 Haymarket since 1720, to Lord Pelham, dated 21 August 1787, states that they 'Make and Sell all Sorts of French Rappees, Spanish, Portuguese, Scotch and High Dry'd Irish Snuffs'. One of the most fashionable snuffs sold here throughout the reign of George III (1760–1820) was Spanish bran at three guineas a pound. This snuff was accompanied by a two shilling phial of vinagrillo, an aromatic rose-scented vinegar imported from Spain. Small quantities were used to moisten the Spanish bran.

Fastidious snuff-takers laid down snuff as they laid down cellars of wine, many reserving a small room specially for storing snuffs and preparing them for daily use. The Earl of Harrington, formerly Lord Petersham and a celebrated snuff connoisseur, left snuff in his cabinets to the value of more than £3,000 when he died in 1829. He prided himself that he possessed a jewelled snuff-box for every day of the year. To a friend who expressed admiration for his snuff-box of light blue Sèvres porcelain, he commented, 'Yes, it's a nice box for summer, but would not do for winter use'. The connoisseur considered that the quality used during the morning was unsuitable for evening enjoyment: his cabinets contained morning and evening snuffs and for each an appropriate spoon.

When snuff-taking was at its height the *Ladies Journal* calculated in 1788 that the habitual snuff-taker took a pinch every ten minutes and this, with the ceremony of blowing and wiping the nose, occupied one and a half minutes. The editor declared that

2

in a snuff-taking life of forty years, two years would be dedicated to 'tickling the nose' and two more years to blowing it. The same magazine in 1823 vigorously attacked the practice of snuffing by ladies, stating that 'it bestows a cadaverous hue upon the complexion; destroys the sense of smell, stops up the nose, leaves a dirty patch on the upper lip, causes snuffing and grunting. In the case of men, ladies can never return a snuff-taker's kiss'.

Professor Ure in the 1830s discussed the prevalence of adulterated snuff despite legislation making this unlawful. He declared that snuff he had analysed contained a large proportion of starch and cereals, peameal, bran, sawdust, malt, rootlets, fustic, even ground glass and the deadly oxide of lead. Also sold ready prepared to snuff-makers were milled refuse leaves such as those of senna and rhubarb, coloured with burnt sienna and yellow ochre and made pungent with ammonia.

More than a century after rasped tobacco had first become established as a pungent perfume the snuff-box became a flamboyant accessory among the fashionable. It was Beau Nash who dazzled the nobility and rich gentry with his elegant handling of jewelled snuff-boxes after he was made Master of Ceremonies at Bath in 1704.

Oliver Goldsmith in his *Life of Richard Nash* recorded that in 1738 the Prince of Wales, in appreciation of the delights of Bath, presented Nash with a large gold enamelled snuff-box. 'Upon this some of the nobility thought it would be proper to give snuff-boxes, too: they were quickly imitated by the middling gentry and soon it became the fashion to give Nash snuff-boxes.' Many ladies at Bath were compulsive snuff-takers. Before stepping into the water the visitor was presented with a small floating dish in which she placed her snuff-box and handkerchief for use whilst traversing the bath.

Snuff-boxes were made in a wide range of materials from costly chased gold to inexpensive pewter and horn. Prior in his *Cupid and Ganymede*, 1709, described a snuff-box 'set with Bleeding Hearts and Rubies, all pierc'd with diamond darts'. Snuff-box design was glamorised by artist-jewellers creating an unceasing flow of new patterns in almost every branch of industrial art. This was ridiculed in a notice published in *The Tatler*, 7 March, 1710, regarding gold snuff-boxes displayed in the shops at that time, stating that 'a new edition will be put out on Saturday next, which will be the only one in fashion until after Easter. The gentleman that gave fifty pounds for the box set with diamonds may show it till Sunday, provided he goes to church, but not after that time, there being one to be published on Monday which will cost four-score guineas. They were made by the celebrated gold chaser, Charles Mather,' who was known as 'Bubble Boy'.

When the elaborate social ritual of the snuff-box had become acceptable in the drawing room, goldsmiths, chasers and jewellers created boxes resplendent with precious stones and gems. Gold and silver were set with flashing jewels as gifts for ladies. Many of these elegant small boxes, however, were intended as bonbonnières, to contain breath-sweetening comfits and it is difficult to distinguish these from snuff-boxes. By the mid-18th century similar boxes might be used, too, to contain sponges soaked in aromatic vinegar. Sir Ambrose Heal's collection of trade cards contains illustrations of several such 'spunge boxes'.

The London Tradesman by R. Campbell, 1747, describes the work of the 'snuff-Man who buys Tobacco from the Tobacconist, and makes it into several Sorts of Snuff, by cutting it small with an Engine, drying it before the Fire, and grinding it in a Mill. He seldom takes an Apprentice, but employs Labourers, who work at so much a Pound. This Trade is abundantly profitable, but now much over-stocked'. Campbell also adds that 'the Tobacconist's skill consists in recognizing the Properties of Tobacco, and his profit arises from the Difference between buying and selling. If they take any apprentices they are taught to cut, with an engine for the purpose, are employed in stripping the Leaf off the Stems and in spinning the Pig-Tail: it requires neither much Strength nor Ingenuity. The Trade is reputable and profitable and requires a large stock to set up with.' Labourers were paid twelve shillings a week for operating the 'engine' and preparing the tobacco for use.

Snuff now began to be ground in factory mills operated by horses walking round in never-ceasing circles. I observed this mode of power in use as late as the 1930s. Several mills might be seen at work in a single factory, each grinding about 30 lb of snuff each day. The tobacco stalks and leaves were first chopped by hand, piled into heaps, moistened and covered with cloths in a warm room where they were left to ferment for several weeks. After high fermentation this mass was reduced to dust in large wood-lined iron mortars, ground by heavy slowly moving pestles. This tobacco dust formed the basis for many types of snuff.

In 1747 too, *A General Description of All Trades* devoted a paragraph to Georgian snuff-box makers. 'The introduction of snuffing gave rise to and made these Artists become necessary, who have not been wanting from time to time to invent a great Variety of Fashions, but also to bring them to surprising degrees of beautiful workmanship, in all manner of Metals, Stones, Shells, who are continually striving to improve and vary them, in order to strike the Taste of the Curious.

'Their Work is easy, but very ingenious, the masters of which are not very numerous, though they take Apprentices. Their working hours are usually from six to nine, in which time a good hand will earn 3s or 4s, but in common not above 2s. A man may set up for himself with about £20.'

The trade card of Anne Vict and Thomas Mitchell, Cornhill, advertised in 1742 that they made 'Snuff-boxes of Gold, Silver, Mother of Pearl, Tortoiseshell, Agat, Amber, Ivory, &c.'. No classification of shapes by period is possible. To speak of the rounds of Queen Anne, the ovals of George I or the rectangles of George II is wrong for these were the prevailing shapes throughout the entire period and nearly every geometrical form is represented.

Snuff-boxes were necessarily carried close to the body as the chill must be taken from snuff to bring out its bouquet. Special snuff-box pockets were incorporated in clothing. Dean Swift in 1712 recorded that when he bought a new gold snuff-box 'the Duchess of Hamilton made me Pockets like a woman's, with a Belt and Buckle, for you know that I wear no wastcoat in Summer: and there are severall divisions, and one on purpose for my box'. Seven years later Tom D'Urfy wrote that 'a wench gave snuff to me out of her Placket pocket' – a small pocket inserted in the skirt. More usually the lady carried her snuff-box in a large pocket tied round the waist under the skirt. Not until the late 1790s did slender fashions require an alternative to this bulky pocket in the shape of the small handbag, known as an 'indispensible'. In 1799 *The Times* noted the new fashion for carrying a small bag to contain handkerchief, snuff-box and other necessities.

George IV was, like his mother Queen Charlotte, a copious snuffer: twelve varieties of fresh snuff were placed upon his wine table each day. During his Regency and reign he collected several hundred magnificent gold and jewelled snuff-boxes, most of which Queen Victoria had converted into personal jewellery. His Civil List expenditure on snuff-boxes was £7,000 a year and complaints were made by Parliament that he presented snuff-boxes to the value of about £15,000 to ministers on the signing of any treaty.

In the reign of William IV (1830–37) snuffing ceased to be a highly fashionable accomplishment associated with the nobility. Costly snuff-boxes were becoming personal accessories of the newly industrial rich. *Hints on Etiquette*, 1835, referred to snuff-taking as 'an idle, dirty habit, practised by stupid people in the unavailing endeavour to clear their stolid intellect and as it is not a custom particularly offensive to their neighbours, it may be left to each individual taste as to whether it be continued or not. An *Elégant* cannot take much snuff without decidedly losing caste.'

Very few snuff-boxes were seen at the Great Exhibition, 1851. Those catalogued were in silver, elaborately ornamented in high relief, then once more hand-worked: there was a renewed vogue for classic scenes such as Daphne teaching Chloe to play the flute. For everyday use the most common size was little more than half-an-inch thick and a couple of inches long. Wooden tobacco pipes came into extensive use during the 1850s bringing about a lessening demand for the fashionable snuffs.

PRICES

The economist Dr Franz Pick affirmed in 1970 that antique snuff-boxes sold in 1969 showed a 75 per cent increase over the values of the previous year. The value of diamonds during the same period rose by only 20 per cent. The magnitude of this appreciation makes it impossible to value closely snuff-boxes that fall within the collector's orbit.

Astronomical prices were reached in 1969. A gold snuff-box made in 1726, its lid set with a tortoiseshell panel enriched with a monogram in diamonds, sold for £23,000. In May of that year Christies sold an ornate gold snuff-box made in 1744 for 16,000 guineas. A millionaire might pay as much as £4,000 for an early Georgian snuff-box of jewelled gold in which to carry his pep pills, whereas his secretary would perforce be satisfied with a mid-19th century box of tortoiseshell set in a silver plated nickel mount costing a pound or so.

Antique snuff-boxes in gold are comparatively rare and always very costly. A George I (1714–27) example, three inches wide, its cover chased with a Mercury and Argus scene enclosed in borders chased with scrolling foliage, was sold in 1970 for 820 guineas. A gold box, chased and dated 1736, bought a few years ago for £2 made 500 guineas in the sale rooms during 1968. Early 19th-century snuff-boxes are sometimes equally valuable. An engine-turned example made by A. J. Strachan, London, in 1803 sold for 440 guineas in 1970 and another by the same maker hallmarked 1827, for 660 guineas.

Here are a few prices obtained by Christies early in 1970 for factory-made silver snuff-boxes of collectors' quality:

Peter & Anne Bateman, London, 1791. Gilt, oval, cover chased with classical figures in relief within a *rocaille* cartouche. Width three inches. 170 guineas.

Samuel Pemberton, Birmingham, 1805. Decorated with scrolls and foliage on an engraved ground within a Greek key pattern border. 25 guineas. Snuff-boxes of this popular type are not rare.

Matthew Linwood, Birmingham, 1808. Plain with moulded sides and the cover set with a jasper plaque. Width 2½ in. 40 guineas.

Thropp & Taylor, Birmingham, 1812. Gilt with incurved sides and panels chased with diapered oak foliage. Width 2¾ in. 150 guineas.

A series of press-embossed views dating from the William IV period fell within the £30–£50 range. The embossment on those by Thomas Spice was so exaggerated that parts of the view projected as much as a quarter of an inch above the lid. Values of these reached as much as 100 guineas.

The condition of the hall-marks on silver snuff-boxes affects their collectors' interest. Examples struck with a set of hallmarks difficult to decipher lose up to 50 per cent of their market value.

Gold mounted rock crystal is now rare. A Mayfair jeweller in 1970 paid 820 guineas for a barrel-shaped example of the late 18th century. Bloodstone snuff-boxes, fashionable throughout the Georgian period, are always costly. A gold-mounted snuff-box set top and bottom with a bloodstone and hallmarked 1740 sold for 350 guineas; a London-made example with its surface engine-turned and dated 1803 was sold in December 1969 by King and Chasemore for 490 guineas; and a month earlier one with its mount bearing the 1840 hallmark sold for 460 guineas.

Agate snuff-boxes are often unrecognised and may be bought for a few shillings. A gold-mounted example of cartouche form with the cover and base each set with a mocha stone agate, and attributed to about 1740, was sold by Christies for 180 guineas in June 1970. A less attractive oval example cut from solid striated agate and gold mounted, dating to about 1800, sold for 50 guineas. A gold mounted onyx bordered with chased flowers and foliage and engine-turned sides, by Charles Rawlings, London, hallmarked in 1823, made 340 guineas.

The knowledgeable collector of pre-1780 pinchbeck distinguishes this metal at a glance from gilded brass. Bargains have been possible for some dealers class such boxes as brass and fine examples have been sold for a matter of shillings. Yet Christies obtained 90 guineas for a rectangular example with bombé sides and a cover set with a jasper ware plaque.

Mother of pearl snuff-boxes with silver mounts and lids painted with scenes command prices ranging between 20 and 50 guineas, but plain early Victorian examples are to be had at a fraction of these prices.

In June 1970 many Staffordshire enamel snuff-boxes of the late 18th century appeared on the market including a rectangular example painted in colours with flower sprays within *bianco sopra bianco* scroll cartouches and trellis work, with mounts of gilded metal. Measuring 2¼ in. wide, this sold for 32 guineas. Two ovals 3½ and 4 in. wide sold for 40 guineas each. A fine Battersea enamel snuff-box, bought in the late 1920s for £2, its approximate retail value at the time of manufacture, sold for 600 guineas. Collectors unfamiliar with this branch of English craftsmanship should inspect and handle some of the fine enamel snuff-boxes in our national museums and beware of reproductions.

Common snuff-boxes in poor condition are valued at no more than £2 each. For instance, a plain surfaced Sheffield plate snuff-box with a badly worn lid revealing large areas of copper was seen in Canterbury priced at £7. It would have been an expensive purchase at more than a pound.

Art and Antiques Weekly in the issue dated 18 July 1970 illustrated a Georgian horn snuff mull. A photograph had been submitted to five provincial dealers for their estimates of its retail value. The prices given ranged from £9 to £30.

Snuff Rasps and their Cases:
Spoons: Handkerchiefs

SNUFF RASPS AND THEIR CASES

MOST SOCIAL customs prompt the development of a highly personalised art of their own. When snuff-taking was transformed from a plebeian indulgence into a fashionable accomplishment by the 1690s, the snuff rasped by dealers from carottes of tobacco tended to be adulterated with titillating pepper, touch wood or one of the sternutatory herbs. This established a need for personal snuff-rasps so that snuff-takers could grind their own powder direct from a carrot-shaped plug of tightly rolled tobacco leaves. These would have been soaked in one of several spiced oils, providing snuff connoisseurs with a range of flavours that successfully masked the bad breath prevalent at the time and was a pungent protection against ill odours. The plug, known as a carotte from early in the 17th century, was drawn a few times over the sharp, jagged teeth of the silver or steel rasp, providing a supply of powdered snuff to be carried in the snuff-box so that a pinch of the powder could be placed on the back of the hand and sniffed up the nose. This freshly prepared snuff was known by its French name *tabac râpé*. The term, anglicised as 'rappee', was long applied to a coarse, inexpensive snuff made from darker, unoiled tobacco leaves.

Of necessity the sharp teeth of the rasp had to be protected by a case or cover of silver, ivory or a wood such as box-wood, walnut or pear-wood which soon became an accepted detail among a gentleman's toilet accessories. Length ranged between about seven and twelve inches, but there were diminutive three-inch rasps, too, for the pocket, kept in wear-resistant cases of leather or embroidered cloth.

The best of these snuff rasps, now splendidly patinated, have become collectors' treasures. Their convex covers may be exquisitely decorated with all-over patterns. The silver may be tooled in relief embossments, the ivory carved, the wood carved or inlaid with ivory or exotic woods of contrasting colour. Some are brightly japanned. Dean Swift recorded in 1711 that he ground his snuff on a rasp fitting into an ivory case.

Subjects for rasp case ornament included the period's favourite Old Testament stories such as Susannah and the Elders and nude figures under the guise of classical tableaux as well as sporting motifs, coats of arms and cyphers and numerous formal patterns. Many cases were designed and made in France. Indeed, some collectors claim that snuff-rasp cases were not made in England. This is contradicted by the fact that they were entered in the 1737 price list of the London Assay Office, the cost of assay being one penny each. Hall-marked examples are recorded.

Silver rasp cases made between 1697 and 1720 were in high standard silver, the hallmarks including the figure of Britannia and the lion's head erased, instead of the leopard's head and lion passant of sterling silver. Only the case was hallmarked: the rasp itself contained more than the legal proportion of copper in order to make the silver harder, springier and long-wearing under daily rasping.

Three styles of personal snuff rasp are to be found: (1) with pivoting cover; (2) with sliding cover; (3) with the rasp fully exposed, needing the protection of a leather case.

In the pivoting design the thin cover was flat and tapering on plan, swivelling on a joint at the wide end. When swung open the cover disclosed the perforated rasp of heavily alloyed silver, iron or steel. At the back of the rasp, to receive the snuff, the silver casing was sunk in a shallow recess with a thin raised rib down its centre. This prevented the rasp from sagging with use and provided two channels for the snuff to flow without clogging from under the rasp at the narrow end and neatly into the snuff-box.

The rasp case, consisting of a sliding shutter concealing the iron rasp, was a narrow rectangle, often with a rounded end. This might be shaped as a scallop shell on each face and covered a small recess into which the powdered snuff was collected from beneath the rasp. More often, however, the end was plainly rounded with a spout from which the snuff was poured into the pocket snuff-box. The rasp was fitted over a fixed back, somewhat rounded to form a long shallow rectangular recess. The shutter that covered it was arranged to slide lengthwise between a pair of grooves and was ornamented with an all-over design matched by that of the rounded back. The exposed type of rasp was merely a grater set into a shallow wooden receptacle shaped to catch the falling snuff.

Mill-ground tobacco snuff appears to have been marketed in bulk no earlier than 1702 when Admiral Sir George Rooke captured from Spanish vessels near Cadiz several thousand barrels of Spanish snuff and a further large cargo of Havana snuff in Vigo Bay. This was distributed throughout the country by sailors who received it in lieu of prize money. Known as Vigo snuff and sold at cheap rates it set the seal on the use of tobacco snuff by the poorer members of the community. From as early as about 1715 the use of personal rasps steadily declined although in 1760 such an individualist as Dr Johnson still preferred to rasp his own rappee, having discovered that the factory-milled product might be adulterated with chicory leaves steeped in tar oil. Some continued the custom to as late as the end of the century.

As snuff-takers turned more and more to factory milled and blended snuff sold under brand names, this meant that the main demand for rasps was among the more exclusive retailers who ground special snuffs and concocted personal blends. The rasps they used were bat-shaped instruments about a foot long. As the black-boy was the tobacconist's shop sign so this style of rasp became the snuff-seller's distinguishing symbol.

The trade card of Fribourg & Treyer, 'at the Rasp & Crown, upper End of Ye Hay Market, London', issued during the 1730s illustrates such a snuff rasp. This was a board tapering from a width of about six inches to four inches with a short handle at the narrow end. The centre was chisel-sunk leaving a narrow rim into which an iron grater was fitted, space being allowed beneath to catch the grated tobacco. This was poured into a mortar and ground to an impalpable powder with a pestle. Snuff-men sold carottes to their customers and charged for rasping. In 1765 Lord Spencer bought '1 Paris carotte £1.1.0; Rasping 1.0; Cannister 6d'.

By the mid-18th century snuff-sellers preferred a rasp in the shape of a half-cylinder fitted into a silver frame with a semi-circular handle. This resembled a kitchen grater and measured from four to ten inches in length, with the top and bottom ends covered, the lower end being hinged to permit removal of the snuff. The frame might have gadrooned rims with a reeded handle. In another design a cylindrical steel grater was set in a silver frame, the side pieces continuing over the top to form a semi-circular handle.

The Sheffield platers in the 1770s evolved a new design in domestic snuff rasps. This measured about a foot in length and had a shallow, flat-based oval body. Two-thirds of this was covered by a convex rasp fitted into a hinged frame. The remainder consisted of a box to hold the unused portion of the carotte.

The rough surface of the rasp consisted of a series of small raised protuberances roughly broken from behind with a steel tool shaped to give them a jagged edge. For silver cases the rasp was of heavily alloyed silver hammered until springy and tough. In about 1740 the sheet iron rasp came into use. This was usually framed in silver to lie snugly within the body of the box, resting upon a ledge formed by a narrow ribbon of silver encircling the interior of the rim. Hammered sheet iron was used until the 1720s when the more efficient, longer-wearing rolled steel came into use. This was thinly tinned to prevent rust, which friction of the tobacco in fact quickly removed. French plating with silver leaf was even less permanent.

From the early 1790s the rolled steel used for snuff rasps was annealed in a bed of hot charcoal about two feet deep, the lower part of the fire being in a state of incandescence, the upper layer at a lower temperature. This caused a condition suitable for the development of oxide colours. After removal from the fire the steel was hardened by being plunged into raw whale oil and then vigorously rubbed with an oil-soaked pad of beaver felt. This process surfaced the steel with a hard blue film capable of resisting the friction of the tobacco. Rasps from this period are always in excellent condition. In the early rasp the jagged-edge piercings were irregularly spaced and appear to have been forced into the metal by means of a sharp punch. Later the perforations were made by raising small hemispheres with a fly-press in such a way as to leave a perfectly flat ground; each hemisphere was then broken by a tool, leaving a jagged edge.

Makers of snuff rasps bought graters by the sheet which they cut to fit their rasp cases or frames, for many a rasp shows severed perforations around the edge.

SNUFF-SPOONS

Many women snuff-takers snuffed from a tiny spoon or nose shovel of sterling silver, often gilded. This fashionably super-seded the more commonly used quill. Spoon and quill kept the nails clean and the custom also meant that the fastidious woman could proffer her personal box with little risk of its coming into direct contact with her fellow snuffer's fingers.

Snuff-spoons or ladles seldom weighed more than five penny-weights and were therefore exempt from hallmarking. The spoon was commonly about 2 in. long with a shallow oval bowl; some bowls were hemispherical and others shaped like shovels. A snuff-spoon was usually included among the fitments of an 18th-century etui and was also an accompaniment of the table snuff-box.

SNUFF-HANDKERCHIEFS

Fashion required that after snuffing one hand and the upper lip should be dusted with a ceremonial handkerchief measuring from 18 in. to 24 in. square. An advertisement in the *London Gazette*, 1694, described a sophisticated snuff-handkerchief as being 'in lawn with a broad rim, laced around with fine lace about four fingers broad'. When the fashion for snuff-taking snowballed during Queen Anne's reign it brought into use more serviceable cambric and cotton handkerchiefs known as snuff-napkins. These might also be spread to protect the neck-cloth, shirt and waistcoat from falling snuff. At this time men's coat tails began to be fitted with capacious pockets in which to carry the bulky snuff-napkin. It was from these loosely hanging pockets that pickpockets for the next hundred years found fine game, extracting lawn and other expensive handkerchiefs for which there was a ready receiver's market. Those who special-ised in diving into coat pockets for sneezers, skins and dummies (snuff-boxes, purses and pocket-books) were known as tail-buzzers. Women carried their snuff-handkerchiefs in linen pockets sewn to straps encircling their waists between the petticoats. It became a fashionable ostentation to carry in the hand an elaborately worked laced handkerchief, the pocket concealing a cotton square for actual use.

Obviously the snuffer called for coloured handkerchiefs, the less to reveal the scant laundering of personal linen in a day of heavily taxed soap. Some were dyed a light brown tint in an effort to disguise snuff stains; others were ornamented with simple wood block printing in bright colours. To protect the decaying wool trade, textile printers were forbidden by law from 1720 to 1774 to use material made entirely of cotton but even then the production of plain blue cotton snuff-handker-chiefs was permitted. Squares of silk began to be used for the first time in 1721.

When the technique of monochrome copper-plate printing began to be applied to textiles in the early 1750s a demand was created for snuff-handkerchiefs illustrating pictorial scenes, first on silk, then on a fabric woven with a linen warp and a cotton weft and from 1774 on cotton. The introduction of Arkwright's water-power loom at this time enabled calico to be woven with a smooth, regular surface upon which clear designs were reproduced in delicate detail.

The only permanent colours so far were black and reddish purple. Printing in red was evolved in about 1800; blue and green a few years later. From about 1815 stippling replaced dark mottled shadow-work in pictures which now displayed more roundly modelled three-dimensional effects.

In 1831 the drastic excise duties long imposed on calico printing were removed. From 1718 a tax of threepence a square yard had been levied on the calico manufacturer and a further threepence upon the printer. From 1782 the printer's tax had been increased to fifteen per cent of the fabric's value, increased to twenty per cent in 1812.

So far snuff-handkerchiefs had been printed singly by hand presses: roller machinery had been invented half a century earlier but was unsuitable for all-over picture work on snuff-handkerchiefs. Steam-driven and enlarged roller machinery now came into use, printing monochrome handkerchiefs at the rate of 9,000 a day, equal to the production of 42 hand-presses. Four standard sizes were made: 21, 24½, 28 and 31½ in. square.

Adaptations to the printing machine during the 1840s made it possible to print snuff-handkerchiefs in black and three shades of four colours – a total of thirteen tint variations. These were later augmented by superimposing one colour over another. Silk and lawn handkerchiefs had long been hemmed by hand-sewing. Cotton handkerchiefs were rarely hemmed until after the invention of the lock-stitch sewing machine in 1851.

The collector of snuff-handkerchiefs will find that they offer vivid glimpses into the pleasures and enthusiasms of their period. They depict a wide variety of portraits and contemporaneous events. Subjects range from popular views of celebrated buildings to representations of the willow pattern. Those printed with such betrothal motifs as hearts and love birds, or with amatory pictures and couplets, were known as flirting squares. Snuff-handkerchiefs will be found bearing the insignia of Orange clubs and Masonry; Niagara Falls with explanatory details; the coronations of George IV, William IV and Queen Victoria. Crimean handkerchiefs dated 1855 embody maxims for a soldier, army signalling, medals for distinguished conduct and long service, the music of bugle calls, and pictures of events in the field.

From 1842 to 1883 it was possible to register industrial designs at the Patent Office, giving protection from industrial piracy for three years upon payment of a fee of one pound. Such a registered picture contained in some inconspicuous place, usually incorporated in the design itself, a diamond-shaped registration mark containing symbols from which the name of the printer may be interpreted by Patent Office officials.

Although calico printers in the 1870s tried to save a declining trade with new effects produced by recently invented synthetic dyes, printed handkerchiefs were issued only as souvenirs, on commemorative occasions, for propaganda purposes, and with illustrated nursery rhymes for children.

CHAPTER 3

Gold: Silver: Miniatures

GOLD

WHEN Beau Nash delighted fashionable Bath with his snuff-boxes of jewelled gold, similar bijouterie had already scintillated for more than thirty years at the Court of France. But now, in the reign of Queen Anne, the English goldsmith began his own contributions to this work, creating snuff-boxes for men and women in precious metals. The English jeweller was particularly in his element designing splendidly proportioned, delicately ornamented and superbly finished boxes in gold and silver, now a joy to the modern collector. Details were considered meticulously. Lids were made to fit tightly yet open smoothly. This important feature was recorded in *Pandora's Box*, 1719:

> *Charming in shape, with polish't rays of light,*
> *A joint so fine it shuns the sharpest light.*

The hinge, too, was made with watch-maker's precision, extending the full width of the rectangular lid. In the oval shape, opening lengthwise, the hinge was positioned about one-fifth of the distance from each end of the box and here, too, joints were virtually invisible. Hinges were external and riveted to the back: not until the 1740s was the integral hinge in regular use. Constant working of an ill-made hinge eventually wore the lugs, causing the lid to become loose and let snuff leak into the pocket. Even the slightest projection of the thumb-lift on the front of the lid was a hazard seldom introduced to pocket boxes intended for snuff, since the projection might catch against the clothing when being lifted from the pocket and spill the powder.

Thumb-lifts when used might be designed and ornamented to match the overall decoration or set with diamonds, sprays of

3

flowers always being fashionable. The existence of the slightest defect in a gold snuff-box of the Georgian period should arouse suspicion regarding its genuineness. The early gold snuff-box was engagingly slender to fit the waistcoat pocket.

Circular snuff-boxes were fashionable, too, at first with hinged lids. From about 1720 circular lids might be of the pull-off pattern. These were made until the end of the century despite the hazard of a jerky movement spilling the snuff. Gold boxes with pull-off lids were more commonly used as containers for breath-sweetening comfits, aromatic sponge or patches – but to collectors 'snuff-box' has become the generic term. When fitted with hinged lids, such boxes are often difficult to distinguish from true snuff-boxes, but minor characteristics, such as a mirror in a patch box lid, may make this possible.

Jewelled boxes of the Queen Anne period had rounded corners: the oval shape, however, outnumbered circular boxes during the reigns of the first two Georges (1714–1760). Engraved trade cards in the British Museum illustrate many ovals, mostly with curved sides, from about 1725 to the late 1760s. Shallow rectangular boxes with rounded corners were also fashionable at this time. Base and cover were encircled with plain moulding, ornament being restricted to the cover. Irregular shapes were numerous too, some designed with an escallop shell outline, others, from 1727, as asymmetrical cartouches.

Until about 1715 lid decoration consisted mainly of engraved armorials or cyphers, sometimes with a colourful hardstone or shell as a central feature. The *Daily Courant* referred in 1705 to a gold snuff-box decorated 'with a large blue onyx stone upon the lid'. Such snuff-boxes were specifically exempted from assay after 1739: examples struck with hall-marks earlier than this date are extremely rare. Classic decoration in relief became fashionable on gold snuff-boxes with the accession of George I. These were low-chased on matt grounds, allegorical scenes and heroic subjects being usual. The relief work became higher from about 1730 and had become customary by the mid-1760s.

Georgian snuff-boxes in gold from about 1760 until 1815 were usually rectangular and from the 1790s the sides tended to be concave or rounded in *bombé* form rather than vertical, depth varying between ¾ in. and 1¼ in. The pointed oval or shuttle shape was a late 18th-century fashion but has proved less enduring than the straight-hinged rectangle. Although these were the prevailing shapes, no real classification is possible for every geometrical and curved shape was approved and goldsmiths worked with freedom of form, material, colour and decoration. During the second half of the century it was customary for winter snuff-boxes to be heavy and those carried during the summer months to be light-weight. Jewelled and lavishly worked boxes were protected from damage with fitted cases, shagreen, ivory and morocco leather always being fashionable.

Many handsome snuff-boxes were bedecked with gold of various hues, as many as four different alloys enriching a single design such as a bouquet in vari-coloured gold in relief against an engine-turned ground, with borders and corners similarly decorated. Golds shaded to blue and green tones against a background of yellow gold were particularly fashionable, with burnished highlights. Silver oxide added to 22-carat gold produced a green alloy; copper oxide, red; and iron oxide, a bluish tint.

A magnificent series of gold snuff-boxes elaborately chased on cover and sides was made early in the George III period. In these the goldsmith patterned the metal by applying various punches to the outer surface. In *repoussé* work the embossed design was raised from the underside. Less common were boxes decorated with *ciselé* work in which the metal was carved as though it were wood. These three styles of ornament, with the addition of engraving, might decorate a single snuff-box.

With the assistance of artist enamellers, London goldsmiths produced some spectacular snuff-boxes decorated with portraits and other paintings upon the gold ground, which enhanced the brilliance of the enamel colours. Others were set with gold plaques displaying pictures commissioned from independent artist enamellers. *Basse-taille* enamelling, seldom seen on English snuff-boxes, consists of cutting designs into the surface of the gold and filling the channels with translucent enamels through which the engraved lines are visible.

Panels of gouache and grisaille painting are to be found set in snuff-box lids. *Gouache* is a term for painting in water colours rendered opaque by the addition of white and gum. The result is a velvety surface reflecting light. *Grisaille* is a term for painting in soft tones of grey, causing solid bodies to be represented as if in relief. *Verre églomisé* decoration on panels of glass set in the lid and sides of early Georgian snuff-boxes is uncommon. This ornament consists of gold or silver foil on the underside of the glass against a ground of red, green or, more often, blue.

Portraits originally held a personal interest only, the sitters for the most part being now unknown. A portrait of a celebrity is usually indication that the box was a gift from the person portrayed. This might be a miniature painted on ivory, often protected by a convex glass. Such ornament is rarely found inside the lid as dust would obscure its delicate lines. The snuff-box intended only for display in a cabinet usually contains a portrait, sometimes a pair of a husband and wife. Celebrities displayed magnificent collections, most of them received as gifts and often inscribed within the lid.

The *tabatière secrète* has a miniature portrait painted on ivory concealed beneath the central ornament of the cover. This is revealed by pressing a secret spring. Others have an erotic painting hidden in this space. In some combined snuff and patch boxes the patches were carried in the small cavity.

From about 1815 gold and silver were used more lavishly than during the years of the Napoleonic wars, heavy castings in high relief superseding the more delicate hand-craftsmanship. This brought about a change in mood: expressed, for example, in the vogue for snuff-box lids displaying scenes adapted from Dutch paintings. These castings were, of course, surface finished by hand-carving and were sometimes set within mounts of gold.

In the majority of instances the framing was cast too. The lid design might incorporate a tiny central escutcheon upon which the owner's crest or cypher was engraved.

Birmingham became the main centre for the manufacture of gold snuff-boxes and, like the London goldsmiths, specialised in engine-turned ornament during the first third of the 19th century. The sides of the fashionable box were concave, usually with surfaces engine-turned in a single matching pattern. Panels of differing designs decorated a long series of gold snuff-boxes. during the 1820s. Wide mounts with flower and foliage decoration in deep relief were the rule: the oak leaf and acorn pattern was popular long after the end of the Napoleonic wars in 1815.

The lid at this period might be set with a cast and chased scene of hunting or other sport. Presentation boxes in gold were elaborately designed, the goldsmith preparing a master drawing illustrating the plan and side views. Several copies might be made.

No further development occurred in the design of gold snuff-boxes until 1854 when the great volume of imported jewellery in heavily alloyed gold urged the Goldsmiths' Company to agitate for a change in the regulations. For the first time in England jewellers were permitted to make use of compound metals, that is, the gold was alloyed. Until 1798 no quality other than 22-carat gold was passed by the Assay Office. The two per cent alloy in this, normally copper, accounts for the reddish tint displayed by gold snuff-boxes made before that year.

The new qualities included 18-carat from 1798: that is, 18 parts gold and six of alloy which might be copper, copper and silver, or copper, silver and zinc. Three differing tints then faced the purchaser of an 18-carat snuff-box, only 75 per cent of which was actually gold. The term *carat* indicates the proportion of gold and not a definite unit of weight as in precious stones. From 1854 snuff-boxes were made in 15-carat gold; in 12-carat consisting of equal parts of gold and alloy; and 9-carat containing 15 parts alloy to nine of gold. Only by long usage of the term can this quality be termed gold, but legally this is permitted. These four standards are indicated by numerals stamped at the assay office. The price of 22-carat gold remained constant at about 84s an ounce throughout the gold snuff-box period.

SILVER

Silver snuff-boxes constitute the most numerous group available to collectors, dating as they do from the reign of Charles II to late in that of Victoria. The precious metal has been preserved: those of base metal and the like for the most part have been destroyed. Chronological classification by form alone is impossible: for instance identical patterns were made during early Georgian and early Victorian periods. Hallmarks, of course, serve the purpose of accurate dating, but frequently the slight continual friction against a chamois-lined pocket has worn the silver until marks have become indecipherable. In dating such pieces reliance must be placed upon methods of craftsmanship and associated ornament.

Few silver snuff-boxes remain that were made earlier than about 1730, but London newspapers of the period record numerous descriptions in the columns advertising lost and stolen goods. The two examples quoted here are taken from among a hundred or more collated from various sources. *The London Gazette*, September 1692, refers to 'a Silver Snuff-Box Guilt on the inside, and the top of it is Engraven with a Cypher and a Garter round it, and a Duke's Coronet'. This style of decoration is characteristic of the period. Silver snuff-boxes might be lavishly decorated, however. *The Daily Courant*, September 1709, described such a stolen example: 'Silver Snuff-Box, on the Lid a Locket compos'd of 10 Garnetts, in the middle an old-fashioned Chrystal under which 2 Angels support a Crown over a Cypher, at each corner of the Box on the same side is set 4 Escallope Shells at the Tail of each Escallope four Stones.' The lid of a two-inch oval snuff-box made by the celebrated Thomas Isod which I recently examined was exquisitely engraved in the limited space with two Comedy figures miming to music against an architectural background with a surround of shells, scrolling foliage and caryatids.

Most snuff-boxes of the early 18th century were constructed from sections of plate flattened from the ingot by the hand-hammer and hard-soldered together and burnished so that seams were invisible. Much more costly was the snuff-box hand-raised from the silver plate as a single unit and fitted with a hinged flat lid composed of a single piece of plate. Shallow circular snuff-boxes were turned in the lathe from solid castings and fitted with hinged lids. Some boxes in each group were given cast lids.

The silver used between 1697 and 1720 was by law required to be of the quality known as high or Britannia standard, containing less alloy and consequently softer than sterling. For this reason the plate was slightly thicker than in boxes of sterling silver. The assay office mark included a figure of Britannia in place of the lion passant gardant, indication of sterling quality.

Georgian silversmiths continued to use hand-beaten plate, but by the 1770s the factory silver refiners and rollers of Sheffield and Birmingham were supplying rolled plate at lower prices and this could be shaped in the press. Circular snuff-boxes began to be spun in the lathe. Small master silversmiths bought snuff-box units from the factories and finished and assembled them in their own workshops. In the early 19th century snuff-boxes were made from rolled plate virtually concealed beneath heavy ornamental castings or rose engine-turning.

In Georgian work topical embossments were fashionable, particularly portrait busts of naval and military heroes and, less commonly, political figures. The Jacobites tended to carry snuff-boxes embossed or engraved with portraits of Prince Charles, the Jacobite rose and other emblems associated with the intrigues around 1745. Hallmarks show these to have been made in Scotland in about 1750; some later examples bear the maker's mark of Collin, a silversmith of Bond Street, London. As with other Stuart mementoes, however, the collector has to be on the watch for Victorian boxes, including the box claiming a cover of oak wood from the famous tree of Boscobel, framed in silver appropriately engraved with the future Charles II peeping from among foliage.

Oval snuff-boxes outnumbered other shapes in silver until the 1760s and displayed almost every variety of ornament apart from precious stones. Trade cards now in the British Museum depict ovals, mostly with curved sides, from about 1725 to 1760, the single exception being a rectangle of about 1750. Rectangular snuff-boxes were made with rounded or canted corners: they were very shallow, some but $\frac{3}{8}$ in. deep. In such a design the lid and base corners were encircled with plain strengthening moulding and ornament was restricted to the top. This might be engraved on the outside with a coat of arms in an expansive ornamental cartouche, or the outside might be entirely plain and a picture engraved within the lid. Irregular shapes were numerous too, some designed on the escallop shell outline, with straight hinges. Among other lid treatments of the period was the casting in all-over high relief of an intricate figure scene, usually adapted from a well-known painting and enclosed within borders. This was finished by hand-carving. Alternatively, cast ornament, chased and burnished, might be applied to a lid, or a raised design might be achieved with embossing and chasing in an intricate all-over pattern. Such effects contrasted with the flat formality of other patterns in rose engine-turning. This formal patterning was widely acceptable over almost a century, the box being ornamented on all six surfaces. The slight roughness in texture prevented the box from slipping accidentally through the fingers and was less easily marred than plain silver by constant handling.

The interior of the silver snuff-box was gilded to prevent discolouring of the metal by the snuff and its added flavouring ingredients. The gold remained brilliantly radiant, a perfect ground against which to offer a pinch of snuff. Embossed lids and sides were lined with gilded plate to prevent accumulation of snuff in the interior recesses created by such ornament. There was a late 18th-century vogue for lining silver snuff-boxes with a thin veneer of highly polished tortoiseshell.

For a time, through the 1760s–80s, comparatively few silver snuff-boxes were made. This was due in part to the popularity of colourful boxes in painted enamels, then at their finest, but more especially to the challenge of Sheffield plate, much cheaper and difficult to distinguish at a glance from sterling silver. The London silversmiths met this competition by loading snuff-boxes with styles of ornament impossible with Sheffield plate: even the shape was a challenge as the rectangular box became boldly rounded in a manner that would render Sheffield plate especially vulnerable to copper-revealing wear.

Regarding other shapes, the octagonal snuff-box had been fashionable from 1690 to the 1740s. It was usually small, about two inches wide, with the lid all-over engraved. Triangular snuff-boxes had a mid 18th-century vogue. They were usually given silver-gilt mounts with lid and base set with hardstones such as lapis lazuli. Heart-shaped snuff-boxes had flat lids crest-engraved and bordered with engraved bands of appropriate scrollwork. These were invariably shallow.

The snuff-box with a sea-shell as a container, its edge cut and fitted with a silver mount, usually reeded, achieved some popularity between about 1790 and the 1830s. Cowrie shells were in considerable use for this purpose. The lid hinged near to the wide end of the shell opening with a thumb-lift near the point. The lid was usually engraved with a wide border of swags and festoons, or foliate scrolls with a central cartouche containing a cypher. Sizes ranged from 3½ in. to 2 in. long. Cypraea shells were also used. Hallmarks suggest that such snuff-boxes were made at the coastal towns of Newcastle, Arbroath and Cork.

The early 19th-century tendency to use silver lavishly and replace costly hand labour with heavy casting was expressed even on snuff-boxes. There was a marked change of mood, but snuff-boxes escaped the disastrous excesses of some table silver. There was, for example, a vogue for snuff-boxes displaying scenes adapted from Dutch oil paintings. Such ornament, cast in high relief and chased, was held in a rim shaped from flat plate which was fashionably engine-turned. In another series the cast frames constituted the major ornament. A plain box made from rolled plate had wide, boldly convex moulding soldered around the lid and covering the sides entirely. The lid might be engine-turned with a central reserve containing an engraved scene, often of a religious nature, or a commemorative motif or inscription. At this time the standard lid decoration might incorporate a tiny rectangle for the owner's crest or cypher.

During the first one-third of the 19th century the lid of a silver-gilt snuff-box made in London or Birmingham might be set with a solid gold plaque upon which a crest, cypher or presentation inscription might be engraved without revealing the fact that the box was basically of sterling silver. The border might be composed of a design of applied vine tendrils on a matted ground and the sides and base engine-turned before gilding.

Many sporting snuff-boxes are associated with the early 19th century. A typical design had rounded corners and projecting rims, the sides vertical and engine-turned, the lid of flat plate displaying an applied cast and chased scene or motif in silhouette, such as a horse or greyhound, with a ribbon above for the animal's name and another below for the occasion and date. Pocket snuff-boxes were also engraved with scenes of prize-fighting and the like.

Silver has always proved particularly amenable for use in combination with more colourful materials. Throughout the period under review jewel-encrusted gold snuff-boxes had their less ostentatious counterparts in boxes of silver-gilt set with gemstones such as emeralds, garnets and amethysts and variegated hardstones. The top and base might be of carved stone and the sides of the box elaborately embossed or cast in relief and chased.

Cheap, pressed light-weight snuff-boxes for ladies were made in numerous shapes and forms: they might be round, oval, octagonal, irregular in outline, or represent hearts, purses, escallop shells, travelling chests, shoes or books. The lids of a long series of post-1815 snuff-boxes were pressed with a range of views of castles, abbeys, national buildings, stately homes. One authority has collated more than 700 such views and states that nine out of ten are struck with the anchor of the Birmingham Assay Office. Makers' marks include those of Nathaniel Mills, Joseph Taylor, John Shaw, Samuel Pemberton, Thomas Willmore, George Bettridge, William Pugh and Joseph Phillimore.

The silver harnessing technique was applied to snuff-boxes from about 1830. The box, carved from colourful hardstone, was hammered with chased silver openwork in an all-over design of birds, animals, flowers, foliage and elaborate scroll-work, so that the lively metalwork and the stone immensely enhanced each other. By the late 1840s birds and other motifs might be set with innumerable tiny glittering gem-stones.

Snuff-boxes of oxidised silver appeared during the late 1840s, ornamented with handsome pictorial relief work. These bas reliefs were electrotypes. Two such boxes with sporting scenes were seen at the Great Exhibition, 1851: a Scottish deer stalker and an angler with a catch of fish on a line.

In the early snuff-box a touch on a small stud operating a catch allowed the lid to open. In the early 18th century it was found that a thumb-lift attached to the front edge of the lid mount was safer and more reliable in its action. These thumb-lifts varied from a narrow plain scroll flange to a wide cast plate with an ornamented upper surface, such as a floral design or scroll and shell.

MINIATURES

Miniature portraits painted in full colour were fashionable ornament on the lids of gold and gilded silver snuff-boxes throughout the 18th century. These pictures, usually the work of expert craftsmen rather than original artists, were painted in water colours, at first on vellum and later on oval slips of ivory which imparted a delicate lustre to the carnation or flesh areas.

The system of painting followed by the majority of early miniaturists was described in *The Art of Painting in Miniature*, 1735. The portraits were painted on vellum stiffened by pasting it to a plate of copper, brass or wood. 'This pasting must be on the Edges of your Velom only and behind the plate; For which purpose your Velom must exceed your Plate. The Part you paint upon must never be pasted . . . there must be a clean white Paper between the Velom and the Plate.' The collector should inspect a miniature that has a metal table to ensure that it has been flattened by the battery method, a point sometimes overlooked by the modern copyist. In copies, too, the paper between the vellum and the plate may be omitted. Until the 1720s miniature painters prepared their own colours from ingredients sold by apothecaries. By 1730, however, fifteen suitable colours could be bought from the print shops for painting 'portraits in little', as miniatures were then called.

The use of thin ivory tablets for this work was introduced to England by Bernard Lens junior (1682–1740) in 1708, but was confined to leading artists until the 1740s. The old ivories were not polished, in fact it was common for the painting surface to be slightly roughened to ensure that the colours would bite. Before use the miniaturist rubbed this surface with garlic juice.

The Georgian miniaturist began by dead-colouring the whole area of the portrait, laying on the paint with smooth clear strokes of a pencil brush. The base for faces consisted of white which was mixed with a tinge of blue for women, vermillion for men, and a little ochre to suggest age. Over this ground the portrait was dotted or stippled. Some miniaturists made round dots and others preferred longish flecks. Those to whom speed of production was important used hatching, that is, short strokes crossing each other in every direction: obviously such portraits tended to be inferior.

Collectors may find snuff-boxes set with miniatures within the lids and, in some instances, portraying a member of the original owner's family. But they should be aware of the fact that forgeries have been abundant for the past seventy years: in 1903 fraudulent Cosways were discussed in an art journal. One may find a miniature set in a snuff-box of an earlier period, or even an antique miniature set on the lid of a much later box. An example from Horace Walpole's Strawberry Hill collection was described in the sale catalogue, lot 101, as '*a fine gold escallop shaped* SNUFF BOX, richly enamelled with flowers, on the top a very fine miniature of James I by Hilliard, and within a portrait of Queen Elizabeth, also by Hilliard, both in the finest manner of this much admired artist, the onyx at the bottom of the box is considered perfectly unique'. These miniatures were painted on the plain backs of playing cards.

The most fashionable painter of miniatures for setting in radiantly bejewelled snuff-boxes of George III's day was Richard Cosway, RA (1742–1821). Ivory played a great part in the success of his technique which allowed it to gleam through the very thinly applied water-colours with remarkable brilliance: in many instances one may note areas of its surface bearing no trace of colour, the curve of the cheek or the rounded flesh of the shoulders and bosom being the creamy ivory itself. He persistently used a cold, clear, bright ultramarine. Early and late grounds are distinguished by a greyish-green tint; work of his middle period by grounds of mottled white or grey. One of his characteristics was his treatment of hair in washes of colour touched with delicate lines and suggesting masses rather than wiry detail. Some of his most exquisite portraits are found in the lids of jewelled snuff-boxes and painted directly on box-lids of ivory.

The Georgian painters whose miniature portraits are found set in snuff-box lids were a numerous group. High among them are the following, but about thirty others were of comparable ability.

Gervase Spencer (d. 1763) painted excellent portraits of which Horace Walpole wrote: 'He greatly favoured a very pale blue background, but substituted for it sometime a dull brown colour.' His water-colour effects display an unusual clarity of definition.

Jeremiah Meyer, RA (1735–89), miniaturist to George III and Queen Charlotte, worked on ivory with transparent water-colours. His draughtsmanship tended towards the angular, the entire surface of the ivory being covered with very fine lines, long and short, and crossing each other at all angles to secure adequate face modelling. These lines are often so fine that it is difficult to see them without a glass. Unfortunately he used a fading flesh-tint.

John Smart (1741–1811) is known by the incomparable textures of his flesh tints in a colour used by no other miniaturist.

Ozias Humphry, RA (1742–1810) usually painted three-quarter face against a background of green, brown or blue, and gave his sitter long, narrow eyes resulting in a sleepy expression.

Samuel Shelley (1753–1808) was a devotee of pale colours and had the personal characteristic of sometimes turning his ovals so that width was greater than height, ideal for certain snuff-boxes.

George Engleheart (1752–1824) is known for his rigidly accurate drawing, and some rich dark cross-hatching on the feminine neck and shoulders.

Andrew Plimer (1757–1822) duplicated Cosway's technique but substituted line work for fleecy hair masses.

John Couler (1768–1805), the first artist to exhibit miniatures at the Royal Academy, was notable for the exquisite delicacy of his portraits on snuff-box ivories.

Many of the more splendid of the Georgian snuff-box miniatures were signed with a full name, initials or a monogram: the majority are unsigned. A full signature such as R^d *Cosway* or Oz^s *Humphry* was usually inscribed behind the portrait, between the ivory and the snuff-box lid. The artist's surname might be inscribed on the front of the ivory, but usually no more than a monogram or initials is found in this position. Microscopic in size and mingled among the hair of curls or wig, or concealed in the fold of a dress, these can only be detected after prolonged search with a magnifying glass in a bright light. When gilt or lead pencil has been used it is essential to hold the portrait at the correct angle to the light. A signature may be so close to the edge of the ivory that it is concealed by the encircling mount.

CHAPTER 4

Sheffield Plate: Britannia Metal: Moiré Metal

SHEFFIELD PLATE

SNUFF-BOXES were the first articles to be made commercially in Sheffield plate. This important material, superficially resembling silver plate but very much cheaper, consisted of a thin layer of pure silver fused over a thicker layer of copper. The process was invented in 1742 by Thomas Bolsover, Tudor House, Sheffield. A year later he established workshops at Baker Hill, Sheffield, and concentrated on the manufacture of snuff-boxes and buttons.

These boxes were shallow and circular, their lift-off covers measuring about $2\frac{1}{2}$ in. across by $\frac{3}{4}$ in. deep decorated with all-over designs in relief. Early ornament was wholly hand-worked and this style continued throughout the period that these boxes were in vogue – to the late 1770s. But from the 1760s designs were commonly raised in relief by pressing with dies made from the newly invented Huntsman tool steel, harder than any metal made hitherto, and finished by hand chasing.

Covers displayed a wide range of relief patterns such as flowers and foliage among rococo scrollwork, classical scenes with draped figures and elaborate backgrounds, hand-chased portraits of celebrities such as William Pitt, 1st Earl of Chatham and Frederick II of Prussia among a trophy of arms, both in Sheffield City Museum. A style that achieved some popularity consisted of a classical scene pierced and set against a ground of aventurine glass (see p. 93) intended to suggest clouds. Snuff-box bases were stamped beneath with expansive patterns in line-work resembling engraving, such as a basket of fruit surmounted by scrollwork.

The sides of the two units composing the snuff-box were made by encircling each of the decorated discs with a strip of Sheffield plate. The strips were bent into a circle and the ends joined to form rings. The rings were attached to the discs by lapping them over the edges and soldering them into position. Ornamental sides for the box were made by swaging a strip of plate into curved shapes. The seams of the vertical joints are always faintly visible.

Copper at this period could be silver-plated on one side only, the reverse displaying the bare copper. A plain disc of plate, silvered side facing downward, was usually placed within the cover to conceal the copper and to keep the snuff from clogging the undulations caused by the embossments. Examples are to be found with the interior gilded, but others reveal the unplated side of the copper. In some instances the entire interior was lined with highly polished tortoiseshell to prevent oxides forming on the copper and tainting the snuff. The tortoiseshell in the silver might be backed with copper to strengthen it. Copper covered on both sides dates from the late 1760s and is usually found in association with stamped pastoral scenes. The base might consist wholly of a disc of tortoiseshell, its exterior surface engine-turned. A long series of snuff-box covers was set with plaques of tortoiseshell in piqué posé (see p. 118).

The majority of Sheffield plate snuff-boxes from 1760 were rectangular, quite plain and tinned inside. A five-lug hinge extended the full width of the lid. Edges and corners of those now remaining are often pocket-worn revealing a tinge of copper. Oval and circular forms with hinged lids and the pinched rectangle were common. These, from about 1770, might have fluted sides edged with fine plated wire. Oblong snuff-boxes might have rounded ends and were usually fitted with thumb-lifts. Those intended for constant work-a-day use were necessarily of strong plate to prevent warping. From about

4

1780 the cover mount might be set with a skilfully painted Staffordshire enamel.

By this time the majority of Sheffield plate snuff-boxes were of Birmingham manufacture. Sides tended to be concave or rounded in bombé form, depth ranging from ¾ in. to 1¼ in. The pointed oval or shuttle shape was a vogue of the late 18th and early 19th centuries. None of these shapes has proved as enduring as the plain straight-hinged rectangle.

Matthew Boulton, Soho, Staffordshire, was a prolific maker of snuff-boxes from 1765. In 1767 he wrote to a friend, 'I have lately begun to make snuff-boxes in metal gilt and in tortoise-shell inlaid' – that is piqué posé. He is known to have made circular boxes in Sheffield plate with hinged lids framing panels of exotic woods, mother of pearl and tortoiseshell. Boulton was the first Birmingham maker of Sheffield plate to adapt and bring to perfection silver edges to snuff-boxes, a technique patented in 1785 by Valentine Rawle.

A popular early 19th-century decoration on an otherwise plain snuff-box was a cartwheel copper penny dated 1796, soldered to the centre of the flat lid and close-plated to match the box. The pennies were minted for the Government by Matthew Boulton at Soho and it has been assumed that these boxes were made by his firm, although no marked example has been noted. A second series was made early in the Victorian period by a now anonymous firm who electroplated the pennies.

By careful examination of manufacturing techniques it is possible to attribute an approximate period of manufacture even if shapes and sizes appear to be identical. The double-lapped copper edge dates from 1768; silver-lapped edges were introduced in 1775; narrow cast silver mounts from 1780; silver edges from 1785; bright-cut engraving was first used during the early 1780s and continued until about 1810. Stamped silver mounts filled with lead-tin alloy were introduced in 1790 and wide mounts stamped in silver in about 1815.

To compete with silver boxes the Sheffield plate box might

have to be engraved with a crest or other identifying symbol. To avoid revealing the copper in the engraved lines a shield of more heavily silvered plate might be soldered in, usually in the centre of the lid. By 1810 a silver shield was sweated on over the Sheffield plate on the area of the lid to be engraved. From about 1810 fused silver plate could be rolled appreciably thinner than formerly, cost being perceptibly reduced.

Table snuff-boxes in Sheffield plate, sometimes gilded, were usually circular with lift-off covers and measuring between four and six inches in diameter. An unusual design was spherical, the lower hemisphere supported by a trumpet foot and the upper hemisphere finialled to serve as a lift-off cover.

BRITANNIA METAL

Concurrently with Sheffield plate snuff-boxes from the 1780s a series of inexpensive snuff-boxes was made from two silvery-looking metals devoid of any coating of silver. These were Vickers white metal and britannia metal, both the invention of James Vickers of Sheffield.

Vickers white metal, dating from the 1770s, is an alloy composed principally of tin with the addition of antimony, copper and bismuth. This alloy so closely resembles sterling silver in colour when new that the casual observer would not be aware of the difference. It is soft and could be cut with a knife. Snuff-boxes in Vickers white metal are rare and those made by the originator are always impressed beneath I. VICKERS in small capitals. The Sheffield Directory for 1787 lists twelve white metal workers.

Early in the 1790s Vickers omitted the bismuth and commercialised this cheaper white alloy under the name of britannia metal. This eventually became very popular, large quantities being made. Brownell's Sheffield Directory of 1817 lists 73 britannia metal makers. Its high silvery lustre with a bluish white tinge was a distinct advance on the current quality of pewter which it superseded. The hardness of britannia metal made it capable of taking a high polish lost only after a long period of neglect but then impossible to restore.

Snuff-boxes, following the prevailing silver outlines, were usually made from thinly rolled metal, bodies and lids being stamped and fitted with hinged mounts of gilded brass. They were rarely decorated with more than simple engraving.

Britannia metal continued to be used for snuff-boxes until about 1850 when it was superseded by electroplated metals. The vast majority were unmarked. Those made by James Vickers and his successors between 1806 and 1817 were stamped on the base I. VICKERS in small capitals and should not be mistaken for his series in white metal; during the next twenty years the letters were larger; and after 1837 the small capitals reappeared with the address BRITANNIA PLACE SHEFFIELD added below. Other Sheffield makers of marked britannia metal snuff-boxes included J. Wolstenholme from 1828, P. Ashberry from 1830, and James Dixon & Sons from 1806, marked DIXON between that year and 1830.

MOIRÉ METAL

Snuff-boxes in shapes prevailing during the period 1816 to the early 1830s were made in moiré metal. Its brilliant surface was closely covered with stars and other geometrical patterns. The process of manufacture was patented in 1816 by Edward Thomason, Birmingham, who had observed that tinned iron plate held obliquely to the light revealed figured patterns, particularly on Pontypool tin plates. Impurities were removed from the surfaces of the snuff-box units by rubbing with nitric acid and salt. This ensured that the designs would be visible from every angle. After washing and drying the plate was immediately coated with clear hard varnish to preserve its silvery brilliance, followed later by several more protective coats and finally polished by hand.

The small crystalline figures providing this ornament were obtained by heating the plate until the film of tin melted.

Whilst cooling the coating of tin crystallised into a mass of graceful designs. Variations were achieved by heating only part of the tin. A granite effect resulted from hammering the plate before treating it with nitric acid. This broke the figures into even smaller crystalline patterns.

CHAPTER 5

Pinchbeck: Gilt Brass:
Lancashire Brass

PINCHBECK

THE NAME of Christopher Pinchbeck (1670–1732) passed into the English language as a synonym for the counterfeit and sham. Yet he was celebrated during his lifetime as the inventor and maker of complicated astronomical clocks, musical automata and church organs. Each year he set up his booth at Bartholomew and Southwark Fairs under the sign of *The Temple of the Muses*, an eye-catching juggler performing on a platform outside. So great was his reputation for melodious devices operated by clockwork that in 1729 his fairground 'Temple' attracted a visit from the Prince and Princess of Wales.

Established originally in St George's Court, Clerkenwell, in 1721 he moved to more central display workrooms in Fleet Street under the sign of *The Astronomico-Musical Clock* with convenient premises nearby. Here he advertised that he made and sold 'Watches of all sorts and Clocks with a variety of musical performers together with a wonderful imitation of several Songs and Voices of an Aviary of Birds so natural that any who saw not the Instrument would be persuaded that it were in Reality what it only represents. He makes musical Automata or Instruments of themselves to play exceedingly well on the Flute, Flaggelet or Organ, Sets of County Dances, Minuets, Jiggs, and the Opera tunes, fit for the diversion of those in places where a Musician is not at Hand. . . . He also Mends Watches and Clocks.'

Pinchbeck's work was mainly for the affluent. In 1722, for instance, he sold an astronomical clock to Sir Robert Walpole for 700 guineas, a musical clock to Louis XV for £1,500 and a mechanical organ for £300 to the Grand Mogul.

Although celebrated as a maker of complicated musical clockwork for forty years, it is a curious fact that to most people Christopher Pinchbeck's name is associated only with a gold-like metal alloy evolved during the last six years of his life. Pinchbeck, real pinchbeck, has such a lovely hue that it is time collectors understood it more fully. He had found, like other clockmakers, that even the finest of English brass was untrustworthy for clock movements. It was pitted by too many microscopic air bubbles buried in the body of the metal. Cogs were weakened by such flaws and tended to crack after little use. He, like other clockmakers, used plates of latten, that is, brass sheets made absolutely solid by long beating with a water-operated battery hammer. This entailed laborious and costly handwork to bring each unit to its final clockwork precision.

During his early years in Fleet Street, Pinchbeck experimented to improve the copper-zinc alloy known as prince's metal, named after Prince Rupert, who was claimed by Daniel Defoe to be its inventor. This metal was defined in 1705 as five parts copper and one part zinc converted into an alloy by direct fusion.

Francis Hauksbee, FRS, a celebrated metallurgist with laboratories only two minutes' walk from Pinchbeck's workshop, succeeded in extracting sulphur fumes from copper, thus producing a highly purified metal known as rose copper. This meant that for the first time unpitted brass castings were possible in England from the late 1720s. Pinchbeck carried the improvement further: instead of incorporating into his alloy English zinc, then containing calamine, he used tutenag imported from China, much of it forming a protective lining to chests of tea. Tutenag was actually pure zinc, a metal then impossible to produce in England. Fused in small crucibles in the proportion of five of rose copper to one of tutenag, these methods produced an unpitted alloy capable of being cast in clear-cut relief.

Pinchbeck's next step was to colour this alloy to match

contemporaneous 22-carat gold, then recognised by the Goldsmiths' Company as the standard quality hallmark for jewellery. This he achieved by processing the cast metal, first by heating until slightly red, then, when cold, pickling it in vitriol. Dust and scale were removed by washing in water and the piece momentarily immersed in aquafortis. Decorative relief work and soft, rounded edges were clearly defined by chasing and then finally burnished with a bloodstone fluxed with oil and whiting.

The new metal was marketed as pinchbeck before 1727. A new trade card designed and engraved in that year illustrated his shop sign, now *Pinchbeck's Head*, displaying a copy of his portrait painted by Isaac Whood and engraved in mezzotint by John Faber. Simultaneously he issued an advertising token, a bust of George II on the obverse, and the reverse with a portrait of Pinchbeck himself surrounded by objects made in his work-shops—a snuff-box, a cane knob, a watch attached to a double chain and a signet ring. This was inscribed around the edge: 'Christopher Pinchbeck Senior, at Pinchbeck's Head in Fleet Street.'

The metal pinchbeck achieved, quite wrongly, the reputation of being untarnishable and retaining its lustre indefinitely. True, oxidisation was a slow process, but objects made by the Pinchbeck family, cast in the solid metal, were such as demanded continual handling or were rubbed by the pocket lining whilst being carried.

Pinchbeck created his own fascinating range of handsomely hand-tooled bijouterie resembling gold such as snuff-boxes, etuis, chatelaines, cane knobs and other personal finery, showing a wholly different approach to the demand of an increasingly sophisticated and discriminating clan of the not-so-rich.

Snuff-boxes were advertised from the beginning as 'so nearly resembling gold that the best judges can hardly distinguish one from the other' and must have been made in tens of thousands. Remaining specimens inspected have the appearance of fine craftsmanship from a period when labour might be considered well-spent in giving to less costly substitutes the exquisite finish expected on snuff-boxes of gold.

The boxes were worked upon in exactly the same way that goldsmiths treated their fashionable jewellery in cast gold and silver. Pinchbeck was used alone in the majority of instances, the relief work being the outstanding feature of design. Shapes included oval, rectangle, octagon, cartouche and shell, duplicating fashionable patterns in gold. The box and cover were cast separately to be finished all over with flowers, foliate scrolls and shells against a matted ground, by a goldsmith using fine chisels, burins and various chasing tools. Punches and stamps were used for background work. The centre of the cover might be decorated with mythological heroes and heroines in the mood of the ancient cameo, with pictorial scenes or musical trophies within ovals. In one extensive series the cover was set with a flat colourful hardstone (see page 87) such as agate, sardonyx, mocha stone or cairngorm, bordered with a scroll and wave design. The sides were usually cast in bombé shape and panelled with fruit and flowers between arched pilasters. The base might be set all over with a hardstone matching that of the cover. The thumbpiece might be plain, serrated or enriched with a shell.

The earliest reference to Pinchbeck's name as denoting this metal was by Henry Fielding in 1734: 'the nobility and gentry run so much into Pinchbeck that he [the jeweller] has not dispos'd of two gold watches this month.' L. Cook in 1744 referred to 'gold, silver and pinchbeck snuff-boxes' and Lady Mary Wortley Montagu in 1755 wrote to the Countess of Bute concerning 'three of Pinchbek's watches'.

Christopher Pinchbeck died in 1732, too soon to know wide appreciation for his gold-coloured brass alloy. He was buried in St Dunstan's Church, a few yards from his retail shop. Nine days later the *Daily Post* announced that 'the snuff-boxes and other toys made by the late ingenious Mr Pinchbeck's curious metal . . . are now sold only by his son Mr Edward Pinchbeck'.

Imitators soon appeared offering an imperfect alloy masquerading as pinchbeck: there was then no legal protection against the use of a trade name. The counterfeit metal contained English zinc and instead of being processed was finished more cheaply with the period's far from satisfactory gilding. This prompted a further advertisement from Edward Pinchbeck in which he announced that he 'did not dispose of one grain of the curious metal which so nearly resembled gold in colour, smell and ductability to any person whatever'. Following the death of Edward in 1766 Pinchbeck's Head came under the control of his elder brother, Christopher II, long established as a maker of astronomical clocks at impressive premises in Cockspur Street. He became a personal friend of George III who appointed him his Principal Clockmaker. He was selected in 1768 to make a four-sided astronomical clock for the Queen's House. This was designed by the King and Sir William Chambers: the clock is now at Buckingham Palace. The Pinchbeck business was discontinued after Christopher's death in 1783.

GILT BRASS

The Pinchbecks at no time manufactured the light gilded brass snuff-boxes and other jewellery such as were made in factory workshops and which passed under the name of pinchbeck for a century or more after 1780 when James Emerson of Henham, Bristol, patented a formula and process for making by direct fusion of copper and zinc a fine brass closely resembling pinchbeck. This was described as 'more malleable and more beautiful and of a colour more resembling gold than ordinary brass.' This golden metal, very much cheaper than the pinchbeck which it superseded, became widely used by the manufacturing jewellers and snuff-box makers of Birmingham and Clerkenwell, who pirated the name of the pinchbeck.

They made their snuff-boxes from Emerson's metal rolled by machinery and shaped with a hand-operated drop hammer patented in 1769 by John Pickersgill, London. A year later

John Smith of Birmingham developed the process to give not only form but clear relief ornament. Little use was made of this stamp in the snuff-box branch of the trade until the mid-1780s.

Production of gilded-brass snuff-boxes no longer depended upon handcraft and personal skill but upon a variety of brass alloys and power-driven machinery. By the mid-1790s the two units of a snuff-box, with provision for hinging and fastening, were stamped with tools made from a new steel, much harder and longer wearing than had formerly been available. This raised impressions in finer and higher relief, three operations being needed, with the metal annealed between each to prevent splitting. In addition to the die-sunk intaglio with the required decoration a 'force' was used. This fell snugly into the die but allowed just enough space for the thickness of the metal being shaped and at the same time raised ornamental detail. Low relief work needed but a single operation.

The units were then chased, polished and burnished or gilded. Two colours of gilding were now possible – yellow and orange. The yellow tinge was secured by the application of zinc-mercury before gilding in the usual way; as many as four coatings might be given. Dating of these inexpensive snuff-boxes is not determined accurately by style alone, since the fashion introduced by the goldsmith might be continued until the tools were worn. Even before 1800 snuff-box men were tending to speed up manufacture through use of the press, by building box and cover from several pressed units that could be quickly brazed together.

Early imitations of pinchbeck snuff-boxes in gilded brass may be found struck with small punch marks resembling the assay marks which were then struck on 22-carat gold. Because of the confusion between assay marks and trade marks on everyman's golden snuff-box, legislation became necessary and from 1798 it was illegal for any identifying marks to be struck on pinchbeck or gilded metal. It was stipulated, too, that in the case of gilded metal the amount of gold, single, double or treble, should be shown. At the same time 18-carat gold was required to show the figure 18 along with the lion passant hallmark.

Gilt-brass snuff-boxes from about 1815 might be decorated with engine-turning, the lid design incorporating a plain surfaced shield, scroll or rectangle upon which the owner's crest or, more usually, cypher might be inscribed. Cover and base were decorated to match. Designs may be counted by the hundred.

The early 1830s saw the beginning of a vogue for decorating gilt snuff-box lids with pictures in high relief, many of them from worn tools used by factory silversmiths. Such pictures included sporting scenes, adaptations of Dutch paintings, designs illustrative of Shakespeare and his works and buildings of national interest such as Windsor Castle, the Tower and London Bridge. Snuff-boxes might be electro-gilded from the early 1840s, a process which covered them with a film of pure gold, varying in thickness and wearing properties according to price.

LANCASHIRE BRASS

When Philip Andreas Nemnich travelled England in 1799 he passed through the watch-making township of Prescot in South Lancashire and noted in his diary: 'Here the best watchmakers' tools are made and all parts of the movements of watches; while one workman is employed solely on the manufacture of watch springs, a second makes the cogged wheels such as the ratchet, minute and hour wheels, a third the barrels and barrel covers, a fourth the balance cocks, a fifth the hands. These pieces go to the clock and watch-making centres of Liverpool, Coventry and London where they are assembled and fitted into cases.'

These hand-made watch units by the early 1820s were meeting direct competition from France where machine tools were producing them at a fraction of the cost possible in England. These tools had been devised by Frederic Japy of Beaucourt, France, in 1776. He established a factory for making parts for watch movements in 1810 and a few years later his sons opened show-rooms and offices at 108 Rue du Temple, Paris. Instruments cut accurately the teeth of cogged wheels, drilled the watch plates and polished the finished parts. These standardised units could be assembled into a movement held between a pair of brass plates. The Japy brothers were selling more than half a million movements a year by 1840 and similar mass production had started in the United States of America. This effective rivalry had created drastic unemployment among the craftsmen of Prescot who had to seek other uses for their idle equipment and tools. Eventually they discovered a potential market for snuff-boxes in brass and copper, many of them fitted with simple but effective combination locks.

Brass and copper plate, in a gauge strong enough to prevent warping, were found long-wearing and inexpensive. But it was the ingenious keyless lock mechanism devised by a Prescot craftsman that resulted in the production of snuff-boxes that still intrigue collectors today. These ranged from table boxes to pocket size. Table snuff-boxes were particularly vulnerable to the petty pilferer, while the pocket box needed to be secure from spilling its valuable contents when constant use led to careless handling. The table snuff-box originally contained a tiny spoon for replenishing the pocket box.

The obvious development, then, was for the Prescot watch men to design many of these locks with combination controls on the lids to delight and puzzle late Georgians and early Victorians. The controls resembled a pair of crudely engraved watch dials numbered from one to twelve and fitted with circling pointers. By setting the pointers to certain pre-arranged numbers the box's catch-fastener could be released. In some instances there was also a third control pointer in the shape of a sun in splendour. The catch for opening the box might be in the shape of the first or last quarter of the moon: this slid back to open the lid and forward to latch it when closed. All joints were soldered to prevent seepage and the surfaces of the solder wiped smooth.

The locking mechanism was attached to the underside of the lid and protected from clogging by a covering plate of brass or iron. This was sealed at the edges with solder made from equal quantities of brass and zinc, to prevent snuff from seeping through the joints. The interior was heavily tinned to prevent the snuff from acquiring a metallic tang.

In many instances a five-lug hinge extended the full width of the pocket snuff-box, securely riveted with brass wire. Constant opening and shutting tended to wear the lugs of the hinge, causing the lid to fit loosely and allow snuff to leak into the pocket.

Shuttle-shaped pocket snuff-boxes such as were fashionable during the fourth quarter of the 18th century achieved renewed popularity in brass and copper. The example illustrated (No. 15 between pages 64–65) is in copper decorated with ornament resembling the bright-cut engraving used on silver plate, wriggled and punched work with an engraved monogram and, around the sides, the inscription *May the Wings of Liberty Never want a Feather*. This suggests that the owner was a supporter of the Reform Bill and that this box was made during the early 1830s. The lid is fitted with a pair of revolving studs: these are marked with short arrows which, when correctly placed, secure or release the catch.

The majority of these snuff-boxes were sold plain, either of brass highly burnished or of an alloy more closely resembling the colour of gold. Others were decorated with simple chasing or punched and wriggled work, or were line engraved with motifs such as sporting and maritime scenes, flowers and foliage, scrollwork and inscriptions. The owner's name or initials and date were frequently introduced. *Memento mori* snuff-boxes in this style may be found. Typically the box was engraved with the deceased's name and date of death accompanied by a suitable text or inscription and an 'all-seeing eye'. Frequently the inscription indicates that the snuff-box was carried by a mourner in lieu of the more usual finger ring.

Coffin-shaped snuff-boxes inscribed with allusions to death

were common. A specimen with a combination lock to its brass lid may be found with sides and base appropriately made from a hollowed-out block of box wood, the lugubrious tone of the piece being completed by an inscription such as *Sacred to the Dust of A.B.*

An interesting series of pocket snuff-boxes intended for the thrifty have a somewhat simpler and less fool-proof form of opening which avoided the use of a hinge. The box sides consisted of a circular, oval, square, hexagonal or octagonal ring of close-grained hardwood such as box wood or lignum vitae, usually stained dark red. This wooden ring was sandwiched between a pair of brass plates riveted or screwed into the wood. The bottom plate was solid but the upper plate was cut with a figure 8 opening and over this was superimposed a second plate similarly pierced and revolving on a central pivot. Such a box was opened by revolving the top plate by means of a stud fitted for that purpose, until the two openings coincided. The finger and thumb were then inserted through the suitably shaped aperture. No more than the smallest of 'pinches' could be taken owing to the inability of the snuffer to separate finger and thumb. The bottom plate might be engraved with an inscription or name and the rim of the static plate beyond the edge of the revolving cover might be decorated with wriggled work or conventional suns in splendour. Engraving filling the area of the static plate revealed when the revolving lid was fully closed served as an aid to the careful snuffer. This simple style of opening may be found, too, on a snuff-box shaped as a brass-bound book.

The table snuff-box with a lift-off lid was typical of Prescot design and craftsmanship. It is in heavy copper plate with its combination lock controlled by three domed dials. These are engraved with the rising sun, the sun in splendour and the setting sun with a crescent moon to operate the catch. Its Prescot origin is confirmed by the rim encircled with hour numerals and divisions resembling a clock dial. The centre is engraved with twelve petals in outline.

A popular type of table snuff-box was hammered into the shape of a large watch case with boldly curved sides and convex lid measuring $3\frac{1}{2}$ to 4 in. across and nearly 2 in. deep, often fitted with a circular bow above the hinge for hanging perhaps in office or workshop.

In some instances a number will be found stamped beneath such a snuff-box. Since these range from the 1500s to the 1900s they are often mistaken for dates of manufacture. But in fact such a number is no more than the craftsman's way of numbering each box he made consecutively in the manner he had used in better days to mark his watches. When a metal ring swings from a small eye riveted beneath the hinge or elsewhere, the snuff-box dates later than the introduction of the double albert in the late 1840s.

Snuff-boxes with combination locks have been reproduced in the present century. They may be recognised by their construction from light-weight rolled brass of more golden hue than the originals.

Many early Victorian snuff-boxes in these designs were made at Wolverhampton, which for more than a century had been the centre of the brass tobacco and snuff-box trade. These were mostly exported to the continent and many are now returning to collectors as Dutch antiques. Self-acting spring snuff-boxes in gilt brass were shown at the Great Exhibition of 1851.

1   Colley Cibber (1671–1757), celebrated actor and dramatist, poet laureate from 1730, taking a pinch of snuff from a tortoiseshell snuff-box shaped as a scallop shell. Mezzotint engraving by Jean Simon (1675–1751) after the painting by Giuseppe Grisoni (1699–1769).
In the British Museum.

2   Sheffield plate table snuff-rasp. Two-thirds of the canoe-shaped container is covered with a hinged grater: the remainder supports a box large enough to carry a small carotte for grating.
In the Sheffield City Museum.

3   Pocket snuff-rasp cases of carved wood. In each example the cover swivels on a joint at the wide end to expose the perforated grater fixed over a shallow recess. The snuff was removed through a grooved channel cut in the narrow end.
In the Victoria and Albert Museum.

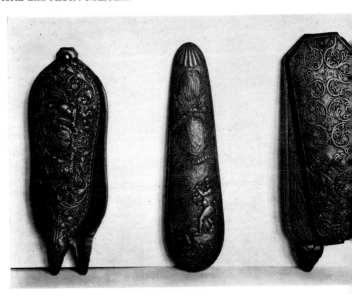

Or since the Parish Clerk said Amen, 〈 Or in a Twelvemonth and a Day, 〈 But continued true and in desire,
Wished yourselves Unmarried again; 〈 Repented not in thought any way, 〈 As when you joined hands in holy quire

The Procession after claiming the Gammon of Bacon at the Monastry of great Dunmow in Essex.

W. Sherwin Sculp.

4 Snuff-handkerchief printed with 'The Procession after claiming the Gammon of Bacon at the Monastery of Great Dunmow in Essex'. Engraved by William Sherwin in the 1780s.
In the Victoria and Albert Museum.

5 Table snuff-boxes of papier-mâché with rimmed lids, each signed 'S. Raven Pinxt. Patronized by H.R.H. the Duke of Sussex and Prince Leopold'. (*Left to right*) Mary, Queen of Scots; Miss Foote, the actress; the Three Graces. Late 1820s.

6   Silver snuff-box set with a medal of Clementina Sobieski, wife of the Old
Pretender, struck in 1719. The border engraved with formal design. Shell and
scroll thumbpiece. About 1750.
Christies.

7   Ivory table snuff-box with lift-off cover set with a portrait of George IV
carved in relief. Diameter $3\frac{1}{2}$ in.
In the Victoria and Albert Museum.

8 (*Above left*) Gold shell-shaped snuff-box, the cover chased with putti playing with doves before a classical colonnade. Interior of the cover inset with a miniature portrait by Gervaise Spencer, signed and dated 1749. $2\frac{1}{2}$ in. long.
Christies.

9 (*Above right*) Gold snuff-box engine-turned, the borders chased with bands of green-gold foliage. By Jacob Amedroz, 1799.
Christies.

10 (*Centre left*) Mother of pearl, carved in low relief, set in a silver box. Late 18th century.
Christies.

11 (*Bottom left*) Gold snuff-box, with slightly bombé sides, the cover set with a plaque of painted enamel. The sides chased with flowers, feathers and scrolls. George II period. $1\frac{7}{8}$ in. diameter.
Christies.

12 (*Bottom right*) Gold mounted snuff-box set with café au lait agate panels. 2 in. diameter.
Christies.

13 Sheffield plate snuff-boxes constructed of copper plated with silver on one side only. The sides are seamed, invisible outside; the covers hand-chased and the bases decorated with die-stamped patterns. Box and cover are lined with tortoiseshell to prevent snuff from clogging in indentations. The example on the right is pierced and set with aventurine. 1750s.
In the Sheffield City Museum.

14 Rectangular snuff-box of sturdy Sheffield plate, set with a copper half-penny of the third issue of George III, struck by Matthew Boulton in 1799. The coin has been close-plated with silver which has proved far more susceptible to wear than the plate box. About 1800.
In the collection of Mrs V. S. Mitcheson.

15 Lancashire shuttle-shaped pocket snuff-box in copper decorated with bright-cut engraving and owner's initials.

16 Lancashire watch-shaped table snuff-box in brass with combination lock operated by a pair of pointers and a sun in splendour.

17 Table snuff-box in yellow Staffordshire enamel, the cover brightly coloured over a transfer print of 'The Corner Game'. Flowers in full colours decorate the sides.
In the collection of H.M. the Queen.

18 Snuff-boxes in Staffordshire enamel. The top box has an inner lid of gilt metal with a loop for holding a snuff-spoon. The double box has two lids hinged at the centre and a gilt central partition. The box on the right is painted with a portrait of William Pitt, Earl of Chatham.
In the collection of H.M. the Queen.

19 Silver-gilt snuff-box, the centre of the cover set with the Sancroft medal 1688 within a border of scrolls, flowers and wave ornament with waisted sides and plain scroll thumbpiece. 1730s. 2¾ in. diameter. Christies.

20 Table snuff-box in 18-carat gold, the chiselled scroll and floral work framing a miniature painted by Andrew Plimer. By A. J. Strachan, 1808. Asprey & Co.

21 Table snuff-box in silver-gilt, the cover engraved with two figures amid fruit, vines and scrolling foliage, the borders chased in high relief with flowers and foliage and the sides and base engine-turned. By Nathaniel Mills, Birmingham, 1827.
Christies.

22 Musical snuff-box with humming bird: early 19th century.
In the collection of H.M. the Queen.

23 (*Left*) Amethyst box of compressed spherical form, the centre of the cover
with an applied gold plaque. 2⅛ in. diameter. Mid-18th century.
(*Right*) Gold-mounted agate, the border chased and pierced with flowers and
scrolls. 1⅝ in. diameter. About 1760.
Christies.

24 Shell-shaped gold
snuff-boxes, covers inset
with amber coloured agate
plaques. (*Above*) Borders
and sides engraved with
birds, fruits, musical
trophies and foliage. Width
2⅞ in. About 1730.
(*Below*) Concave sides
chased with fluting and
wave motifs on a matted
ground. Width 3¼ in.
About 1740.
Christies.

25   Gold mounted snuff-box, the cover and base of mocha agate, the sides engraved with festoons of flowers and foliage on a hatched ground between key pattern borders. By Elias Russel, London, 1768. 2¾ in.
Christies.

26   Set with panels of translucent and mottled grey and brown agate, overlaid with chased cartouches of gold cage-work. About 1770.
Christies.

27 Table snuff-mull made from a ram's horn with silver snuff-box and fittings.
Height 8 in. About 1820.
In the Victoria and Albert Museum.

28 Pontypool japanned snuff-boxes, all with pull-off covers. Mid-18th century. In the National Museum of Wales.

29 Clouté d'or or nailhead piqué on ivory. The hand-worked facets are virtually touching. About 1800.

30 Table snuff-box in Sheffield plate with pull-off cover of tortoiseshell ornamented in silver posé piqué. Made in about 1750 by Thomas Bolsover, the inventor of Sheffield plate.
In the collection of Mrs V. S. Mitcheson.

31 Double snuff-box of agate with gold mounts hinged centrally and chased with scrolls, flowers and wave ornament, the sides with eight pilasters. About 1740.
Christies.

32 Double table snuff-box in silver, one of a pair. By John Edwards, London, 1802. Length 4¾ in.
Prestons Ltd.

CHAPTER 6

Painted Enamels

ONE OF the most delightful manufactures of Georgian artist-craftsmen was the snuff-box in painted enamel. These are as brilliantly colourful today as when they left the workshop bench. Essentially this wholly English craft met the needs of innumerable men and women who adored elegant little trifles to match their studied graces but could never afford the exclusive creations of goldsmiths and jewellers. They delighted in tiny enamelled boxes for snuff or breath-sweetening comfits or fragments of sponge soaked in aromatic vinegar.

It has been established that some of these trifles were made at Bilston in Staffordshire as early as the late 1740s and the craft continued unceasingly for about a century, snuff-boxes being produced in their hundreds of thousands. In contrast, the Battersea factory that has given these enamels their most popular collector-name lasted no longer than three years, 1753–56.

Painted enamels were produced by fusing what amounted to opacified flint-glass to the surface of paper-thin copper and adding coloured decoration by brush, often over transfer-printed outlines, lasting brilliance being given by firing in a muffle kiln. Edges were rimmed with metal neatly hand-tooled and gilded: assembly was so perfect that none of these snuff-boxes ever required a fastener.

The Battersea factory established by Stephen Theodore Janssen at York House, former London residence of the Arch-bishops of York, no doubt materialised because the sponsors were confident of the commercial advantages of decorating enamels with transferred prints, a process evolved at Battersea.

The basic white enamel used at Battersea was probably entirely hand-prepared. Soft, in several tones of creamy white with

5

warm, brilliant surface qualities, this enamel proved an excellent ground for hand-painted decoration carried out in full but not heavy colour with fusible pigments. Colours melted over it with delightful translucent effect, and transfer prints copied excellently. The high glaze on Battersea snuff-boxes suggests that lead oxide played an important part in its composition.

The colours found in Battersea monochrome transfer printing were mauve, near-black, crimson and brick red. The copper plates were cut with deep incisions sunk in such a way that they held the enamel oil-ink firmly, yet permitted printing on paper with clear-cut, even lines when plate and ink were warmed to an equal temperature. Considerable additions were sometimes made by the enamel painter: in others there is evidence of touching up with pencil brush work in a matching shade. But the majority required no such subsequent tinting.

Stylistically their treatment mainly reflected cultivated French taste of the mid-18th century. Their decoration was dominated by the wholly graceful, slightly effeminate engravings of Simon-François Ravenet who is prominent in Battersea work. He and his fellows catered for a sophisticated enjoyment of daintily illustrated classical lore, and a knowledgeable appreciation of high-quality single-colour printing over lustrous enamel. Artists painted as thinly as possible as thick applications tended to split during cooling after firing: the labour cost of preparing the coloured enamels was high. On Battersea snuff-boxes the decoration usually covered the whole surface of the lid, without the gilding characteristic of subsequent South Staffordshire work.

For their subjects the engravers most frequently turned to the popular prints of the period. Portraits of royalty and other celebrities were executed with masterly precision on snuff-boxes: the reverse of a lid might be decorated with another print, its subject not necessarily associated with that on the outer surface. On the sides of the box, and perhaps on the base too, might appear painted flowers or such recurrent printed motifs as Ravenet's cupid groups and representations of the arts.

Among the few known decorators at Battersea were the Irishmen John Brooks, first to apply the idea of copper-plate printing to industrial purposes, and James Gwin who, John Williams has stated, arrived in London in 1755 when he 'got his livelihood by making designs for the lids of snuff-boxes, which he did for a manufactory at Battersea under the direction of Sir Stephen Janssen.' But the most important associate in the venture was Robert Hancock, himself an engraver of copper plates who is credited with introducing transfer-printing to the ceramics industry.

The final stage in the production of a Battersea snuff-box was the fitting of the hinged mount to rim and lid. The enamel, applied to both faces of the thin copper with a spatula, could not be made to adhere to the sharp edges of the copper. This problem was solved by binding all exposed edges in thin frames of copper or copper alloy. In the announcement of the sale at York House, Battersea, there is reference to 'copper frames for mounting the enamels' but in the list of enamels sold from Janssen's City home the description of the snuff-boxes includes 'mostly mounted in metal, double-gilt'.

After the closure of the Battersea factory early in 1756 the *Daily Advertiser* announced that a sale of Janssen's household effects included 'a quantity of beautiful enamels, colour'd and uncolour'd . . . consisting of Snuff-boxes of all sizes and in a great variety of Patterns'. The sale of the stock-in-trade at York House also included 'a great variety of beautiful enamell'd snuff-boxes'. Painted enamels still continued to be made in London. In 1760 J. Morris of Norris Street, Haymarket, advertised that he 'Manufactured all sorts of Enamel'd Work in Snuff Boxes'.

Painted enamels pre-dating the Battersea productions were made by John Taylor, a Birmingham button maker who in 1755 employed some 500 persons. Taylor, no doubt the pioneer in the manufacture of cheap enamelled snuff-boxes and the like, was probably established in the trade before 1750. Not only was he fully equipped with the basic facilities for making the copper blanks and mounts, but he was also a partner in a flint-glass works at Stourbridge.

William Hutton, a contemporary of Taylor and well-known to him, in his *History of Birmingham* published in 1781, wrote: 'To this uncommon genius we owe the gilt button, the japanned [?] and gilt snuff-boxes, with the numerous race of enamels. From the same fountain issued the painted snuff-box, at which one servant earned £3 10 0 by painting them at a farthing each.' If such a painter worked a six-day week and the 14-hour day of the period, this rate of production approximated 30 boxes an hour. Obviously this suggests that he must have employed an assistant, but even with such help his work at the best must have been extremely crude. The basic enamel on these snuff-boxes was applied by spatula. It is probable that speedy production and incomplete understanding of the processes involved resulted in snuff-boxes from which the enamel soon flaked and chipped off the copper base so that few are encountered by collectors.

Taylor himself was a successful man of business, unlikely to take up an enterprise which did not promise profitable results, as may be gathered by the comment of James Watt in a letter to Matthew Boulton in 1775: 'John Taylor died the other day worth £200,000 without ever doing one generous action.'

Taylor was by no means the only Birmingham enameller. Basil Palmer is recorded in the 1767 *Directory* as an enameller and button-maker. The craft continued unceasingly in Birmingham until the 1840s. *Robson's Directory*, 1839, lists three enamellers: Charles Gwynne, 16 Mott Street; J. Abrahall, 4 Caroline Street; and John Brown & Co., 69 Bull Street.

Matthew Boulton, trading as Boulton & Fothergill, is usually referred to as of Birmingham, but actually was at Soho in South Staffordshire. His trade card of the 1770s illustrated his premises. Confirmation of enamel manufacture is plentiful and includes a reference in a letter written to James Adam in 1770. Queen Mary possessed a double snuff-box by Boulton with a gilded silver mount struck with the hall-mark for 1783.

For some years prior to the establishment of Janssen's

Battersea factory, South Staffordshire and Birmingham were the most important producers of enamel snuff-boxes. Early collectors established the fame of the Battersea work, but only recently has there been a long over-due evaluation of South Staffordshire enamels.

The craft of japanning on iron had been established in Bilston as early as the reign of Queen Anne and it has now been confirmed that a group of enamellers from France arrived in this town some time before 1745 and taught the local japanners what was hailed at the time as an improved art of decorating. Contemporaneously, and throughout the first half of the 18th century, the Bilston parish registers refer to a number of snuff-box makers.

Here in Bilston, with the flint-glass centre of Stourbridge only a few miles away to the south-west, was an obvious centre for anyone wishing to produce decorative enamels on a commercial scale and requiring rolled copper, metal mounts, enamel colours and decorators. With reasonable certainty the 1740s have been credited with the circular snuff-boxes of japanned iron with detachable lids inset with painted enamel plaques.

The earliest industrial enameller of whom any personal record exists was Dovey Hawkesford of Bilston. He was described in 1741 as a chapman, but at the time of his death in 1749 the news columns of *Aris's Birmingham Gazette* reported him as having been an enameller. This is confirmed by the fact that at this time Benjamin Bickley bought a fully equipped enamel factory in Bilston, advertised as possessing 'a pair of millstones and two mills for grinding enamels.' This was almost five years before the Battersea venture was launched.

From the examples that remain today it is clear that the main development of Bilston enamelling dates from about 1750. At once it is necessary to reject the old idea of one or two individual enamellers whose hand may be detected in all the major South Staffordshire productions. It has been established that more than eighteen master enamellers operated at Bilston. These included the Bickley, Perry and Becket families, James Brett,

John Buckley, J. Hoo Foster, John Green, S. Hanson, Thomas Knowles and Isaac Smith. Local directory records tell their own tale of the rise and fall of the trade.

Enamelling was established at near-by Wednesbury in 1776 by Samuel Yardley who obtained the necessary equipment from the sale of the Bickley factory in that year. It has not been fully appreciated that this marked a distinctive new phase in the development of enamelling. Yardley found that costs could be cut drastically by dipping the shaped copper into thick liquid enamel. At the same time enamelling furnaces became more efficient and were enlarged. By 1780 other enamellers were established in Wednesbury, all using the dipping process and improved furnaces to the detriment of the Bilston enamellers who continued applying the viscid paste to the copper by means of spatulas. Soon a second coating of fine quality enamel might be applied over the basic layer: the two qualities are visible in cracks.

The men associated with the manufacture of Wednesbury enamels include three generations of Yardleys, the families of Holden, Ross, Baker and Snape. There are several contemporaneous references to the excellence of their work. It was James Ross who evolved the formula for the delicate pink tinted enamel and for many years he was the sole maker. Many of these enamellers made snuff-boxes, in some cases sending them out to independent decorators for painting or transfer printing, receiving them back, already muffle-fired, for mounting and finishing. At the same time several mount-makers bought decorated lids of good quality from one supplier and second quality bodies from another source, fitted them together and sold them to merchants at competitive prices. Snuff-boxes are often found with the basic white enamels on body and lid of obviously different qualities.

Snuff-boxes in what is sometimes described as the Battersea style usually have their lids enriched with pictorial decoration and the sides with additional pictures or hand-painted posies. Some elaborately mounted snuff-boxes are brightly but somewhat laboriously painted with subjects adapted from engravings such as that by De Larmessin of Lancret's 'L'après-dîner'. These constitute a distinctive group preceding the more mechanical style of painting associated with factory productions. Colours are usually bright with particular emphasis on yellows and reds over red-brown printed outlines.

At this period the most highly decorative style of picture was largely the province of French artists and it is scarcely surprising to find the works of Watteau, Lancret, Boucher and Nattier copied on snuff-boxes. For instance, a rectangular snuff-box lid might display one or other of Antoine Watteau's gay scenes such as his *Fêtes Venitiennes* or *Le Colin Maillard*. Other frequently copied works are Nicolas Lancret's *Flute Lesson* and *Tea Party* (the latter in many extremely fine adaptations), *Les Amants* by Jean-Marc Nattier and *Pensent-ils au Raisins?* by François Boucher.

Among the mezzotint engravers whose work was adapted by the South Staffordshire enamellers may be mentioned Richard Houston who popularised Philippe Mercier's series *Morning, Afternoon* and so on: the vivacious study of a woman holding a mask from *Night* in this series is frequently encountered on snuff-box lids. François Vivares produced several engravings of classical landscapes by Claude Lorraine and others which, more or less standardised, appeared on innumerable painted enamels.

The classical landscapes decorating South Staffordshire enamel boxes are pleasantly drawn and carefully coloured, but they are unambitious routine pieces of work in line with the contemporary demand for pillared ruins and pastoral scenes. Only very occasionally do people and animals come to life.

Not until the 1760s were enamelled snuff-boxes given gilded decoration, which could not be burnished to a rich lustre and lacks the brilliance of later gilding. Even when new this gold was slightly dull in appearance and would not withstand wear. South Staffordshire gilding from the 1780s involved the use of mercury and was a serious health hazard.

During the period of South Staffordshire's finest production, the 1760s to the early 1780s, a painted enamel snuff-box might be a truly handsome possession. The outer surfaces of box and lid were smooth and flawless. Superimposed upon this background, which might be tinted in such colours as blue, green or pink, there might be a raised diaper pattern of criss-cross lines interspersed with dots, all in white or one or more harmonising colours.

The slightly convex lid of the typical snuff-box was decorated with elaborate scrollwork applied in raised white enamel covered with gilding; sometimes this might embody tiny flower posies painted in full colour on white reserves among the scroll-work. The central white reserve of the lid, within the irregularly shaped rococo scrolling, was painted in full colour with or without the basis of a transfer print, and on each side of the box a white reserve among more gilded scrolls contained another tiny picture painted in full colour – often by a different hand on the finest snuff-boxes – or a simple flower posy. In some examples the base carried another posy in colour or a single flower in gilt. A peculiarly straggly gilt flower is probably the trade symbol of an individual firm and other symbols which may eventually be identified include central dot-and-dash designs on raised white, applied like the diaper work covering the rest of the box.

Slight embossing on enamel snuff-boxes dates from the late 1760s: a box decorated in this way has been noted with an inscription dated 1769. By 1775 deep press-embossing had become fashionable, such as is seen in the snuff-box with a rose embossed on the lid, each petal painted in detail. (Some of these closely resembled Meissen porcelain).

Until the French Revolution the majority of Staffordshire enamels went abroad, principally to France and Italy. With these markets lost, the final phase of these delightful snuff-boxes was dominated by the need to cut costs. By the 1790s quality was being sacrificed disastrously and the market flooded with innumerable tiny snuff-boxes in no way comparable with the early issues. The collector must look beyond these intriguing but unambitious trifles if he is to appreciate the English painted enamels' colourful contribution to 18th-century manufactures.

Typical of the late mass production work were the little boxes in dullish colours, usually oval, less well-hinged and lacking applied base rims, which nevertheless were so well constructed that they never required fasteners to secure their contents of snuff. Even at the time these were regarded largely as souvenirs to be sold or presented by shop-keepers at fashionable watering places and holiday resorts. Many were printed with local views and the inscription *A Trifle from* – Tunbridge Wells, Cheltenham, Bath, Harrogate, Evesham, Worcester, Stafford, Stone, even Wolverhampton, to name only a few towns. Some bore, in addition, painted in, the name of the shops that presented them to favoured customers.

A small snuff-box, transfer-printed and hand-coloured with a portrait of Queen Caroline, was issued early in the reign of George IV (probably in 1821) when according to *Parson and Bradshaw's Directory*, 1820, only two South Staffordshire enamellers were operating: Isaac Becket, Duck Lane, Bilston, and John Yardley, Church Hill, Wednesbury, both entered as enamel box makers.

Early snuff-box mounts are notable for their superb craftsmanship. They were fitted to the edges of the enamelled body and lid and known to the trade as 'jointed mounts'. Specialist mount-makers in Bilston served the painted enamel trade and there were several in Wolverhampton and Birmingham. Decoration on the earliest mounts, made from thin ribbons of pinchbeck, was restricted to short tooled lines and punchings such as the craftsman's time and ingenuity allowed. The first technial improvement came in 1768 with the introduction of the steel swage block through which a ribbon of soft brass could be drawn so that its cross section could be of any desired ornamental shape. These swage-shaped ribbons were too flimsy to be used alone as mounts and were therefore hard soldered to slightly heavier plain ribbons which were fabricated into hinged mounts. Such built-up mounts are distinctive and are associated with enamels made before the era of cut-price production. Edge decoration on this ribbon was still hand-worked with such simple motifs as beading and gadrooning. The inevitable irregularities of handwork distinguish it from machine-made patterns. These date from 1779 onward when William Bell patented a process for decorating the outer surface of profiled ribbons by means of 'rolling cylinders, the cylinder being shaped to suit the design. These are of great benefit to the toy trade'.

Hinges were usually four-jointed, but in the case of rectangular and square boxes they extended the full width of the box. Hinges on inexpensive souvenir snuff-boxes had three joints. Most hinges were carefully made to withstand the severe wear of a snuff-box being continually opened and shut. From about 1790 a slight deterioration in craftsmanship may be noted. A shapely lifter or thumb-piece was fitted to the front edge of the lid.

Careful examination of suspected London reproductions reveals the marks of press tools around the hinges, some of which have a small central projection. But reproductions made by Samson & Co., Paris, do not have this defect.

CHAPTER 7

Musical Boxes: Singing Birds

MUSICAL BOXES

GEORGIAN elegance found expression in many a tiny snuff-box exquisitely enriched with embossments and jewels. But even more splendid was the snuff-box which, with slight pressure upon a concealed button, chimed and tinkled a melodious accompaniment to an invitation to participate in the ceremony of snuffing. Such boxes provided precisely the quality of surprise that fascinated and delighted rich Georgians.

Musical snuff-boxes in England date from the early 1770s to the 1860s and are usually cased in hallmarked silver or silver-gilt: rarely in gold before the mid-1850s. Queen Mary possessed several that had formerly belonged to Queen Charlotte in which the aroma of Georgian snuff still lingered.

Shapes, sizes and decorations resembled those of fashionable pocket snuff-boxes, but many were designed for the table. Early examples were of plainly polished silver, followed by chasing. During the 1780s and early 1790s there was a fashion for bright-cut engraving, followed by cast and chased decoration from 1800, and, in the early 19th century, by engine-turning. From about 1820 the cover design usually incorporated a cartouche for the attachment of a cast and chased coat of arms or crest.

The majority of early cases were hallmarked in London: on those made between 1790 and the mid-19th century Birmingham hallmarks are common and some of Glasgow.

In the 18th century the cover opened directly to the snuff compartment. The musical movement beneath was separated by a plate of semi-transparent polished horn through which the mechanism was visible. This was always sealed. The flat base was hinged and highly polished. From about 1800 the positions were reversed, the cover opening to the musical movement with the snuff-box beneath. Dimensions approximated 3 in. by 2 in. by 1 in., the silver case weighing about 5½ oz and the movement about 2½ oz extra. The movement, the work of a skilled watchmaker, covered the entire area of the case and was about ¼ in. deep. At first only a single tune could be played but the number was gradually increased until by the 1830s as many as six tunes could be played within the confines of a small snuff-box.

Until about 1815 movements were simple, a 1¼ in. brass disc set with twenty steel striking pins radiating fan-wise from a central point on each side. These plucked a resonant metal comb cut with fifteen to twenty-five teeth tuned to scale. By about 1810 mechanism began to be improved and the disc was superseded by a revolving cylinder of brass from which steel pins projected. Cylinder and comb were placed parallel and provided with a spring to wind and thus operate the automatic music.

Specialists in Geneva, such as comb-makers, cylinder prickers and spring-makers supplied parts for the movements. In London the makers and assemblers of movements often worked as garret masters. Benson & Hill, London, were spring-makers late in the 18th century whose signed work is sometimes discovered. Complete movements were imported from Switzerland and Germany throughout the period by agents in Clerkenwell and Birmingham who fitted them into boxes made by English jewellers.

Less expensive musical snuff-boxes were made from about 1815 with outer cases of jet black horn. Covers were often decorated with impressed views, classical scenes, oval portraits of celebrities, or sometimes scrollwork enriched with gilding long since worn away. Engine-turned decoration was also used. These sold in large numbers for more than half a century.

Wood snuff-box cases became popular from the mid-1820s, such as maple, palm-tree, olive wood, amboyna, coromandel, rosewood, fruit woods, with covers attractively grained: lignum vitae was also used. In one popular series the cover was inlaid with a design composed of trumpet, tambourine, music sheet and other musical trophies accompanied by an olive branch.

A musical snuff-box typical of a series recorded in the *Penny Magazine for the Society for Diffusion of Useful Knowledge*, 1838, 'usually plays two tunes repeatedly, the pins being fixed and immovable. However, pins could be fixed to play almost any tune desired: usually they come in fancy boxes with the mechanism visible under a sheet of horn. Some of the larger snuff-boxes can play as many as six different tunes.' A cheap musical snuff-box sold the world over from 1835 was operated by a worm screw and had neither spring nor speed regulator. The boxes were of japanned iron hand-painted in colours or, from about 1860, decorated with coloured transfers. These snuff-boxes played but a single tune and were also counted as interesting toys for children.

Popular tunes were used almost exclusively until the 1830s, often selections from operas. Waltzes were in continual demand from the 1830s together with ballads and patriotic and folk songs until about 1850. Airs from oratorios date from about 1845. Musical snuff-boxes inspired at least two musical compositions: *The Snuff-Box Waltz* by M.S. in 1830 and *The Musical Snuff-Box* by Anatul Liadov.

Musical snuff-boxes may be dated by the style of the case, the type of ornament used, the progressive improvement in the mechanism and the selection of tunes. For instance, the positions of the steel pins, until about the middle of the century, were marked off by hand and holes bored into which they were fitted. This was a tedious process, costly in labour, for only very skilful craftsmen with a thoroughly accurate musical ear could be employed. Every cylinder was separately marked and careful inspection will reveal the scriber lines. Hollow punches ensured that the pins were accurately and firmly positioned. Warm sealing composition was then run into the cylinder and its ends covered with brass.

During the period 1810–60 amber-coloured tortoiseshell musical snuff-boxes were made with gold or silver mounts and embossed medallions set in their covers. At first these were imported from Jacquard Brothers, St Croix. These progressively played two, three, four and, by the early 1830s, six tunes. Thereafter they were made in Birmingham by William Hall, Newhall Street and Heeley Harris & Co., Lemon Street, both of whom imported Swiss movements. The name of the maker might be scratched microscopically beneath the brass plate of the mechanism, such as A. Bordier, Geneva, on a series of exceptionally fine musical snuff-boxes made from about 1785; C. Friderico, Geneva, a specialist in small watches who supplied mechanisms for musical snuff-boxes from about 1800 to 1820; and C. Brugercia, London, 1820–24. J. H. Heller, Berne, supplied good quality mechanisms from 1870 to the 1890s. The winding key was usually concealed in a tiny compartment in the bottom of the box, invisible because covered with a slide matching the case. Music was produced on opening the lid.

Musical snuff-boxes for the table contained larger movements than the pocket variety. The majority were in black horn or papier mâché and early examples even play two tunes. A depression in the dividing horn near the fastener and extending the whole width of the box accommodated a snuff-ladle.

SINGING BIRDS

A particular treasure among a collector's snuff-boxes is the specimen with a hidden spring in the side which if lightly touched opens a trap door in the cover releasing a brilliantly plumaged bird that turns and flutters in an ecstasy of trilling song and then as suddenly disappears again. Such boxes were made in materials ranging from plain blonde tortoiseshell to jewelled and chased gold. No technique at the jeweller's disposal which added to their splendour was considered too costly.

The trap-door which released the tiny bird, seldom exceeding $\frac{3}{4}$ in. overall, was fitted into the centre of the snuff-box lid and was usually enriched with a colourful picture in enamels such as a portrait, posy or coat of arms. This panel was encircled with pearls, diamonds or other precious stones. The melodious song was accomplished by applying the basic principle that a whistling note could be created by air pressure, first demonstrated in 300 BC by the engineer Philo of Byzantium. This was applied to singing bird boxes in the late-1760s and to snuffboxes in about 1790, a whole range of notes being produced with a series of flutes similar to those on a pipe organ, but other integral parts were crude. Ten years elapsed before virtual perfection of mechanism was attained.

These delicate creations are found in a variety of detail, but there is no variation in the mechanical principle. The bird song is generated by forcing air, by means of tiny bellows, into a tube with a whistle outlet. In this tube operates a piston, its motion controlled by cam wheels. These movements modify and vary the tone and volume of the whistle sound. Motive power is provided by a coiled spring, the speed at which it uncoils being regulated by a governing mechanism.

The tiny bellows, less than one-inch square, is constructed on a copper wire frame covered with fine skin of the chicken-skin variety, so prepared that it is air-tight as well as exceptionally supple. When the spring operates the bellows air is forced through the piston tube. This produces a single long-drawn note which the intricately designed mechanism converts into the characteristic extensive tone range.

The tiny bird itself contains further mechanism causing the head to turn from side to side, beak to open and shut, wings and tail to flutter and the whole body to turn from side to side. The real master stroke was to make the bird flat so that it could be concealed in a shallow box until pressure upon a tiny lever made the cover spring open. Immediately the bird rises upright it begins to sing. At the end of the song it returns into the box and the lid snaps shut. All these automatic movements were timed to a split second. Birds of the 18th century were enamelled and not feathered, nor could they turn their heads.

In the manufacture of singing bird boxes time did not count. The making of a single example required the services of a master watch-maker to supply the mechanism; a first class jeweller and goldsmith; an artist enameller and bird-maker, additional to the assembler.

Singing bird boxes were first made in about 1770 by Peter Jacquet-Droz, a celebrated Swiss watch-maker. Eventually he reduced the mechanism to miniature proportions suitable for fitting into snuff-boxes, by replacing the series of flutes with a single piston moving backwards and forwards in a tube. This discovery was copied by the watch-makers of Geneva. It is known that before 1790 at least two dozen master-men had overcome the intricacies of manufacture and were engaged in their production until about 1830. A second series was made between 1860 and the 1930s. The earlier signed singing bird snuff-boxes were made by Jacob Frisart between 1790 and 1812: during ten of those years he worked in London. Boxes marked FR were made by Rochat et Fils, Brassus, Switzerland, founded in 1802. They moved to Geneva in 1810 and traded as Frères Rochat until 1825. These snuff-boxes imported into London repeated the elegance of early Georgian snuff-boxes ranging from specimens in 22-carat gold, chased, jewelled and enamelled to those of plain amber and tortoiseshell.

A simplified mechanism was devised in about 1860 and singing birds enhanced less expensive snuff-boxes. Their cases might be in silver-gilt, silver or gilded brass, stamped from the plate and outwardly resembling vinaigrettes or early 19th-century snuff-boxes. Those made in the 1930s sold in London at fifteen guineas each.

CHAPTER 8

Jasper Ware: Pottery and Porcelain

JASPER WARE

WHEN Josiah Wedgwood, FRS, in 1766 outlined his proposals for establishing a new pottery at Stoke-upon-Trent, he specified that production should include 'snuff and other boxes'. He did not market snuff-boxes, however, until he had developed the fine white stoneware that he named jasper ware, so called because its density and hardness made it possible for the lapidary's wheel to produce a polish as brilliant as that of the natural stone. It was not until 1776 that he was able to declare 'we are now absolute with jasper'.

Jasper ware is basically a vitreous semi-porcelain converted into a close-textured stoneware by the addition of barium carbonate. Its smooth non-porous surface was secured without the application of glaze and when pressed thin it revealed translucency. At first it had a creamy hue. Experiments continued and by 1780 a perfectly white jasper was made. Wedgwood's log detailing thousands of trials still remains.

Variations in the quality of jasper ware permit snuff-boxes to be dated with some accuracy. The jasper body ranged from the dry and opaque to the waxen and translucent: that made between 1780 and 1795 feels almost like satin. During the early 1780s a slightly glossy variety was made. Until 1820 texture was fine and uniform of grain and never chalky in appearance. Yet it was porous enough before firing to be stained throughout its substance by mineral oxides to almost any desired colour. Seven ground colours have been noted in snuff-boxes: dark blue, lavender, sage green, olive green and the bluish pink known to collectors as lilac, an intense black and an attractive yellow. These hues varied in tone for technical reasons such

6

as impurities in the oxides used and variations in kiln temperature.

At first the jasper was coloured throughout the mass of its fabric: such snuff-boxes often display spots which appeared during firing. In 1777 Wedgwood discovered that the front of a panel of white jasper could be coloured by dipping into a slip of coloured jasper. From 1780 all snuff-boxes were coloured by this method.

Skilfully worked white jasper embossments were applied to these lustrous coloured backgrounds, against which they stood out clearly in relief. Tiny plaques, cameos and medallions were also made for insertion into the lids of snuff-boxes in ivory, gilded silver, gilt brass and tortoiseshell. Jasper plaques suitable for pocket snuff-box lids measured up to $2\frac{1}{2}$ in. diameter or 2 in. by $1\frac{3}{4}$ in. and cost about sixpence each. The finer of these were protected from damage with a covering of glass.

From originals, moulds were made in plaster of paris or fired potter's clay. The moist white jasper was pressed into such a *pitcher* or intaglio mould until every line and dot was filled. Superfluous clay was then scraped off level with the face of the mould with a modeller's tool. After drying for a few minutes the white jasper relief was extracted, wetted with water and applied by hand to the coloured jasper panel. The reliefs were then tooled and edges undercut to sharpen shadows. The subsequent firing was a skilled operation.

The obvious defects in jasper ware snuff-boxes such as slight warping prompted Wedgwood to use the same technique for their ornament, pressing reliefs separately and applying them to flat panels. His bas reliefs were also set into lids of table snuff-boxes. After 1790 attractive snuff-box lids included tricoloured specimens, constituting some of the most elaborate of Wedgwood's art work. The ground might be pink, the border blue, and the relief white. The borders enclosing the jasper relief might be reticulated to show the colour of the panel beneath.

Snuff-boxes might be decorated with contemporaneous

portraits classed by Wedgwood as *Heads of Illustrious Moderns*: about a thousand subjects were issued, but few of them on snuff-boxes. The Wedgwood catalogue of 1787 lists 229 names. Portraits are usually in white profile against a blue ground, very occasionally against green or black. The rare full faces include Dr Erasmus Darwin and Flaxman's portraits of Captain Cook, William Pitt and Charles J. Fox. If fitted into a colourful frame of jasper the price of a snuff-box reached one guinea. Snuff-boxes with commissioned portraits were ordered in numbers of not less than ten, usually for presentation purposes and cost three to five guineas each.

John Flaxman, RA, celebrated for his classical work and portraiture, received his first commission from Wedgwood in 1775 and for twelve years produced designs for reproduction in jasper, such as *Muses with Apollo*, 1777. Portraits by Flaxman found on snuff-box lids include George III and his family, Sir Joshua Reynolds, the Duchess of Devonshire and the popular admirals Rodney, Howe, Duncan and St Vincent.

Eliza Meteyard in her *Life of Josiah Wedgwood*, 1865, illustrates a circular table snuff-box set with Flaxman's masterpiece of 1775, *Muses Watering Pegasus in Helicon*. Of this she writes: 'The horse is so instinct with life that it seems to snort and move: and the Muse standing beside it looks as though she lifted her water-bearing vessel to its lips. The life-like attitude of the Muse who seeks to wash the foot of the immortal steed, and of the one who caresses it, are equally remarkable. Even the water breaks into waves. The ornamental setting shows in masterly detail one of the finest borders peculiar to Wedgwood's bas reliefs.'

William Hackwood joined Wedgwood in 1769 and immediately became his leading modeller of bas-relief subjects, some of which are found on snuff-boxes. Josiah Wedgwood considered Hackwood of 'the greatest value in finishing fine small work' suitable for snuff-boxes. He remained with the firm until 1832.

Among the many jasper medallions incorporated into snuff-box lids the more important included: Aurora, the Goddess of the Dawn, 1773; Priam Begging the Body of Hector, 1774; Hercules overcome by Love, 1774; The Philosopher, 1777; Nymph with Garland, 1784; Sacrifices to Victory and other sacrificial subjects.

Jasper reliefs were often set in ormolu or silver mounts thought to have been made by Matthew Boulton. These might be skilfully worked with scrolls or cast with floral sprays and birds. Wedgwood wrote of his jasper cameos that 'these are set in gold and cut steel mountings for snuff-boxes . . . and other trinkets which have lately been much worn by the nobility.'

The facets on hand-wrought cut steel were cut in diamond-shapes, highly burnished and rust-resistant. Most of the remaining examples reflect light as brilliantly today as when they were taken from the wheel. These mountings might also be enriched with an inner fillet of gold, sometimes with the addition of polished jasper ware beads.

Wedgwood jasper snuff-boxes from 1772 to 1780 were impressed *Wedgwood & Bentley* in upper and lower case letters of various sizes: in 1772 he recorded 'going on a plan to mark the whole'. The soft clay beneath the box was impressed with ordinary printer's type of the period, such marks being entirely durable after firing. From 1780 the name *Wedgwood* in any of six varying sizes was impressed.

William Adams, a favoured pupil of Josiah Wedgwood, left his master in 1769 and established a pottery at Greengates, producing jasper snuff-boxes from 1787 to 1805 impressed *Adams*.

Humphrey Palmer of Hanley claimed to have been earlier in the field of jasper reliefs than Wedgwood. But for the impressed marks it would be difficult to distinguish between their work, but Palmer's mounts were probably the work of a Wolverhampton maker. Palmer's modeller cleverly imitated Wedgwood's patterns immediately they appeared in the London shops. Copyright in design was then limited to three months.

John Turner, Lane End, and his son produced from about 1790 some excellent, fine textured jasper, slatey-blue, green and black.

Several snuff-boxes have been noted marked *Mayer*, crudely made of poor jasper.

POTTERY AND PORCELAIN

The first ceramic snuff-boxes made in England date to the late 1740s and were the work of Thomas Whieldon, Fenton Low, Staffordshire. He improved the existing pottery known as agate ware, variegated throughout its texture with colourful markings and stripes resembling those of the then fashionable agate stone displayed in snuff-boxes and jewellery. The surface of this pottery, glazed by sprinkling with galena, was covered with minute granulations in which snuff tended to accumulate. For the same reason white salt-glazed stoneware was found unsuitable for snuff-boxes: examples seen are of modern manufacture. By using the newly evolved liquid glaze Whieldon produced a smooth surface. He also altered the composition of his agate so that it more closely resembled the real stone.

Whieldon used a white burning clay stained with metallic oxides. By piling flat bats of different coloured clays one upon the other and heavily beating them to drive out enclosed air pockets, he caused the separate clays to adhere to each other in a solid mass. This was cut into slices with wires. This process of laying, beating and slicing was repeated again and again, the run of the grain being preserved. The fine wavy lines of coloured clays were disposed in countless folds with irregular striations giving a picturesque effect yet avoiding violent contrasts. As workmen became skilled in this work the striations became thinner and the effects more attractive.

This mass of vari-coloured clays was almost non-plastic and inclined to split if shaped by throwing on the wheel. The difficulty was overcome by pressing the clay into shaped moulds. After firing the snuff-boxes and lids in their biscuit state were smoothed by hand-polishing and then dipped into the transparent liquid glaze that was introduced in about 1750. By 1760 the glaze was faintly tinged with cobalt, the snuff-boxes then more nearly resembling natural agate. Whieldon sold the units to merchants in Wolverhampton and Birmingham who fitted them into gilded metal mounts, that is, hoops, hinges and spring fasteners. So closely resembling agate stone, these snuff-boxes were in great demand. Eliza Meteyard has recorded that Whieldon also made small oval snuff-boxes painted with flowers on white earthenware.

Snuff-boxes with screw-on covers were among the first articles to be made by the Leeds Pottery. These were in deep cream-coloured pottery and thickly glazed, with an embossed design on the cover. At about this time, the 1760s, snuff-boxes were being made at Bristol in tin-enamelled earthenware decorated in blue, usually painted, sometimes spattered.

Porcelain snuff-boxes in the 18th century were mainly Continental. Factories such as Meissen and Vienna were constant sources of supply in hard paste porcelain from the 1740s, the finer examples set in gold mounts. This porcelain was much tougher than the soft paste porcelains of Bow, Chelsea and Derby which were not strong enough to withstand the strains of snuff-boxes in hourly use. Porcelain snuff-boxes may be found simulating folded letters sealed with red wafers impressed with British coats of arms and inscriptions in English. These are hard paste porcelains from Germany.

English bone china, much stronger than soft paste porcelain, was used for snuff-boxes, which were made in the Staffordshire Potteries from about 1815. Box and cover were fitted into gilt metal mounts such as had been used by the Bilston enamellers. Some were carefully and neatly painted in polychrome enamels; less expensively they were decorated with bat-printed flowers, foliage, shells and the like in black or purple.

Snuff-boxes of the much more durable felspathic earthenware known as stone china were made from about 1815 until the mid-19th century. These were usually decorated in colour under the glaze and were capable of withstanding the rough and tumble of everyday usage.

CHAPTER 9

Hardstones

THE COLOURFUL materials used to create individual character in early Georgian snuff-boxes included thin plates of
crystalline hardstones. These were cut and polished and set in
hinged mounts or frames of gold, silver, pinchbeck or one of the
gilded brass alloys. London jewellers assembling these brought
together some of the finest work of the period from gold chasers
and lapidaries.

Agates with their fascinating veins of colour and vitreous
lustre decorated snuff-boxes throughout the 18th and 19th
centuries. This hardstone is immediately recognised by its
flowing colour bands alternating in light and dark colours –
white, yellow, orange, grey or brown. Single colour agate was
also used for snuff-boxes in a variety of tints, mainly by early
Victorian makers. Other varieties of English and Scottish
quartz noted in snuff-boxes include onyx, sardonyx, bloodstone
and cairngorm.

Agates or veinstones, a form of chalcedony, are all more or
less porous and could be stained in vivid colours by soaking in
red, blue, green or brown dye. In addition agate plates, ready
dressed and polished, were imported by the snuff-box makers
from Oberstein, Rhineland. This source was exhausted long
ago but German lapidaries for more than a century have worked
agates from Brazil and other South American states.

Lapidaries in Aberdeen prepared agates from Angus, Mon-
trose and the Ayrshire coast and hardstones from the celebrated
Cairngorm mountains in the Grampian highlands. From here
and three other mountains they obtained quartz crystals in
white, pink, yellow, reddish and dark brown, and black.
These, known to collectors as cairngorms, were found in rock
cavities and among river debris. Of these quartz crystals, the

deep yellow, skilfully cut, were – and still are – sold as Scottish topaz, the darker varieties as smoky topaz. Other native hardstones set in Georgian and Victorian snuff-boxes included porphyry from the Forest of Glenorchy on the Marquess of Breadalbane's Perthshire estate; heliotrope or bloodstone, a dark green chalcedony spotted with red; cornelian, a red chalcedony, stained naturally with oxide of iron.

Derbyshire produced some outstanding hardstones, particularly the blue fluorspar of Castleford with fascinating zig-zags of colour ranging through deep blue, amethyst, tawny brown, pink and honey gold. Derbyshire's marbles in a range of subdued tones were used too. In 1791 William Hutton visited Derby and observed in the shops a wide array of snuff-boxes in Derbyshire marbles and marvelled at their export by the thousand to China and South America. Petrified sponges forming rich patterns are found in stones from the Isle of Wight and the Sussex beaches and these too may be noted in snuff-boxes, cut and polished by local lapidaries.

Perhaps the most highly fashionable of the hardstones imported by the jewellers for setting in snuff-boxes was aventurine. Snuff-boxes set with chrysoprase, a pale green chalcedony mined in Koseinitz, Silesia, became fashionable from about 1740. Mocha stone, an Arabian agate displaying tree-like markings, was set in snuff-boxes throughout the Georgian period. Petrified wood from Austria was also imported by the snuff-box men.

Hardstones were cut on a horizontal wheel of lead dressed with emery powder, a natural mixture of corundum and magnatite, made into a paste with olive oil or water and spread on the flat of the wheel. After grinding, the stone was polished on a tin wheel with tripoli and water, and finished on a zinc wheel with putty of tin and water. Final polishing was carried out by hand and was the work of children. The stones were passed as perfect when water splashed upon their surface made no improvement to the lustre. Stones were polished on both sides so that the interior surface of the box did not clog the snuff.

In many instances snuff-box lids and bases were in hardstone, the mounts being in gold or silver. A fashionable shape was a rectangle or square with clipped corners which required eight vertical side panels of hardstone. Occasionally both lid and base were hinged with a horizontal partition between, intended to contain two qualities of snuff. In another pattern a deep rectangular box was divided centrally with a vertical partition on which hinged a pair of lids. A circular box might be fitted with a cover enriched with a mosaic of vari-coloured agates set in a formal radiating design, each stone separated by a thin, flat ribbon of gold. The central point was emphasised with a contrasting gem such as an amethyst which itself might be encircled with paste diamonds or rock crystal.

Throughout the 18th century there was a demand for the snuff-box carved from a single hardstone, fitted only with a hinged gold mount encircling rim and lid. The earliest hard-stone snuff-box of this type recorded so far was mentioned by Francesco Zucchi in 1636. This was made from a solid block of rock crystal. Until about 1750 such snuff-boxes were usually in the shape of escallop shells, although cartouche and trefoil shapes are known as well as circles and oblongs. These stones were for the most part of German origin.

Some London gold chasers traded as specialists in making gold and silver mounts and fitting them with hardstone plaques. George Vertue in 1732 noted that 'of late years in London have been several Chasers of Snuff-boxes' and named Parberry as being 'accounted the best gold chaser' at that time. He referred also to 'a Frenchman named Mr Capheire who died in London *c*. 1710' as a specialist in this work, but rarely is an example found that can pre-date the Queen Anne period.

Until about 1790 hardstone snuff-boxes set with highly polished agates of fine quality might display small masterpieces of the gold chaser's craft, cover and sides being lavishly har-nessed with exquisitely worked openwork *à cage*, in gold or silver, the latter usually gilded. Some examples contain recur-ring motifs of hounds and exotic birds enclosed in a closely scrolled framework all chased in high relief and leaving little of the stone to be seen.

Later came the picture design with mythological subjects incorporating ancient buildings with figures, animals, birds, enclosed in a simple asymmetrical framework of flowers, foliage and C-scrolls. These were more graceful than formerly and less confining of the lustrous hardstone which formed a splendid ground for the precious metal, each enhancing the other. In some snuff-boxes the pictorial design was reflected in the side panels which might form a continuous all-round scene.

From about 1760 the lid mount might extend from the edge of the lid, over the stone in a wide border often depicting birds amidst scrolling floral swags, a matching mount encircling the base of the sides. These mounts were wide and sometimes ostentatious, such as chased floral and acanthus leaves in green gold. Later came narrow mounts pierced and chased with flowers and scrolls hung with garlands, but reeded mounts became more common.

The hardstone plaque set in a snuff-box lid might be further ornamented with a central carved motif such as an ivory or mother of pearl medallion bearing, for example, a classical scene – even profile portraits were fashionable, sometimes signed. From about 1760 to the 1780s it was customary for such appliqué work to be gilded. Carved birds in hardstone of contrasting colour inset with tiny diamonds or other glistening precious stones or gems were considered highly elegant.

For a short period from the early 1740s a series of resplendent snuff-boxes appeared. The lid of light-coloured chrysoprase over pink foil was mounted with carved mother of pearl or ivory with handsome effect. From the early 1770s an oval agate lid might be set with a blue and white jasper cameo such as the Three Graces, Sportive Love, Venus chiding Cupid, the Nine Muses and a hundred others.

Hardstone snuff-boxes of the Georgian period are rarely hallmarked. An Act (12.Geo.II) of 1739 exempted from assay 'snuff-box rims, whereof tops and bottoms are made of stone or shell'. The hallmarks had tended hitherto to deface chased mountings. But the mounts for hardstone snuff-boxes were again required to be assayed from 1797 no matter how elaborate the chasing. For this reason little spectacular work dates later than that year.

A few hardstone snuff-boxes were made during the first quarter of the 19th century, highly effective but with much cheaper openwork in cast silver which might be gilded. This covered lids and sides in all-over designs in the early George II style. The fashion for decorating hardstone covers with appliqué birds and other lively motifs was repeated, with enrichment by innumerable small gems. Hallmarks show that such snuff-boxes were made in white and gilded silver until the 1870s. Another type, usually mistaken for solid silver, was made with mounts stamped by the factory silversmiths and filled with a lead-tin alloy. This was followed by perforated and engraved mounts cut from thin flat silver plate.

Less costly than the Scotch pebbles, as native agates were termed at the time of the Great Exhibition of 1851, were cut and polished blue granites from Aberdeen and Peterhead, used for much small jewellery, sometimes in imitation of intricately inlaid marble, or etched with fluoric acid. Serpentine from the Lizard district of Cornwall, red spotted and white veined, or red veined on an olive ground, was soft and easy to work. By then even the hard rosewood marble from Derbyshire could be cut into plaques for snuff-box lids.

MARBLE INLAY

An interesting use of hardstones is to be seen in inlay work, the agate, fluorspars, jasper, cornelian and so on being selected for their depth of colour and brilliance. Some light-coloured stones were stained to produce a desirable intensity of hue. These were inlaid in the style of the Italian *pietra dura*, that is, to form a mosaic panel. The English version was developed in Derbyshire during the late 1830s by John Adam of Matlock. Channels were cut into plates of vein-free black marble measuring $\frac{1}{8}$ to $\frac{3}{16}$ in. thick. These depressions, arranged in geometrical and curvilinear patterns, were fitted with colourful marbles or quartzes, sliced and saw-cut to the required shapes, forming gorgeously plumaged birds, vivid butterflies and other insects and sprays of flowers and foliage, among which sprigs of jessamine were notable. The Duke of Devonshire permitted his wonderful collection of Italian stonework to serve as models.

The pieces were embedded in jeweller's cement and rubbed down and polished. Unlike Italian work, this inlay could be finished as a single smooth surface. The extreme delicacy and accuracy of the fitting can only be appreciated by inspection. Eventually, however, Derbyshire inlaid work lost its purely local character in snuff-box lids by including malachite from Russia, soft marbles from Northern Italy and ornamental glass from Venice. Signed examples of such inlay are not infrequent, the name of the maker being engraved in some inconspicuous corner. The names of J. Tomlinson, J. Turner and Selim Bright have been noted.

FLORENTINE MOSAICS

Snuff-box lids from the 1820s might be set with mosaic pictures constructed from tiny cubes of brightly coloured marble and known as Florentine mosaics. These minute blocks of marble measured about $\frac{1}{32}$ in. long and were laid down and cemented to a flat surface, as a veneer over a base of gold or gilded silver which formed the main surface of the lid. In some instances the surface of the finished mosaic was slightly convex. The marbles were selected in colours to form such scenes as Roman temples, fountains and classical architecture and portraits, animals, birds and flowers. Copies of original Roman mosaic floors were reproduced in miniature. Colours were restricted, resulting in designs being necessarily stiff, although the palette for later mosaics was increased by using dyed tesserae. The earliest

Florentine mosaics displayed on snuff-boxes were the work of
Parisian hardstone workers, soon to be rivalled by craftsmen in
Naples and Rome. Complete pictorial plaques were imported
by English jewellers and mounted into snuff-box lids. Between
the early 1850s and the late 1860s Derbyshire marble-men
worked Florentine mosaics for Birmingham jewellers. These
were more meticulously finished than the Italian imports.

AVENTURINE

A brownish tinged glass flecked with gold-coloured spangles was
used to make snuff-boxes displaying an unusual glittering effect.
It was named aventurine when it was discovered by chance by a
member of the Venetian glassmaking family of Miotto, early in
the 17th century. It was, of course, only an artificial imitation
of the form of quartz known as aventurine.

Snuff-box units were exported from Murano to London early
in the 18th century when gold chasers fitted them into gold
mounts. More than a century passed before Birmingham glass-
men were reproducing this artificial aventurine and in the
1850s were selling snuff-box units at about six shillings a pound.
Their substance was prepared by fusing for twelve hours a
mixture of 300 parts crushed flint-glass and 40 parts iron filings.
This when shaped and slowly cooled resulted in an excellent
imitation of aventurine. Frequently octahedral flakes of copper
were enclosed in a readily fusible glass: according to some
authorities the correct name for this is 'gold stone'.

Genuine aventurine is a translucent quartz, yellowish-
brownish-red in colour, containing small flakes of glittering
mica, which give a gold-spangled appearance to a polished
surface in reflected light. This is not known to have been
imported until early in the Victorian period. Single stones were
cut with flat or slightly rounded surfaces and set into snuff-box
lids, gold or silver mounted with substantial rims elaborately
chased.

Snuff-boxes were also carved from whitish-reddish-brown

aventurine-felspar flecked with golden particles and known as sunstone. This is much harder than quartz.

CANNEL COAL

Brittle cannel coal is a bituminous mineral which burns with a bright flame. It is so inflammable that, being lighted with a taper, it burns like a candle and is smokeless: its name is a corruption of candle coal. Known to the Georgians as 'parrot coal', it can be cut and highly polished like jet which it somewhat resembles and is perfectly clean to handle. It is found in the coal seams of Lancashire, Yorkshire and Scotland. A valuable seam was worked in the Wigan coalfield during the 19th century by the Ince Hall Coal & Cannel Co., Wigan.

For nearly two centuries the material was used for snuff-boxes. In 1697 Celia Fiennes visited 'Newcastle Underline [near Wigan] where is the fine shineing Channel Coale . . . that is hard and will be pollish'd like black marble for salts or snuff-boxes or such like, the only difference it will not bear the fire as marble does else it resembles it very much'. James Arbuckle in *Snuff*, a poem written in 1719, refers to snuff-boxes of coal. The *Gentleman's Magazine* reported in 1764 that at Sheffield were made 'snuff-boxes of a sort of coal called kennel, or cannel coal, by Mr Joseph Hancock who is the present Master Cutler'. Hancock was already making snuff-boxes in Sheffield plate. At the Great Exhibition, 1851, carved snuff-boxes in cannel coal were displayed by G. H. Ramsey, Derwent Haugh, Newcastle.

Cannel coal snuff-boxes were fitted with silver mounts and carved in shapes resembling those of contemporaneous hard-stone boxes. The jet black made an excellent ground for gilding: others were painted with floral designs in bright enamel colours fired in a low temperature muffle kiln. Some were coloured with paint. A cartouche-shaped example in the collection of HM Queen Mary, gilded and painted, was made and signed by Joseph Angell, 10, Strand, London.

SLATE

Snuff-boxes of slate proved formidable competitors of Derby-shire marble inlay which had been entirely superseded by about 1860. Slate was so processed that it closely resembled fine marble. It was decorated with black japan and painted in colours with designs adapted from Florentine mosaics. This painting was stoved for several days, making the colours so permanent that pocket friction had no effect. Fitted with electroplated mounts, such snuff-boxes were comparatively inexpensive.

CHAPTER 10

Papier Mâché: Composition: Japanned Iron

PAPIER MÂCHÉ

COLLECTORS of papier mâché snuff-boxes must distinguish between the three products that were made under that name: the original made in London from the 1740s as *papie machie* and in the 19th century as *carton pierre*; paper ware from 1772; and *papier mâché* japanned ware from 1836. Although created by different processes, themselves subject to progressive improvements, the three groups are now classified in collectors' terminology under the single term of papier mâché, a French expression literally meaning 'masticated paper'.

The early Georgian variety, named papier mâché – variously spelt – on a number of London trade cards, consisted of a composition of rags reduced to a fibrous pulp with glue, chalk and fine sand. This was shaped into snuff-box and lid forms by hand pressing into oiled boxwood moulds. When dry these were stoved until hard and then japanned at a low temperature. Die pressing of these forms dates from about 1780.

The papier mâché snuff-boxes preferred by collectors were made by a technique patented in 1772 by Henry Clay, Birmingham. He evolved a process for making a tough, heat and moisture resisting material capable of withstanding the heat of oven japanning to acquire a surface finish which by the 1780s had become as lustrous as oriental lacquer. It was made from sheets of porous textured paper saturated with a mixture of flour and glue. Snuff-box lids and boxes, each as a single unit, were shaped by applying the sheets to a metal mould rather smaller than the required sizes of box and lid. Each layer

33 Silver-gilt snuff-box in the form of a mask of Lord Nelson. The cover is of oak from H.M.S. *Bellerophon*, inscribed 'CALVI, Copenhagon, Trafalgar, Oct. 21. 1805'. Height 3½ in. In the Victoria and Albert Museum.

34 Gold snuff-box presented to Sir Arthur Wellesley by the Borough of New Windsor in 1811. London hallmark for 1805. Width 3⅜ in. In the Victoria and Albert Museum.

35 (*Left*) Silver-gilt snuff-box set with plaque embossed with a horse and lion in a jungle. Maker's mark W.S., Birmingham, 1830. (*Centre*) Triangular snuff-box in silver inscribed with the name JOHN BEAZLEY NEWTON. (*Right*) Silver with an all-over checker design. Maker's mark W P & B S 1800. Bracher & Sydenham.

36   Silver-gilt snuff-box, the cover chased with a view of Battle Abbey, borders of scrolling foliage, the base chased with an unidentified historic building. By Matthew Linwood, Birmingham, 1810.
Christies.

37   Silver snuff-box, the cover chased with a view of Windsor Castle, set against a ground of engine-turning and a chased floral border. By Nathaniel Mills, Birmingham, 1827.
Richard H. Everard.

38 Silver snuff-box, the cover chased in high relief with an all-over scene of a huntsman and hounds in a wood. Base of mother of pearl; engine-turned sides. By Nathaniel Mills, Birmingham, 1840.
Christies.

39 Silver-gilt snuff-box, chased with the portrait of a greyhound named on ribbon above. The inscription below reads 'The property of the Earl of Moray. Gain'd the highest prize at the Downe Coursing Club. Oct.R 1818'.
Brufords of Exeter.

40 Silver snuff-boxes with engine-turned sides and covers set with chased and embossed views. (*Top*) Bath and Wells Cathedral by Rawling & Sumner, London, 1835. 3⅜ in. by 2¼ in. by 1⅛ in. deep. (*Centre*) gilt, with a hunting scene, by Ledsam Vale & Wheeler, Birmingham, 1828. 3⅜ in. by 2⅜ in. by ⅞ in. deep. (*Bottom*) view of Abbotsford by Francis Clark, Birmingham, 1837. 3 in. by 2 in. by ⅞ in. deep.
Prestons Ltd.

41 Silver table presentation snuff-box with applied flower and foliage decoration. By John Shaw, Birmingham, 1844.
Richard H. Everard.

42 Table snuff-box in 18-carat gold, engine-turned in basket pattern with chased oak leaves and acorn edging in coloured gold. Interior of cover set with a miniature portrait. By A. J. Strachan, London, 1813.
Asprey & Co.

43   Presentation table snuff-box to a major of the 96th Regiment: in the form
of a field mess tent with guards.
N. Bloom & Son Ltd.

44   Silver mounted table snuff-box
made from a hoof of the
cavalryhorse *Midnight*.
N. Bloom & Son Ltd.

45 Silver snuff-box, engraved with carrier's wagon and horses before a village scene. Maker's mark I H between two stars, 1685. $3\frac{3}{4}$ in. wide. Victoria and Albert Museum.

46 Gold snuff-box, struck with the London hallmark for 1814. Maker's mark ILWA. Presented to the Duke of Wellington by the Borough of Hertford in 1814. $3\frac{1}{16}$ in. diameter. Victoria and Albert Museum.

47 Engine-turned gold snuff-box with raised borders, the centre applied with the crowned monogram of George IV in rose diamonds on an oval panel of royal blue enamel. 3¼ in. wide. Marked T B London 1820. Christies.

48 Presentation snuff-box of tortoiseshell lined with gold. Cover inset with carved portrait of George IV when Regent. The gold cover is chased with the Prince of Wales' feathers and scrolling foliage. The border chased in green-gold with laurel foliage. Inscribed 'The Gift of His Royal Highness George Augustus Frederick, Regent of England, to John Watier, 1815.' 3⅜ in. wide. Christies.

49 (*Above*) Classical scene on a silver snuff-box, its shape and treatment adapted from the earlier rococo period. Made in 1823 by William Elliott, London.
Victoria and Albert Museum.

50 (*Left*) Silver-gilt 'pedlar' box, the cover modelled in high relief with a pedlar of beverages wearing a plumed hat, against an engraved background showing roisterers outside a tavern. Maker's mark J.L. London, 1820.
Christies.

51   Four bijou snuff-boxes
such as were carried by
ladies from 1815. The
cover of the example
decorated in relief (*third
from top*) is cast: the
remainder are from rolled
plate. The covers are
designed with escutcheons
in which a crest or cypher
could be engraved.
N. Bloom & Son Ltd.

52 Silver-gilt snuff-box, its cover set with a mosaic panel of London origin: the base and sides engine-turned with chased foliage borders and thumbpiece. 2½ in. wide. By Nathaniel Mills, Birmingham, 1835. Christies.

53 Gold and tortoiseshell snuff-box, base and cover piqué posé in gold with birds upon baskets of flowers and fruit, with key pattern borders. The sides are similarly decorated with gardening trophies interspersed with insects. 3 in. wide. Mid-18th century. Christies.

54   Silver snuff-box with cover chased in high relief with a view of Dryburgh
Abbey, Scotland, the sides engine-turned with chased foliage borders. 2¾ in.
wide. By Joseph Willmore, Birmingham, 1833.
Christies.

55   Silver-gilt snuff-box with rounded ends, cover chased in high relief with
three hounds pursuing game amid hills. Base and sides engine-turned.
3¾ in. wide. London, 1824.
Christies.

56 Gold-mounted snuff-box of grey marble, the cover applied with chased gold figures, the surround of gold cage-work pierced and chased. The sides similarly bordered. The cover rim chased with foliage on a matted ground. 3 in. wide. Early 19th century.
Christies.

57 Snuff-box in 18-carat gold with engine-turned panels and shell and foliage thumbpiece. The borders and corners chased with flowers. Struck with the London hallmark for 1825.
Christies.

58 A Lancashire *memento mori* pocket snuff-box with hardwood sides and brass plates at top and base. The figure 8 opening ensured that only the smallest pinch of snuff was taken as finger and thumb could not be separated. Dated 1847.

59 A pinchbeck example of the 1750s.

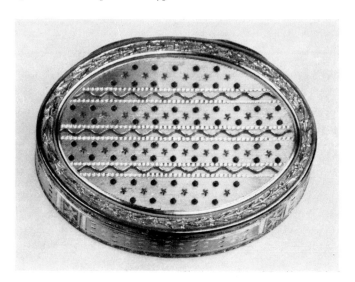

60 (*Left*) Gold snuff-box, centre of the cover inset with a panel of lapis lazuli, the border chased with birds, flowers and scrollwork on a matted ground. The moulded bombé sides similarly decorated on the lower part. Dated 1857. Christies.

61 (*Right*) Gold snuff-box, the centre of the base and cover chased with scrolling foliage on a matted ground within a shaped oval with pellets at the cardinal points. The interior of the cover set with a miniature portrait. About 1790. Christies.

62 (*Left*) Gold-mounted tortoiseshell snuff-box, the cover set with a gold coronation medal of William and Mary, 1689. Reeded mounts to rim and sides. 3¼ in. diameter. Early 18th century.

63 (*Right*) Gold snuff-box, with engine-turned panel, the border chased with foliage on a matted ground. Centre of the base and cover chased with a swirl of foliage. 2¾ in. diameter. Maker's mark G H London 1798. Christies.

of paper was glued into place and dried at 100° F between each addition. When the correct thickness was reached, the shape was removed from the mould and filed.

A different technique was used for complicated pieces such as the 19th-century shoe snuff-boxes. The paper was applied over a shaped core until half the final thickness was reached. A clean cut was made with a sharp tool, dividing the potential snuff-box into two sections. These were separated and the core removed. The halves were then brought together and several more layers of prepared paper applied. The joint was thus strengthened and made invisible.

Japan varnish was then laid on and the piece stoved at japanner's temperature and undulations removed with pumice stone. This was repeated several times. Black was the most common background but crimson or green was obtained by adding appropriate metallic oxides to the japan varnish. The adhesive used between the sheets of paper was similarly coloured.

The snuff-box was then decorated with colours or gilding, over-painted with clear shellac varnish. This was stove hardened and polished by rubbing with rotten stone and oil. Fine work was given a brilliant silken lustre by women rubbing with their bare hands. This feature is found only on English work.

An excise duty was levied on manufactured paper ware which could be produced only under licence; this ended in 1836. Papier mâché japanned snuff-boxes constructed from machine-made panels date from 1838. The blanks were treated as wood and could be planed and carved: snuff-boxes were assembled from several units. From 1847 this papier mâché was of denser texture.

Paper ware has a flat-smooth texture and is lighter in weight than the later papier mâché which is brittle in comparison and reveals a slightly undulating surface when held in an oblique light.

Decorations until about 1815 were painted in colours often enriched with gilding. Then in 1812 sparkling metallic powders known as bronzes in various colours were patented by Thomas

Hubball, Clerkenwell. Within three years pictures and designs on the lids of table snuff-boxes might be composed of bronzes made in about eighteen colours from powdered metals and alloys such as brass, copper, zinc and Dutch metal. Some were chemically stained.

These bronzes were painted over a tacky surface of gold size with wool or cotton waste swabs wrapped around a slender handle. Delicate shading effects and fine lines were painted with a tool made from a fragment of leather tied to a thin string passed through the hollow of a quill so that the leather formed a tiny pad at the tip.

A second bronze period began in 1843, atmospheric effects being obtained by blending gold-coloured bronzes with oil colours. Fascinating lighting effects were created, particularly outdoor scenes with brilliant sunshine. A rare silvery bronze made from powdered aluminium enriched moonlit prospects. Henry Perks painted sumptuous pictures using this technique, signed with a microscopic monogram.

Vividly coloured flowers painted realistically delighted ladies and snuff-boxes so decorated were fashionable from the early 1830s to the 1850s. They were introduced in 1831 by George Neville, Birmingham, who specialised in painting 'flowers on the black'. His signature flower is easily recognised – a blue convolvulus with one petal curled over in contrasting colour. Other distinctive flower painters were Grimes of Wolverhampton, noted for his snowdrops and hawthorn blossom given glowing brilliance by being painted on a ground of gold or silver leaf. Alfred Harvey was notable for his tiny posies of mixed flowers and W. Wylie was an outstanding all-round flower painter who signed his finest work with a tiny monogram WW. Luke Amner was celebrated for his splendid tulips; William Jackson for lilies of the valley; and William Bourne for the radiance of his verbenas. J. Breakspeare of the firm Jennens & Bettridge, Birmingham, was a skilful mid-century flower painter notable for his miniature adaptations of Dutch old master flower paintings. He taught this industrial art to his son with such success that when the papier mâché trade declined from 1860 he moved to London as a professional artist and became an exhibitor at the Royal Academy.

Frederick Newman became celebrated for the magnificence of his peacocks and William Hamson for his resplendently plumaged parrots. Persian designs on snuff-boxes were created in 1855 by John Hinks of McCullum & Hodgson, Birmingham, and had a five-year vogue. These ornate patterns resembled a Persian carpet, leaf gold outlining vari-shaped spaces filled with vivid colours.

George Evans of Fribourg & Treyer wrote in 1921 describing early 19th-century snuff-boxes with which he was familiar. Their 'lids often bear paintings, subjects generally being landscapes, figure and genre scenes, the latter being often of a coarse nature'. The interiors of some of these box-lids might be painted with nudes or risqué subjects.

There was a considerable demand for 'ceremonial' snuff-boxes after the death of the Prince Consort in 1861. These were decorated in mauve and grey associated with mother of pearl. In 1862 the papier mâché men succeeded in copying hardstone effects at a fraction of the price of the originals. Malachite was introduced in that year by Alsager & Neville, Birmingham, who were also responsible for some superb agate and marble effects, the invention of Peter Jones. Tortoiseshell was also imitated.

Table snuff-boxes in paper ware and japanned papier mâché contributed a delightful radiance to late Georgian and early Victorian homes from about 1815 to the 1850s. A fashionable type made extensively in Wolverhampton and Birmingham, and also imported from Austria and Germany by the thousand, was the circular, flat-lidded box measuring from 4 to 8 in. in diameter and between $\frac{1}{2}$ and 1 in. deep. The lid formed a field for colourful, all-over painting in oils. The early lid had no raised encircling rim, the painting occupying the entire surface. From about 1830 the cover rim was made slightly higher than the flat surface framing the picture in black. All-over paintings are usually the work of more skilful artists than the later series. The paper ware boxes are also more strongly constructed.

The manufacture of such snuff-boxes was a specialist branch of the trade. The majority of covers displayed miniature copies of well-known paintings taken from engravings in colours that could scarcely be considered accurate. The head artist in the workshop would paint a commercial version from which assistants made copies at speed, leaving him to add the finishing touches. On paper ware boxes the collector will sometimes find an original painting: these are highly valued.

An early master painter of such snuff-boxes was Samuel Raven, Birmingham. He is believed to have learned the technique of painting on papier mâché in the workshops of Small & Son, Guest, Chopping & Bill, severing his connection in 1816 when the firm was taken over by Jennens & Bettridge. Raven set up as a freelance painter, but was soon buying snuff-boxes and cigar-cases in the black, decorating them with notable skill and selling them to merchants. After about 1830, in the face of competition from Wolverhampton, his paper ware was of a poorer quality supplied by another firm. Like many another freelance industrial artist Raven was capable of adapting his skill to a wide range of painting techniques to suit the limitations of size and shape imposed by snuff-boxes.

Table snuff-boxes painted by Raven after 1826 are inscribed in red script within the cover *S Raven Pinxt. Patronized by H.R.H. the Duke of Sussex and Prince Leopold of Saxe-Coburg* – sometimes omitting the words 'of Saxe-Coburg'. When the painting is entirely from the hand of Raven it is signed in script so small as to be scarcely visible without a magnifying glass. The title of the picture is inscribed in cream paint.

An apprentice artist employed by Raven from 1820 to 1827 recorded that his master specialised in painting pictures on box lids. During those years he noted that all pictures painted in Raven's studios were copied from engravings. David Wilkie's early works, unprotected by copyright, were popular subjects copied unceasingly. These included *The Blind Fiddler, Rent Dor,*

Blind Man's Buff, *The Cut Finger* and *The Village Politicians*. John Burnet's painting *The Young Bird* and *The Beeswing* by Kidd were in demand consistently. *The Proposal* and *Congratulations*, after G. H. Harlow and engraved by H. Meyer, were endlessly repeated by Raven's pupils, who reproduced the pictures in colours of their own choosing.

In the Victoria and Albert Museum is a grand communal snuff-box by Raven, excellently painted with Sir Thomas Lawrence's celebrated portrait of George IV. The interior of the lid is inscribed *J. Machin/Union Commercial Room/S. Raven Pinxt*. John Machin became landlord of the Union Inn, Cherry Street, Birmingham in 1825. Several unsigned examples are known, usually, but wrongly, attributed to C. H. Stobwasser & Co., Berlin. Communal snuff-boxes were a feature of the period in most places where groups of people met; and in the case of a guild or company were identified by a painted coat of arms. Even the House of Commons possessed a set. By 1830 the demand for these painted table snuff-boxes had spread to a wider, less monied public. German imports satisfied their less discriminating needs and to meet the competition Wolverhampton japanners responded with boxes of the new papier mâché japanned, cheaper of construction and for the most part less skilfully painted. The subject of the painted decoration might be religious, royal, sporting, or a female or theatrical figure.

A copyist expert in reproducing William Etty's figures was employed by Edward Perry, Jeddo Works, Paul Street, Wolverhampton and from the 1840s paintings on many lids were adapted from Titian's *Venus* in the Uffizi Gallery, Florence. Many copies of R. Westall's *Venus with Doves* came from the Perry factory. As the custom of offering snuff from table boxes declined these circular lids were often framed and hung – usually three lids to a frame.

Line engravings were transfer-printed on inexpensive snuff-boxes from about 1845. The picture was printed in black oil or varnish ink on a special tissue paper and transferred to lids of cream-coloured japan coated with a special varnish. The line engraving, showing clearly against the light surface, was then coloured and gilded. Finally the picture was coated with transparent varnish, a brilliant lustre being secured by rubbing with a woollen cloth dipped in mastic. Later it became customary to paste a paper disc with a printed engraving to the lid.

William and Andrew Smith of Mauchline (see page 124) from the early 1850s made wooden snuff-boxes japanned and decorated in imitation of papier mâché.

Papier mâché snuff-boxes were not long-lasting, the hinge attachments being weak spots. Collectors should be aware that papier mâché snuff-boxes have been reproduced. Close comparison with an original will show that these fakes have not been japanned, varnished, stoved and polished by the appropriate old methods and the paints differ in quality and brush work. Fingers travelling lightly over the glossy surface will meet with undulations absent from original paper ware.

COMPOSITION

Obadiah Westwood of Birmingham evolved and patented in 1785 a process for making a tougher, harder composition to supersede the earlier pressed *papie machie* (see page 96). Westwood's method consisted of 'cutting and bruising or grinding rags (linen, silk, hemp, flax or cotton) until of a fine texture which are then mixed with a strong paste of glue, flour and water'. Into this was kneaded a small quantity of colouring matter such as Spanish brown, red lead, umber or black. After varnishing and stoving this composition displayed a really fine surface finish resembling japanned work, but was much less costly to produce. Snuff-boxes pressed from this composition continued in production for more than sixty years.

Snuff-boxes with views embossed upon the lids with boxwood moulds in the style of early 19th-century silver were made in tens of thousands annually and bore a superficial resemblance to pressed horn. They were fitted with narrow metal-gilt mounts. Impressions on the lids were very clear until about 1850 when they began to deteriorate. The boxes were all rectangular or oval in shape and weighed about three ounces.

Early composition boxes might be more elaborate and examples have been noted with lid, sides and base inlaid with gold and silver such as trophies of arms and cyphers. The lid of an example sold at Christies in 1967 was fitted with a silver-gilt mount set with a Florentine mosaic (see page 22) of a spaniel beneath a tree stump, attributed to about 1800.

JAPANNED IRON

Japanned snuff-boxes date from late in the 17th century. The parish registers of Bilston, Staffordshire, record several births dating from 1702 onwards in which the fathers were described as makers and decorators of japanned snuff-boxes. These boxes were in hammered iron plate, circular, oval or oblong with pull-off lids, usually black with some gilding. Similar snuff-boxes were already being manufactured in Sheffield and by about 1720 the trade had extended to Wolverhampton. These snuff-boxes, sold by the 'snuff houses' at about threepence each, are now extremely rare. They may be recognised by the slightly undulating surfaces of the heavy gauge iron plate.

The second group of japanned iron snuff-boxes dating between the late 1720s and the 1780s were made from heavy gauge tin plate rolled into thin sheets, even surfaced on both sides. This was iron soaked in molten tin which penetrated its texture and gave the metal a silvery white colour. Pure grain tin from Cornwall was used in the form of shot. This process gave a slight radiance to the japanner's ground colours. The finest snuff-boxes of this period were made by the Allgood family of Pontypool. They developed a process which gave the japan and its decoration a highly durable, granite-hard surface, lustrous and silky to the touch. Pontypool also made snuff-boxes of apanned copper, wi th hinged lids.

Tortoiseshell snuff-boxes (see page 116) were fashionable

throughout the George II period. Japanners of Pontypool and Birmingham produced snuff-boxes decorated to imitate tortoise-shell. These were inexpensive and the demand was considerable. Robert Dossie in 1754 reported that the tortoiseshell effect was 'not only the japanned ground for snuff-boxes and other small pieces, but was also decorated with painting and gilding in the same way as any other varnished surface and which is best done after the ground has been duly hardened by the hot stove: but it is well to give a second annealing with a more gentle heat'. Dossie added that this stoving required to be continued for three weeks or a month. The japan was applied over silver leaf or a white ground. This was clouded and stained with yellow to resemble tortoiseshell. It was given numerous coats of clear varnish, each being stoved.

An inferior quality was made at Wolverhampton, circular splashes of gold and silver leaf being immersed beneath semi-transparent yellow or crimson japan. Against this tortoiseshell effect ornamental motifs were painted in colour such as flowers, fruit or foliage.

Early Pontypool snuff-boxes were also japanned in chocolate colour and the celebrated glowing crimson which was given its impeccable finish by applying gold or silver leaf over a white ground. The Pontypool palette was extended from the late 1770s to include dark green, puce, tomato red, orange, canary, grey and ultramarine blue. But by 1760 Wolverhampton and Birmingham were japanning snuff-boxes in yellow, vermillion, red, lake, blue, indigo, green, brown, purple and flesh white. Not until about 1820 was an improved green japan made: this was costly and is found only on snuff-boxes of the highest quality, often with a basis of block tin.

In 1756 Bishop Pocock visited the Pontypool workshops and noted in his diary that they 'adorned all kinds of boxes with Chinese landscapes and figures in gold only, and not with the colours as Birmingham. This [Pontypool] ware is very much better than the Birmingham, but it is dear', an opinion expressed in 1781 by the Hon. John Byng who recorded in his diary:

'Chepstow. I bought a Pontypool snuff-box, a beautiful and dear ware much to be admired.'

Decorations were now painted in full colour, mainly rustic groups incorporating figures of shepherds and woodmen, and sporting subjects. The celebrated artist Thomas Barker of Bath was born at Pontypool where he was for a few years employed by the Allgoods as a painter of scenic views on snuff-boxes and trays.

The third group of japanned snuff-boxes consisted of boxes made from tin iron plate invented in 1784 by a Wolverhampton ironmaster specially for the use of japanners. This was made from best bar iron in which charcoal was an ingredient instead of coke. This increased malleability enabling it to be rolled to a thinner gauge than formerly. The shaped boxes and their lids were scoured by women and stored in tubs of water until such time as they could be dipped in molten grain tin. Only the surface of the iron was coated with a film of tin, resulting in a great saving of the costly metal.

When hinged mounts were fitted to japanned snuff-boxes they were of cast brass, gilded. From about 1795 mounts might be cast in soft leaded pewter disguised by mercury gilding.

Horn: Scottish Mulls

HORN

CHEAP, tough and extraordinarily adaptable, for centuries horn was one of the basic materials in the English home. Whether his need was a window or a button, an inkwell, a comb, a tip to his bow, or, from early in the 17th century, a snuff-box, the Englishman called upon the ancient, specialised skills of that little-lauded craftsman, the horner. Master horners tended to occupy small workshops, often employing only members of their own families. Because of 'the grete and corrupt stench' emanating from their premises 'to the grevous annoyance of neighbours', London horners in 1455 were directed to transfer their workshops to the city outskirts. They selected the Petticoat Lane district with which they were continuously associated for more than four hundred years.

Snuff-taking until late in the 17th century was mainly a plebeian custom. It was found that horn boxes made the most suitable and inexpensive containers for the finely powdered 'tobacco-snuff', a term then used to distinguish it from various popular herbal snuffs such as crushed camomile flowers. Two distinct branches of the horner's craft were recognised. These were the horn pressers who prepared the green or raw horn and pressed it into plates of convenient thickness, and the moulders who bought unused tips and roots of horn and scraps from the pressers. Until the 1660s the supply of horns from tanners and butchers fully met the needs of the trade. By the end of the century buffalo and other horns were imported from America. In 1696 John Houghton estimated that the horns of 350,000 beasts were needed annually to satisfy the twenty-four master horners then operating in London.

There was a great demand for the horns of Scottish rams from about 1700. When processed these displayed an amber tint and could be easily dyed in attractive shades of red, green, blue and brown. A jet black, which could be highly polished, was achieved by sanding the horn snuff-box and painting it with 50 or 60 grains of nitrate of silver dissolved in one ounce of distilled water. This was colourless. When dry the boxes were placed in the sunlight where they soon turned jet black.

The *Dictionarium Polygraphicum*, 1735, described the process of 'casting horn in a [brass] mould like lead. Make a lixivium of calcin'd tartar and quick lime; into this put scrapings of horn; boil them well together in a copper cauldron of hot water until they come to a pulp; tinge this with what colour you would have it and you may afterwards cast it in a mould and make of it anything of what form you please'.

The horn presser made his plates from the central portions taken from the horns of English cattle, clear and free from striations and other blemishes. The horns were boiled until soft and malleable, then split lengthways with a curved knife and immediately pulled open with a pair of broad-bladed tongs held by another worker. These strips were then placed beneath heavy stones which held them flat until cold. They were then re-softened in the boiling cauldron and each was placed between two iron plates smeared with grease and of considerably greater area. A number of these were pressed vertically into a trench dug in the ground. At one end a narrow space was left for inserting a wooden wedge which was hammered down with a heavy wooden beetle, thus forcing the iron plates against the pieces of horn which gradually expanded into flat plates. After being pressed as tightly as possible they were left in position until cold. These plates were bought by snuff-box makers for cutting into suitable strips.

Until the 1660s the majority of horn snuff-boxes were made from plain-surfaced plates. Then came the vogue for impressing the lids with coats of arms, portraits of royalty and celebrities, classical and sporting scenes. Trimmed sections of sheet horn were softened in cauldrons of hot water and impressed with relief ornament by means of steel moulding tools. The impression needed to be taken quickly to ensure that the relievo was sharp and clear in outline. Oval and circular snuff-boxes were preferred, but rectangular boxes were made also, the two sides folded vertically in a piece, the ends incurved and welded whilst soft. The sides usually remained plain but could be decorated by carved, incised or pressed work. In some instances the horners produced spiral grooves by winding a copper wire around the box whilst it was soft.

Several workers in this medium are known to have engaged in the ornamental pressing of horn, but apart from John Obrisset their reliefs tended to be blurred. Obrisset (d. 1731), son of an émigré Huguenot ivory carver from Dieppe who settled in London and Anglicised his name, followed his father's skills in ivory and eventually became an engraver of ivory, the term then denoting one who carved. But he specialised in sinking steel dies with patterns to be impressed in relief upon small tablets of horn and tortoiseshell suitable for use as snuff-box lids, also supplying similar dies to silversmiths. Obrisset was not an approved silversmith, however, for his mark was not registered at Goldsmiths' Hall.

He specialised in portraiture, usually profile busts or full-length equestrian figures, and for a quarter of a century was acknowledged as a craftsman of outstanding ability. Little is known of his personal life but he was twice married, first in 1690 and secondly in 1717 to Susanne Brisson, the register describing him as of St Martins in the Fields. Formerly he had occupied workshops in Wheel Street, Spitalfields. Contemporaneous records in the possession of the Huguenot Society refer to the family as 'a middling sort of people'.

Much of Obrisset's work was signed, usually with the initials OB or I OB, often accompanied by three, five or seven petalled flowers. A few were impressed with his name in full, some being a combination of OB in capitals and the remainder of his name in script at a period when silversmiths used the first two letters of their surname when marking Britannia standard silver. Six patterns have been recorded with dates, the earliest being a portrait of Queen Anne, 1705. Her consort, Prince George of Denmark, appears on a box impressed I * OB * F *1708*; the Drake box is impressed *John Obrisset Fecit 1712*; a negro's head, with a slave's collar encircling his neck is impressed · 1720 · OB · FECIT. The equestrian portrait of George II dated 29 October, 1727, commemorated the king's attendance at the Lord Mayor's banquet. This function took place, however, on the 30th, the king's birthday. The last of his dated pieces was a sporting subject impressed De^{bre} · *14* · *1728 OBrisset*, the six final letters in script. Lid interiors might be pressed with the initials OB suggesting that John Obrisset was at once the die-sinker, horn worker and craftsman who made the box.

With very few exceptions Obrisset's horn snuff-boxes have an even surface on the underside of the lid, a few being slightly concave; inner and outer surfaces of the base are smooth and even. Rims are usually without metal mounts, the cover being attached by a flanged hinge riveted to one of the long sides. The portrait or other design is usually rimmed with a pressed border, plain or scrolled.

The relief design from 1715 might be framed in a silver mount hinged to the rim and usually reeded. The curved hinge attached with silver pins to the oval or circular box projected outwards by as much as $\frac{3}{16}$ in. and was liable to catch on the fabric of the pocket until special wash-leather snuff-pockets were introduced. A strengthening plate of thin tortoiseshell might be fitted against the hinge inside the lid. A thumbpiece for lifting the lid was fitted opposite to the hinge. Another design had vertical or slightly bombé sides of silver: the base, at this time, was of tortoiseshell. Boxes wholly of silver have been noted, the lid set with a horn portrait and a plain inner lid of ivory. The silver might be double gilt, but this is now badly worn. In some instances a pair of pressed plaques were fitted as lid and base of a snuff-box.

One series of Obrisset snuff-boxes have flat lids mounted centrally with cast and chased silver portraits in high or low relief, against matted grounds. Silver relief work might also cover the entire field such as the several versions of Charles I in plain armour. On other boxes the portraits were struck from very thin silver plate. The silver used was of the high or Britannia standard quality from 1697 to 1720 when there was a reversion to sterling.

Obrisset's subjects were for the most part profile portraits and full-length equestrian figures in armour; often the ground was matted. Many were adapted from the works of medallists, portraits of English monarchs from James I to George II being a speciality. Snuff-boxes displaying portraits of the Stuart Charles I, his consort Henrietta Maria, and James II were carried by Jacobites. His bust of Charles I was adapted from a medal engraved by John Roettiers: seven variations have been collated, all signed OB.

The monarchs Queen Anne and George I appeared on many Obrisset snuff-boxes. Queen Anne was engraved at least twenty-five times, each with a minor variation. One has the base of the box pressed with the Garter Star, centrally placed, its pointed rays extending to the rim. George II, taken from the medallion portrait of Ehrenreich Haninbal, master of the mint at Clausthal-Zellerfeld, Hanover, was made to commemorate his accession in 1727. Collectors also value jugate portraits of William III and Mary II and such subjects as Prince William of Denmark, Queen Caroline, Philip V of Spain, Peter the Great, the Duke of Marlborough and Oliver Cromwell.

Snuff-boxes with the arms of Sir Francis Drake impressed in sharp relief are met with in several variations each of which required a fresh die to be sunk. It is probable that the earliest were issued as souvenirs commemorating the death in 1696 of Drake, the first Englishman to circumnavigate the world. They were in demand by seamen and other frequenters of waterside inns and taverns displaying such signs as Sir Francis Drake, Admiral Drake and the Drake Arms. This accounts for the fact that so many existing specimens are in common horn. These are often offered as historical relics purporting to have been the personal property of Sir Francis and have long been exhibited as such, despite the large number in existence. A series of exquisitely embossed Drake snuff-boxes are marked *John Obrisset Fecit 1712*: two examples are in the British Museum. Lady Elliott-Drake in 1911 recorded that these presentation boxes were made to the commission of the third baronet who was a candidate in the Taunton parliamentary election of 1713.

Obrisset also issued Biblical subjects such as the conversion of Saint Paul after the relief by Sir Francis Bird on the pediment of St Paul's Cathedral. This was pressed in 1710 to commemorate the opening of Wren's new cathedral building. A silver-mounted oval snuff-box in the British Museum is signed ** OB * ACTES YE IX X*.

Snuff-boxes exist displaying evidence of long and vigorous use, the relief work virtually obliterated by pocket friction. This defect is not apparent on patch-boxes, counter-boxes and bonbonnières made by Obrisset in horn or tortoiseshell.

Horn snuff-boxes produced by craftsmen impossible to identify might have their covers enriched with colour. These include: gilded designs incorporating birds, insects and beasts within foliage borders; relief work heightened with gilding; faceted lenticular crystals, agates, cairngorms or other native stones set in the centre; ivory medallions similarly set, these being engraved with cypher or inscription. From about 1750 engine-turning, too, might be introduced.

From the mid-18th century snuff-boxes were made from horn shavings ground into powder, then softened by boiling in strong potash lye. The resulting paste was moulded into the required shape by tools in a fly press. When dry the box was polished by rubbing with subnitrate of bismuth applied on the palm of the hand. Shapes and sizes of snuff-boxes made in this way for more than a century are too numerous to collate. However, temperature variations caused these moulded horn snuff-boxes to become speckled and mildewed and quickly crumble so that few of them remain.

Snuff-taking was a well-established social custom in Scotland from the late 16th century, originally valued for its supposed medicinal virtues such as curing catarrh, tooth-ache and 'naughty breath'. Scottish snuff at this time contained no tobacco, consisting of the dried and powdered leaves of *Achillea ptarmica*, a member of the yarrow family known by the 1590s as sneezewort and long used as a sternutatory. To the Scotsman this herbal powder was known as *sneeshin* and to take a pinch of snuff was *sneesing*. Macgill in *Old Ross-shire*, 1659, alludes to a 'sneeshin maker' named Walter Denune. Howell in his *Letters* of the same year noted that sneeshin 'mightily refreshed the brain,' adding that 'one shall commonly see the [Scottish] serving maid upon the washing block, and the swain upon the ploughshare when they are tired with labour, take out their boxes of sneeshin and draw it into their nostrils with a quill; and it will beget new spirits in them, with a fresh vigour to fall to their work again'. Hall in 1761 differentiated between tobacco snuff and the herb sneeshin: 'I have sent you a little Provision of the best Preston-Paris snuff with a bottle of Highland Snishon.'

Highlanders who accompanied the Court of James I to London in 1603 introduced the sneeshin miln, known to collectors as a snuff-mull, following a Scottish pronunciation of mill. This has always been made from a ram's horn, the point curled artificially into a scroll to prevent it from rubbing a hole in the pocket or bag. The exterior of the horn, sometimes stained black, was scraped smooth and highly polished and the interior cut vertically with closely spaced sharp ridges. These abrading edges enabled the snuff-taker to grind his own snuff from a plug of tobacco or sneeshin.

The rim of the horn was usually fitted with a hinged cover of horn; from the 1670s the cover might be of silver or pewter with an upward-curving thumbpiece. This was most usually plain but often enriched with a centrally placed facet-cut gemstone excavated from the Scottish mountains, such as light or dark cairngorm, colourful agate or transparent crystal. On silver the gem was usually encircled with thistles or foliage embossed in high relief. In Georgian examples the surface of the horn was carved with an ornamental motif, subjects ranging from a laughing Scotsman with long hair and bonnet or a thistle between a pair of leaves, to a duck or an elephant's head.

Differentiation between the Georgian snuff-mull and snuff-box continued. In 1771 Tobias Smollett noted: 'The lieutenant pulled out, instead of his own Scottish mull, a very fine gold snuff-box.' From about 1760 and throughout George III's reign snuff-mulls might be carved from ivory, bone or wood, the latter often displaying the laughing Scotsman motif. By this time serrations within the horn were no longer required by those who bought ready-ground tobacco snuff or sneeshin.

Many a Scotsman, from about 1700, carried with his snuff-mull a tiny spoon, instead of a quill, for applying the snuff to his nose, and a hare's foot for wiping his upper lip afterwards. These were attached to the lid mount by fine chains of silver.

The pocket snuff-mull measured between 1¾ in. and 3½ in. overall, but the collector finds the same design on a more lavish scale in the table snuff-mulls constructed from the horns of highland cattle. These were designed for communal use in the home, tavern or club, richly appointed specimens being intended for guild ceremonies and masonic banquets. Such a table snuff-mull, with a tortoiseshell cover and silver mounts, was sold at Christie's in July 1968. Originally this was the property of the Crossgates Chicken Pie Club, founded in 1760 with the object of improving the breed of horses and cattle. For seventy-four years members met over suppers of chicken pie and in May 1834 became incorporated with the Dunfermline Agricultural Society.

Shaped in a bold spiral of one-and-a-half turns and measuring 8 to 10 in. in height, as much as 18 in. overall and 3 in. wide at

8

the mouth, the table snuff-mull was fashionable from late in the 18th century to the 1860s. Its use was restricted to the service of good quality tobacco-snuff. The oval mouth of the horn was fitted with a capacious snuff-box of silver, its lower edge attached to the rim with silver pins concealed beneath a circuit of beading or reeding. The cover was hinged and fitted with a narrow thumbpiece, plain multi-scrolled or with a scalloped edge. The cover was usually topped by a figure in the round cast in solid silver, such as a Highlander, lion or horse, or an eagle with outspread wings alighting on its kill. This was commonly used as a handle for lifting the lid. On fine examples from about 1820 a ball and tongue hinge was fitted; otherwise a plain five-lug butt hinge was used. An identifying shield-shaped plaque was usually applied to the horn below the box, but might be replaced by an embossed thistle flower between a pair of leaves.

The long conical end of the mull was fitted with a protecting sheath, usually of smoothly plain silver with an applied edge matching that of the box. A paw or ball foot was attached to the outer curve of the horn below the box by means of an expansive lion or other mask. This gave stability to the mull and permitted it to be pushed smoothly across the table. Attached to the lower part of the mount by slender silver chains might be a snuff spoon, hare's foot, pricker, rake and mallet. All the silver mounts and accessories might be gilded.

Table snuff-mulls from early in the 19th century might be mounted with Sheffield plate, the finials in solid silver; from 1835 in British plate (silver fused to a nickel alloy); and from the late 1840s in electroplated silver on copper.

Ram's head table snuff-boxes, also, are associated with Scotland. The skulls, richly ornamented with silver and Scottish gemstones, became a fashionable conceit from about 1840. An example made by Walter Baird, 72 Argyle Street, Glasgow, shown at the Great Exhibition, 1851, was catalogued as 'a Scotch ram's head, each horn measuring 3 ft 5 in., mounted as a snuff-box and cigar case, in gold and silver, adorned with a cairngorm and Scotch amythyst stones'. Another, made by M. McGregor, Perth, was mounted with a silver snuff-box on top of the skull with a full set of accessories, the end of each horn carrying a thistle-shaped mount set with a Scottish amethyst.

CHAPTER 12

Tortoiseshell: Piqué: Mother of Pearl

TORTOISESHELL

TORTOISESHELL in warm translucent yellows and amber tones finely mottled with brown tints made fashionable snuff-boxes and other minor personal accessories in Stuart England. The craft of working tortoiseshell into sheets and moulding it into relief patterns had long been understood by English jewellers. This delightful shell exists as a surface layer on the back of the hawksbill sea turtle (*Testudo imbricata*) found off the Brazilian coast. The shell, weighing five to 25 lb according to size, is separated from the turtle's external skeleton by placing smokeless fire beneath it. The plates then lift from the bone and may be levered off with a long knife. Tortoiseshell of inferior quality is taken from the *Testudinata* which produce five large horn-like plates from the middle of the carapace or shell and four smaller scales from each side. These are known commercially as blades. In addition there are 25 smaller scales, known as feet or noses, taken from the margin.

The material consists mainly of a substance resembling gelatine, with a small quantity of inorganic matter. It is found as naturally compressed cells, but under heat and potash these become spherical. The shell then becomes plastic and may be shaped, pressed or moulded as desired, these forms being retained when cold.

Tortoiseshell was welcome for snuff-boxes because the powdered snuff did not cling to its smooth surface. It could be embossed in screw moulds after softening by immersion in boiling salted water, the pattern being impressed with tools cut in intaglio as with horn. Hunting and genre scenes, floral and scrollwork patterns, geometric designs, masonic and other devices were all popular.

Pocket snuff-boxes were constructed from sheet tortoiseshell rarely more than $\frac{1}{8}$ in. thick: table snuff-boxes were stronger, the plate measuring about $\frac{3}{16}$ in. thick. Pieces of shell could be welded together by the application of low heat from smokeless court charcoal, later from peat charcoal. Heat tends to darken tortoiseshell, hence a low temperature is essential. Seams are invisible. The material had to be handled gently, however. Horace Walpole noted the risk of sudden disaster when he commented to George Selwyn, in a letter of 3 August 1760, 'Hearts do not snap like a tortoiseshell snuff-box'.

All-over incised ornament on the thin tortoiseshell was introduced by Matthew Boulton in the mid-1760s when he was commissioned to make several engine-turning lathes for Josiah Wedgwood. He then manufactured them for sale. With this machine tortoiseshell could be cut with intricate patterns.

The lids of tortoiseshell snuff-boxes were often enriched with elaborate designs in gold, but more usually the plain, handsomely grained shell was considered adequately decorative. This was dark in colour until the 1770s when honey-blonde shell became fashionable.

A long series of tortoiseshell snuff-boxes made between the 1770s and about 1820 even lacked metal mounts, consisting wholly of shell, the lid fitting securely over the box opening and including a tortoiseshell thumbpiece for lifting. Lids might be decorated with pressed work, in contrast to engine-turning beneath the base. A favourite all-over pattern was basket-work.

During the first quarter of the 19th century oblong snuff-boxes with clipped corners and ribbed or slightly concave sides were fashionable, with plain gold mounts and ornament in gold lines. The cover might be of plain, attractively marked blonde tortoiseshell or might be set with a cast gold or gilded silver plaque displaying a profile portrait in low relief, subjects including royalty and naval, military and political celebrities. Other plaques were of ivory painted with miniature portraits, classical subjects or scenes in colour; mother of pearl exquisitely carved with ornamental subjects; fine stoneware known as jasper usually in blue with relief decoration in white. The plaque was usually framed in a narrow gold fillet and often protected by glass (see under *Piqué*).

Large tortoiseshell snuff-boxes for table and mantelshelf were made from sheet tortoiseshell made by welding together pieces of shell by the application of smokeless heat so that seams were invisible. Motifs in relief could be saw-cut separately by hand and punched into the softened shell and welded into position, giving a three-dimensional effect to the design on the lid, comparable with the period's embossed silver, while the sides were decorated with all-over patterns in relief. Only when held against the light can this welding be detected as irregularities of pattern fail to correspond with surface markings.

PIQUÉ

The fine texture and translucency of tortoiseshell made it a splendid material to be lit with touches of gold. Scintillating effects were achieved by piercing the shell with tiny metal rods of graduated sizes until the surface appeared to be dusted with golden spangles outlining human figures, exotic birds, insects, flowers, vine patterns, peculiarly elaborate escallop shells, coronets and monograms. This notion was created late in the 17th century by one Laurentini, a jeweller of Naples. France and England adopted the craft so skilfully that it is known today in both countries by its French name, *piqué*. There is no English term for this exotic decoration. Light delicate work is known as *piqué d'or*. Patterns in large points were given the name of *clouté d'or* or nail head piqué; *foulé point d'or* consisted of points crowded into intricate patterns.

The term *piqué posé* is now applied to the style more exactly known by its old name of inlay. In this the ornament is more emphatic, being formed with inlays of strip gold or silver, sometimes still with the piqué patterns for background diaper, trellis work and leaf outlines among the heavier solid scrolls. Occasionally a really elaborate snuff-box may be inset with solid panels closely chased with shells or similar detailed relief work set off by delicate many-pointed shells of gold inlay surrounding diapers in different sizes of gold piqué so that the whole gold-lined box – lid and sides and even base – possesses a mellow, golden glow far richer and lovelier than solid gold. It is possible to find a piqué d'or snuff-box with minor flower borders around a splendid peacock outline in the smallest size of gold points with six or more sizes of point upon its tail.

Some of the earliest piqué was applied to snuff-boxes of both tortoiseshell and ivory, sometimes with matching watch cases. Both made excellent vessels for snuff, preserving its varying delicate aromas more perfectly than any metal except gold, seldom warping to spill in the pocket or fail to open in the hand and offering constant delight to fingers and eye.

Advertisements in the *London Gazette* in 1700 for stolen property included two piqué snuff-boxes: 'a round Tortoise-shell Gold studded Snuff-Box with a Gold joint' and 'a large Gold Snuff-Box, the outside Tortoiseshell with Gold Studs, and the inside solid Gold'. These and other advertised descriptions suggest that piqué point was the more usual technique. Then fashion demanded the many variants of palmettes and strapwork in piqué posé.

A collection of piqué snuff-boxes pre-dating 1715 may include an extensive range of design adapted from those of contemporaneous precious metals, cartouche and shell shapes figuring considerably. An early snuff-box may open with a small drop hinge but the projecting pin hinge came into use early in the 18th century, high quality of craftsmanship being a feature of English piqué. Even the plainest repetition of these points of light distributed evenly over the surface of the tortoiseshell created an effect of shimmering restrained beauty.

By early Georgian days posé d'or was being used alone. Some specimens may appear almost overladen with golden chinoiserie scenes and figures among pillared ruins, pastoral and hunting groups, pavilioned gardens, tea parties and music parties and cloud-borne cupids in scroll and leaf borders. Even the Paris balloon ascent of 1773 has been commemorated on blonde tortoiseshell snuff-boxes. Often the gold mounts are chased, a refinement that adds greatly to the delicacy of the effect.

The English piqué craftsmen developed hairline posé d'or in the early 18th century. Seascapes and other pictorial scenes were achieved in lines of gold or silver as delicate as pen drawing, subjects becoming more elaborate in the early 19th century. Such work on snuff-boxes is uncommon.

Gold and silver for piqué work were used in a pure state without any alloy whatsoever. The metal was thus soft enough to be rolled or beaten to paper thinness. Cut to shape it was pressed upon the surface of tortoiseshell heated by court quality charcoal, then tool-worked into position. The contraction of the tortoiseshell in cooling held it firmly in place without jeweller's cement which would mar the clarity of the inner surface of the shell. The surface was made perfectly smooth by scraping away superfluous tortoiseshell, then polishing and burnishing the whole. The metal was so soft and thin that it could be shaped by hand tools over embossed tortoiseshell, but in this case a hard varnish adhesive was used. For hairline piqué posé a thin shallow groove was cut into the heated tortoiseshell, the strip of metal was inserted into this and given a light hammer blow. When the shell cooled it was held permanently in position. In ivory the piqué work was hand-tooled into the surface and fixed by a cement.

The majority of piqué snuff-boxes found today reflect the change to more formal patterns in the second half of the 18th century. One or two pseudo-classical motifs might be developed with exquisite delicacy – such as an oval patera with a swag of husks on a plain oval box or a conventional honeysuckle flower or an urn flanked by loops of drapery. The ellipse or oval with pointed ends was popular in the late 18th century. Lids were usually piqué edged with cable pattern with a posé motif at their meeting points. In the centre might be a miniature portrait framed in piqué posé, an oval patera, or a silver panel engraved with the owner's crest.

Such pioneers of factory silversmithing and jewellery as Matthew Boulton included piqué work among their manufactures. In a letter to James Adam in 1770 Boulton confirmed that production was in progress and ten years later he acquired the workshops of John Gimblet, a considerable maker of fine piqué posé who operated at Snow Hill, Birmingham, from the early 1760s to 1780.

Substantial gold inlay continued as a successful branch of the Birmingham and Sheffield factory trade well into the 19th century. One result was that the hand-craftsman in piqué turned to ivory as the loveliest gold stud work of piqué d'or was developed more extensively than formerly on this equally inviting surface, often vividly stained green, red, blue or black which set off the points of gold or silver. This work continued through the late 18th and early 19th centuries.

Star ornament is characteristic of this period, probably adapted from the French hand-workers, but popular with the factory piqué men of Birmingham. The sprig pattern was usually associated with factory worked stars and small double circles until about 1800. Some heavy nail head or *clouté piqué* suggests Boulton craftsmanship, the star-head facets shaped by hand as in his cut-steel work: in Victorian specimens from 1872 they were machine-worked. Designs on ivory in posé d'or were seldom in more than simple line work. No signed piqué snuff-boxes have been recorded.

Imitations of piqué snuff-boxes were made during the late 19th century. These are in celluloid, cleverly simulating tortoiseshell and decorated with gilt nail heads and stars fixed with adhesive. Sooner or later one falls away, revealing the deception.

MOTHER OF PEARL

The splendid opalescence of mother of pearl snuff-boxes was acknowledged by Georgians of the 1790s and early 1800s, a period when precious metals suffered from war-time scarcity. In addition to their fascinating chromatic effects these snuff-boxes were a delight when opened, when the inner pearly surfaces of the shell panels were revealed, for the metal setting was restricted to narrow mounts, usually of silver-gilt.

The mother of pearl for boxes came from the linings of three varieties of haliotis shell, known to manufacturers as great snails, ear shells and buffalo shells. After being sawn into convenient sections the pieces were flattened on a horizontal grinding wheel, smoothed with a mixture of pumice stone and pumice powder, and given their final brilliance with buff leather and rotten stone. This was the work of craftsmen who took a pride in finding shells which could be cut in series of matching panels. The *London Directory*, 1797, lists about twenty mastermen in the pearl trade who worked upon the delicate substance with saws, files, drills and sulphuric acid. There was a revival of mother of pearl snuff-boxes during the early Victorian period by the pearl workers of Birmingham and Sheffield.

Mother of pearl panels were set in the lids, bases and sides of snuff-box frames. The lid panel might be slightly convex or flat and carved in three-dimensional relief with an all-over design. A typical pictorial scene might include figures such as dancers against a rural background surrounded by a border of flowers and foliage, itself encircled with a plain formal edging. The lid interior might be decorated with a picture in transparent paint which was illumined by the underlying radiance of the pearl, or set with a miniature portrait painted on ivory.

The peacock iridescence of mother of pearl snuff-boxes, displaying a colour range of reds, yellows, purples and browns, coppery greens and steely blues, is caused by the shell structure embodying microscopic furrows which run across the surface.

Snuff-boxes in every fashionable shape were assembled by goldsmiths who stocked sets of pearl panels and carved, engraved or painted them to the customer's commission and fitted them into silver-gilt mounts.

CHAPTER 13

Scottish Tartan Boxes

SCOTSMEN were prohibited by Act of Parliament from wearing their multi-coloured tartans between 1747 and 1782 when the ban was lifted. During this period tartans were considered by Englishmen to be badges of outlawry and Scotsmen wore grey shepherd's plaid. The wearing of clan-tartans was revived, however, at the time of George IV's visit to Scotland in 1822 and by 1828 clan-tartans were again fashionable. This gave James Sandy, a poor mechanic of Perthshire who had lost the use of his legs, the idea of making snuff-boxes of white wood with hinges also of wood. Each was decorated on the lid with a tartan design and the sides with sketches in indian ink protected by clear varnish. These snuff-boxes came to the notice of Charles Stiven, Laurencekirk, Kincardineshire, who pirated the idea and decorated snuff-boxes with sketches of huntsmen and hounds such as were fashionable on serving jugs in brown salt-glaze stoneware, recognisable views and rural scenes. Designs of meandering lines known as 'worming' followed and naturalistic subjects such as the fruiting vine. These were soon joined by designs in checks, at first in black, later in colours, a great variety of diapers being produced. From these developed the celebrated clan-tartan boxes in full colours.

The craft spread to Ayrshire and by 1832, according to *Chambers's Gazetteer of Scotland*, more than one hundred persons were employed in the clan-tartan woodwork factory of William & Andrew Smith at Mauchline, Ayrshire. This village was an obvious centre for souvenir work, being the home of many of Robert Burns's friends and of characters in his poems. The old kirk yard was the scene of his 'Holy Fair' and half a mile away was, 'that lovely cot Mossgoil'. Scotsmen at the time of William IV's coronation in 1831 carried colourful clan-tartan snuff-boxes enriched with gold or silver name plate. The Smith brothers' clan-tartan snuff-boxes and other articles, known contemporaneously as Laurencekirk boxes, were soon in such demand that a wholesale warehouse was established at 61 Charlotte Street, Birmingham.

The wood of the sycamore (*Acer pseudo-platanus*) was used exclusively because of its close even texture and light weight which gave the articles all the advantages of contemporaneous papier mâché. A length of rough wood costing 25s made snuff-boxes to the value of £3,000. This block was drilled with a series of circular depressions which were then squared out with chisels, filed and finished with glass paper.

Craftsmanship was notable for its excellence. The cover was attached by an integral hinge hand-carved and fitted partly to the box rim and partly to the lid with a precision equal to that found on some of the finest gold snuff-boxes. These well-fitting joints never worked loose and ensured a tight lid through which snuff could not permeate. The box and lid were lined with heavy tin-foil to prevent scent from the wood affecting the snuff. The ingenuity with which the large number of component parts of some snuff-boxes were assembled is remarkable. A small octagonal box, for instance, might consist of twenty-six different pieces, yet appear to be carved from a single block, so exactly were the parts fitted together.

The exterior surface was prepared for ornament by covering with ground colour. Until the mid-1840s a white ground was used for the tartans in lighter tones but it was found that black gave greater depth and brilliance to the overlaid water colours. Several coats of ground colour were applied, each rubbed with fine glass paper. The article was then ready to receive its decoration in imitation of a clan-tartan, about one hundred varieties being used, with Royal Stuart the most popular. An invaluable reference work for collectors is *The Clan-Tartans of Scotland* compiled and published by William & Andrew Smith.

A mechanical method of drawing tartans in colour was patented by William Smith of Mauchline in November 1853

(No. 2639). By fitting a single drawing pen into a simple hand-worked machine and using water colour it was possible to draw straight lines with ease and precision. The workman, with his pattern before him, could regulate the lines and spaces by means of a notched wheel. All lines in one colour were completed, the pen cleaned and the workman continued with a fresh colour. The patent specification states that Smith's snuff-boxes possessed three advantages over those designed by competitors: 'perfect securing when the box is closed; facility of fully opening and closing; exposure of the snuff to a greater or lesser degree as may be desired'.

The patent was superseded in August 1856 by a second patent (No. 1845) granted to Andrew & William Smith. In this, instead of ruling pens small wheels or rollers were used and for the first time oil and varnish colours could be introduced. This improved machine, operating several rollers simultaneously, was able to draw all the parallel lines of one colour at once. The patent specification noted that tartans could be drawn by this machine more cheaply than by former methods.

The colours used were selected to harmonise and the half-tints were created by laying on successive lines of pure colour, results being attractively rich in tone with a pleasing transparency. Although this method continued in use some less costly tartan patterns were printed by lithography from about 1860.

Snuff-boxes of fine quality might be ornamented more elaborately in this manner. Typically, the cover would carry a miniature painting in oils of a scene set against its appropriate tartan. A view of Scone Palace, for instance, might appear on a box decorated with the Murray tartan; Balmoral with the Royal Stuart tartan; Melrose Abbey with the Hunting Stuart tartan. The scenes were painted direct on the wood before the application of the tartan. They were restricted largely to Scottish views, particularly places celebrated in history and song, and to more generalised scenes of the chase and copies of Landseer's pictures rendered into colour from engravings.

After being titled and given its background tartan the article received two coats of clear varnish. This was smoothed with fine sandpaper and five more coats of varnish similarly treated. The article was then hand-polished to a highly glossy surface.

Men employed in this work were paid wages ranging between 16s and 24s for a 70-hour week, dependent upon their skill. Women earned 7s to 9s a week and children 2s. Artists skilled in copying in oil colours from black and white engravings were paid about 30s a week. Outworkers were employed also to carry out inexpensive diaper checkerings: these date from the mid-1840s and were catalogued as tartans. They were ruled on paper which was glued to small articles of wood. Circular table snuff-boxes, painted black, were decorated and varnished in imitation of papier mâché; their lids might be ornamented with tartans or with line engravings overpainted and varnished.

The Smiths labelled much of their finer clan-tartan work with their name and the words *warranted genuine*. Other makers' labels include those of Davidson, Wilson & Amphlet of Mauchline, who until 1841 displayed the royal arms of William IV (d. 1837) and the legend *Makers to His Majesty*. From 1841 the royal arms of Queen Victoria with the words *Makers to Her Majesty* appeared on the labels of Charles Stiven & Sons of Laurencekirk, often with the inscription *inventors and manufacturers*.

William & Andrew Smith also made snuff-boxes advertised from about 1850 as 'Scoto-Russian'. These imitated the costly enamelled boxes for long imported from Russia. The wood box and its cover were first covered with heavy tin foil. This was painted and when dry was placed on a ruling machine fitted with a sharply pointed scriber which traced an intricate pattern of curved and straight lines in imitation of engine-turning. These lines penetrated the paint but only scraped the tin-foil which was left shining bright, the effect resembling inlaid silver. Several coats of copal varnish, each polished down, completed the box. The Jury of the Great Exhibition, 1851, awarded the firm a gold medal for 'accuracy of workmanship, high degree of finish and beauty of varnish' in connection with Smith's 'Scoto-Russian' snuff-boxes. Their prices ranged between 22s and 168s per doz.

Clark & Davidson, also of Mauchline, from about 1835 issued a series of expensively finished tartan snuff-boxes painted with portraits of Prince Charles Edward inside the lids. These must not be confused with the valuable Jacobite propaganda snuff-boxes of the 1740s and later, which were in heavy wood but with hinged mounts of gilded brass.

CHAPTER 14

Miscellaneous

AMBER

AMBER snuff-boxes were fashionable intermittently from the time of Queen Anne until the 1850s. The material had the great advantage of remaining warm and pleasant to handle in cold weather when a hardstone would chill the snuff and diminish its flavour. It was also conspicuously light to carry. The earliest reference so far noted is in Pope's *Rape of the Lock*. Boxes might be in solid amber but more usually frames of 18-carat gold were mounted with plaques of polished amber, the lid being slightly convex.

Amber, a substance traditionally regarded as a charm against witchcraft and magic, was long believed to be a semi-precious mineral, although Pliny described it as a resinous juice which had oozed from extinct coniferous trees and discharged into the sea. It is not of so great an age as hardstone: agate, for instance, is three times harder. Linnaeus confirmed Pliny's attribution in about 1750, declaring that amber was the fossilised resin of the prehistoric *Pinus succinifer* tree. This discovery brought about a decline in the use of amber in fashionable jewellery. The greater part of the amber used in the construction of snuff-boxes came from the Pomeranian coast of East Prussia, the king holding the monopoly and regulating the supply. Amber is of two kinds, marine and terrestrial. The former is thrown ashore during the autumnal storms and is either fished from the tideless Baltic with small nets or picked up by wading. Terrestrial amber was excavated in the form of small, crude fragments from alluvial deposits of sand and clay in mines sunk on the sea-shore.

Baltic amber is found in all shades of yellow, from the palest primrose and brown and red and often encloses the remains of small insects. In clarity it varies from a vitreous transparency to absolute opacity, some specimens suggesting ivory. This is rare and is used chiefly for carved appliqué work welded to a darker amber plaque for setting in a snuff-box lid. Amber from Sicily has a light reddish hue; Chinese and Burmese ambers are either yellow or red and usually cloudy.

Amber intended for snuff-box lids and bases was first split by a lead plate revolving in a lathe. The surfaces were then worked over with thin scraping tools, smoothed with a Swedish whet-stone, polished with vegetable oil or chalk and water and finished by friction with a flannel held in the hand. During these proces-ses the amber tended to become charged with electricity, very hot and even liable to fly into fragments. For this reason the pieces were worked in rotation to keep each cool and but feebly electrified. They were then ready for the jeweller to fit them into gold mounts. If the amber in a snuff-box breaks it may be repaired invisibly by smearing the edges with caustic potash and pressing them firmly together when made warm over a smoke-less charcoal fire. The union is so perfect that no trace of the join is visible. Very few early Georgian amber snuff-boxes remain.

Terrestrial amber was of lesser quality, the fragments being fused into pressed blocks at the Dantzig finishing works. These blocks could be cut and worked into snuff-box lids. Snuff-boxes composed of amber throughout were cast in a piece and not carved as commonly believed. The process was outlined in *The Polygraphic Dictionary*, 1735: 'To melt Amber and cast it into any figure, with flies in it, as seen in those valuable pieces of Amber sold at a great price. Crush your amber and sprinkle it into hot turpentine, stirring it with a piece of fir wood until you find no resistance . . . keep stirring until the powder Amber is dissolv'd and thick enough to pour into moulds. When it is cold, you will have what figure you propose remain as hard as amber itself, with all the qualities of amber.'

Gold or silver snuff-box frames set with plates of amber were

9

fashionably carried in the daytime and might be circular, oval, rectangular, shell-shaped, or in basket form, the latter commonly of German manufacture. The amber lid was sometimes set with a gold-framed miniature. The sides of others were in gold skilfully chased in elaborate patterns.

As the century progressed gold and silver mounts became less elaborate and lighter in weight. Until 1798 the gold was always of 22-carat quality. Mounts in the early part of the 19th century might be cast in rather heavy metal and gold was of 18-carat quality. From 1854 gold of 15, 12 and 9 carats was used by the factory silversmiths; hand-worked mounts were in 18-carat gold. The majority of factory work incorporated plaques of pressed and polished amber from the Danzig workshops: these might contain insects of existing species. An amber snuff-box set in gold, made by C. W. Hoffman of Danzig, won for him a prize medal at the Great Exhibition, 1851.

Collectors must beware of imitation amber. This is made by melting together one part of pine resin, two parts of lacca in tabulis, and 15 parts of white colophony. This synthetic amber has none of the electrical power that lies latent in genuine amber.

DAMASCENING

Damascening decorated some early and mid-Victorian snuff-boxes. The name was derived from Damascus, once celebrated for the quality of its intricate ornament on steel. This was a craft in which line designs or devices of gold or silver were sunk into black or oxidised steel, iron or copper. Fine line channels were undercut on the exterior surfaces and into these were hammered wires of contrasting colour until they were thoroughly incorporated with the metal of the snuff-box. The entire snuff-box was finished with a uniform level surface.

Very few gold snuff-boxes made in England were damascened. A well-known maker in gold and silver gilt fancy patterns during the 1860s and 1870s was the London goldsmith Barkentin. His work is always fully hall-marked.

ENGINE-TURNING

Decoration on snuff-boxes from the mid-1760s might include intricate but wholly impersonal lines in geometrical patterns mechanically incised. This appeared soon after William Baddeley, Eastwood, Staffordshire, had established workshops for the manufacture of engine-turning (known also as rose engine-turning) lathes adapted for use by craftsmen of the jewellery and fine stoneware pottery trades. The engine-turning lathe had long been in use among wood turners, however, and was fully described and illustrated in *L'Art de Tourner* by Charles Plumier, 1701. This lathe rotated the objects to be decorated with an eccentric oscillating movement, the cutting tool remaining still. The machine could be so adjusted that the tool would incise clear-cut shallow lines on any shaped surface in an almost unlimited range of geometric patterns composed of complicated chevrons, chequers, zig-zags, dice and so on. Lid, base and sides of a snuff-box might be ornamented in this way, each often displaying panels of different design.

NIELLO INLAY

A little-known series of silver boxes display inlay ornament. Niello decoration was fashionable in England for about a century from 1780 although fine Italian work dates to the 15th century. This art consisted of cutting patterns with an engraver's burin into the lid and sides of the snuff-box, such as scrolls and associated designs. The deep incisions were filled with a black semi-hard composition prepared by heating together oxides of lead, copper and silver with sulphur. When cold this was ground to a fine powder which was sprinkled upon the engraved surface. A little borax was sprinkled over this and it was melted over a charcoal fire, the mixture flowing into the lines cut into the snuff-box. When cold the surface was smoothed and burnished, so that the niello produced the effect of a drawing in black on gold or silver.

This process was not carried out in England until about 1840, a snuff-box lid often being worked with a presentation inscription. Some niello designs were engraved by Daniel Maclise, RA, with great delicacy, shadows being hatched with fine lines. In Georgian days the niello process was termed tulla-work after examples imported from the Russian town of Tulla.

POTATO SKINS

Snuff-boxes composed of potato skins are recorded by George Evans in *An Old Snuff House*, 1921. Carried in the pocket, they could be relied upon to keep the snuff at its correct temperature for, as Mr Evans states, 'snuff is like claret – it needs the chill taken from it to bring out the bouquet. . . . These snuff-boxes were ornamented with a greenish lacquer, with a few fine threads of red or gold. The lids of some were hand-decorated with a crest, monogram or other means of identification.' The gilded hinges and fastener were, however, rather clumsy. Such boxes cost about twelve shillings each with little gold ornament. In the account books of Fribourg & Treyer they are entered as vegetable boxes. Mr Evans illustrates a rectangular example with bombé sides and a chased thumbpiece.

BASSE-TAILLE

This decoration is only occasionally found on snuff-boxes. Colour designs were made by chiselling into the gold or silver and filling the incisions with coloured enamels brought flush to the surface and smoothed. Subjects were usually pictorial, including figure groups, landscapes, pastoral scenes and views of castles and great houses.

WALKING STICK HANDLES

Long before the days of tobacco snuff a spherical pouncet box of gold or gilded silver containing perfume might decorate the head of a gentleman's walking staff. By the end of the 17th century walking sticks had become more slender and made of exotic woods. The cane-head remained a fashionable form of perfume carrier, usually spherical, occasionally urn-shaped. In Queen Anne's day it became a conceit among the exquisites to carry a pouncet-box or sponge-box in the snuff-pocket and use the cane head as a snuff-box. The hinged cover was opened by slight pressure upon a catch. Such boxes had become common by 1730. Doctors and apothecaries used them as receptacles for 'nutmeg or ginger to warm the stomach of the valetudinarian, or sugar candy for the asthmatic'.

Snuff-box heads on walking sticks were at first hand-raised from gold or silver-gilt plate and from about 1705 the lid of the spherical body might be secured by a simple bayonet fastener. Later some were of cast and chased prince's metal and from about 1730 of pinchbeck. The ivory crutch handle for a walking stick appears to date from about 1700 and from the early 1720s might be sliced horizontally and hinged, the interior excavated and fitted with a pair of utility snuff-boxes or with a snuff rasp.

INDEX

Illustration numbers are indicated in italic

CONFESSIONS
OF AN
UN-COMMON ATTORNEY

A. Ostade Pinx.^t

L A W.

R. Houston fecit.

Deep, read, in all the Arts of Chican'ry —
With grave important Phyz the Lawyer see!

Is it for Justice he pursues the Laws?
Or is not Gold the first Essential Cause?

London Printed for Carington Bowles, next the Chapter House in St Pauls Church Yard.

A SEVENTEENTH-CENTURY LAWYER

CONFESSIONS
OF AN
UN-COMMON ATTORNEY

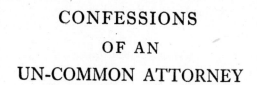

REGINALD L. HINE
F.S.A., F.R.Hist.S.

LONDON

J. M. DENT & SONS LTD.

J. M. DENT & SONS LTD.
Aldine House · Bedford St. · London

Made in Great Britain
by
The Temple Press · Letchworth · Herts
First published 1945
Second edition 1945
Third edition 1946
Fourth edition 1949

KNOW ALL MEN BY THESE PRESENTS

THAT

I DEDICATE THIS BOOK

In the firſt place to myself, having written it for my own pleasure.

In the second place to my brother solicitors, for their 'use and enjoyment,' and in self-defence of our much-maligned profession.

Then to the intelligent reader, who will know how to discover those better things in any book that lie hidden between the lines.

And, laſtly, to the general reader who, though he may shun the law and all its works as he would shun the devil, may care to consort with the writers, doctors, schoolmaſters, and parsons, who are depicted in Part Two of the book.

▼

ACKNOWLEDGMENTS

(1) To the secretary and to the librarian of the Law Society for perusing, revising, and approving the draft of this book as submitted.

(2) To my sometime master and present mentor, E. E. Kellett, M.A., for hearing my confessions in camera, and for his indulgence in regard to my more literary sins.

(3) To Messrs. Hawkins & Co., solicitors, of Hitchin, for leave to quote certain passages from my unpublished *Chronicles of a Country Firm (Messrs. Hawkins & Co., of Hitchin), 1591–1942.*

(4) To my friends, Margaret Kirk, Frederick Gordon Wood, M.A., and Arthur Fellows, for presenting plates to this work.

(5) To my secretary, Miss K. E. Foster, who for twenty years has been struggling with the handwriting stigmatized on page 88.

(6) Last, but not least, to my wife, for redeeming the manuscript from many faults, and for reading the proofs.

CONTENTS

vii

PART TWO.   LIFE OUTSIDE THE LAW

LIFE AS A MAN OF LETTERS

ILLUSTRATIONS

IN COLOUR

IN HALF-TONE

IN LINE

*Tailpieces by Samuel Lucas and Charles E. Brock.
Initial letters by the Pelican Press.*

There is no description so hard, nor so profitable, as is the description of a man's own life.—MONTAIGNE.

This is the best of me; for the rest I ate and drank and slept, loved and hated like another; my life was as the vapour and is not; but this I saw and knew; this if anything of mine is worth your memory.—JOHN RUSKIN.

We are not content to pass away entirely from the scene of our delight; we would leave, if but in gratitude, a pillar and a legend.—R. L. STEVENSON.

I mentioned that I was afraid I put into my Journal too many little incidents. Johnson: 'There is nothing, sir, too little for so little a creature as man. It is by studying little things that we attain the great art of having as little misery and as much happiness as possible.'—BOSWELL'S *Life of Dr. Johnson.*

One book amongst the rest is dear to me.
'Tis when a man has tired himself in deed
Against the world, and falling back to write,
Sated with love, or crazed with vanity,
Bemused with drink or maimed by fortune's spite,
Sets down his Paternoster and his Creed.
PROFESSOR SIR WALTER RALEIGH.

I have had nothing worthy to be called a life; only moments of living.—REGINALD L. HINE.

Vera Effigies Viri   clariſſ EDOARDI COKE
Equitis aurati nuper   Capitalis Iuſticiärij
ad Placita coram   Rege tenenda aſsignati

THE AUTHOR
From a photograph by Frances Coombe

INTRODUCTION

I will not make an over large gate to my little city.
                ARTHUR WARWICK, *Spare Minutes*, 1637.

I

OON or late, by time's gentle admonition, or by the harsh reminder of war, the day comes when every mortal man is constrained to set his house in order. Forty years as a country attorney have I been winding up clients' affairs. Thirty years as an historian have I been writing the lives of others. Now, at three score, I have the uneasy feeling that I should tidy up the over-crowded curiosity shop of my own brain, and render an account of my own stewardship.

I wish I could have compiled a life in three proud volumes; packed with matters of political importance or social consequence; it would have gratified my vanity. But the truth is, mine is a 'little city.' It has only two gates. Over one is written *Law*; above the second stands *Literature*. In a day of terrible things I have been 'the common man,' or at least 'the common professional man,' happily, and not, I hope, too selfishly, busy in my day of small things.

But who, asked Zechariah, 'who hath despised the day of small things?' That is a comforting assurance, and the prophet adds to it by declaring that the meek and lowly have good reason to rejoice. Certainly there are advantages in obscurity, and Montaigne goes so far as to raise it to a virtue: 'All the glory I claim in this world is that I have lived quietly.' He would have all but princes, magistrates, and a few sleek favourites of fortune, content to be content: to abide in a happy stillness of mind and in humble stations of life. The troubles of this world, argues Pascal, arise out of man's inability to sit quietly in one room. Foolish, restless, insensately ambitious creature, he must always be up and doing: questioning all things,

xv

quarrelling about all things, conquering if he can the whole wide world.

At the outset of this book I, too, would stake out a quietist's claim. Throughout my days I have laboured in one parish, and kept to my native homestead of thought. In this I have followed the affectionate attachment of Plutarch, who once remarked: 'As for myself, I live in a little town, and I choose to live there lest it should become still less.' If I am remembered, it will be as the devoted chronicler of the little town of Hitchin in Hertfordshire. But let no critic on that account write me down as parochial. The corner of the universe wherein a parish historian seems to sit alone whispering to himself is the universe itself; or, as old writers were fond of saying, *speculum mundi*—a little mirror of the world. Let such a man hold up his head, for the story of an English town is the history of England itself. Truly may he say: 'I have beaten the parish bounds and found them to contain the whole creation. I have stood by a stall in the market-place and trafficked with the Indies. I have gossiped with John Stiles in the street, and heard in his voice the voices of all the children of men.'

There is another advantage enjoyed by the private citizen. He belongs to himself. When the little man in the little city looks out upon the huge and thoughtful night, fame loses its allure; he has no envy of counsellors or kings. His tributes as first, second, or third citizen must be paid: 'Render unto Caesar the things that are Caesar's.' But when that has been accomplished he is freer than most men to follow his own whim, to taste the delights of human tranquillity, to cultivate the muses, to make innumerable friends. That way, even in the brief hour-glass of one man's life, much happiness can lie; there may be no sand-storms, but there will be many golden grains of blessed gaiety, some fireside ease, cool spaces of leisure sitting at peace in 'the middest of one's books.'

How sane was the advice of the philosopher-statesman, the first Marquess of Halifax (1633–95), 'that you should live in the world so as it may hang about you like a loose garment.' It is not easy. More and more the modern world encroaches upon the liberty of the subject. 'A truly free Englishman,' as Sydney Smith complained, 'walks about covered with licences.' But with a little ingenuity it can be done. The art of living is to play hide and seek with life: 'Thou shalt hide them in the secret of Thy presence from the pride of man.' Yes, by the grace of God, it is still possible for a mere individual man to make his private world within the world, 'a pavilion from the strife of tongues.'

II

The aim of this book is to make known what one such man has seen, heard, and done in his own secret pavilion, and to share some of his happiness—'the days that in the folded past were beautiful'—with men of like passions with himself. Years ago, in a book entitled *The Cream of Curiosity* (Routledge, 1920), I cleared some of my conscience by sharing with bibliophiles some precious literary and historical manuscripts of the seventeenth, eighteenth, and nineteenth centuries which, after a youth of prodigal collecting, and throughout a miserly middle-age, I had been hoarding for my own pleasure. And now, to all or to the few whom it may concern, I would make another distribution out of the fading manuscript of my own life: sayings, doings, and dreamings that ought not to go down with me into the grave, or be left to the caprice of literary executors, *disjecta membra*, fallen leaves, delicate in colour but decaying fast, whirled here and there by the blind wind of fate, doomed if not pressed within the pages of a book to drift in obscurity down the gutters of time.

I could wish that these memoirs of mine were less a medley of disjointed things! But I am one of those to whom the same Lord Halifax referred: 'Some men's memory is like a Box where a man should mingle his jewels with his old shoes.' Here—for shoes can talk as well as walk—are memories of my life's pilgrimage in the law, a profession rich in human and inhuman contacts: murders recollected in tranquillity, homicides, justifiable and unjustifiable, the strange sorry spectacle of a world of wrongdoing, crime, and its punishments. Here, too, have been recalled many unusual cases that have come my way, and tales of ancient tenures and jocular customs, such as—once upon a time—obliged the lord of the manor of Archers Court near Dover 'to hold a bason under the King's head

B

whensoever he should pass over to Calais'—no sinecure in medieval days—and the holder of an estate in Yorkshire 'to render a red rose at Christmas and a snowball at summer.'

The law, precisely because it is not an exact science, is a most exacting profession, and you will find its practitioners driven to do other things—preferably illegal—to preserve their health of mind.   For my own part, I saw, before I was out of my articles, that I should have to lead a double life, and accordingly I apprenticed myself to the muses, whom, more especially Clio, I have served with fidelity ever since. Certainly, for the happiness and enrichment of my life, I had decided wisely, for, in the art and craft of local history, one has not only to pore over parchments in one's pavilion; one needs to be out and about in the streets, consorting with 'the substantialest men of the parish,' or studying Tom, Dick, and Harry, at first-hand.   Worthies and un-worthies, saints and sinners, magistrates and mountebanks, all and sundry must be walked with and talked with if the multi-coloured character of one's townsfolk is to be faith-fully recorded.   Once again, something of value to a writer, tied to retiredness, is lost, but he will gain in other ways by mixing with his fellows.   A man shall be known by his friends and, as Frederick the Great observed about his connection with Voltaire, one can profit even from un-friendly men: 'On peut apprendre de bonnes choses d'un scélérat.'   It takes all sorts of men and women to make one man, and that is why, in compiling my own memoirs, I have thought it right to describe some of the parsons, doctors, poets, schoolmasters, scholars, and scoundrels who, for good or evil, have left their mark on my life.

III

Such are the 'old shoes,' stowed away for luck, in the box of my memory; and let no Benvolio scowl upon me for tying them with new ribands.   But what of the jewels that lie, higgledy-piggledy, beside them in the box?   There I have not been quite so fortunate, unless, as Ford suggested, 'experience be a jewel that I have purchased at an infinite rate.'   Some men are born with a silver spoon in their mouth, and a precious jewel in their head.   It was not so

with me.   But I have picked up a few brilliants: the fiery
opals of fancy, emeralds—'green thoughts in a green shade'
—rubies of riotous imagination, amethysts of chaste and
sober hue, diamonds of scintillating thought.   These gems
have their setting in commonplace books that I have kept
from my youth up.   Others have been presented.   In my
'flaming and canicular days' I kept company with poets who

> quoted odes, and jewels five words long,
> That on the stretch'd forefinger of all Time
> Sparkle for ever.

Nor am I yet so old and so austere that I would 'give my
jewels for a set of beads.'

I promised not to make an over-large gate to my little
city; and the words of Francis Bacon—a model of brevity
—are already ringing in my ears: 'Prefaces are great waste
of time, for though they seem to proceed of modesty yet
they are bravery.'   Very well then; I will cease.   Here is
the box I spoke of: the old shoes and the jewels.   There is
the table of contents.   You may pick and choose at your
fancy.   You may rummage for yourselves.

PART ONE
LIFE IN THE LAW

Then welcome business, welcome strife,
Welcome the cares, the thorns of life;
The visage wan, the pore-blind sight,
The toil by day, the lamp by night,
The tedious forms, the solemn prate,
The pert dispute, the dull debate,
The drowsy Bench, the babbling Hall,
For thee, fair Justice, welcome all!

BLACKSTONE.

LIFE IN THE LAW

I

OD!' expostulated the Emperor Charle-
magne on a memorable occasion, 'God!
my life is hard indeed'; and *sotto voce*
or with vituperative words solicitors
likewise are wont to rail upon their lot.
It is the aim of this book to show that
I myself, as an un-common attorney,
have been more fortunate than my
brethren, but one must recognize that the profession is not
what it was. No longer, in this pestering age, are there the
lucid intervals the early practitioners enjoyed. Who in this
hustling age could obey the golden rule Sir Edward Coke
(1552–1634) ordained: 'Give six hours to sleep; as many
to the study of righteous laws; for four hours pray; devote
two to meals; and what is over bestow upon the Sacred
Muses'? His was a counsel of perfection more suitable
to his time than ours. After our exhausting labours six
hours' sleep is not enough. Nor could any modern solicitor
spare six hours for the study of laws, whether they be
righteous or unrighteous. Besides, as young Henry, afterwards Sir Henry, Hawkins used to say: 'If you spent all
your time poring over the law there would be none left for
breaking it.' Then again, where in this irreligious era
would you find one single solicitor of the Supreme Court
four hours *per diem* upon his knees in prayer? It is sad
that it should be so, for, as Sir Matthew Hale observed in
Taylor's Case: 'Christianity is parcel of the Laws of England.'
Such is the frugality and urgency of modern times that the
allotment for meals is more than they require who can but
dash at midday into a snack-bar and swallow in haste, still
in their minds considering and chewing 'the nice, sharp
quillets of the law.'

Last, and undoubtedly least, there are the Sacred Muses:
'Sacred,' as one solicitor observed, 'because nowadays never
touched.' Here and there, however, you may find some
un-common attorney eager to devote 'what is over' to the
service of Clio, the muse of history, particularly to the

3

history of English law, as traced through the centuries in the tomes of Bracton, Fortescue, Selden, Blackstone, Maitland, Pollock, and Holdsworth; and certainly you would find any solicitor of standing proud of the history of his own firm.

Gone, too, is that ruminating, spider-like existence that a lawyer used to lead in his be-cobwebbed chambers. Nowadays, what with telephones, and callers hurrying in by train or omnibus or car, life in the law is one long interruption; nor is modern conveyancing, though said to be simplified, as simple as it seems. When I became an articled clerk in 1901, the documents of title, elegantly scrivened on sheepskin, not vulgarly typed as now on parchment paper, were still being composed in the grand style with elaborate recitals leading up to the climax of the *Testatum* and *Tenendum*, and then, as in a dying fall, brought to a close with gracefully written *Powers* and *Provisoes*.

For centuries, laymen like Izaak Walton had sighed after 'those times when there were fewer lawyers, when men might have had a lordship conveyed to them on a piece of parchment no bigger than your hand.' And when, to our resentful surprise, and by the Law of Property Act, 1925, deeds were reduced to a mere handful of their former size and shorn of their ancient splendour, men of the old school declared that conveyancing, as a fine art, was dead. It was natural that they should mourn the passing of copyholds, of tenants in common, of other incidents of tenure dear and profitable to old-style conveyancers. To them the attempt to master 'the lawless science of our law,' under the holy name of codification, did but create fresh complications and a burden of new forms and precedents. Hardly were they recovered from this shock when a second world war brought in a spate of emergency legislation passing the wit of ordinary men to understand, with government by proclamation, and the invasion of the realm of law by an army of bureaucrats. It is now the lawyer's turn to sigh for the simplicity of days gone by, ruefully admitting with the melancholy Burton: '*Ut olim flagitiis, sic nunc legibus laboramus*—as in times past we were sicke of offences, so now are we of lawes.' Common law, case law, statute law, our poor tired heads are dazed with the daily accumulating burden of it all. Once upon a time—just think of it—the House of Commons could meet and debate and do nothing. At the close of one such session Queen Elizabeth asked the Speaker what its members had passed. 'An it please your Majesty,' he replied, 'we have passed two months and a half.' *O si sic semper!* In the next reign, it was said that 'the books of the common law might all be carried in a wheelbarrow.' Whereas, now, our Halsbury and Hailsham *Laws of England*, our forms and precedents, our statutes and reports, are hauled to our offices in huge pantechnicons.

Gone are the care-free days when country attorneys, tossing aside all 'weightier matters of the law,' would forgather in provincial societies or in private dinner parties, and make merry over the foibles of their clients, or the *jeux d'esprit* of lightly learned counsel, such as he who, in the defence to an action for seduction, set up the mock-serious plea of 'contributary negligence,' or the diabolical ingenuity of articled clerks who are wont to propound such posers as this: 'Sir, does the phrase *en ventre sa mère* mean the same thing as *in loco parentis*?' Gone are the days of the market ordinaries when, for two solid hours, one could feed and fraternize with the farmers. Gone are the days when solicitors, like Armigel Wade of Hitchin, could post up champagne in their book of petty expenses.

II

My good fortune lay in the fact that, for thirty-five years, first under articles, then as assistant solicitor, I was attached to one of the oldest firms in the land, that of Messrs. Hawkins & Co. of Hitchin. Some day my history of that firm, from 1591 onwards, will be published; and it would be a pity to quote at large from it now. But the best of my days were spent half doing my duty in a state of life into which it had *not* pleased God to call me, and by the good nature of my master and father-in-the-law William Onslow Times [1] devoting the other half to the discovery of manuscripts for the history of a royal and ancient manor.

For the sort of life I had in mind to follow, the conditions were ideal. The office in Portmill Lane (sometimes, in

---

[1] It is hoped to include the account I have written of him in a companion volume to my *Hitchin Worthies*.

pleasant banter, ſtyled Chancery Lane) was housed in a comely Jacobean building. It had two front doors, and several bolt holes or back doors. A ſtranger, ringing the bell, would be puzzled by the lack of any apparent welcome. Somewhat myſteriously, the door would open, but only half an inch, the catch being released by a wired device, worked by a clerk far too busy and superior to descend from his high engrossing ſtool. If the ſtranger entered at his peril, and, in his ignorance, asked to see 'Mr. Hawkins,' he was once again abashed. 'Sorry you can't, he died in 1877.' But there was a deferred welcome within, and ſtrangers became clients, and clients developed into friends.

It would not be correct to describe the interior as comely. Like moſt lawyers' offices (but why, why, why!) the rooms —littered with files, the duſt of ages upon them—looked dishevelled and untidy. The wall-papers were of the mock varnished and grained pine in favour a century before, though if you explored with a penknife you might light upon five or six other specimens, each more attractive than the one above. The windows were made to open; but a ponderous legaliſtic atmosphere hung about the chambers: a curious conglomerate of parchment, sealing wax, corroding ink, calf bindings, ſtale tobacco, escaping gas, and myriad decaying matters. But very soon one became 'part and parcel' of all this; one accepted, one even liked one's surroundings; they were all of a piece with the antiquity of the firm; one was proud to be able to smell one's way back to Elizabethan times.

Then there were other attractions. One's fancy was caught by the double doors of some of the principal rooms, an inner door of baize, warranted to muffle the guiltieſt of intimate confessions. The room I occupied possessed a secret chamber, opened by a hidden spring in the wall, large enough to conceal a confidential clerk if earshot evidence of a ticklish interview were needful. Everywhere one came upon cupboards, some of them undiſturbed for centuries, filled with family skeletons and other surprising things. One of the firſt I opened contained the reports and the account books of the celebrated McAdam (1756–1836), whom the firm, as clerks to the local Turnpike Truſts, had called in to macadamize and improve the Hitchin-to-Welwyn and Hitchin-to-Bedford roads. In another cup-

OFFICES OF HAWKINS AND CO., PORTMILL LANE, HITCHIN
From a photograph by Harry Meyer

JOHN HAWKINS
From a photograph by Maull & Fox

board I came upon a marked catalogue of the sale of Byron's furniture and books, and I remembered that on 13th July 1824 his funeral cortège passed through Hitchin, with a black slave and a Greek attendant, and that some of Hawkins & Co.'s clients had been privileged, for one memorable moment, to take up the precious casket enshrining the poet's heart, and hold it in their hands, and that one of the women Friends was 'scandalously reported to have kissed it.' Tied up with a bundle of title-deeds in another cupboard I found two letters from the Cromwellian and Restoration poet, Andrew Marvell, written when member for Hull in 1670, and complaining that no one could expect promotions, spiritual or temporal, unless he made his court to the king's mistress, the Duchess of Cleveland.

On a shelf in that same cupboard, deep in dust, reposed the draft of a Bill introduced into the House of Commons in 1770, forbidding any woman 'to impose upon, seduce, or betray into Matrimony any of His Majesty's subjects by means of scent, paints, cosmetic washes, artificial teeth, Spanish wool, iron stays, hoops, high-heeled shoes, or bolstered hips.' Any marriage so contrived was to be null and void.

Another amusing commentary on the wiles of women came to light amongst the probate papers of a client stowed away in yet another cupboard. It was a paper cutting dated 31st May 1775, and read as follows: 'On Saturday May 20th, a Tanner, who lives within twenty miles of Hitchin Back-Street, returning late from his Work, found his Wife was gone to Bed, but had forgot to lock the Door. The Husband, blundering in in the Dark, just gave Time to another, who had supplied his Place, to get under the Bed. The Husband had put off his Clothes and was getting also into Bed when his Wife complained she was exceeding ill, and should be glad of some Aniseed Water, but feared the Publick Houses were all shut up except the Sun Inn which was at the greatest Distance. The honest Man put on his Clothes, and went into the Sun, where, putting his Hand into his Pocket for a shilling to pay for the Water, the Waiter returned it to him, telling him he could not change his Guinea. The Man, amazed to hear Mention of a Guinea (as knowing he had but a few shillings), hastily put his Hand again into his Pocket and pulled out

nine more, with a Ten-Pound Bank-Note, and on further
Examination found he had got a new Pair of Breeches
and a fine Watch. Comprehending the whole then in an
inſtant, he observed, with the coolness of a Philosopher,
that the affair was over before this, and that what was done
could not be undone. As his Wife, therefore, had been
so induſtrious in putting him into so much Ready Money,
he would have a Bottle of Wine firſt, and then carry her
the Aniseed-Water. The Tanner had the Breeches cried
on Tuesday in the open Market, but has not yet found
an Owner.'

III

In two shelved recesses of my room, lingered the remains
of the original library; and to a bibliophile like myself it
gave perpetual pleasure to gaze upon its lordly folios—Star
Chamber reports, High Commission Court reports, manuscript books of precedents compiled by dead-and-gone practitioners, and a hundred others. And how I loved to run
my hands over their ribbed spines and calf and vellum
bindings! But sometimes I would dislodge a huge tome,
shake off the top inch of Jacobean and Georgian duſt from
the open window on to the surprised heads of those walking
the ſtreet below, and settle down beside the fire to read.
Moſt of all I liked to dip into *Coke upon Littleton*, marvelling
at the misguided talent of that young poet who, doomed to
take up law, turned this very learned and laborious treatise
into rhyming couplets. One marvelled, too, at the baſtard
Law-French, in which moſt of the early black-letter reports
were written, and that it should have continued for so long.
During the interregnum, Cromwell, that maſter of verna-
cular English, had his dictatorial way. But no sooner was he
dead than the cuſtomary language was revived. 'The
Law,' said Roger North, 'is scarce expressible in English.'
With that acid comment the lawyers of England heaved a
sigh of relief at the Reſtoration, and once again, in reporting,
it was possible to concoct sentences like the famous one of
1631, so dearly beloved of our profession: *Il ject un brickbat
a le dit Juſtice que narrowly miſt.*
I remember earning my firſt money as a writer (four

guineas from the *Evening News*) by an essay on 'Swearing,' in which, after delving into these same reports, I was able to show how far one could go in the gentle art of making enemies without incurring the displeasure of the Courts. The reports of Sir Francis Moore, for example, reflect the nice discrimination of the judges of the Elizabethan age in the matter of malediction; and if, as seems just possible, these cases would hold good *mutatis mutandis* to this day, they provide a fairly comprehensive code of the strong language one may with impunity use. For example, you may say of the Archbishop of York, if it pleases you to do so, that he is a 'covetous and malitious bishop.' Of an inn-keeper that 'he is a caterpillar, for he liveth by robbing his guests.' You may walk up to a person and say: 'Thou art a goose,' or 'Thou art a wood-cock,' but if you place your hand on his shoulder as you repeat the words then you are lost.

Lawyers and attorneys have possessed such a bad repu-tation from the beginning that you may revile them at your pleasure. Here are a few phrases of abuse that the judges have allowed: 'He is the falsest knave in England and by God's blood I will cut his throat,' and this: 'Thou art a common maintainer of suits and a Champerter. I will have thee thrown over the Barre next term.' And magis-trates, too, have had to put up with some rough usage in the exercise of the king's commission. Of one it was said: 'He is a vermin in the commonwealth, and a hypocrite and a dissembler in the Church of God.' Of another: 'He is a blood-sucker and thirsteth after blood; but if any man will give him a couple of capons and a score of wethers he will take them and be his friend.' In each of these two cases the magistrate had to swallow the insult, as likewise did a much more exalted personage, the Lord Keeper, Francis North, of whom it was disrespectfully alleged, in that fourth figure of rhetoric called *sauce malapert*, that 'he had been seen riding on the back of a rhinoceros.' This 'most impudent buffoon lie,' with 'the brazen affirmations of truth to it,' are said to have 'roiled him extreamly.'

IV

On the top shelves of the same room ſtood some volumes of early ſtatutes, bearing the book - plate of Sir Henry Hawkins, afterwards Lord Brampton, which was surprising for, though articled to his father, he had been turned out of the firm for perpetrating praćtical jokes at the expense of the clients, and sent up to London 'to sink or swim.' Not till Henry achieved fame at the Tichborne trial was 'Old John' reconciled, and even then the visits to Portmill Lane were few and far between.[1]

Not only was Hawkins's book-plate inserted, but it is evident that he had perused these statutes of the realm, for numerous marginal notes expressed delight in the quaint titles, more particularly of those that applied to Scotland: 'Of playing at the fut ball' (football); 'For the away putting of sornaris [beggars], fulis, bardis, and sic lik utheris runnaris aboute'; 'Anente reſtriccione of sumptuose clothing'; 'Againis [againſt] superfluus banquetting'; 'Anent thame [them] that refuse to tak gold that is crakkit'; 'Anent the dampnable opunyeouns of heresy'; 'Anent the youthe suspećtit to have declinit from the trew religioun'; 'Aganis children that becomes papiſtis when they are out of Scotland'; 'Aganis persounis quilkis [which] makis perturbacioun in the kirk the tyme of devine service'; 'Addićtioun to the aćt of cursing'; 'For punishment of the blasphemy of goddis name and utheris horribill aithis'; 'Of slauchteris, murthouris and byrningis'; 'For remeid of the falssete and ignorance of sundrie notaris.'

A flight of ſtairs led from this room into two attics, where often in busy idleness I would apply a remedy 'aganis' my

---

[1] The account I wrote of Henry Hawkins's association with the office, and the separate account of 'Old John,' his father, can be read in *Hitchin Worthies*, pp. 290–300, 201–8. In the *Hiſtory of Hitchin*, vol. ii, p. 325, I have told how, from this same room, he forged a letter to the *Herts Mercury* in his father's well-known writing, announcing the sudden and lamentable death of John Curling, chairman of the Hitchin Bench, and I described the subsequent aſtonishment and rage of the editor who heard, four days after printing a suitable obituary notice, that Curling was presiding as usual at Petty Sessions. It did not ſtop there, however, for Hawkins, as soon as the hunt had died down, procured two other insertions announcing the premature deaths of Miss Beaumont and Miss Chriſtiana Times. He felt that all these people *should* be dead, and that the flutter of even a false alarm might possibly shorten their days.

HENRY HAWKINS, Q.C.
From a caricature by Spy

MR. JUSTICE HAWKINS
From a painting by George Richmond, R.A.

own ignorance, for the boxes and the shelves contained nearly all I needed to know of my adopted town and of those who, in their brief day and generation, had sojourned in it. In summer it was stifling under the roof, for the windows refused to open, and at each movement, however stealthy, clouds of dust would arise. But like Sir Henry Chauncy, the first historian of my county, I could always spend fascinated hours in 'the study of old ledger-books, the ransacking of mouldy parchments, and examining over-worn and blind records,' and I never tired of spying into the history of the foremost Hertfordshire families. Once you were able to prise open the narrow wooden boxes—so reminiscent of coffins—there, when the dust had died away, there it all was, from the cradle to the grave; extracts of baptism from the parish register, pedigree notes and achieve-ments of arms on vellum, the first stilted essays 'much after' Cicero and Addison submitted to the family tutor and pre-served by doting parents, college reports of a later date, bills 'for sumptuose clothing and banquettings' incurred at Oxford or Cambridge, the resettlement of the estate at twenty-one, batches of love letters,[1] letters of a more scandalous character from the black sheep of the family, which 'family skeletons,' if brought to the light of day, had to be tactfully reinterred, myself retaining a funny-bone just for remembrance, settlements upon mistresses, main-tenance of natural children, abductions, seductions, black-mailings, breaches of promise, letters in dishonourable exile from the uttermost parts of the earth, first at frequent, then at infrequent, intervals, fading at last into silence; records of the more reputable members of the family; their pre-arranged matches with heiresses of estates that marched with their own; the begetting of sons and heirs; household account books vividly reflecting their style and manner of life; farming accounts accompanied in many a box by advisory letters or the essays on the *Management of Hogs* (1769), or the *Essay on Manures* (1804), or the *General*

---

[1] The letters in one bundle I opened were in French and addressed not to a client, but to an eighteenth-century partner in the firm who, before he gave up the ghost, had endorsed the packet: 'To be destroyed after my death.' It would be unfair to blame the executors for a breach of trust, and prudish to condemn the solicitor for being 'engaged at some length' on pressing business abroad. Those who dip into these sparkling and enchanting letters will fully understand.

View of the Agriculture of Hertfordshire (1804), by Arthur
Young who, despite his experimental knowledge, and with
the authority of the Board of Agriculture behind him,
farmed at a heavy loss near by at North Mimms; notes of
evidence taken in the squire's private 'Justice room';
calendars and notes of cases heard at Quarter Sessions;
voluminous accounts of expenditure over the honourable
but much-to-be-avoided office of High Sheriff, with hundreds of pounds to pay for hogsheads of port for the gentry
and barrels of strong beer for the javelin-men, the ringers,
and the link-men, tobacco and snuff for the prisoners,
sirloins of beef, capons, sack, and music for the judge's
lodgings, and five guineas for printing the Assize sermon;
still more voluminous accounts of those aspiring landowners
who ventured to stand for the county, with not hundreds
but thousands of pounds to fork out in ale-houses and
market ordinaries on the Tom, Dick, and Harry forty-
shilling freeholders (two guineas for a plumper) for the
securing of their votes [1]; records of a more retired, country-
house character in the squire's mature and later years,
the catalogue of his growing library, correspondence with
Kent or Capability Brown in home - made attempts at
landscape gardening, game, archery, and pigeon-shooting
books, hunting diaries, the making or enlargement of
parks, the marrying off of daughters, and at the latter end
the solemn last will and testament not only signed but
sealed, the last Polonius-like instructions to the son and
heir, the last bedside words of farewell to the family re-
tainers, the ejaculation *in articulo mortis* of those pious
sentiments which the family chaplain would quote and
enlarge upon in the funeral sermon, to be printed in due
time with double lines of mourning on each tearful, lauda-
tory page.   And so, with the hatchment of arms by ancient
custom suspended from the window of the death-chamber,
and subsequently borne aloft in the carefully marshalled
procession to the church, and the family coach and the
deceased's charger draped in black, another Hertfordshire
squire would be gathered to his fathers, proclamation would

[1] When I went through the papers of John Radcliffe of Hitchin Priory,
who served as member in three parliaments, I counted up to £9,000 in
respect of the 'douceurs,' or 'encouragements,' that his agent lavished on
the voters in St. Albans alone; and that was a trifling part of the whole
election expenses.

be made for his heirs, and another wooden box of muniments would be opened for the next 'estate-holder' by the solicitors in Portmill Lane.

v

Death is a great leveller. Side by side with these remains of the nobility and gentry one came upon box after box throwing light on the common people, the short and simple annals of the poor. Some contained the evidence they had given before the Inclosure Commissioners in the last pathetic attempt to save their holdings and their commons. Others preserved the statements of ancient inhabitants, up in arms because some village tyrant had ploughed up their church path, or denied their right to glean. Others were crammed with copies of Court Rolls, the originals of no fewer than thirty manors being housed in a room below; and many a long luncheon hour, passing like a minute, have I spent sitting on the floor, cushioned with loose papers of common-form conveyancing that had slithered from the shelves, unwinding and rewinding the Rolls, absorbed in the community life of husbandmen and tenantry in centuries gone by.

By such means best of all you may learn the rules of good husbandry as followed on the open fields, the upholding of customs that have 'immemorially been or ought to be kept,' the concern of the Court Leet over matters of town regulation and town improvement, and its 'presentments' and punishments of petty delinquencies and domestic, manorial crime. From parchment to parchment one was lured on by the antique flavour of the phrasing and the whimsical entries that were found. Thus Sleep Dearmer of Hitchin was presented 'for leading his geese into Butts Close and for speaking slightingly of the jurymen'; Galbraith Tarleton 'for cutting down great limbes from his apple trees contrary to good husbandry'; Joan Terrier 'that she is a common garrulatrix et perturbatrix, and should have the judgement of the stoupe' (i.e. ducking stool); the widow Roberts 'that she shall not att any time or times hereafter throw or cause to be flung out of her window any Chamber Pott or Potts whereby it may be an annoysance to Edward Rumbald and the rest of her neighbours upon pains to

c

forfeite 6*s.* '; and laſtly as an 'annoysance' to a court digni-
tary it is 'Presented that Humphrey Woolcot did exclaim
and rail againſt Boſtlock Toller, Gentleman Steward of this
manor, as a mountebank attorney and the Lord's hireling

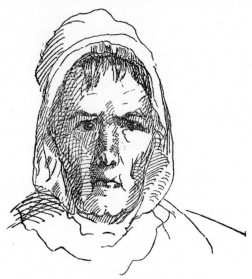

A HITCHIN SCOLD
From a drawing by Samuel Lucas

creature, and that he would have the court-books out of
his hand and caſt them on the common layſtall (i.e. dunghill), and often as the bailiff cried the court he did sing out
luſtily: *Come, come away to the Tavern I say*, so that none
that ſtood by was able to hear.'

VI

Occasionally, if I wanted a change in the relaxation of
lunch-time reading, I would forsake the attics and go down
into the cellar, a murky, damp, spider - infeſted place,
housing the records of the archdeaconry, in which eccle-
siaſtical area the firm had held office as regiſtrar for more
than two hundred years. In the fitful gleam of a candle
it was difficult to make out the faded script, and I marvelled
at the scholarly devotion and the good eyes of William
Urwick, who had spent a whole year in the same cellar

digging out material for his *Nonconformity in Herts* (1884). To the sinful layman, who is often preached at, at least by innuendo, in church, there is a wicked pleasure in prying into 'sacerdotal enormities' and priestly peccadilloes. Here, indeed, on these grimy shelves there was the devil's own plenty, so that whenever I fell out with the vicars of Hitchin I was in a position to say: 'Very well then, if you take that line, I shall compile a book revealing the private lives of your predecessors and wind up with your own.'

Being, at this present, at peace with Holy Church, and hoping for Christian burial, I shall rake up none of these clerical misdemeanours, and, besides, there was so much good old vintage stuff laid down in that cellar that one could drink it all in, and be not malevolent, but merely merry. It was fascinating to turn over the papers relating to excommunications, penances, accusations of witchcraft, presentments for heresy, licences for midwives, apothecaries, and schoolmasters, informations against 'prophane swearers,' and the like. It was interesting to discover that parsons were at one time obliged to furnish the State with weapons of war, according to their means: 'Petronells, corseletts, halberdes, black-bylls, and Skottish Capps,' and already I knew, piece by piece, the armour taken down from the north wall of St. Mary's at the time of the Armada.

In the next century one could observe Archdeacon Laud, like a sleuth-hound, hunting down the Brownists and Independents in cottages, barns, and woods, the attacks by the Puritans in the sixteen-thirties and -forties on the popish altar rails, their insistence on receiving the sacrament sitting, their endowment of lecturers to preach the word of God in the market-place in opposition to the sermons and homilies of the regular clergy in the parish church near by. Here, in one document that I found, is a presentment typical of what was happening in many parishes at the outset of the Civil War: 'That Henry Harlowe of Ashwell, tailor, then being lay parson at Tharfield, spoke divers scandalous words to William Turner of Tharfield, clerk, in derogation of the book of Common Prayer and the administration of the Sacraments and other ceremonies of the Established Church, namely, "that the said book of Common Prayer was partly God's and partly man's hotchpotch, and if he [William Turner] chose to bury the dead according to the same book of Common Prayer he [Harlowe] could not answer for the same."'

One must admit that the laity come out badly in these records. A barber is presented for that he 'did trim several persons on the Sabbath Day during divine service'; a publican and sinner for 'suffering divers persons to sit up drinking overmuch in his house on the Lord's Day'; one Adam Brock (1610) of Shenley for that 'he in an unseemly manner did lay a henne under the book of John Meade the parish clarke'; Thomas White (1674) of Pirton 'for not coming to the church service, and for inscribing texts of Scripture in the chancel over the Communion-table "Ye worship ye know not what," and over the door, "In vain do ye worship me."'

VII

It was to be expected in such an office that the clerks would be in keeping; nor was I disappointed. To me, as a mere junior, the senior members of the staff, in manners, countenance, and clothes, belonged to a bygone age. I marvelled at their solemn, dignified demeanour, their courteous but firm refusal to be hurried. Though time might be 'of the essence,' they preserved an even pace with the slow majesty of the law.

Within five minutes of my arrival, and again it seemed meet and right, I was being offered a pinch of snuff from an eighteenth-century snuff-box by a conveyancing clerk with an eighteenth-century face, and it was he who showed me the cupboard where, aforetime, the sherry and the snuff had been stored for the better sort of clients. In Jacobean and early Georgian days, as I found out later, the firm had provided Christiana, White Lisbon, and 'gold-Pippen Syder' as 'refreshers' for their clerks, and many a grateful client had contributed to the office cellar. The family of Bowes of St. Paul's Walden Bury, from whom our present queen is lineally descended, behaved in a manner still more open-handed. On one occasion, when posting a cheque in payment of the year's account, they enclosed a key—no doubt a spare key—of the Bury cellar as though to confer the freedom of their choicest wines upon their family solicitor. That key still hangs, as a trophy or exhibit, upon a nail in Portmill Lane, but unfortunately it does not fit the lock of the modern Bowes-Lyon cellar. I have tried it.

The clerk (James Inskip Bloom) who initiated me into the office with a pinch of snuff could not tell me much of its history; for he had been taken over with a practice at Baldock whose principal had committed *felo de se* a mere thirty or forty years before. Therefore, as I was curious to know, he passed me on to the head cashier (Henry Jeeves), a mid-Victorian man with mutton-chop whiskers who, before he retired, was to spend sixty-eight and a half years in the service of the firm.[1] Looking upon this courtly and stately man, so long established in the confidence of the partners, it seemed hard to credit that once upon a time, as a mere terrified office boy, having by accident spilt a bottle of ink over an important deed, he had leapt out of a lower office window, and had lain in hiding for a fortnight for fear of what the 'old master' would do.

That fear remained rooted in him. By the time I entered the office, John Hawkins had departed this life four-and-twenty years, but often while Jeeves talked with me he would glance nervously over his shoulder as if he heard the dread figure coming down the stairs, and his voice would sink to a frightened whisper. For that reason he preferred to talk not of 'old John' but of those who went before—Wilshere, Tristram, Draper, Skynner—and with tearful solicitude, he would implore me, as he had implored generations of other articled clerks, to do nothing to lower the traditions set up and maintained by such men. Standing beside him that first day in St. Mary's Church, I felt that he was right; one after another the predecessors in title of our principals had been honourable and indeed remarkable men. Jeeves pointed out the monument of the founder John Skynner (1570–1660), 'consultissimus,' so his epitaph declares, in all the affairs of the town, and 'studiosissimus,' to promote the good feeling of the neighbourhood.

Of John the younger (1596–1669) another monument declared that 'he was a man of great learning and commended by all. He was deeply read in Common Law,

---

[1] Not by any means a record. Messrs. Burges, Ware & Scammell of Bristol have a clerk (Edwin L. Wyatt) who has been with them for eighty years.

which he practised for a long time, and defended the causes of his clients with great industry, integrity, and fidelity. In foreseeing the events of his causes none, far or near, could surpass him.' Similarly, of the bachelor brother Ralph Skynner (1607–97) posterity was to know that 'he was for many years a Publick Blessing, not only to this Parish but to the neighbourhood; so truly good that the most censorious could spy out no occasion for Detraction, his Charity so great, publick and private, and so well placed, that he was indeed the Patron of the Poor. The Widow and the Fatherless were his Wife and Children, for whom, as in his life so at his death, he made a bountiful provision. In the communion of the Church of England he lived sincerely up to his profession and received the character of a true primitive Christian.'

The epitaphs of the eighteenth century are not so bountifully phrased, but of Richard Tristram (1714–85), whose monument was allowed to be erected in the chapel of his friends and clients the Radcliffes, it is certified that 'during the course of a long life spent in the profession of the law, he maintained the most unbiassed and unsuspected integrity, nor was he less exemplary in the discharge of every other religious and moral duty.' As an unregenerate articled clerk I smiled at the 'unsuspected integrity,' but Jeeves could see no wrong and had no sense of humour.

Leaving the church, we sauntered along Bancroft, a street of many mansions, one of which the founder of the firm had acquired from John Gaddesden in 1616, as was evidenced by the original grant, with its huge pendent seal, still displayed on the walls of the office. At the further end of Bancroft Jeeves wanted to show me the almshouses provided and endowed by John and Ralph Skynner, with the arms and crest of the benefactors emblazoned over the gateway (see illustration facing p. 21). To me it was a comforting thought that, if later on I became 'aged and poor,' I should have a strong moral claim to sink into the firm's own almshouses, subject only to the condition, originally imposed, 'to live orderly and go constantly to church.'

VIII

In my work as a budding conveyancer I was placed under the order and disposition of the managing solicitor, William Hammond Hanscombe, who slashed my drafts about, as I considered, just for the sake of slashing, or to keep a mere articled clerk in suitable subjection. But I said nothing, because he sprang from a twelfth-century family that was already laying down the law when my people as hinds, or horny-handed tillers of the soil, were still tied hand and foot (*glebae adscripti*) to the lords of their manors. Also he was a fine figure of a man, especially in the morning, when he appeared at the office in a silk hat and a morning coat. In the afternoon, such was his custom, he walked in wearing a short black coat and a bowler. After tea he strolled in with a lounge suit and a cap. When I discussed these descending degrees of dignity with my master-in-the-law, Mr. Times, he replied that Hanscombe was right; the gentry always made appointments in the morning; clients grew less distinguished as the day wore on. Being already on this theme, he proceeded to call attention to my own reprehensible habit of cycling in the nine miles from Newnham Hall with no headgear at all. In his view that was not seemly, for, however little I might feel was due to the firm, I should bear in mind that Hitchin was a royal manor, and furthermore that it was locally governed by an Urban District Council of which, and of the earlier Local Board, he had had the honour to be the clerk for close on fifty years. He would not greatly mind what I did and what I wore in the rural district where the clerk of the council was a rival solicitor, but for the future would I please put on a cap the moment I crossed the boundary?

As though to increase my respect for Hitchin and my acquaintance with its worthies, I was asked to abstract the marriage settlement (1831) of Frederick Peter Delmé-Radcliffe, at one time its leading citizen and squire. I looked upon this prodigious document of title, with skin after skin engrossed in a crabbed and chancery hand, and my heart quailed. Was it really necessary—I wondered—to have signed, sealed, and delivered such a monstrous deed in order to get married? The parchment was brittle and wrinkled with long folding. Try as one might, it would not lie down flat. To deploy it on the table—shared with another articled clerk—was out of the question; so I dragged it down to the floor and examined it flatwise there, remembering that in the eighteen - sixties the firm's eminent conveyancer, William Hawkins, when he occupied the same room, had favoured that position. But it takes a better Christian than I to kneel and kneel for ever, and I was relieved when my brother articled clerk suggested suspending the deed from the gas bracket well placed above our heads.

Then with a happy sigh I settled down to my task, having already discovered that one could trust one's right hand, mechanically, to carry on with the writing whilst the mind, or perhaps half the mind, went free. In the unpunctuated [1] wilderness of the attorneys' craft it was just possible to keep sane by inventing prettier names for the 'pieces or parcels of land' and the 'messuages and tenements' I was having to describe, by listening to the imagined song of birds in the 'coppices and spinneys,' by clothing the so-called 'corporeal hereditaments' with the sheer loveliness, the seasonal splendours of the changing year.

For such unfortunates as are 'staked down purely to the drudgery of the law' there is a still more effective escape gained by taking an interest in the personal life of the 'parties.' This man Delmé-Radcliffe, for example, was tremendously worth knowing. The time was to come, though little did I guess it then, when I should spend the Sunday mornings of two years in the muniment room of his mansion, working and worming my way through thirty thousand of his ancestors' letters and papers. The day would come when I should print a short but long-pondered account of his career (see *Hitchin Worthies*, pp. 209–17). But even as I laboured through this settlement, I was beginning to discover the variety of inherited character referred to by Bulwer Lytton when he introduced the 'settlor' to Mr. Dallas, the American ambassador, as: 'a country gentleman able to hold his own in every field of sport, and no less qualified to take his seat in the cabinet of the statesman, or the closet of the scholar and philosopher.'

[1] The stock answer of a solicitor, when clients complain of unpunctuated deeds, is this: 'How would you like the title to your estate to depend upon a comma?'

FREDERICK PETER DELMÉ-RADCLIFFE AND HIS HARRIERS (1833)

From a painting by the Rev. Charles Delmé-Radcliffe

A LAWYER'S ALMSHOUSES

From a drawing by J. C. Buckler (1832)

Still living in Hitchin town were men who had cheered him on as a famous gentleman-jockey, who had joined in his *Hunting Song* at the hunt dinner, and applauded his *Guardsman's Grave* at the farmers' audit feast. Some had watched him in the part of Old Knowell when *Every Man in his Humour*, with Charles Dickens, Douglas Jerrold, Mark Lemon, John Leech, and other famous people in the cast, was played at Knebworth House in 1850. To my surprise no one of my acquaintance possessed a copy of *The Noble Science* (1834), a book on the practice and philosophy of hunting which, by the purity of its style and the profundity of its instruction, had taken its place beside Somerville, Beckford, Smith, and Vyner as a classic of the hunting field. But before my abstract was finished I had exchanged three of my school prizes in vainglorious tree-calf for a quietly bound copy in morocco of Radcliffe's first edition.

IX

Not long afterwards, I was entrusted with the making of a *Terrier*, or schedule, of an estate at Chesfield belonging to the trustees of Mrs. Poyntz-Stewart, and by way of introduction was asked to supply biographical notes of its manor lords onwards from Domesday Book. That was a 'matter in hand' much more to my liking, involving as it did the consultation of the county histories. There, also, the mere fatigue work was mitigated, almost forgotten, in the delights of discovery. One day, for example, when I was unable to reconcile the boundaries of the home farm showing differently on various plans, I was fascinated to find that in medieval times a dispute over boundaries in that same parish had led to fatal results. My eye had lit upon a passage in Chauncy describing the unneighbourly relations of Chesfield and Graveley: 'whence such contentions arose between the Incumbents that they, meeting together upon Perambulation [i.e. at Rogation-tide], one Parson killed the other.' The site of their encounter was subsequently known as Parsons Green.

It was in Chauncy, also, I found this attractive pen-portrait of William Clerke, one of those lords of Chesfield

manor with whom my introduction was concerned: 'He
loved a country life, delighted much in the Pleasure of
Hawking, and would be very free, brisk and merry in all
Companies. He suffered much for his Loyalty to King
Charles I when the factious Party was prevalent, and in the
Height of those troublous times he rose one evening from
Supper, sat down in his chair by the Fire and dyed.' The
cause of death, and Chauncy should have noted it, was
hearing the news of Naseby Field (14th June 1645). Ten
months later—and that also should have been stated—the
king, disguised as a servant, and with his hair cropped,
passed by Chesfield and Graveley, and so on to Newark
to surrender his royal person to the Scots.

At intervals, manor Courts were held for these land-
owning clients, and by a beneficent office custom articled
clerks were allowed to accompany the steward. By my
time much of the dominion, the power, and the glory of the
manor lords had disappeared. And so, alas, had many
courses of the customary dinner. I remember sighing with
envy over the menu of the banquet ordered by the firm for
the royal manor of Hitchin in 1592: '2 dozen tarts, a capon,
3 geese, 2 dozen pigeons, 2 couples of rabbits, 4 dishes of
boiled meat, 2 double ribs of roast beefe and half a mutton,'
with a sweet course to follow of 'warden-pyes and fruet,'
two gallons of wine, and about as much beer as would flood
out the river Hiz; whereas in mere village manors, and in
modern times, one had to rest content with what the local
inn could provide. It was not much, but one helped it
down with claret and port of one's own choosing.

What one relished best of all was the drive in a high dog-
cart up and down country lanes, breathing out the smell of
parchment from one's stifled lungs and breathing in the
marvellous air for which (as Fuller noted in his *Worthies*)
buyers were wont to pay 'two years extra' on the purchase
of Hertfordshire land. 'Drest in a little brief authority,'
one liked also to stand on the steps of the village inn and
bawl out the opening of the Court: '*Oyez, Oyez, Oyez*, all
manner of persons who have suit or service to perform to
the Lord of this manor draw near and give your attendance.'
As the words died away in the wind, one would see the
cottage doors opening and the customary freeholders and
the copyholders come flocking up the street. Then, when

the Court was opened, there would be the swearing in of
the homage, or jury, composed of the more substantial
tenants, who had to be marshalled at the table according
to the dignity and measure of their holdings.

The 'day out' was not spoilt—not for the last hundred
years—by any great burden of business. Eating and
drinking were the business, and later on the burden, of
the day. A few notes would be jotted down in pencil
for formal minutes of the Court that could be worked
up at leisure in Portmill Lane: presentments of individual
offenders, e.g. for 'stealing brush wood out of the lord's
new coppice,' or 'for rescuing cows as they were being
driven to the Pound,' or 'for oppressing the common' by
turning out to grass more beasts than their holdings allowed;
notes, too, more numerous of proclamations for heirs, sur-
renders, and admissions. By the middle of the afternoon
the steward and the clerk, heavy and somnolent with a skinful
of wine and a paunchful of unaccustomed provender, would
be hoisted and strapped into the front seat, with the Court
Rolls at the back, and jog back to Hitchin with the satisfaction of an alcoholiday well and truly enjoyed.

As a budding antiquary I took a special interest in these
'ancient tenures and jocular customs.' It was pleasant to
remember, whenever we held the Court of Much Wymond-
ley, that the lord of that manor 'from time whereof the
memory of man runneth not to the contrary' had enjoyed
the right of presenting the first cup of wine to the kings of
England upon their coronations. When we held the Court
of Great Bradley in Suffolk we reminded the tenants of
their obligation 'to render a pair of red silk hosen on
Michaelmas day to the bedchamber of the Lady of the
manor.' The manor of Potton Much Manured amused us
by its whimsical title. Of the manor of Welwyn Rectory
we possessed a fascinating sixteenth-century relic, for the
steward had evidently forgotten to bring any parchment for
the Court he was holding in the nave of Welwyn church,
and must have torn a page out of a service book in the
chancel. On the reverse of his minutes can still be seen
the square musical notes and the words of the Te Deum.

X

'The Law,' said Coke, 'is the perfection of reason.' But reason can be very dry-as-dust and dreary. Human beings, on the other hand, are seldom dry-as-dust, and it is precisely the irrational element that makes them so attractive. At the day's end one does not recall the conveyances, assignments, mortgages, leases, and tenancy agreements that one has drafted or dictated, though these are the main concern of any solicitor's office. One thinks rather of those out-of-the-ordinary clients, the fantastical, hysterical, unreasonable, half-certifiable sons and daughters of iniquity or obliquity who climbed the stairs and asked for one's advice. It is they who make their indelible mark on the memory, and redeem the tedious hours of what might prove a humdrum profession.

Some clients, of course, are more than unreasonable; they are downright angry: 'chafed and irritable creatures with red faces,' as Emerson well described them. With such, one has a difficult tête-à-bête, but one learns in time not to lose one's temper. If I am provoked beyond bearing, I make an excuse to leave my room, take a turn round St. Mary's Church, practise deep breathing, and, as I come back, repeat the words of that long-suffering and sweet-natured lawyer Sir Walter Scott: 'If God bears with the very worst of us we may surely endure one another.' Then if the client is still impossible I show him the door and charge up a double attendance fee.

It will be appropriate here to set down some of the strange cases met with during the thirty-five years I spent in Portmill Lane, and the much stranger cases that have come my way since.

One of the queerest of those half-certifiable clients above referred to was a woman whose habit it was, the moon being at the full, to get out of bed at midnight, take off her night-gown, descend the stairs, open the door, proceed along the pavement for two hundred yards until she came to a red pillar-box; and then, falling reverently upon her knees, she would pray fervently to that strange postal deity. This was all very well so long as the devout lady remained unobserved. But one night the local police constable caught her in the act of praying naked and unashamed and, after thumbing his note-book, decided that, under section 28 of the Town Police Clauses Act, 1847, his duty was to take her into custody; after which I was called in and consulted. It was a case that required careful handling, with the co-operation of a psycho-analyst, and a priest; and let me say in passing how wise solicitors would be in such circumstances to make more use of the friendly offices of the Church.

Many a time, at my wits' end, I have been driven to say: 'This is a matter not of law but of conscience. Take my advice. Go to your parson, make your confession, and be led by his more sanctified and enlightened counsel.' For many years I kept at my elbow a French manuscript of the sixteenth century privately instructing the priests in the diocese of Avranches in the hearing of their confessions. It was an eye-opener to me that godly people should be so conversant with the depths to which our so-called human race could still further descend. But I could not but admire the complete understanding, the tolerant and fatherly outlook, the solution set down for every possible predicament and problem in which frail and erring mortals found themselves entangled. I like to think how many anxious and diseased minds I have comforted, quoting verbatim, and I am ashamed to add without acknowledgment, from this manual of the good old Catholic bishop.

XI

About the same time, and all this is many years ago, an attractive little man, but with trouble written all over his face, was shown into my room, and so raging was the fever of his mind that he could not be still or sit down. Up and down he paced, blurting out fragments of the old familiar tale of brotherly and sisterly and cousinly disaffection:

> Jealousies, strifes, heart-burning disagreements,
> Like a thick scurf o'er life.

Then, quite suddenly, he ceased, and his countenance cleared. The burden had been lifted, or as the vulgar say, 'he had got it off his chest.' 'Before we go any further, Mr. Hine,' he asked—and with an appealing smile—'do you mind if we both pray about my case?' The question caught me unawares. Never in my longish experience had I been asked to do such a thing, and there was a shameful split-second of hesitating thought. Then I summoned up grace to say: 'By all means. It should help spiritually, and might even help materially in such a difficult matter.' So, side by side, we knelt down on my beautiful carpet, made at a hand loom in Bokhara by a far better praying man than either of us, to wit a Mahommedan, some fifty years before.

In what precise terms my client lifted up his heart I do not know, for he prayed in secret as we are bidden in Holy Writ to do. Nor will he ever know that, for lack of inspired utterance, or even of halting words, I fell back upon the noble prayer composed by Dr. Johnson for our profession—a prayer fixed in my memory since the day I discovered that William Wilshere of Hawkins & Co. (1754–1824) had had it engrossed and framed to stand like a guardian angel beside him on his desk: 'Almighty God, the Giver of wisdom, without whose help resolutions are vain, without whose blessing study is ineffectual, enable me if it be Thy will to attain such knowledge as may qualify me to direct the doubtful and instruct the ignorant; to prevent wrongs and terminate contentions; and grant that I may use that knowledge which I shall attain to Thy glory and my own salvation for Jesus Christ's sake. Amen.'

'The fervent prayer of a righteous man availeth much.' My client, as I found out later, was a righteous man, and in the matter we were dealing with he was undoubtedly in the right. What followed was another instance of the efficacy of prayer. One by one the apparently insuperable difficulties and the dissensions disappeared. The letters that had been so bitter became surprisingly friendly. The opposing parties came together to compose their differences. The irreconcilables were reconciled. The family feud was ended. Feeling that my client's prayers had done far more good than my own conduct of his case I was chary about sending in a bill, but I did so eventually with the covering, apologetic letter that I commonly employ: 'I

A SIXTEENTH-CENTURY LAWYER'S OFFICE

From a painting attributed to Jan Verbeeck

dislike sending in professional charges to friendly people, but we have a saying here that offices like individuals have to live.'

Some of my clients, looking upon the Queen Anne cabinets, the Sheraton chairs, the two grandfather clocks, the Persian runners, the Canaletto and Pannini paintings, the Samuel Lucas water-colours, and Mr. Justice Darling's silver candlesticks, in what is commonly known as 'Hine's Museum,' are of the opinion that the office lives beyond its means. But this particular client was a man of taste. He had not spent twenty years with William Morris's firm for nothing. He paid up like a Christian. I took his hand and his cheque. We parted the best of friends.

The tale does not end upon that mercenary note. There was a charming sequel. Four years later, in came the same little man with the same big heavenly smile. 'You will have quite forgotten me,' he modestly began. 'Not in the least,' I broke in, 'you are Sheldrick. We don't forget the interesting clients.' 'There's no business to bring you this time,' he explained, 'but I have a month's leave from the firm, and should like to spend it making you a piece of tapestry. If you haven't forgotten, I haven't forgotten either. I want you to have from me something more lasting than mere money.'

To every country attorney I hope there come these gifts in kind, usually in the shape of game, poultry, butter, fruit, and flowers. Aforetime, it was a custom still more generously observed. The picture of 'A Sixteenth-century Lawyer's Office' ascribed to Jan Verbeeck which hangs in my partner Reginald Hartley's room, and is here reproduced, portrays a group of country clients rewarding their family solicitor with the fattest of capons, the ripest of grapes, and score upon score of eggs, whereas the client who ventured in empty-handed is left standing, and likely to stand, by the door. When I delved into the records of Messrs. Hawkins & Co. I found there, too, many acknowledgments of 'haunches of venison,' 'cock turkeys,' 'partridge, woodcock, and snipe,' and even a litter of pigs, that clients had bestowed upon the office that had brought them successfully through 'the glorious uncertainty of the law.'

Books without number have been showered upon me; many a grant in aid for expensive volumes that I had in preparation; a cycle,[1] and even a car. But no one had ever thought of a piece of tapestry, and I was deeply moved. Better still, I was to have my own choice of a subject, and, assisted by a book of designs that my friend and client submitted, I chose, on a scarlet background, No. 5 of the famous Unicorn tapestries at the Cluny Museum, depicting the richly gowned and bejewelled lady of the manor of Fresne, in a gracious setting of medieval flowers and domestic animals, with her left hand supporting the standard and banner of her proud family of Le Viste, and with her right hand at rest on the head of the unicorn. A month later there was a formal presentation in the donor's house, and a promise, on parting, that I should be constantly remembered 'at the throne of grace.'

XII

It is a natural transition from prayers to parsons, and it leads me to cite the case of a clergyman who, thirty-five years ago, was carrying out palaeographical research work for me into some early Hitchin charters. To pick his clever brains more closely I resolved to visit him. Walking up to his west-country rectory from the station, I reflected that I had never inquired whether he possessed a wife. To me he had been just a man of learning: *mens et praeterea nihil.* Anyhow his private life was no concern of mine. But the house, as I approached it, looked forlorn and neglected, as though no woman had lived in it for years. The windows had not been cleaned. The creepers were running wild. I tried the bell, but it refused to ring. I hammered on the rusty knocker, but it summoned neither man nor maid. At last the rector himself appeared in shirt-sleeves, somewhere from the back, and gave me such a hearty welcome, such excellent fare, and later on such a

---

[1] The bicycle was given to me by William Thomas Wylie, who farmed all day and wrote poetry all night, at Ashwell in Hertfordshire. When I was making his will he said: 'They tell me you are the worst driver of a car anywhere in the county. As you are bound to kill yourself, and perhaps some of the king's lieges too, I want you to accept a bicycle from me. Now promise me, give up the car.' I told him I could not promise, but I would, from that time forward, lead a treble life—car, and cycle, and Shanks's mare —and use his gift on every possible occasion. In the second world war, when petrol was so scarce, my Golden Sunbeam was, indeed, worth its weight in gold.

comfortable bed, that I hardly noticed the absence of any angel in the house, and murmured to myself: 'Here indeed is a successful bachelor.'

Rising early the next morning, I sauntered round the village and fell in with a tenant-farmer, who once upon a time, so he said, had been people's warden. When he heard where I was staying he shook his head, and asked me if I knew, and what I knew. Then slowly it came out that not only was the rector married, but his wife and daughter had had to leave him, and there were rumoured to be four or five unofficial wives kept in widely separated places. Possibly that accounted for the fact that the congregation at matins was limited to the gardener and myself. But who was I—a clerk in unholy orders—to sit in judgment on a clerk in holy orders? Whatever his twentieth-century misdeeds, we spent an innocent, studious Sunday afternoon over thirteenth-century deeds, and I went back to my own parish knowing much more of its history than when I left it.

Thirty years later I offered a lift on the road to a most attractive woman, and was soon putting all manner of leading questions to her about her present and her past. As she was not on oath, these were parried with much vivacity and wit; and, before I knew where I was, I, in my turn, was being cross-examined, and made to tell just who and what I was. Suddenly, from a chance word that fell from her lips, I discovered that she was the daughter of my old palaeographical parson. It was a joyous meeting.

At once we were friends, and soon she was one of my clients. On her own account, and in spite of terrible handicaps, she had done astonishingly well in the world. But her father had, long since, been suspended, at his own request, and I was to consider whether I could invoke the cumbrous procedure of the Clerical Disabilities Act, 1873, and get the aged sinner back into the bosom of the Church. Perhaps in appealing to the Archbishop of Canterbury I overstated my case. Was I not writing on behalf of a fine scholar and a friend? But the primate's reply was chilling. My client's record, black-listed at Lambeth, had made 'distressing reading.' It was 'impossible to reinstate him in the exercise of his ministry.'

Before I reached the end of the epistle, a wicked thought,

D

a scandalous rejoinder, had flashed into my brain.   It was
too good a chance to miss.   This is what I would say:
'Your Grace, we grieve to learn that you should despair
of our client's spiritual condition, and that you should
entertain little or no hope of a genuine repentance.   All
that we can say to convince you is that, whereas in our
client's prime he kept five concubines, now at the age of
eighty he has reduced the number to two.   Is there not
here a reasonable ground for hope?'

It is one thing to write such letters.   It is another thing
to post them.   Alas! the best letters are those that one
does not send.

XIII

The next file from which I would remove the red tape is
concerned with the winding up, the unwinding, and the
re-winding of the estate of a cottager in one of the Hitchin
hamlets.   Upon hearing of his death, I took the view that
there could be no estate worth proving.   The man dwelt
alone in a four-roomed house hardly better than a hovel;
he had no visible means of support; his clothes would have
disgraced a tramp.   However, the neighbours spoke of a
secret hoard, and I promised to go down and search.   They
were right.   In the oddest hiding places, in a soap dish,
a discarded bowler hat, and a copy of *Pilgrim's Progress*, I
found treasury notes, money, and securities for money,
worth £1,400.   What I did not find was a will.

It is foolish of people to die intestate.   It gives so much
more trouble.   In this case it took months to establish the
family pedigree, and to account to the claimants; and even
then one of them, a sister, could not be found.   Apparently
she had been on the road—a wanderer on the face of the
earth—for close on forty years, and no searching for her
marriage, or her death, and no amount of advertising in the
News of the World and the *People* brought in a trace or a
clue.   So we gave up trying, and deposited her share—a
goodly sum—at the bank.

And then a strange thing happened.   This very woman,
for whom we had been searching all over England, came,
all unknowing, and died, as it were, on our doorstep.   She

was found in a ditch near by, with a few pound notes stitched into her ragged clothing, little guessing, poor dear, that a few steps further in the direction of our office would have put her into possession of £283.

Two months later I was about to divide the money amongst the tramp's next-of-kin when a message came through the telephone from a woman who declined to give her name. Did I know that the deceased, when a young woman, had given birth to an illegitimate son? If not, then I ought to be informed, though where in the world he was now she could not say. Then, before I could fire off the dozen and one questions that rushed into my brain, she dropped the receiver.

If there *was* a natural son living, then under the Legitimacy Act, 1926, he would inherit his mother's share to the exclusion of mere brothers and sisters. So another series of searches and inquiries had to be set on foot, which eventually confirmed the anonymous message on the telephone. Step by step, the life-history of the son was traced: his infancy in the workhouse; his apprenticeship to a newspaper firm; his reporting jobs in London; his emigration to South Africa. But the tragedy of it all was that, when we discovered him at last in Durban, he was a dying man. The mother's fate was to repeat itself in the son. There was just enough strength left in this journalist to compose his last article, the account that we required of his own life, and for which, if it satisfied us of his identity, we should be paying him the largest fee (viz. the £283 or what was left of it) he had ever earned.

That article will never be printed, but it was brilliantly written, and with the lucidity and sense of proportion that comes to dying men as they look back over the days of their pilgrimage. His, for the most part, had been happy; it was only in the closing stages that the clouds had gathered over his head. Within three months of his marriage his wife was taken from him by tuberculosis. Within three months of his second marriage he himself was smitten with the same disease. Then, dreading lest the curse should go further, he, for some queer reason, insisted upon his wife's divorcing him, and went off to Durban to die. By the time his long autobiographical letter reached me he was dead, and under his will the mother's share had passed to the hospital sister who nursed him through the last sad weeks and days and hours.

A month later I went down with pneumonia. 'Do tell me,' I asked my nurse when I was getting better, 'at which hospital you were trained.' 'Nowhere that you would be the least interested in,' she replied, 'as a matter of fact it was right away, as far away as Durban.' 'But I *am* interested,' I persisted, 'was it possibly the —— hospital?'— and I gave the name. 'Why, that's extraordinary,' she exclaimed, 'there are dozens of hospitals in Durban, and you've picked out the very one I belong to.' 'I can do better than that,' I went on, 'I can give you the Christian name and the surname of one of the sisters.' And I did so. On hearing it, she almost jumped out of her uniform with delighted surprise. 'You're not a solicitor,' she cried, 'you are a wizard. It's amazing. Why, she and I were probationers of the same year and shared the same ward together. Only last week she wrote to me for my birthday.'

It is indeed a small world. It is getting smaller every day. Yet, if you want to find anybody in this absurdly small world it can cause you a deal of trouble. *Probatum est.*

XIV

One afternoon, in the year 1920, there was shown into my room Edward Smithson, at one time a barrister at York, and much addicted in his retirement at Hitchin to the making of books on the Baconian theory. 'I'm very troubled, Hine,' he said, 'and, I don't know why, but I felt I must come to you as a brother writer and tell you what's wrong. The fact is that, for the first time in my life, when I begin a sentence I can't foresee the finish of it.' I was beginning to smile, but I checked it on the instant. The expression on his face was far too tragic. 'Don't worry,' I replied with an attempt at comfortable words, 'lots of us are like that. I certainly am. I just go on in blind faith that somehow the confounded sentence will come right in the end. After all, it's a more romantic way of writing, and I'm pretty sure that Sir Thomas Browne, when he set out in the proud full sail of his great prose, hardly guessed where or when he would be able to make port.'

As there was something that frightened me in Smithson's eyes, I walked home with him. But somehow my words returned unto me void. He would not be comforted. At the door of his lovely house I said: 'Take my advice. Forget all about Francis Bacon for a time. Get some fun out of the plays. Does it really matter who wrote them? Promise me to laugh your way through *Henry IV, Part I*, this very night.' That was the last I saw of Edward Smithson. He shot himself a few hours later.

The saddest thing about this tragedy was that he left no letter of explanation or farewell. Sarah Smithson was inconsolable. She could not follow him, but she could not live without him; his guidance was essential for so many things. In my account of her (*Hitchin Worthies*, pp. 334–8) I have shown that it was from this time that she resorted to mediums, though only to such as were beyond suspicion, and so, by her serious and scientific practice of spiritualism, she kept in touch with her husband, and ruled her life by his counsel.

It was a pity that she required me to destroy the records of his communications. Some were of an impersonal character, and might with advantage have been filed in the archives of the Society for Psychical Research of which she was a member; particularly Edward's description (she showed me thirty pages of it one day) of the natural history of the other world, and his amazement and joy at finding the daylight split up into its prismatic colours. The particular problem to which he was devoting his time, or rather his eternity, concerned the behaviour of ants in the spiritual world, and unfortunately it was divulged that he was being assisted in his studies by a woman of whom Mrs. Smithson strongly disapproved. I well remember her consulting me as if I ought to be able to do something practical in the matter. It was a curious predicament, and one for which, as a lawyer, I could find no precedent in the books.

In another series of communications I was of more service. A message came through that Edward Smithson would like to have the valuable meadow in front of his house (42 Tilehouse Street) made over to the town of Hitchin as a recreation ground. On the second sitting he directed that I should be called in to advise. My chief hesitation was as to user, whether, for example, cricket or football should be allowed; and it was when my queries were communicated to him through the medium (the daughter of a well-known professor) that Edward expressed his wish to have the ground limited to women and girls, and enjoyed by them solely as a rest-garden; a stipulation, the first of its kind in England, and one which was warmly commended in due course by the Ministry of Health. At a later sitting, just before the opening, Edward announced that he would be there on the day, 'looking through the front bedroom window'; and all the time Sir Joseph Priestley, K.C., was speaking Sarah Smithson kept turning her head that way.

This is no solitary case. I have had three clients who, whilst expressing the fullest confidence in my opinions, have submitted them through a medium for the consideration of dear ones departed. It puts one at a disadvantage. One simply cannot argue legal points with the blessed dead, and one has the uneasy feeling that, from their superior knowledge or revelation, they are more likely to be right.

Nor has this been my sole experience with a suicide. Indeed it would be strange if it were so. Hardly a year, hardly a month, passes in any solicitor's office, but some threat of suicide is made. The routine attack by any neurotic woman, for example, is first blandishment, then, if that fails, a flood of tears, and if the horrid lawyer still hardens his heart, she resolves to make an end of it all, and 'you, you, you will be held responsible.' Self-threatened men and women are apt to live long. But sometimes one is mistaken, and the worst befalls.

Fortunate is that lawyer who has no such case of conscience on his mind. I have but three, but after twenty years they still rankle and twinge. In the night watches I think of the doctor who took his life one hour after receiving a private letter from me, the bitterest, the most savage, that I ever penned. I think of another distracted man with whom I paced up and down the streets of Hitchin, wrestling as I went with his self-determination upon self-destruction. From the outset his was a hopeless case. Three of his brothers had committed *felo de se*. There was a family curse. In his pocket (he took it out to show me) was his justification or death warrant: the work of John Donne, Dean of St. Paul's, entitled *Biathanatos*. *A Declaration*

*of that Paradox or Thesis, that Self-homicide is not so naturally
Sin that it may never be otherwise* (1644). But instead of
talking, talking, talking, I ought to have placed that client
under my own personal care and protection. So likewise
with another whom I knew to be making inquiries into the
time that the different poisons took to kill, and the respective
degrees of agony involved. Suicide pacts are common
enough amongst lovers. But only once have I met with a
suicide pact between a husband and a wife. And when
everything had been nicely arranged the husband found
that he did not love his wife sufficiently to die with her.

Another curious suicide should be recalled. Once upon
a time I was negotiating the purchase of a cottage in
Cambridgeshire, and, though there was neither electricity nor
gas, and only a well for water, I was puzzled that the widow-
owner should be asking a price considerably below the
market value. Then slowly, as I gossiped with the neighbours, it all came out. Two or three weeks before my call,
her husband had drowned himself in the aforesaid well, and
she wanted at all cost to get away. For her a message had
been left: 'I am going to seek for the truth'; that, and
nothing more, scribbled on a half-sheet and pinned to the
kitchen table. Why, I wondered, had not the coroner's
jury brought in as their verdict that the deceased met his
death by too much dwelling on the old adage that 'Truth
lies at the bottom of a well'?

XV

From strange cases let me turn aside to consider some
of the strange callers I have had—a motley crowd, yet I
would not have been without them; each brought a touch
of unexpectedness and colour to my office's drab routine.
Hard pressed one morning, for example, I heaved a sigh
when a clerk announced: 'A man from the sewage farm.'
'What does he smell like?' I asked, 'oh! never mind, show
him in.' To my astonishment, the man was charming,
and smelt much sweeter than my parchments. I went on
being astonished. In the first five minutes he had quoted
from St. Augustine, from the poet Vaughan, and from
Pascal. He was (*inter alia*) a practising herbalist, a healer,
and an occultist. He came with instructions for a will to

be made for his wife, and told me in advance the day and the hour when she would die. He proved right in the day and only four hours out in the time. As a favour he offered to tell me when I myself would die, but, said I, 'it's more exciting not to know.'

Another morning, when I was still more busy, a weird creature forced her way through the barrage of my clerks (you can throw a man out, but it is not seemly to throw out women), and appeared, without any announcement, in my room. Coming straight to the point, she asked me if I was saved. That was a query I could dodge, for my old master-in-the-law, who had likewise suffered, had taught me the rejoinder, and in the original Greek. It nonplussed her, but only for a moment. Looking at her armful of tracts meantime, I knew that I was lost. She would keep me half an hour at least. I stood up as though to close the conversation. She sat down. I strode to the door and flung it wide. She ignored the gesture. 'You cannot refuse these tracts,' she said in the firmest of tones, 'for they are by Judge Rutherford, and are only thirteen shillings for the eight volumes.' 'I much prefer the Bible,' I countered, 'to any verbal inspirationist like your Pastor Russell or Judge Rutherford, or to any Jehovah's Witness like you, upon the Bible.' 'But you can't tell,' she urged, 'unless you have read them first. Come, I'll recite you some of the best-known pages from *The Harp of God*.' I groaned, and gave up the unequal battle. She strode to the door and shut it. Then, standing guard over me, she declaimed passage after passage, till my ears were dinned and my brain was dizzy. In ten minutes she had reduced me to submission. In my weakness I even admired a cover illustration which caricatured the Catholic Church as the Great Beast of the *Book of the Revelation*. Then, to be rid of her, I purchased the whole bundle of tracts, escorted her out of the office, hurled the writings of Judge Rutherford at the heads of the offending clerks, and told them that, for their sins, they deserved to read the lot.[1]

---

[1] Office life is full of coincidences. This was the first Jehovah Witness I had met in private or public life; yet the very next day I was consulted by another who wished to know what the law would say if she deserted her husband and children and dedicated herself to the religious life. For a short and critical examination of Russellism see *Beliefs of To-day: a Review of Modern Cults and Creeds*, by Edward T. Vernon, pp. 116–34.

That was an unlucky day, for in the afternoon another woman, pleading urgency of business, obtained admission to my room. One glance was enough. In the law one has to make swift and shrewd judgments, and by experience in face-reading one does not often err. 'Good and evil,' said Cabell, 'keep very exact accounts, and the face of every man is their ledger.' With this face in front of me I could have no possible doubt. The woman was either evil or mad.

'I want to know,' she opened, 'what opinion you hold of the late Canon Hensley.' 'What an odd question!' I exclaimed, 'and really I can't imagine why you should ask me. Anyhow, he was far and away the finest character in Hitchin. Everybody would tell you that. An all-round scholar, not only a senior wrangler but a senior classic. The devoted vicar of Hitchin for over fifty years. A godly man, a man of blameless life if ever there was one . . .'

'I thought so,' she broke in, 'you are just like all the rest, deceived, and taken in. I hoped, as you had not included him in *Hitchin Worthies*, you might have discovered the truth.'

'Well,' I said, 'I am not too old to learn. What was the horrid truth?'

'He was a murderer,' she screamed.

I gasped.

'Yes, your paragon of virtue was a hypocrite and a criminal. If you will put on your hat and follow me, I'll take you to the old vicarage. I'll prise open a floor-board in his study, and under it I'll show you the skeleton of the pupil whom he murdered.'

That was quite enough for me. 'The whole thing is fantastic,' I shouted back, 'what you need is not a lawyer but a doctor. Come, I'll take you to Marshall Gilbertson next door.' But when we reached the bottom of the stairs she bolted.

XVI

One grieves when the character of good men is taken away; but who grieves when solicitors are told they have no character to be taken away? Often I wonder why our profession is so much abused. There are black sheep to be found in every flock. But what of the ninety and nine that went not astray? I may be a prejudiced party, but I have known hundreds of practitioners who were large-hearted, open-handed, fair-minded men; tolerant, perhaps too tolerant, of human frailty; quickened in their own sympathies by being called upon to advise all sorts and conditions of men in all sorts and conditions of trouble; devoting some of their office time and much of their leisure to philanthropic, intellectual, and social work.

Yet even my old master indulged 'the lurking suspicion that, of all the professions called honourable, the Law is the least entitled to that appellation,' and Sir Henry Hawkins, who gained a vast fortune and a coveted notoriety in the practice of the law, used, in his nineties, to warn all and sundry to have nothing whatever to do with it. Even such able men may have been mistaken. But it is difficult to rebut the age-long suspicion of solicitors who can twist words and meanings as they please, harder still to escape the reproach of Holy Writ: 'Woe unto you, lawyers! for ye have taken away the key of knowledge.'

Clearly, the poor reputation of our profession springs not from its conveyancing, constructive, reconciling side, but from the contentious, the litigious. 'Nine-tenths of the attorneys,' as Sir George Stephen pointed out, 'live by guarding their clients from litigation instead of by fomenting it.' But in the best regulated office litigation is bound to come, and it is when clients lose that they become scurrilous and bitter. From abusing the other side's attorney, they turn to the rending of their own. Both, in some mysterious way, are held responsible for 'strict statutes and most biting laws,' for penalties exacted with the utmost rigour of the law. Though they themselves may have besought us to sail to the windward of the law, yet, if they suffer shipwreck, the blame is none of theirs. They prefer to think of themselves as poor innocents fooled and fleeced by

> what dark insidious men
> Have cumbrous added to perplex the truth
> And lengthen simple justice into trade.

Here also I have been fortunate, having had a partner to whom the more vexatious matters could be passed. If pleasant letters were to be written, they were composed in the style of Cicero in my room. If unpleasant letters had to be written, they were dictated, in a Draconian style, in his room.   But even the wariest attorney is bound, sooner or later, to fall foul of his personal, un-passable clients, and I have had a share, though not by any means my rightful share, of 'contumelious words.'

There was a caller one evening—a man with a wasp in his bonnet—who came buzzing into my office just to sting me with the poison of his tongue.   Throughout his divorce case he had been very trying, calmly expecting a solicitor of the Supreme Court to make detailed arrangements for the sordid hotel evidence that would be wanted.   Eventually the petition broke down through his own foolishness, and he was furious.

'The law is an ass,' he began.

'And why not?' I snapped, 'does it not legislate for fools?'

'Call me a fool if you please,' he snarled back, 'but I 'm wise enough to know that when our revolution gets going it 's lawyers like you who will be the first to be hanged. And I hope I shall live to see it.'

'Perhaps you 're right,' I answered, 'it certainly was so in the Peasants' Revolt of 1381, and again in Jack Cade's rebellion of 1450.   That was a fine bloodthirsty line Shakespeare had about it, put, you remember, into the mouth of Dick the Butcher: "The first thing we do, let 's kill all the lawyers."   At the time of the English Revolution (1688) there was a judge who hoped he might live on to hear a rule applied for in Court that solicitors should be hanged for the quite sufficient reason (without further proof of guilt) that they *were* solicitors.   And I suppose, at the time of the French Revolution, they chopped off the heads of *les avoués* before they started on the aristocrats.   That reminds me.   Do let 's stop quarrelling, for I 'd like to tell you of our office association with the French Revolution.'

'I 'm listening,' he muttered.

'Very well, then,' I continued, 'this was at one time the private house of William Wilshere, the lawyer, who practised in Portmill Lane.   He began building it at the end of 1789; and so sure was he that the revolution would spread to England that he prepared for the worst.   Accordingly, in a hollow of the front wall, he inserted a secret chamber, with shelves for food, drink, and valuables, air-tubes for ventilation, and a massive iron door.   When I saw that hiding-place for the first time, it brought home the haunting terror of those years better than any book. Yes, you can take it from me, if we didn't have a revolution then, we 're not likely to have one now.'

XVII

In our profession one is constantly learning, or one should be learning. Sometimes it is law itself, always it is human nature, now and then it is customs that were observed in

'THE KEENNESS OF THAT PRACTISED EYE'

From a drawing of the solicitor William Bentley by Samuel Lucas

days gone by—common people's law outside the law—and sunk long since into desuetude. Years ago, before the passing of the Law Reform (Married Women and Tort-feasors) Act, 1935, a shabby hen-pecked little man called upon me to advise if he was responsible for his wife's ante-nuptial debts; and I had to tell him that he was, but only to the extent of the property or fortune that he had acquired through her. 'What a fool I 've been,' he burst out, 'I ought to have married her in her shift.'

It is fatal, of course, to betray any sign of ignorance or incomprehension in the presence of a client.   Nothing muſt diſturb

> The keenness of that praćtised eye,
> The hardness of that sallow face.

But, though his ſtrange words ſtirred a diſtant echo in my memory, they did not rouse it.   'Of course you should have done,' I pronounced with deep convićtion, and hurried him out of the room.

In my ſtudy at night I found the clue.   There it was lying all the time in my commonplace book and shamefully forgotten.   'When a man designs to marry a woman who is in debt, if he take her from the prieſt clothed only in her shift, it is supposed he will not be liable for her engagements.' Or in the words of Thomas Middleton, the Elizabethan dramatiſt:

> . . . he should take a wench with her smock-dowry,
> No portion of her but her lips and arms.

That this cuſtom was widely praćtised is evident from the entries in many a parish regiſter.   In that of Chittern All Saints (Wilts) one Annie Selwood is recorded as having been 'married without any clothes or head-gear on.'   At Whitehaven in 1766 a woman aćtually ſtripped herself to her shift in the church, 'and in that condition ſtood up in the chancel and was married.'   A ſtill more remarkable entry occurs in the regiſter book of St. Chad, Saddleworth: 'On Tuesday se'nnight was married at the parochial chapel of Saddleworth Abraham Brooks, a widower of about 30 years, to Mary Bradley, a widow of near 70, but, as the Bride was a little in Debt, the Bridegroom obliged her to be married in her shift, and the weather being very severe threw her into such a violent fit of shaking as induced the compassionate miniſter to cover her with his coat whilſt the marriage was solemnized.'

It was the same hen-pecked little man who forced his way into my private house on a Sunday, if you please, and demanded to know on the spot if the law allowed him to chaſtise his wife.   It was an outrageous queſtion to put to a solicitor on the sabbath day (*Dies Dominicus non eſt juridicus*), and I was resolved not to help him.   Besides, it needed but one glance at his puny frame to see that he would come off second-best. This was not the he-man to whip a she-woman into subjection.

'At one time,' I replied, 'the law did allow a man to administer moderate correction to his wife, or, as an old writer put it, "with a stick no thicker than the husband's thumb." But that would scarcely hold good nowadays.' Then, taking down my commonplace book from its shelf, I went on: 'Look, here, in the eighteenth century, is the great Dr. Johnson saying this: "Nature has given women so much power that the law has very wisely given them little." Since his day, husbands have been losing ground all along the line. Our wives still exert their unnatural influence over us, and now Parliament has conferred on them rights as well. You take my advice. Go home and, if only for peace and quiet, give in to that termagant of yours every time that there is trouble.'

From the 'penniless bride,' so called, let us turn to a penniless poet, 'an eager, meagre servant of the Muses.' Most poets, declared Mrs. Browning, are 'scant of gold,' and we have it on the authority of Wordsworth that 'poetry has never brought in enough to buy shoe-strings.' Certainly that had been the experience of the fine, dedicated bard who, one day, climbed my stairs, for he was one of those inflexible spirits in the authentic, proud tradition

> who never made a poorer song
> That they might have a heavier purse.

I liked him at first sight, for he had an eye with a fine frenzy rolling, and, besides, it was a splendid gesture to come in and make a will having nothing to leave. No doubt he had treasure laid up in heaven, or in the *Paradyse of Dainty Devises*, but, so far as I could make out, all he possessed in the world terrestrial was a bank overdraft, a bundle of unpayable bills, and sundry unsaleable clothes. On the other hand he had great expectations. Some day his poems would take the world of letters by storm, and his plays, he was confident, would be accepted. I, too, when I read them, was circumspectly sanguine, though I knew better than he what that great beast the public was like, and I had seen something of publishers and had heard what actor-managers were like. So we drew up a will, much in the subjunctive mood, but bequeathing copyrights and royalties as though they might run into millions. As it seemed vulgar to speak of a bill of costs, I said, smilingly, that I would accept one of his poems in satisfaction, and here, phrased in the rich Elizabethan manner, is what he tendered:

TO ——

Amongst the shades I shall not see
Your beauty languish and decline;
Nor trace the first, faint fatal line
On your body's pale, cool ivory.
For still youth's potent magic sways
The April pageant of your face;
Your limbs have yet the casual grace
Of childhood's long, enchanted days
For me was this brief splendour made,
The shy, young petals of the rose,
Before its fragrance fainter grows,
And all its golden glories fade.
I shall not see the brigand years
Creep with their soft assassin's tread
To bow your exquisite small head,
And dim your shining eyes with tears.
Others may watch your springtide go,
Squandered at last by spendthrift Time;
But some more subtle pen than mine
Must mourn for Beauty's overthrow.

It isn't decent to weigh the immortal gossamer of verse in avoirdupois or even troy weight, or to think of it in terms of filthy lucre, but it seemed to me that these lines were worth more than the two guineas I should have charged, and therefore some change was due. So, to make us square, I sent him a translation of my own rendering which I knew to be worth a guinea, having once sold it to the *New Statesman* at that price:

THE GOOD THINGS OF THIS LIFE

(*From the French of Christophe Plantin,* 1514–89)

Give me an house, convenient, clean, and fair;
An old-world garden with its fruitful walls;
Orchards and spreading vines; a few tried thralls;
A faithful wife unspent with children's care.

No debts, no quarrels, lust or lawyer's snare;
No irksome sharing of ancestral halls;
Desiring little, deaf to ambition's calls,
Or aught beside that simple folk forswear.
Grant me to live in low estate at ease,
In true devotion telling out my days;
Give me a soul at peace from passionate ways,
A fearless mind unmoved by man or fate.
So, praising God, I'll graft and prune my trees
Till Death comes softly to my garden gate.

XVIII

It used to be said by John Skynner, founder of the old firm in Portmill Lane, that nowhere does the character of a man come out more conspicuously than in the making of his will. That was truer in his day and generation than in ours, for you had then, in the forefront of the will, and generally in Latin, an elaborate statement of belief, and throughout the rest of the document, in English, you became aware of the testator's pride and prejudice, his remorse and the recompense he sought to pay, friendships, enmities, family feuds, all summed up with that intensity of vision which comes to a man who is about to die. Yet will-making is still the most pleasing and human part of a lawyer's practice, and by the harsh reminder of wars it has become a more prominent and profitable part. Indeed, if I were purchasing a lawyer's business, one of my first inquiries would be: 'How many wills have you in safe custody in the strong room, and in how many of these have the partners been appointed executors?'

In my time I must have drawn a couple of thousand wills, but naturally the pace quickens in times of pestilence or peril. When I wrote the *History of Hitchin* I was interested to see how clients flocked into the office of Ralph Skynner, at the time of the Great Plague of 1665, to make their wills, which he was wont to begin with that grim and significant phrase: 'Now in this frail time of mortality.' Even so, some would-be testators were smitten before they had time to sign. Here, for example, is the will of Richard Swansley who, as parish clerk, ought to have been up and doing, but could only gasp out his wishes to those terrified people who

THE MAKING OF THE WILL
From an engraving by Crispin de Passe

REBECCA COLLINS MAKING HER OWN WILL
From a drawing by Samuel Lucas

ſtood about his bed: '*Memorandum* that about the 25th September, 1665, Richard Swansley, the parishe Clerke, being visited by the peſtilence in his house, and very sicke and weak in body with the sayd disease, did declare his laſt will and teſtament nuncupative [oral] in these words, or the like in effeƈt, *viz.* he speaking to William Swansley his brother who was then present in the house with him sayd, "I will that you shall have all the goods which I have, to take all and pay all," but, being informed that the said William was fallen desperately sicke, he then declared his minde in these words: "I will that John Swansley my brother and Rebecca the wife of William my brother shall be my executors and take all my goods and parte them betwixt them without any diſturbance." . . . All this he did declare with an intent that it should ſtand for his laſt will and teſtament in the presence of Jane Marshall the keeper of him in the sayd sicknesse.'

It is rare nowadays for any but sailors, soldiers, and airmen on aƈtive service to make nuncupative wills. But I well remember the will-making rush of 1940 when the 'peſtilence that walketh in darkness' and 'the deſtruƈtion that waſteth at noonday' were decimating England; a bomb that fell one night in a nearby village brought me three terrified teſtatorial civilian clients the next morning. Not knowing what another night might bring, they all demanded to sign there and then.

XIX

To any old-fashioned person like myself there is much to miss and deplore in the form and subjeƈt-matter of modern teſtaments. One felt happier, legally and religiously, about wills that opened with the hallowed invocation: 'In the name of God. Amen.' Nor was His name taken in vain when the teſtator went on to 'bequeth my soule unto almightye god and to all the holy company in hevyn.' In course of time, however, the form had to be modified to suit the religious innovations of the age. By the end of the fifteenth century, 'oure blissed lady Saint Mary the Virgyne his glorious modre' was joined as legatee. After the Reformation, 'the holy company of hevyn,' and 'oure

E

blissed lady' were cut out; testators put their trust instead
in 'the death and passion of Jesus Christe,' or threw themselves upon the mercy of 'the Comforter.'

With the seventeenth century this religious testimony
began to wane. More wills were drawn by the lawyers,
and fewer by the priests. Whatever the testators believed
or expected in the next world, they kept it to themselves.
The Quakers, in death as in life, maintained a strict reserve;
they went down into the darkness with not a word vouchsafed about their 'Inner Light.' It seems a pity to have
nothing said. But what can you do, in this irreligious age,
with people who are doubtful if they possess a soul to be
bequeathed or saved? If we solicitors were to ask for
instructions on such a matter they would smile.

Another change for the worse is the gradual displacement
of the old family-solicitor-executor by the bank trustee and
the public trustee. No doubt there is an advantage in
having a trustee who does not die, and who never would
play ducks and drakes with the estate. And one must
admit there was an atom of truth in the old rhyme:

> Women be forgetful, children be unkind,
> Executors are covetous and take what they can find.

But in the office of a personal representative what you
need is not a cold, correct official, an impeccable machine,
but a human being, even if he be a fallible mortal, someone
who has been the confidant of the testator and his household, the repository of the family secrets, the trusted adviser
and friend. If he has seen the deceased through all the
troubles and trials of a lifetime, surely he is the best person
to see him into the next world, and watch over the interests
of his widow and the children. Besides, bank trustees and
the public trustee insist on having every detail of the execu-
torship considered in London town; they are not at beck
and call, on any daily and hourly emergency, like the
solicitor in the next street.

And again, what distant official would dream of carrying
out all the hundred-and-one requests and secret trusts con-
fided to a family executor and friend? I am thinking of
the pledges I have given to many a dying person to make
sure, when the end came, that life was really extinct. I
have been asked to place love letters, tresses of hair, and

even food, in the coffins of my clients. I promised a lady, whose husband had deserted her, that she should be buried in her wedding dress. I promised a poet that he should be laid to rest with his unpublished poems as a pillow for his head.[1] I have seen the light come back into a dying woman's eyes as I undertook to look after her Shetland ponies and her cats. I have committed breaches of trust finding homes for pets I had been directed to destroy. I have taken many a last message—the secret of a lifetime—to a parson or a priest.

Like every family solicitor, I have gone through hundreds of thousands of papers—some of them very private papers—not consigning them in a blind hurry to the everlasting bonfire, but dealing with them in the way the testator would like best. And once, having found an unfinished manuscript—and there is no more pitiful sight to a man of letters—I completed the work in the style of the deceased and published it posthumously. These are things that no bank trustee or public trustee, even if capable, could fairly be asked to undertake.

In nearly every town, there are to be found friendly and trustworthy people—quite apart from solicitors—willing to act as executors, and something more than executors, in delicate matters of this kind. At Hitchin, a hundred years ago, a certain John Morgan was much in demand for the purpose, because, as parish clerk, he could see the funeral through; as a printer, he could prepare the black-edged memorial cards; and, as a poet, he was always willing to throw in a 'copy of verses' for the relations, e.g. 'Lines on the very sudden and affecting death of Miss Laura Stanton of Hitchin which took place there on Saturday, January 21, 1832, after a short but severe illness, aged 20. Written on the day of her funeral.' He certainly earned his reward: 'I give to my friend John Morgan for his trouble my best Nite Gown and my Bigest Boots.' Unfortunately, I do not possess Morgan's talent in elegiac verse. But, at the risk of becoming a professional necrologist, I have composed many 'personal impressions,' and 'character sketches' of my client-friends to supplement the formal obituary notices

---

[1] In 1938 the Dean of Westminster gave me a graphic account of the exhumation and opening, at the dead of night, of Spenser's coffin, but, alas, there was no trace of the poems said to have been buried with him.

printed in local papers. So many of them have deserved a good remembrance, and of 'the laſt sad offices' it is the one I have liked beſt to do.

XX

Then, too, in modern will-making, it seems a pity to resort as much as we do to general terms. I suppose one should be pleased to simplify, to shorten. Anything to avoid prolixity and tautology. But 'all that my personal eſtate,' 'all my furniture and personal belongings,' 'all my personal chattels as defined by section 55, 1 (x), of the Administration of Eſtates Act, 1925'—how dull and unspecific and unsatisfying such formal phrases be—especially in wills, which ought to express the teſtator's wishes, as far as can legally be allowed, in his self-chosen words. Besides, the legatee likes to know, on the face of the will, juſt what he is getting. And pieces of furniture too—though classed as goods and chattels—have a life, a personality, of their own. In a poem on *Solitude* my friend Harold Monro wrote of these so-called inanimate objects with underſtanding:

> The large and gentle furniture has ſtood
> In sympathetic silence all the day
> With that old kindness of domeſtic wood.

But there is more in it than kindness. In course of time, ſtanding and serving us generation after generation, these miscalled 'pieces' become friends of the family, and ought, with a loving particularity, to be mentioned by name in the will. How often do I turn aside from our bleak and precedent-prepared modern teſtaments, and dip into my glorious collection of Hitchin wills in medieval, Stuart, and Georgian days, when beds and coffers and tables, 'silver sponys,' 'platterys and pewter dyshes,' saucers and candleſticks, and even warming-pans, were handed down to children and grandchildren with tender care as though each prized possession were an heirloom.

So likewise—and even to a later period—was it with the doublets, gowns, kirtles, and cloaks with which our forefathers arrayed themselves when they were 'in the body.' Agnes Hemmyng (1533) gives 'to Thomas my girdell of friers knottys, and to Robert the girdell I was married in.'

Elizabeth Joyce enriches her sister-in-law with 'my best
beaver hatt, my Damaske gowne, and Damaske petticoat of
a sea-green colour.' Mary Corrie (1762) passes on to
brother George 'a Bible and a pair of sheets.' Mary
Swain, spinster, of Preston hamlet (1764), has no one to love
and very little to leave: 'To my niece Mary Swain my best
stays and my worst, together with the nutmeg-grater and
the jack and spit. To May Doggett my second-best stays,
my red cloake, and a frying pan.' The beginning of modern
generalization can be seen in the will of Margaret Albury
(1800), who, if only she had been more specific, would have
saved a deal of trouble: 'My books to be divided amongst
the family as they can agree, but I hope there will bee no
words, and pray dont sell none of my books.'

Years ago, at the end of a lecture that I had delivered on
medieval England to a village audience, a fine old country
couple came up to me and said: 'Muster 'Ine, we proper
fancied what you said about them 'dieval wills, and if you
dunt moind the missus and me 'ud loike to 'ave ouren dun
arter ther same fashun.' For a moment I was taken aback.
It rather looked as though I had been touting for business.
So I hurried my new clients out of the hall, had a whispered
conversation in the porch, and then the three of us, linking
arms for safety in the dark, jogged down the lane to their
cottage so that I could make an inspection of their treasures.
They had been quite right in their 'feelings.' Along with
the tawdry trinkets, the oleographs, the hand-stitched
scriptural texts, and the terrible photographs, there were
some admirable pieces: a Dutch dower-chest, a Welsh
dresser, a red-lacquer corner-cupboard, a copy of the
Breeches Bible, and a portrait of John Bunyan that looked
like an original. Having taken instructions how to share
these amongst the sons and daughters, I inquired about
grandchildren, and learnt that there was but one. 'What
can we do for Hannah?' I asked. The old man scratched
his head. But the old woman looked suddenly bright.
'I have it,' she declared, 'I have it. You mentioned bells,
sir, in your talk.' 'Yes, indeed I did,' I replied, 'I told
you about Edward Pryor, barber-surgeon, who died wondering what he could do to amuse his little girl when he
was dead and gone, and how he slipped into his will: "I
give my daughter Mary bells for a child to play with."'

'That's it,' she broke in, 'that's the very thing.' And with that she flew to the corner-cupboard, and fetched out a miniature set of hand-bells, made at Biggleswade of all unmusical places. We tried playing *The Bailiff's Daughter of Islington* upon them, with very poor results.

'But Hannah will do better,' I declared. And then, muddling up my modern and medieval notes, and drinking to their long life in nauseous cowslip wine, likely to shorten my own, I took my leave.

XXI

Yet another change in will-making has been brought about by the Inheritance (Family Provision) Act of 1938, which has curbed the freedom of husbands and wives to cut one another, and the children, off with the proverbial shilling. In future there must be a 'reasonable provision for dependants.' The Court, however, 'shall have regard to the *conduct* of the dependants, and to any other matter the Court may consider *relevant*.' It is those two words in italics that have worked the mischief. They have thrown open the floodgates of 'divers unhappy differences' and bitter family feuds. In cases likely to be affected by the Act some solicitors advise that a Statutory Declaration should be prepared of even date with the will. But I hold the view that the relevant considerations, justifying a testator in cutting out his near-yet-not-dear ones, should be embodied in the will. There they operate with more force and solemnity; and no great harm is done, because the respectable Probate, Divorce, and Admiralty Division takes care to exclude any scandalous matter from the grant. In the mere will, therefore, you can be as scandalous as you please. Certainly, the testator has no scruples. By the time the will is opened he will be safely shut up in his coffin. Meantime, with malice prepense, he is resolved to have his fling. Sitting at your table, he will pour out the gall and wormwood of a lifetime, dictating—relevant or irrelevant —the shameful incriminating charges that are to be recorded.

Here I will cite nothing from modern instances; the Act is far too recent. But there were wills being made after this fashion long ago; and with time as the great healer, there is no harm in quoting from them. Here, for example, is a clause from the 1869 will of a Hitchin solicitor, Thomas Gorham Pierson, declaring that 'my wife Christiana Jane, having withdrawn herself from me without my consent, and petitioning for a separation on at best trifling grounds, and having rendered to me next to no assistance, but on the contrary proved herself to have been very artful, designing,

THE SOLICITOR THOMAS GORHAM PIERSON
From a drawing by Samuel Lucas

provocative, grasping, and overbearing, she deserves and I desire that she may have nothing more than she can legally obtain for her life.'

There is nothing so implacable and incurable as hatred between husband and wife; it will flare up even on a death-bed. Once upon a time I went to see an old, old Quaker die, and it was an experience I am not likely to forget. Like many a birthright member of this select society, he had a religion within a religion; it was that of ancestor worship. Year in and year out, he worked away at the family pedigree, and pored over the family letters. From Joseph Besse's *Sufferings of the Quakers* (1650–89), and from Quaker minute-books, he knew to a day how long his forbears had spent in 'the stronghouse' for their faith, and to a farthing how much had been taken from them by distress, that the 'hireling-priest' might have his 'wages.' True, he had spared time to marry, and some further time to beget children. But this was done simply to add to the pedigree. He did not love them. In return, they hated him. So inhuman was he, so little concerned about *their* sufferings that, one after another, they left him to follow their own 'creaturely activities.'

As no one answered the door, I walked in. Such was the silence, I wondered if the crotchety old housekeeper had 'walked out.' Knowing my way up the stairs, I opened a landing door, and there was the old man propped up on two pillows, his eyes wide open and staring into space. The room itself was indescribable, littered with bottles of unavailing physic, the debris of two or three days' meals and ablutions, dust and dirty linen everywhere. The windows were hermetically sealed. There was a heavy smell as of oncoming dissolution. On the floor beside the bed were bundles of title-deeds and account books; and on the bed itself, to be within reach to the very end, were the boxes of family letters.

All the thirty years I had known him the old man had possessed a deathly pallor (had he not been living always with the dead?). But now the face had gone as white as the snow-white billy-goat beard; and to crown all he had donned a white night-cap or death-cap with grotesque lappets standing out like horns above each side of his head.

Slowly and painfully his wits travelled back from the eighteenth to the twentieth century. And at last a gleam of recognition and of pleasure flashed into the eyes. He even smiled, for, in an attempt to chaff him back to life, I had reminded him of the day, sixty years before, when attired in a frock-coat and a top-hat he had ridden round and round Hitchin market-place on the back of an elephant. But the smile soon waned. There was no time to lose. Above all, he wanted to entrust me with those letters: 'You and I, Hine, you and I, are the only ones who care.' With that, a dark shadow drifted across his face, and the eyes glowed with fury as he thought of those who ought to have cared. There was a lull, an ominous, un-Quakerly silence, a silence before a storm. Then, summoning his reserves of strength, he sat up straight in bed and, looking for all the world like an Old Testament patriarch, he cursed his wife by her names and he cursed his children by their names, cursed them one and all, and went on cursing. It seemed such a piteous, indeed wicked, way to die that I could bear it no longer. I took up the letters, and tiptoed out of the room, followed down the stairs by the raving incantation of those curses.

Many a long year has passed since then. But neither God nor man has provided me with the leisure to edit and publish those family papers as the old Quaker expected me to do. Whenever I come upon them in my study, I wonder if he has any power—from wherever he may be— to lay a curse on me.

XXII

Let me turn to another death-bed scene, one that I was not privileged to witness for myself, but which I had at first hand from a professional man who was present. In this particular case the dying client was a considerable landed proprietor. But his wife had committed the unpardonable sin. She had failed in the one thing needful, viz. to provide him with male heirs. Instead, she had given birth to a succession of daughters whom he never wanted. When at last she died, he was anxious, but almost too old, to re-marry and to beget sons. There were some written pro-posals in a shaky hand; but the letters were intercepted by the daughters. He was foiled and furious. Then he, too, was summoned to that world where, as it is said, we neither marry nor are given in marriage. The rector, the family, the lawyer, the agent, were hoping for a quiet and godly end, for in his time the squire had been a good churchman, and in support of the Tractarian Movement had written many a pious and learned pamphlet.

But it was not to be.

'James,' he commanded, 'fetch me my Wellington boots.'

'The master must be crazy,' said the butler to himself, but the habit of unquestioning obedience was too strong. He did as he was told. Then, glowering upon the assem-bled company, the old man took hold of each heavy Welling-ton by the thong, mustered every ounce of available energy, paused awhile for breath, then hurled the boots at the heads of his daughters as they stood beside the bed.

'I hate you all,' he screamed, sank back upon the pillows, and expired.

At one time I meditated writing a monograph on Hitchin death-bed scenes; and the mention of 'boots' reminds me of one that would certainly have been included. It can be

'A CONSIDERABLE LANDED PROPRIETOR'
From a drawing by Samuel Lucas

told truthfully in the very words of the niece who communicated it to me: 'Years passed by, and William grew so frail and feeble that he could not take off his boots. So he went to bed in his boots. Months passed. Still more feeble he grew, and unable to take off his clothes. So he went to bed in his clothes. Then came his siſter and said: "This will not do, William. Thee muſt have a night-nurse, the doctor shall order thee one to-day."'

'The sick man shook his head. "Never," he expostulated, "sooner than have a night-nurse would I die." And the next afternoon, at four o'clock, just as the night-nurse tapped upon the door, the obstinate old man yielded up the ghost, and slept with his fathers, clothes and boots and all.'

In the hour of death, as in the hours of life, women can be ministering angels. Yet not all men believe them to be so. I remember visiting the death-bed of a clergyman who—like William—would not have a woman near him in the house. It was a baffling, piteous, rather sinister case, for the client was suffering from the third and last of his strokes, and could neither speak nor move. Yet I could tell from his eyes, and from the fumbling of his hands, that he wanted me to find something, or to do something urgently before he died. Yet with all my questioning and prompting I could not interpret his dumb anguish; and he slipped out of this world with his message undelivered. It was only when I went through the papers in his bedroom that I came upon the clue. There it was—a horrible collection of obscene photographs that, ever since his days were numbered, he must have been longing to destroy. As I burnt them, and as I thought what agony of conscience the parson must have endured, the dreadful warning of Oscar Wilde sprang into my mind: 'He who lives more lives than one more deaths than one must die.'

XXIII

It seems to me that the art of dying is fast dying out. Nowadays, few people, be they Christians or pagans, die 'according to plan'; whereas, in the eighteenth century, it was almost an article of religion to pass out of this life in a manner befitting. If you read the four volumes of *Piety Promoted*, collecting testimonies and death-bed sayings of Quaker elders and ministers (some of them Hitchin people) from 1657 to 1854, you will come to the conclusion that their affecting last words must have been long and carefully rehearsed. Though they disdained all the arts of living, they were past masters in the art of dying. Over the death-bed scenes of other people there is an exasperating

uncertainty. At school, for example, I was made to copy
out the pathetic utterance of William Pitt: 'Oh, my country!
how I leave my country!' When I left school I was told
that he had said nothing of the kind, that his laſt words
were: 'I think I could eat one of Bellamy's veal pies.'
What and where is truth? Such doubts and misgivings
made me the more careful about my references when I was
writing the lives and deaths of my Hitchin worthies and

Thos Shillitoe

From a silhouette in Friends House Reference Library

unworthies, many of whom made a good, and some a
glorious, end.

It was teſtified of Thomas Shillitoe that, as he neared
the farther shore, he caught sight of a better land and
cried out joyfully: 'Mine eyes have seen Thy salvation and
Thy glory; when shall I feel Thy presence?' The same
authentic vision was vouchsafed to another Quaker miniſter,
Thomas Thompson: 'To them that may Enquire concerning my end,' he exclaimed, 'let them know that I die in the
Faith that saves and triumphs over death and hell, finding
no cloud in my way, but perfeċt peace with God, the
presence of whose glory is with me.' The Rev. Samuel
James, paſtor of the Baptiſt church that Bunyan himself
had founded, died with a triumphant and radiant expression

and with the cry of 'Victory, Victory' upon his lips. There is a quieter note, but no less confident, in the valediction of Samuel Spavold: 'The truth,' he assured those who stood about his bed, 'the truth is a precious thing; it is worth seeking for.' Then, taking each of them by the hand in turn, he said: 'Farewell, I love you, I love you all.'

It is only the elect who can die in a manner so sanctified. Of the great majority it must be confessed that the world and all its cares were with them to the end. In the delirium of his last moments John Hawkins, the solicitor of Portmill Lane, was stammering over the speech that he had written for the annual meeting of the Hitchin Friendly Institution. The last words of Frederick Peter Delmé-Radcliffe were touched by no commiseration for himself, but for his physician who would soon be losing the best patient on his books. 'Ah! doctor,' he said chaffingly, 'you 've killed the goose that laid the golden eggs.' As for my old friend Kit Nash, the female poacher, she too died in character. It had to be in the workhouse, but the master was a sportsman and an understanding friend. Knowing her ruling passion, strong in death, he went out and bought her a pheasant; and as she lay in bed, reciting from an unfailing memory the parable of the prodigal son, she would run her fingers over and over the soft and silken feathers, blessedly content. It was a fine end to a fine old poacher.

XXIV

When a man is mortally ill, it is the doctor and the parson who should be in attendance. But most men happen to be testators, and though solicitors are seldom guilty of what, in Scots law, is called 'vicious intromission' or, in the vulgar, 'butting-in,' you will frequently find that, at the request of the family, they are present at the end which, for them, is a new beginning.

So is it after death. You might expect the undertaker to be in sole charge. But in point of fact the family solicitor is constantly asked to choose the hymns and the lesson, to interview the parson, and to marshal the procession. Indeed, you may judge the standing of a solicitor with his client by observing whether he meets the mourners at the church, or whether he follows the body from the house, and —another subtle distinction—whether he follows in his own car or sits amongst the mourners. By undertaker's custom he comes last; but in the estimation of the mourners he stands first, for he holds a secret which all are dying to know.

One should be pleased at the comparative simplicity of modern funerals. Sometimes, when I read through my early Hitchin wills, I marvel at the change. In medieval days it was not easy for a rich man to enter heaven without 'a thousand masses,' and poor men would starve themselves to death in order to have a splendid funeral. Listen to Lawrence Bertlott the lawyer who began his will (1471) in common form as we begin a sermon: 'In the name of the fadre and son and Holy Goost, Amen.' He would have a 'prest be founde to singe for me in the chirch of Huchyn by the space of 8 yere, saying daily after the offertorie of the masse thise wordes at the aulter ende "for the soulez of Lawrence Bertlott and his faders and his moders and for all cristin sowles *De Profundis*."' Bertlott stipulates that his 'Executors or their assignes also shall worship God during the yeares above rehersed,' and make sure that the priests and the poor people get their money after the close of each commemoration service.

John Pulter, 1485, was a little more modest in his requirements: 'I wol that my funerall be honestly made and done to the laud of God and not for the pomp and veyne glory of this miserable world.' Nevertheless, 'for the remission of myne offenses,' he made provision for a 'trentall plenar after the ordinance of St. Gregory' (i.e. for one mass to be said daily for thirty consecutive days), and that 'for the space of xxx days they sing daily *Placebo*, *Dirige* and *Commendacions* all by note' (i.e. with music).

After the Reformation there was an end of obits, trentals, and month's minds, of candles, torches, and processions. When Thomas Cartwright, the champion of English Puritanism and the foster-father of the Hitchin Puritans, came to die in 1603, he directed that his 'bodie shall be layd up in the churchyard of the place where it shall please the Lord to call me out of this life without pompe and superstition used in the Popish Synagogues in times past.'

Simplicity more and more was to be the executors' rule for burying 'God's creature,' the body.

Yet it is not easy for any Christian soul to part in silence from the inseparable companion of its sojourn upon earth. And why should that be called 'vile' which is, or might be made, the temple of the Holy Ghost? One testator asks rather tenderly that it may be 'buried in the churchyard of

'A SOLICITOR IS SELDOM VERY FAT'

From a drawing of the Hitchin solicitor William Bentley by Samuel Lucas

Hitchin amongst my oulde frendes.' John Field (1725) could not bear the thought of having to be buried in woollen according to the Act of 1667. You can almost hear him muttering Pope's line: 'Odious! in woollen! 'twould a saint provoke.' '*Item,*' he puts down in his will, 'my mynde is that my executors shall bury me in *linen only.*' They must risk the fine of £5 which the law imposed. What troubled Henry Taylor (1748) was lest his grave should not be wide enough, for he was a big man and he knew how careless sextons were: 'I give to my Grave Digger one ginne that he take kare to make my grave full large, and as sum In-curidgement to Mow down the Weeds in the Summer season. It is my desire to have a strong oke coffin without any Super Fluishes but to be full large.[1] I would have Wine and Ale to all the people to drink, and they that are bearers to the ground my will is that they be Invited to Super.'

XXV

Women, as might be expected, were more particular than men about appearances. Mary Swain (1764) required 'to be carried to the Grave in a Hearse with 4 horses, and the mourners to be carried in post-chaises, and the relations to have hat-bands, ribbands and gloves.' Barbara Gregory (1776) wished 'to be buried between my 2 husbands, to have a good substantial elm coffin lined with white, a Breast-plate with my name and date, to be decently nailed, and 6 of the best handles used on coffins. And that my executor set down a neat pair of grave stones to my memory and some suitable epitaph.' Ann Trigg (1769) begged that her age should not be disclosed. Gloves were to be given to all that came to see her, including the washerwoman. The neighbours were to have two bottles of wine.[2]

By another clause in Ann Trigg's will, her executors were directed, 'as soon as conveniently may be after my decease, to cause the body of my late uncle Henry Trigg to be removed into Stevenage Churchyard from the place where he now lies, with as much privacy as possible, and I do hereby give and leave the sum of 40s. for that purpose.' To those not living in Hertfordshire it should be explained that, by

---

[1] The same thought must have troubled the mind of Joseph Scholes, ancestor of my friend, Dr. Percy Scholes, for it was written of him in the *British Weekly Express* of 19th February 1814: 'Joseph Scholes was a man of gigantic stature and exceeded the ponderous weight of thirty-seven stone. . . . His coffin measured two yards six inches in length, and nearly three yards in girth. In point of size, strength and action, with exact symmetry in all parts, he stood unrivalled.' 'A solicitor,' says Leman Rede in *Portraits of the English* (1840), 'is seldom very fat.' But in the *Obituary* of Richard Smyth (1590–1675) you may read of 'Mr. Cornwall, attorney, who died at Reading; being dead he was so extreamly fatt as he weighed 392 lb.,' which is twenty-eight stone.

[2] The vicar of a parish near Hitchin, whose name I must suppress, thought it a pity that his mourners should have all the wine. He had a bottle of port buried with him when he died. Nor did his eccentricity end there. He directed that he should be buried on the very edge of the churchyard beside and above his garden, which stood on a lower level. One side of the coffin was to be glassed, and exposed, so that his beloved flowers might still remain in view.

his will, proved at Hitchin on 15th October 1724, Trigg committed his body to the west end of his hovel, where it was to be decently laid 'upon the purlin.' There it was to stay for at least thirty years, or until 'the General Resurrection when I shall receive the same again by the mighty power of God.' The body was accordingly enclosed in a coffin, and the coffin placed upon the cross-beams of the said 'hovel' at the back of the Old Castle Inn. The fact

From a drawing by Charles E. Brock

that tens of thousands have gone on pilgrimage to see the coffin speaks volumes for the curiosity of mankind. It has been an open question in Stevenage whether Ann Trigg's executors did remove the body. But the coffin remained (and still remains, 1944) on the cross-beams, and I believe the body to be within. My client John Moore told me, just before he died in 1927, that in his youth, he had spoken with an old carpenter who had been called in to make a new coffin, bound with iron, in place of the old one which was perishing. In transferring the skeleton, the carpenter abstracted a lock of hair and a tooth, just to satisfy himself, and all others whom it might concern, that Trigg was still above ground.

I hope it may not be disturbed, for the wishes of any

F

deceased should be respected, and Trigg had good reasons for what we are pleased to consider eccentric. According to contemporary accounts, he and Richard Tristram were standing one day in the churchyard of St. Mary's, Hitchin, watching the sexton dig a grave, and were both so horrified at the way in which the bones of earlier interments were tossed about that they resolved, there and then, not to be buried in consecrated ground. Accordingly, Trigg, when he died, had his body hoisted between heaven and earth as aforesaid, and Tristram directed his son to bury him in a field some two hundred yards from the Folly Brook in the parish of St. Ippolyts. 'To the intent that his father's remains might never be disturbed or the land ever alienated,' Tristram's son, who, as a solicitor, held the practice in Portmill Lane, executed and enrolled a Bargain and Sale, dated 14th December 1768, whereby the field in question was vested in trustees 'upon trust to dispose of the yearly rents and profits on every Christmas Day amongst the sixteen poor persons in the almshouses founded by John and Ralph Skynner.'

To conclude this section on burials, let me quote once again from the will of the solicitor Thomas Gorham Pierson (1869): a remarkable document that, in clause after clause, illustrates the 'whimsical and splenetic schemes of disposition,' the 'resentments that sleep not in the grave,' described by Hayes and Jarman in their classic *Forms of Wills*. Evidently, this uncompromising attorney was furious that St. Mary's churchyard had been closed, and that he would not be able to sleep in the sepulchre of his fathers. 'Having been deprived by an Act of the Legislature, in conformity with a Misfounded National Prejudice, of the right of interment with those of my family who have gone hence before me, I direct that my remains be interred in the vault I have constructed in the hill of the estate bequeathed by me to Stephen William Clarkson Pierson, having no faith in the merits of consecrated ground, no hope of salvation from the Burial Service, but only in and through the only One Triune God Jehovah I AM and the Blood of His Son once shed for man, and not continually in the Memorial observance thereof.' In death, as in life, Pierson was thwarted, for his body was not allowed to be buried in the Cave of Machpelah, as his hill-side vault was called.

XXVI

When taking instructions for a will, I have always insisted on a *Direction for burial*. Some testators smile, or shrug their shoulders and say: 'How old-fashioned you parish historians are! When I am dead and gone, I don't care a damn what happens to my body.' Others are glad to save their executors the slightest uncertainty. Some have curious ideas about the disposal of their corpses. I have known village people order new suits of clothes in which to be interred. I knew a Crimean veteran who insisted on being dressed up in his uniform, with all his medals displayed. My old master, Mr. Times, had a client who commanded that he should be buried in an upright position, as warriors, in primitive days, were wont to be. I once made a will for a man who had been four times married. It bothered him so much to decide with which wife he should lie that I advised him to be buried in celibate seclusion by himself. He was also troubled about the future. Whose husband should he be 'in the resurrection'? That was a moot point, out of my jurisdiction as a lawyer, and on which I could but refer him to St. Matthew xxii. 24-30. Only twice have I made wills bequeathing bodies to hospitals for dissection; one for a hospital matron—the other for a Quaker, who had spent her life in useful service and wished to be useful in death.

On several occasions I have been asked not to advertise the death, lest some personal enemy, or some black sheep of the family, should attend the funeral and make a scene. But there is not much fear of brawling nowadays; we are all so respectable and so restrained. Oddly enough, the last 'scene' at Hitchin was in connection with the funeral of the solicitor William Wilshere, from whose private house, as aforesaid, I now dispense the law. So much was he respected, that men followed him in thousands to his grave. They mourned for him as one man, all save his own brother John, whose hatred pursued him even after death, the more exasperated because the victim was now beyond his corporal power. 'Such was his tenacity and resentment,' writes William Lucas in his diary, 'that he attended and publicly rejoiced at his brother's funeral. I saw him, dressed as usual in rags, on his old pony, and attended by all his spaniels and greyhounds, watching for the coffin to

JOHN WILSHERE
From a drawing by Samuel Lucas

be brought out, and endeavouring, though in vain, to conceal by bitter jests the turbulent conflict of his own feelings. As at his father's funeral he gave the "death-halloo."'

XXVII

Gradually, the *Direction for burial* is giving place to a *Direction for cremation*, and in spite of the opposition of the Catholic Church the time cannot be far distant when cremation will become compulsory. Either the deceased or his executors must express a wish for cremation; but it is curious that, if the executors disagree with the wishes of the deceased, they can have their own way, as the law does not permit a man any property in his own body when dead. In this matter also I like explicit instructions. Too many solicitors copy the customary phrase: 'and the ashes to be scattered,' without considering that there might be some spot of earth very dear to the testator where those ashes ought to be scattered. At the risk of being thought an incurable sentimentalist, I ask the question every time, and sometimes, sooner than leave such a delicate commission to an undertaker, I do the scattering myself.

I remember, once upon a time, being co-executor with two others for a man who was devoted to his garden. To him it was dearer than wife and children, and he had stocked it with rarities from near and far. When he died—there being no precise direction—I besought my co-executors to allow the ashes to be scattered in the garden; but they would not agree. 'No,' they replied, 'it does not say so in the will; they must be scattered at Golders Green.' I smiled assent; but inwardly I resolved to be a villain. That same night I paid a secret visit to the undertaker, who was a friend of mine. Moreover he was a passionate gardener, and sympathized with my point of view. 'Just *pretend* to scatter the ashes at Golders Green,' I urged, 'but hide the casket in your private car, and I will call for it at your office the following day.' Everything went according to plan. The next afternoon I took up the casket, hurried off to the garden, and with loving care placed little particles of ash round the roots of the more precious of the plants. I was just finishing this labour of love when, to my astonishment and dismay, one of my co-executors came up the drive. 'I want to see the garden,' he explained. 'But,' I countered, 'surely you can leave that to another day? I simply must have your help now in going through the papers.' Then I took his arm and manœuvred him up to the house. When we left, an hour later, I was not so lucky. He was determined—after all—to see the garden, and when we came to that part of it where I had been busy he stared, and stared, and said: 'I can't think who's been liming the garden.' Very faintly, I could hear myself responding: 'Yes: isn't it strange.' But at that moment I was aching to have said:

'Why, man, don't you know, that's all that is left of our lamented friend.'

There was another case in which I was concerned, though not as an executor. There the will specified that the executors were to take the ashes out to sea; and some of the residuary legatees decided that they also ought to go if merely as a mark of respect. On the day appointed a sou'-wester was blowing. All were horridly sea-sick. And when at last the ashes were flung out, a gust of contrary wind caught them and blew them back into the faces of the family. All his life, the deceased had been of a sardonic and tempestuous disposition, and he lived down to his reputation, even in death.

'So like the old man,' the relations said, as they brushed his dust and ashes off their clothes.

I had another similar case in which a flight-lieutenant directed that his ashes should be thrown out of a bomber. This also was arranged, but not very cleverly arranged, for when the ashes were dropped through the bomb doors, the wind, by suction, threw them back again, and there was no end of a difficulty sweeping them up and collecting them for a second attempt.

It was fashionable at one time to have ashes scattered from the peak of a mountain. But I do not suggest this course when I happen to be an executor; it is no fun climbing up a mountain with a casket. Moreover, dead men's ashes can be surprisingly heavy. There is one will I prepared which, if I survive, will oblige me to scale many thousand feet to do this last, steep office for a Quaker, and the odd thing about Quakers is that they make more ashes than any other kind of men. Being less inflammable than ordinary mortals, I suppose they take longer to burn.

The service at a crematorium can be in any form the family prefer. But, service apart, the ceremony is simple, reverent, and touching. Only once have I known it otherwise. By some incredible mistake, when a client of mine was being cremated at Golders Green, the resident chaplain was given the wrong name. As the coffin vanished from view, he blessed it with the Christian names and surname of the widow, and again referred to the corpse as that of 'our dear sister here departed.' The poor widow, hearing herself committed to the flames, tried to scream, but her voice died away in her throat. Nor would she be comforted till the vicar came to her own house and read the service for her husband in proper form as appointed.

XXVIII

After death the burial, or, if you please, the cremation; and after that the reading of the will, though this time-honoured custom is less and less observed. It seems to me a pity, for it gives one the opportunity of social intercourse with the family over the sherry and biscuits or the tea; and, before the mourners disperse, one can advise or arbitrate on many a point of possible dispute. The modern habit of solicitors is to post copies of the will to the residuary legatees, or if the relatives are few, they are, in the alternative, invited to the office. At last the solemn moment arrives for the breaking of the seal. The family solicitor, who knows everything, looks with slow, scrutinizing eyes upon the terribly expectant faces of those who know nothing; and then, with agonizing deliberation, spreads out the fatal document, adjusts his spectacles, and reads.

There is some risk, I admit, in the reading of a will, for, once the body has been laid in the grave, the sense of awe and the respect due to the dead vanish. Tongues are let loose. Passions and prejudices reappear. I have often thought how much wiser it would be to follow the Welsh custom and have the will read before the burial, with the deceased present to give a solemn and truth-compelling character to the proceedings. Only twice, however, in an experience of forty years, have my readings been interrupted; and on the second occasion I had been anticipating trouble. There was a black-sheep, or rather black-ewe, daughter; so black that the rest of the family would have nothing whatever to do with her. To make things easier I offered to meet her at the station, and escort her to the funeral in my private car. I remembered that she had come three parts drunk to her mother's funeral; and I guessed she would be in a worse condition at her father's. But she was merely in the excessively polite first stage, and possibly hoping for the best. We kept a discreet distance from the funeral cortège, nor would I let her stand too near the others at the grave. At tea-time the ninety and nine juſt persons who 'went not aſtray,' and 'needed no repentance,' sat round the dining-room table. We two were shown into a separate room, where we talked (for she was a cultivated woman) of Alice Meynell's poems, and Bridges's *Teſtament of Beauty*.

After tea we joined the juſt persons for the reading of the will. By that time the emotional atmosphere was tense, almoſt electric. Unfortunately, the clauses that concerned the reprobate came at the end of the will, which meant that she had to liſten, with growing impatience, to the clauses rewarding the good sheep of the family. Her countenance darkened. Then, very soon, it changed from the black of malevolence to the crimson of indignation, for, though I rushed through the sections relating to her at headlong speed, she realized that she was not going to touch a farthing of capital. There would be nothing for the moneylenders, nothing for the drinker's paradise she had promised to herself; nothing but income doled out at the discretion of a brother whom she loathed. At her time of life, to be tied up by 'protective truſts' was a disgrace too deep for words —even for *her* words. There rang out, inſtead, peal upon peal of wild, hyſterical laughter. She sprang to her feet. Caſting an evil eye, with one comprehensive glare of fury, upon the family, and then looking daggers, with a special pointed glance, at me, she swept like a deposed queen out of the room, and slammed the door. It was only a little slam. But a moment later, as she left the house for ever, there was a grand slam that shook the home of her fathers to its very foundations, a slam that reverberates in the memory of a sensitive lawyer ſtill.

XXIX

Let us pass from laſt wills and teſtaments, and deaths and burials, for I would not have it thought that life in the law is a lugubrious and woebegone affair. It should be the reverse; especially in a country practice, where one has, not a mere bowing acquaintance, but a pleasant and jocular friendship with the majority of one's clients. One calls them by their Chriſtian names. One knew their fathers, sometimes their grandfathers. As a parish historian, I am at a strong advantage. For good or evil I can relate things about the ancestors of my clients for a long way back. I can tease them. I could blackmail them. It was surprising the number of townsmen and townswomen who came secretly to the office when I was known to be writing *Hitchin Worthies*, and cajoled, entreated, and would have bribed me to suppress this or that scandalous incident in the past history of their families. Had I been more hard-pressed for money, I could have made a not-very-pretty penny. Not without warrant did I claim, in the conclusion of that book, to be a monument of discretion. 'Though I have received a generous meed of thanks for what I have written,' as I pointed out, 'I ought to have received much more for what I have *not* written.' [1]

Sometimes this kind of knowledge can be of practical service. By investigating a long sequence of wills, I was able to prove that the family of Huckle of Hitchin had been bakers in straight succession from Elizabethan times, with the result that the present holder of the business can boast on his bill-heads: 'Established 1575.'

It follows that no country attorney need be what old Bishop Earle called 'a meer formal man.' If he chooses, he can save hours of dull letter-writing by walking up and down the streets, where he is certain to meet his clients, or he can transact business with them at the club or at a tavern. For my own part, though I have taken instructions on golf courses, and in cricket pavilions, I prefer in half-idle moments to consort with my clients, after the eighteenth-century fashion, in coffee houses. [2] Sometimes, in the office, when I am faced with a difficult problem, and wish to gain time to think, I break off the interview with this remark: 'Let's go out and have some coffee. It will clear our wits.' And it does. A few paces in the sun, or in the

[1] So likewise with this present book, though it will never be known with what care I have studied the susceptibilities of the living and the memory of both the blessed and the un-blessed dead. Truly a book of this character has but one perfect reader, to wit, the author. He remembers the many delightful but possibly derogatory passages he excised from the manuscript. He recalls the still more inflammable material that lies smouldering in his notes.

[2] I noticed, when I was writing the history of Messrs. Hawkins & Co., how frequently the firm made use of the London coffee houses, not only for appointments with London clients, but for completions. One of their most favoured resorts bore the title 'The Signe of the Golden Spectacles.'

fresh air, can be helpful in themselves: *solvitur ambulando.*
And, undoubtedly, there is a stimulus in this particular
drink. 'Free yourself,' said Cobbett in his *Advice to
Young Men,* 'from the slavery of tea and coffee and other
slopkettle.' Doctors tell their patients never to touch it;
yet it is odd, whenever I go into a coffee house, they themselves are coming in, or sending in, for coffee. It was a
doctor, I remember, who passed on to me the oriental
secret for the making of coffee, that it must be 'as sweet as
love, as black as sin, and as hot as hell.' Any man of
letters would instinctively side with Francis Bacon against
the medicals, and I would make a statutory declaration
any day affirming the truth of his words that 'this drink
comforteth the brain and heart and helpeth digestion.'

Another blessed comfort lies in the unusual character of
many of one's office matters. I had a client, for example,
John Beagarie by name, who made two outstanding Bunyan
finds. The first was the anvil which Bunyan acquired, on
being disbanded from the army, in order to take up his
trade as a tinker; it bore his name, the date 1647, and the
name of his village 'Helstow.' The second was an iron
fiddle which also bore his name and place of origin in the
same rare, aspirated form. It was my difficult but fascinating task to trace these discoveries back, decade by decade,
and generation by generation; to establish their pedigree
by affidavits and declarations of marine - store dealers,
cottagers, and farmers, so that Sir Leicester Harmsworth,
in buying them for presentation to the Bunyan Museum at
Bedford, might rest assured that they were genuine relics
of the immortal dreamer.[1]

XXX

The word 'pedigree' recalls many pleasant hours spent in
village churches, and sometimes, by the courtesy of the vicar,
sitting outside in the sun, poring over parish registers on
behalf of claimants to estates. Sometimes I have been
lucky. I have discovered quickly what I was hunting for.

[1] The authenticity of the anvil was maintained by Frank Mott Harrison,
a leading Bunyan authority, in *Apollo,* vol. xviii, no. 104, pp. 122–3; that
of the fiddle in an illustrated article by myself in the *Bedfordshire Times* for
16th March 1934.

Then, feeling that I had an hour in hand, I have put off the lawyer, and, as an antiquary, have settled down to a more careful and general inspection.

'Surely,' said one of my clerks to me as we were shutting up the office towards the end of a Saturday morning, 'surely, you 're not going to spend your one spare afternoon poring over musty, parish registers?'

'Oh, yes, I am,' I replied, 'I 'm determined to trace that William Cain baptism we want. And, even if I don't, I shall not have wasted my time. In my quiet way I shall probably have as much fun as you will over your football.'

By two o'clock, after a bread and cheese lunch at the 'Olive Branch,' I was comfortably installed in the parlour of the friendly vicar of St. Ippolyts; and the early vellum- and russia-bound volumes of baptisms, marriages, and burials lay ready for me upon his refectory table.

On the fly-leaf of the first book, beginning in 1625, there was set down a receipt 'To make ye best inke,' too faint to decipher in full, but 'gum Harabick' and 'white wine' were amongst the ingredients, and evidently the wine had been lavishly poured in, for the script was the colour of old Sauterne.

I turned a few pages, and in Charles the First's reign caught sight of some indulgences and licences to certain women 'being greate with childe to eate fleshe' on fast days, and even on the additional Wednesday and Saturday fast days imposed by Elizabeth in 1563 for the sustentation of the fishing industry.

Another few pages brought me to the Civil War and, whereas in other parishes one frequently found a gap until the Restoration, in this sequestered place folk appeared to have carried on much as before. At any rate, amongst the burials, there were no soldiers mentioned as having been slain, as at Hitchin two miles away, and none of the bastards who were baptized were accredited to the three thousand parliamentary soldiers quartered in that town. In the period of the Commonwealth a parish registrar was elected, and one came upon his entries of the marriages performed by the local magistrates: '1654. 25th January. John Sibly and Elizabeth Hopkins, their intended marriage published three Lords Daies and no man contradicting, were marryed by Sir Brocket Spencer, Knt, Justice of the Peace.' It is clear that these out-of-church weddings were not considered binding by the vicar, for he adds: 'Marryed also again by Henry Sykes, Vicar, February 2.'

Here, as in other registers, it was the burials that contained the most singular memoranda. On Christmas Day, 1669, for example, it is recorded that 'Susan, wife of Edmund Papworth of Charlton Mill was there buried in St. Hippolettes Church at the upper end of the middle space neer the pulpit, under the planks.' This note was not in the vicar's hand, but in that of Papworth himself, who went on to occupy a page or two of the register by collecting the genealogical data of his self-important family, which, after making money as woolstaplers for three hundred years, had since been prospering as millers.

Turning over the pages to August 1749, I met with vicar Finch's eulogy on little John, 'the son of Henry Lofft and Mary his wife—a Beautifull Blossom this, betwixt two and three years of age, for Sprightliness and Sense not one in ten thousand equal to him.' Another few folios brought me to the burial, on 21st May 1778, of 'Moses Ozier, son of a woman out of her mind, born in the ozier ground belonging to Mr. Craft of Hichen.' This Moses in the bulrushes had been baptized only six days before.

Throughout these Ippolyts register books one lit upon odd and attractive names, such as: Ann Almond, Woolmardine Plumb, Daniel Element, Abraham Tibbs, Old Norwood, William Barefoot, George Turpin, Mary Bouse, Lydia Bodkin, Mary Gulliver, Sarah Single. Is it not a shame that names like these should have vanished out of village life, and that the tribes of Smith, Brown, and Robinson should have usurped their places?

XXXI

My friend and brother-solicitor, William Brigg, of blessed memory, neglected his clients and devoted most of his career to parish registers.[1] That, alas, was not possible for me, but in and out of the law I have seized every chance

---

[1] The author, *inter alia*, of *The Herts Genealogist and Antiquary*, 3 vols. (1895–9), truly a quarry of learning for those who are building up the history of this particular county.

that offered to transcribe and edit the registers of my own county. Nor, for the domestic history of the English people, do I know of any records more illuminating, vivid, and racy.

It is a theme beyond the scope of this book, but in passing I will cull a picturesque thing or two from my ever-growing collection. At Therfield, for example, against the burial of John Groom (1793), the vicar has caustically noted: 'His executors have not proved his will.' At Ashingdon (Essex) under the year 1717 a bridegroom is stated to have done penance for marrying his deceased wife's sister. It is explained in the Anstey register that the affidavit required by the Act of 1667, certifying burial in woollen, could not be made in the case of Edward Wheeler (1693) because 'he was put into the coffin quite naked.' Among the register books of Middleham I found this remarkable entry: 'Burials. October 29th, 1792. I enter under the head of burials, as spiritually dead, the names of John Sadler, clerk to Mr. John Breare, Attorney-at-law, of this place, and Christopher Felton, clerk to Mr. Luke Yarker, Attorney-at-law, of this place: first, for irreverent behaviour a second time after public reproof on a former occasion of the same sort; and secondly, when mildly admonished by me not to repeat the same, they both made use of the most scandalous and insolent words concerning myself, for which I thought proper to pass a public censure upon them after sermon—though they were wilfully absent—in the face of the congregation, and I enter the mention of the same in this book that the names of these insolent young men may go down to posterity as void of all reverence to God and his ministers.'

When I dipped into the early register book of Stondon (Beds), I came upon a slip of paper referring to the case of a rector who, in the time of James I when William Laud, afterwards archbishop, was archdeacon, was presented for having taken a service without wearing a surplice. His plea was *in forma pauperis*: 'I have only one surplice and it was in the wash.' [1]

Another slip of paper at South Mimms throws a cruel

---

[1] It is interesting to note that Laud gave great offence at that same time (1617) by wearing a surplice at a funeral in Scotland (Nichols's *Progresses*, iii. 344).

light on the period when rich people were 'interred,' common people 'buried,' and paupers 'cast into the grave.' For the old and the unfortunate it must have been bitter, indeed, to come at last to a parish 'shell,' and the little bell tolling hastily, and the 'wukkus carte' jog-trotting irreverently along the road:

> Rattle his bones over the stones,
> He's only a pauper whom nobody owns.

Here, from that parish, is the cost of Will Grimes's 'putting to earth' in 1729:

to a coffin	8s. 0d.
to a affer david	1s. 0d.
to minister and clarke	3s. 4d.
to bere and bread and cheas	5s. 0d.
to sroud	1s. 6d.

XXXII

By instinct one looks to the sixteenth and seventeenth centuries to provide the unusual and amusing entries, for many a rector and vicar of that age was wont to add some telling biographical touches. One learns something of the parson and something of the deceased. I remember, once upon a time, making an office journey to Great Amwell to trace the family of Warner, and in the register of that parish, all through the fifty-eight years the Rev. Thomas Hassall was vicar (1599–1657), I found his people being portrayed to the very life. Naturally I pounced on the entry of 'Master William Warner, a man of good yeares and of honest reputation, by his profession an Attornye at the common please, author of *Albion's England*, who diinge suddanley in the night in his bedde without any former complaynt or sicknesse on Thursday night being the 9th daye of march was buried the Satterday following' (1608). But Hassall was at his best with children and with the wastrels of his parish. I liked the tender description of Master Walker's son—'a pretty, ingenius and hopefull child.' Again I halted at the marriage of 'William Harth and Mary Magdalen alias Skinner October 11, 1614' and

wondered what less honeſt reputation lurked in her Christian names. Amongſt the short and simple annals of the
poor I noted the burial of 'George Soveraigne an owlde
man, a bagpipe player, of no certagne dwellinge'; of
'Phillipe Winchly, an owlde notorius bedlam roge, died
suddenly in the field within our parish as hee travelled
along'; of 'William Robinson, a miserable poor man
commonly called "Wicked Will"'; of 'Edward Shadbolt
of above three score and ten yeares allwayes a good laborer,
no spender, without children, seldome eate good meate or
drank good wine or wore good clothes, yet lived and dyed
very poor and miserable'; of 'Elizabeth Wilkinson by birth,
Elizabeth Sheafe by marriage, Elizabeth Davis by common
fame, Elizabeth Chandler by usual appellation, neyther
mayde, wife, nor widdowe, after an unquiete lyfe a lan-
guishing sicknesse and a desyred death was buried the
nyneth of Julye 1632.'

Hassall indulged the habit of be-scribbling the regiſters
with Latin tags and scriptural quotations as though to
mitigate the miseries of this present life: the doubtful
blessing of being born, the perils and disillusions of the
married eſtate, the inevitability of dying (*Statutum eſt
omnibus mori semel*); and so likewise did Thomas Tipping
the curate of another parish (Little Hadham) whose regiſters
I needed as a lawyer to examine. The marginalia of this
scholar were in Hebrew, Greek, Latin, French, Italian, and
English. For example, in the marriage regiſter, you will
come upon these obvious but laudable sayings:

> Quicunque non habet uxorem non eſt homo.
> Bona mulier eſt bonum donum.
> The wife whom choice and passion both approve
> Sure every wise and worthy man will love.

When he comes to the burial regiſter there is a dying fall
in his ſtyle, nor can he forbear to point the finger of warning:

> Hodie hic, cras in sepulchro.
> La triſte maison vous eſt ouverte.
> Vous mesme, vous serez bientôt envelopé dans cette nuit qui
> envelopera tout le monde.

One can have too much in this moralizing ſtrain; it is
apt to give one the creeps. As a relief, one looks for

scribblings of a more secular character, like one I found
on the fly-leaf of the register book (1666–95) at Eckington:

> Our Grandfathers were Papists,
> Our Fathers Oliverians,
> We their sons are Atheists,
> Sure our sons will be queer ones.

XXXIII

That little word 'queer' leads one on to consider the
extraordinary surnames that are to be met with in parish
records, especially in the Puritan period. Already I have
cited some attractive examples from the St. Ippolyts
registers, but these would pale into insignificance beside
many I have found. Here are a few taken from parishes
in the Hitchin region: Ankle, Balaam, Bawcock, Breeding,
Childermass, Chuck, Coalblack, Collop, Damosell, Ditch,
Drawsword, Eaw, Evilthrift, Freelove, Fogg, Funeral,
Giggle, Grave, Guzzle, Hadduck, Huzzy, Indeed, More-
speed, Mouse, Outlaw, Pipkin, Pitchfork, Pretious, Rapier,
Sacbut, Scurfy, Sex, Silverside, Sipsap, Slimehead, Slow,
Sorry, Thickpenny, Topcoat, Triplet, Tuppeny, Typtoe,
Wedlock.

Keeping good things to the last, let me set down a short
list of names in combination—all from my own county—
where both the Christian and the surname are outlandish,
Old and New Testamentish or grotesque: Gabriel Angell,
Abednego Atkins, Giver Battell, Ghost Butteridge, Pater
nell Bunne, Lamentation Caudle, Plampin Cooley, Matthew Divine, Radulphus Doffer, Adam Eve, Youthful
Eyres, King Fisher, Obsingoldsbey Humblebee, Repentance Peacock, Susannah Sparrow, Zilpher Spittle, Lazarus
Stops, Greediana Tarboy, Tobias Trim, Adored Tuffnail,
Wigmore Wiskin.

Sometimes land-development companies or urban district
councils write to the office asking me to make suggestions
for the naming of new streets; and from field-names or
famous land-holders' names in tithe or enclosure awards,
or from manor rolls or early charters I can supply what they
need. Now and again, clients come to me for help in the
naming of their children; and I provide them with some

strong Christian name which I know to have been used in their family in days gone by, or with something quiet and Quakerly like Felicity, Fidelity, Humility, Mercy, Melody, Prudence. Those gracious names remind me that, in working through the registers of Waltham Holy Cross, I came upon *Love, Peace, Unity*, and *Concord* as the baptismal names of the four children of Benjamin and Ann Sears (1803). Such predestined little angels could hardly expect to flourish in this fallen world, and God took them all to Himself in 1805.[1]

Occasionally, I am approached by novelists and play-wrights at their wits' end for the naming of their characters or *dramatis personae*; and when I post a selection I am care-ful to point out that morally, if not legally, the names are my particular property; findings are keepings. It was all very well when Clifford Bax stuck my Battalion Shotbolt, sometime Steward of Hitchin Manor, into a London play. He, as a friend of mine, was immune from any injunction; but I have bid other writing men beware. Sir Walter Scott, I have begged them to remember, used to fork out a guinea very cheerfully to any one who produced a surname or dialect word not known to him before. It would, I always urge, be a proper custom to revive. I have left it to their courtesy and conscience, but though some glittering words have been showered upon me, I have touched no golden guineas. As for my best discovery—Humiliation Scratcher of Ware—I would not sell him, no, not for five guineas.

'What 's in a name?' you may murmur, and wait for no reply. But let no one lightly assume that these hours spent over registers are mere idle or whimsical pursuits. Often they lead on to substantial and exciting business, as any lawyer knows. By an odd coincidence, since this section of my book was begun, I have been handed a file of three hundred and fifty pages of foolscap—the labour of fifteen years, building up, from a hundred different sources, the case of a claimant to an English dukedom, and all now depends upon tracing the movements of a younger son of

---

[1] In the same registers I came upon the surprising surnames *Want, Pain*, and *Death*. In 1674 a marriage was solemnized in the church between a *Goose* and a *Swan*. In 1626 eighteenpence was paid out 'to three women to fetch home *Aminadab* when she was in labour in the fields.' A diligent student will discover many other entries to his liking.

G

the family, after fleeing from the battle of the Boyne on the first of July 1690, and his marriage with a Hitchin Quakeress.

XXXIV

Often, as a man of letters, I complain of 'that ass the law' braying into both my ears, consuming my time, exhausting my energies. But there are many alleviations, or as old Camden termed them 'mollifications,' that temper the asperities of the profession. For the thoughtful-minded there is always 'the gladsome light of jurisprudence' which Coke so often commends to the student. For the practical common lawyer there are the distractions of new faces and new cases.

Once or twice a day, for example, complete strangers will climb the stairs in search of a commissioner for oaths. Such men are to be welcomed, for they break, if only for a breathing space, the heavy diurnal routine. One gains a new acquaintance; at parting there is a far-too-small but easily earned fee which, by legal custom, is looked upon as a windfall to be spent instanter on books, or flowers for the office, or on wine that maketh glad the heart of man. The taking of an oath should, of course, be a solemn, indeed a religious, occasion; and one of our earliest codes, the Laws of the West-Saxon Ine (A.D. 690–3), made the oath of a communicant worth twice as much as that of a man who was not. It is a pity, therefore, that commissioners should be so perfunctory in administering the oath, and that deponents should, so often, swear sitting, or with their gloves on, or with a forbearing smile. My friend E. B. V. Christian, who wrote a history of solicitors, used frequently to deplore the unhallowed manners of the modern age. 'I was often bewildered,' he said, 'by the unpunctuated gibberish of the clerk in Judges' Chambers who swore me to affidavits thus, as I tendered a coin to pay his fee of 18d.: "Swear - thisyername - handwritin' - 'tents - thisyer - afdavit - true - s'helpyer - God - half - crown - haven't - got - change - go - downstairs - and - get - it."'

My master-in-the-law, a deeply religious man, was once taking the oath at a solicitor's office in Luton (at one time a very godless town), when, glancing at the book in his hand, he found it was not the New Testament, but a copy of Shakespeare's works. When he remonstrated, he was pertly answered: 'Well, what's the difference; wasn't Shakespeare inspired?' My own conscience is none too clean in this matter for, being a great lover of bindings, and not having a New Testament up to my standards, I took to swearing my clients and callers on a superb and early edition of the Prayer Book in seventeenth-century morocco, with silver bosses and silver clasps, and exquisite patterning, technically known as gauffering, in the top and fore-edge gilding. There was no title to the richly tooled back, and I was always hoping that no one would force open the clasps and discover what was within. But it happened half a dozen times; objections were raised; and I was driven to the ingenious but doubtful defence that, as the Prayer Book contains the Epistles and the Gospels, it might be held sufficient for the purpose.

On one occasion, having to administer the oath to a Jew, and not having a Pentateuch handy, I went to the bookcase where I keep light, non-legal reading, and fetched out the lovely 1602 edition of Josephus's *History of the Jewish War and the Destruction of Jerusalem*. To show that I was an honest Gentile I explained what I was proposing to do. But, so thrilled was he that I possessed Lodge's rare translation of his race's historical masterpiece, that he made not the least demur. As my conscience was still uneasy I declined to take any fee, so it was arranged that he should, instead, lend me the same author's *Discourse on the Martyrdom of the Maccabees* and the *Treatise on his own Life*. These were delivered the same afternoon, and inside the *Discourse* I noticed that my friend had slipped in a complimentary copy of the Pentateuch for future office use.

XXXV

Another exciting caller is the postman, morning and afternoon, for who knows what he may bring? Many of the letters, it is true, the lawyer opens with a sigh: more deeds to be drawn and in a violent hurry; more requisitions on title to be answered; apportionment accounts to be checked; tenancy agreements to be attended to; imperfect people asking to be supplied with perfect houses; well-to-do debtors protesting they haven't a penny; undertakers demanding payment before the will is proved; unsatisfactory administrators expecting their lawyer to become their bondsman; pages upon pages from petty people on petty points and imagined grievances—such *mutatis mutandis* is the curriculum of a common attorney's day. Constantly, by reason of the post, the lawyer needs to readjust his engagements. At a moment's notice he is called away to an inquest, to a Petty Sessional, or to a County, Court. Disputes over rights of way, party walls, or fences have to be investigated on the spot and without delay. Schedules of dilapidations have to be resisted. Problems of shared houses, with kitchens and bathrooms and lavatories said to be 'enjoyed' in common, have to be considered, and peace by arbitrament imposed.

Most of these matters are trifling, and interrupt more steady and remunerative business. Many a lawyer, chafed with callers and oppressed with correspondence, must be tempted to display the haughty, stand-offish legal maxim, *De minimis non curat lex*, over his outer door. In our case there would need to be a slight variation, for, the name of both partners being Reginald, we should substitute *De minimis non curat rex*. Yet it would never do. Solicitors sigh and common attorneys curse; then they shoulder pettifogging jobs, knowing that little things are wont to lead on to larger things: 'Because thou hast been faithful in a very little, have thou authority over ten cities.'

In the form and style of letters there has been a sad declension, for it requires an unusually well-furnished and confident brain to dictate a good letter at top speed to an impatient and uninterested stenographer. When I looked over the seventeenth- and eighteenth-century letter-books of my late firm I was amazed at the difference. In those ages of longhand, when the lawyer had leisure for long, long thoughts, a letter was 'composed.' 'Fixed in cogitation deep,' he could take time to consider and send 'an advised answer.' Often it was modelled on manuals of the epistolary art. If you read *The Gentleman's Assistant, Tradesman's Lawyer, and Country-Man's Friend* (second edition, 1709) you will learn what can safely and appropriately be addressed to correspondents in their respective walks of life.

Now that there are no schools or academies of polite letter-writing it is a case of each man for himself. The result is chaotic. But there is one countervailing advantage. Where no mask of formal style is worn, you can see your man more clearly. From his untutored writing you

A CAMBRIDGE SOLICITOR TAKING TIME TO CONSIDER
From a drawing by Samuel Lucas

can read his character the better; and that, in a solicitor's office, is of prime importance.

In this plain-speaking period it is so rare to have a flowery epistle that one instinctively suspects the writer's intentions. The style is too good to be true; and if the writer be of the male sex one suspects and dislikes it the more. 'It is a great grace of God in a man,' said Brother Giles of Perugia, 'to have no graces at all.' Still more wary should one be of the client who protests in his opening sentence that he is being actuated by strong religious motives. In like manner spake the Pharisees. Some years ago a young woman wrote to say she would give her soul to possess a certain Samuel Lucas water-colour, 'Snaring Sparrows at Oughton Head,' that she had coveted in my partner's room. Our reply was to the point but cruel: 'Dear madam, before acceding to your request, we should like to know how much your soul is worth.' The people with the best souls never talk about them. Certainly they do not wear them on their sleeves. 'Let us be silent,' said a wise man, 'for so are the gods.'

XXXVI

A sad proportion of the letters one opens comes from the niggling, cantankerous, litigious, lesser breed of solicitors who gain a catchpenny or catch-six-and-eightpenny reputation for smartness but do our profession no good. Alas, from time immemorial, we have been plagued with these 'brabbling and tumultuous lawyers,' who specialize in 'the chicane or wrangling or captious part of the law.' With such men it is impossible to pursue the gentle arts of compromise. Their breast-pockets are stuffed with writs. Their dictated letters are dictatorial, each sentence barbed with a threat. Argument with them soon degenerates into the kind of staccato, bellicose correspondence reported to have passed between two Irish chieftains:

'Pay me the tribute,' wrote the one, 'or else . . .'

'I owe you no tribute,' replied the other, 'and if . . .'

A resounding battle of words, in the good old divinity style, is quite another thing; but here again, in the matter of malediction, we are but pale, ineffectual creatures compared with our grandfathers. They could flare up in an instant, and keep it up, and not repeat themselves. We smoulder but we do not take fire. Even in our contentious practice, we use circumspect, pusillanimous words. 'Tis the same with clients. I remember a letter directed at me by one of my more intimate enemies—a writing man furious because, for services, if I may say so, not badly rendered, I had dared to send in a bill. 'I acknowledge a benefit of clergy,' I had already told him, 'and for poets I have an affection and indulge a lawyer's licence. But I don't see why writers in prose should escape.' Incidentally, I hinted that his prose was poor. Yet, with the whole of the English language at his command, the best this disgruntled fellow could do

'THE WRANGLING OR CAPTIOUS PART OF THE LAW'
From a drawing by Samuel Lucas

was to steal the thunder of the Ettrick Shepherd for the opening, 'Damned Sir,' and the ending, 'Believe me, Sir, with disgust,' of his rejoinder. Though appropriate passages are intended to be appropriated, I too must plead guilty of petty larceny, for twice I have wound up a peppery letter with a phrase of John Bright's that I should like to have claimed as my own: 'I am, Sir, with whatever respect you deserve, yours respectfully.'

For ordinary civil letters it should be possible to improve on our 'truly,' 'faithfully,' 'sincerely,' for these are qualities inherently possessed by any professional man. One need not labour the point. As for 'very truly,' 'very faithfully,' 'very sincerely' the less said of them the better. Here, too, the eighteenth century displayed more taste and ingenuity. Each man would have his own seal, and his own fashion of subscribing. Best of all, I like the letter-endings of George Draper, the solicitor in Portmill Lane: 'I am, Sir, your friend to serve you.' In a 'very truly' democratic age, also, we should get rid of the once-upon-a-time distinguished and now meaningless 'Mr.,' and the still more meaningless and abused 'Esquire.' In this the Quakers, with their plainness of speech and testimony against salutations and titles of honour, have shown a more excellent way. I was pleased to see how particular William Lucas of Hitchin was in requiring to be called by his name and nothing but his name. In 1831, when this rich brewer and landowner received a business letter from John Iliffe with an 'Esquire' after his name, he erased the offending title, returned the envelope, and noted in his reply: 'As a common tradesman I have no pretensions to the title of Esquire.'

XXXVII

The letters one likes most to receive are those conveying the gratitude of clients, for, as wise solicitors never send out a bill of costs without a covering letter, so do they seldom receive a cheque without a covering reply. Some clients go so far as to pay double the amount of the bill, a practice we commend to others less impulsively appreciative. Some to a cheque for the exact amount add a *douceur* of 'very sincere' and golden words, which kindle our hearts (though lawyers are said to be heartless) and make us feel we have, after all, done some good in our day and generation. Some send honeyed words, too sweet to be sincere, but do not include a cheque. It would be improper, it would be self-advertising, even to quote from such letters. But I may safely cite a letter or testimonial of 1818 that I found framed in the waiting-room of one of many firms I have employed as London agents: 'Copy of the inscription on a Silver Table Centre-Piece presented to Thomas Holme Bower by a Lady and Gentleman, his clients, in testimony of their sense of the distinguished ability, gentlemanly attentions, and honourable conduct evinced by him on every occasion, more particularly during a long and arduous Suit in Chancery, conducted by him to a favourable con- clusion.' The feelings so admirably expressed lie latent, or struggling for outlet, in the minds of innumerable clients, and in estimating our rightful place in human society are a set-off to the libellous 'three degrees of comparison in a lawyer's progress: getting on; getting on-er (honour); getting on-est (honest).'

I have one client—the novelist Ursula Bloom—who on the conclusion of a matter sends me an appreciation, or valediction, in verse. But then she is a law unto herself, for, often, the original instructions will come tripping along in witty, well-turned couplets, and she waits for a witty reply. In the wear and tear of office life, and at the uninspired hour of nine in the morning, it can be rather trying. But, with the assistance of nimble-minded clerks, and with *The Rhymers' Lexicon* by Loring at my elbow, I do my best; and, when the bill goes in, the gracious lady will find this special item: 'To mental strain replying to your letters in verse.' I have often meant to ask the Law Society what one could rightly charge in such abnormal cases. If it would sanction three shillings and sixpence or even one shilling a rhyme, I would turn poet and compose all my letters in verse.

In *No Lady Buys a Cot* (Chapman & Hall, 1942), Miss Bloom published an amusing account of her experiences in purchasing a house, or cottage, or 'cot.' It was an engaging theme, one that only a woman could efficiently handle. All went swimmingly well to start with. The price was a bargain. The house and garden were a dream. But from the moment the contracts were exchanged everything began to go wrong. The area being 'restricted' there was trouble over the introducing of a housekeeper. There were misgivings about the drains. The boiler refused to boil. The electric heaters declined to heat. The housekeeper would not keep. The falling garden did nothing but fall into the highway. The 'cot' had an indwelling evil spirit.[1]

No writer of repute could possibly write in it. No words, nothing but oaths and curses, would come. And so it went on, from bad to worse, until one Sunday morning,

---

[1] Some dwellings undoubtedly have. In such cases, I advise that the house should be 'blessed,' and every room in it sprinkled with holy water and 'censed.' In both the Roman and Anglican liturgies services have been prescribed for the very purpose, and have 'laid' many a ghost, and set many a client's nervous mind at rest. In the *Rituale Romanum* you will find separate forms for the blessing of houses (*Benedictio domorum*) and for the casting out or exorcizing of demons (*Ritus exorcizandi obsessos a daemonio*).

when her thoughts should have been in heaven, the clever lady had a bright idea in church, and, with a few well-directed words later in the porch, succeeded in planting her bargain on to a fellow worshipper in search of 'the perfect thing.' Thereupon the clever but disillusioned lady leased an expensive service flat in the metropolis, where she is resolved to live and write happily ever after. In that merry volume (not so untrue a tale) her devoted, if in this one transaction misguided, solicitor is represented under the character of 'The Law,' the copy presented to the office being inscribed: 'To The Law, with love, from the Lawless, U. B.'

XXXVIII

It would be a welcome diversion if not only letters but some of our wills and deeds were likewise composed in verse. There is precedent for it. In the Dark Ages charters were frequently put into rhyme by enlightened men to ensure a more lasting remembrance. Every time I held a Court for Potton Much Manured I recited the grant to the family that for four long centuries had persisted as its manor lord:

> I John of Gaunt
> Do give and do grant
> To Sir John Burgoyne
> And the heirs of his loin,
> Both Sutton and Potton
> Till the world goes rotten.

In will-making, verse might be still more effective. When the poet Clifford Bax asked me to become his executor, I consented provided that his will was prepared in heroic couplets. There are good enough models in Villon's *Grand Testament* and Donne's *The Will*, and a man of Bax's pleasant wit, by the device of ironical, allusive, or even malicious bequests, could make huge sport with the Philistines and critics who have misunderstood his work or ruffled the peace of his existence. In the same way, those anti-clerically disposed could follow, but in rhyme, the precedent of Richard Cœur de Lion, who by his will is said to have given 'my pride to the Templars and

Hospitelers, my covetise to white monks, and my lecherie to prelates of holy cherches' (see Trevisa's *Higden*, viii. 159).

In forty years of research I have discovered only three metrical wills, and they were more rhyme-doggerel than verse. Here is one, duly proved at Doctors' Commons in 1737, that passed a considerable personal estate. It ran, or rather ambled on, as follows:

> The fifth day of May
> Being airy and gay
> And to hyp not inclined
> But of vigorous mind,
> And my body in health,
> I 'll dispose of my wealth,
> The which I must leave
> On this side the grave
> To some one or other,
> And I think to my brother,
> Because I foresaw
> That my brethren-in-law,
> If I did not take care,
> Would come in for their share,
> Which I nowise intended,
> Till their manners are mended,
> And of that, God knows, there 's no sign.
> I do therefore enjoin
> And do strictly command,
> Of which witness my hand,
> That naught I have got
> Be brought into hotch-pot,
> But I give and devise
> As much as in me lies
> To the son of my mother,
> My own dear brother,
> To have and to hold
> All my silver and gold
> As the affectionate pledges
> Of his brother John Hedges.

Letters, be they in prose or in verse, are of precious little value if they cannot be read, a predicament often occurring in a country practice where typewriting clients are rare. It is hard to advise on instructions one cannot decipher. Also it takes a wise man to write a short letter. Illiterate people always write the longest, and as for village folk they find it difficult to make an end. Sometimes, owing to shortness or sickness of staff, a solicitor is obliged to write his own letters; and though this is tedious it is a source of profit, for clients are then compelled to call and ask what the letter means. To my native Hineiform hieroglyphics, which have shortened the days of many devoted secretaries (some of them now in heaven), I have added a perverse and studied ambiguity, enabling me to maintain, even against a palaeographer, that any particular word is not to read as it might appear to read and as the other side would like to have it read. In contentious correspondence this gives one a considerable advantage. But it exasperates the recipient. On one occasion a letter so disguised was returned, with this *Recipe for the deciphering of Hine's handwriting* endorsed in red and indignant ink: 'Take a quart of patience, 3 spoonfulls of guesswork, 1 handfull of imagination, 3 pints of insight, and 1 magnifying glass. Then, when you have failed with all these adventitious aids, send the letter back to the writer, and ask him in God's name or the Devil's to have the damned thing typed.'

But not even typists are infallible. Far from it. There be 'typists' most treasonable errors' just as there are 'printers' most treasonable errors.' I shall not be so mean as to give my own staff away, though I hold a private list of their particular crimes and previous convictions. Let me rather share with my readers a true malaprop story told by my brother-in-law, Jonathan Ayliff, who practises in South Africa. It chanced that he was dictating a letter to a client of his in financial difficulties. 'You must set your teeth,' he urged in conclusion, 'and pay off your creditors.' When the clerk brought the typewritten letter to be signed, this is what Ayliff discovered: 'You must *sell* your teeth and pay off your creditors.' As the client's dentures were enriched with the best South African gold, the clerk deserved to be, and was, for the fun of it, forgiven.

That was what Matthew Paris used to call *offendiculum*, a very trifling offence, but I doubt if that other typist was forgiven who, being trusted to send to *The Times* the obituary notice of a bishop, wound up with this tiny but devastating slip: '*Fiends* will please accept this as the only intimation.'

XXXIX

The hardeſt thing to read is not handwriting, but human beings; and of human beings the hardeſt to make out are those 'united contradiĉtions,' husband and wife. Yet muſt no lawyer give them up as 'paſt underſtanding,' for, particularly in wartime, he has to live on the sexual sins of the people, which, according to advocates, make a good ſtanding dish. Every day brings its fresh problems of divorce, separation, reconciliation. Singly, doubly, trebly, the parties in the eternal triangle appear for separate or corporate advice. In our office we possess both a firſt- and a second-class waiting-room, and in placing clients according to financial ſtanding or moral behaviour our clerks have to discriminate as beſt they can. Seeing parties in turn of necessity causes waiting, for as Stendhal observed: 'There are four kinds of love, seven ſtages of it, and ten ways for its ending.'

In Georgian and Viĉtorian days it was simple for the praĉtitioner to dismiss each and every case with the inevitable *Cherchez la femme*. But, in this more enlightened age, we are trained to view domeſtic discords from every angle of the triangle. It is no good depending on the parties to tell the truth, the whole truth, and nothing but the truth. By slow and painful cross-examination it has to be extraĉted, here a little, there a little, then sifted, collated, and assembled into that approximation to the truth which is all we can hope for in a fallen world. 'You muſt always explain matters frankly and explicitly to your lawyer,' so ran the golden rule, 'and it is for him to embroil them afterwards.' But what man and what woman, in such a predicament, is either frank or explicit? It is an odd thing about this universe that, though we all disagree with one another, we are all of us always in the right. It is that fixity, that selfish obliquity, of vision in clients that makes our work as reconcilers so impossibly hard. Man is a one-eyed monſter. He sees juſt what he wants to see.

Then, too, in matters of love or luſt one is confronted with something primitive, something outside the jurisdiĉtion of the law. *Amantes, amentes*, lovers and lunatics! I once perused the three hundred pages of Burton's *Anatomy* discoursing upon love as 'a species of melancholy,' but I think Dorothy Osborne came nearer to a correct diagnosis when she classed the disease as 'a refined degree of madness.' Therein lies the difficulty; you cannot reason with people who have lost their reason; and when, as occasionally happens, one is dealing with homosexualists, Lesbians, and the like, the degrees of mania are very far from refined.   In my own records, and in the Hitchin records, there are strange cases of men taken into custody 'in the apparell of a woman,' one of which foolish, effeminate creatures, on being arrested, showed fight like any man; also of women going about in the disguise of men.   Perhaps the maddest husband and wife case I ever heard of was brought to my notice by a client when I was engaged on this part of my book.   First of all, the husband, on the ground of adultery, obtained a divorce against his wife.   Very soon she wearied of living with her paramour and, being conscience-stricken at the thought of her late husband having to fend for himself, she offered to become his housekeeper.   As the house was going to rack and ruin, the offer was accepted.   Then, after a time, proximity and opportunity revived the husband's original feelings.   Accordingly he proposed to her, for the second time, in marriage and was, for the second time, accepted.   Unhappily the course of true love did never yet run smooth, and something caused the 'master' to alter his mind.   The jilted housekeeper was furious. She sued her fiancé and former husband for breach of promise, and stung him for substantial damages.   After which—and as though nothing untoward had happened— they settled down once more in the humdrum, masterly and housekeeperly way.

When you remember that such and such things have been happening in this crazy world ever since the moment when our first forefather politely introduced himself to our first foremother Eve: 'Madam, I'm Adam,'[1] you will not wonder at the *obiter dictum* of the learned and devout judge Sir Matthew Hale (1609–76): 'There is no wisdom *sub cingulo*.'   And you may recall Roger North's comment or

---

[1] Perhaps there is need to point out that this 'Madam, I'm Adam,' is a palindrome, a sentence that reads the same whether it is spelt forwards or backwards.   Amongst the twenty or so examples I have collected in the course of a lifetime is another that can appropriately be put into the mouth of the sons of Adam: 'Lewd did I live, & evil I did dwel.'

SIR MATTHEW HALE
From a painting by J. M. Wright

JOHN DOE & RICHᴰ ROE.
Brothers in LAW.

gloss that there was a home truth in Sir Matthew's 'excuse,' for 'he married his own servant maid.'

XL

The fact is that this creature called man, this so-called *homo sapiens*, is by instinct a pluralist. He is not content with 'the happy commerce of domestic tenderness.' He wants the moon and the stars, and a whole constellation of beautiful women. The prospect of a lifetime of grim, unremitting monogamy appals him. No one woman can fill his life. With all disrespect to the law, what he would really prefer is to have five wives, each to provide for his selfish comfort in a separate category. There is an old saying that expresses his sentiments exactly: 'A French-woman in a dance, a Dutchwoman in the kitchen, an Italian in a window, an Englishwoman at board, and a Spanish a-bed.' You may argue with wayward men—as I have often done—till you are blue in the face, but it has not the slightest effect. If the old adage be true—that 'beauty draws more than oxen'—how shall that ass the Law hope to draw men away from their women? You may quote the sages: 'A beautiful woman is a heaven to the eye, a hell to the soul, and a purgatory to the purse of man.' You may quote the essayists, the moralists, the divines: 'Happiness is not a feverish pleasure, it is a peaceful rapture.' You may quote the poets:

> Beauty vanishes; beauty passes;
> However rare—rare it be. . . .

But the man's thoughts are far away. He is not listening. His eyes are haunted by a face you cannot see. It is like talking against the wind, a wind which bloweth where *it* listeth. Sometimes, after a wasted hour of endeavour, I make the obvious retort: 'Well, you 'll come to your senses one day.' But when a man repents it is, as a rule, too late. That is the worst of learning from experience; it takes too long. Often it takes a lifetime. 'Experience,' said Sainte-Beuve, 'is like the pole-star; it only guides a man in the evening, and rises when he is going to rest.'

I fear our profession stands in much danger of holding an unbalanced view of the married estate. We see the worst side of it. Sometimes we are invited to the silver weddings and golden weddings of our clients, and we rejoice the more because unadulterated marital happiness is rare. But too often solicitors are cynics. One hard-faced advocate said to me: 'Whenever I go to a wedding I give the happy pair about three years. You remember, Hine, that Lady Mary Montagu used to speak of the advantage of a septennial bill, providing that all married persons should have the liberty of declaring every seventh year whether they wished to live together in that state for another seven years or not. But she should, of course, have made it a triennial bill.'

It has, rather surprisingly, been left to the bachelors to say the most spiteful things about marriage. 'It doesn't matter,' sneered Samuel Rogers, 'whom a man marries; he is sure to find the next morning he has married someone else.' Dr. Johnson spent his lifetime halting betwixt the two opinions: 'Marriage has many pains, but celibacy no pleasures.' It was my bachelor master-in-the-law, as I remember, who gave me a book on this very theme the moment I became his pupil. Its quaint old title runs: '*Religio Jurisprudentis*, or the Lawyer's Advice to his Son in Counsels calculated to prevent the Miscarriages of Youth, and for the Orthodox Establishment of their Morals in years of Maturity.'[1] To this day I can repeat the opening words of the chapter 'De coelibatu et conjugio': 'Critical it concerns us to be in the right Understanding which of those two contrary Conditions of Life are most Eligible and Advantagious, especially since we are bound to believe that it is not good for Man to be alone, and that it is good for a Man not to touch a Woman, for doubtless in some cases 'tis best for a Man to be alone, and in other cases good enough to touch Women *in sano sensu*, and not only lawful but expedient and adviseable to cleave unto her *intus et in cute*. But a Sage Jurisprudent will narrowly look on the Mare before he leap into the Saddle, for aboundance of Injoyments, Postures and Conditions of Life that are lawful enough are woundily inconvenient and bloodily inexpedient.' After which argumental tossing to and fro,

---

[1] Published anonymously in 1685, but in fact written by the father of the Rev. Mark Hildesley, a much beloved vicar of Hitchin, who afterwards became bishop of Sodor and Man. There is an account of the bishop in my *Hitchin Worthies*, pp. 143–64.

the learned author goes on, with a grudging acceptance of Pauline opinion, to suggest that it might be wiser 'to Marry than to Burn.'

After I had served twenty-five years as clerk to the clerk to the Hitchin Justices, watching, each Petty Sessional Court day, the wreck of so many marriages, and the results of less hallowed alliances, my considered judgment would have been: 'Rather let them all burn.' But life has to go on, and lawyers too should go on reconsidering and revising their opinions. In this matter the customary stages are, first, in early manhood or womanhood, the instinct for a celibate life, then, midway in the twenties, a high regard for the sacrament of marriage; then, as a rule in the thirties, there sets in a period of cynicism and disillusion, followed by a lazy, tolerant attitude towards human frailty—to every dog one bite, to every bitch one ——; and finally the broad, pragmatic conclusion that the only thing that matters is happiness, and if clients cannot be happy though married it is better to 'loose them and let them go.'

XLI

The maddening thing is that, so often, when the respective solicitors have decided on that course, and taken written instructions for a separation or divorce, and even after the petition or the deed of separation has been signed, the parties will meet clandestinely and change their stupid minds. Solicitor A. to solicitor B.: 'Sir, I regret to inform you that there is a danger of an agreement breaking out between our respective clients.' That is no mere, imagined jibe. It is what often vexatiously happens.

In these matrimonial causes the practitioner must have patience, for time can be a great persuader. Advice contemptuously rejected has a way of sinking in after a season; conscience works tardily, but inexorably; at the worst, soon or late, comes the day of reckoning: God pays, but He does not pay every Saturday.

What we find in the law, however, is that there is no cure for the disease of jealousy. You cannot compromise or make terms with it. You cannot reason it away. Once the green-eyed monster takes possession, there is no casting

H

him out. Slowly he poisons the whole system. Time is
no healer. The disease is progressive. It develops into a
raging disease. 'The ear of jealousy heareth all things.'
So said Solomon who had considerable experience. The

'ADVICE SINKING IN'
From a drawing by Samuel Lucas

mind shapes faults that are not. The eye imagines what it
cannot see. Jealousy is 'cruel as the grave.' It is the
'injured lover's hell.' Said a French *curé* once: 'I believe
in hell, but I do not think there is anybody in it except
Voltaire.' He was mistaken. If you ever get there (I
crave your pardon, gentle and most Christian reader) you
will discover it swarming with jealous husbands and
jealous wives.

Never shall I forget being called in to interview a man
accused of murder, a jealous husband if ever there was
one, nor jealous without cause. As I sat there in the cells,
taking preliminary instructions for the defence, much em-
barrassed by two prison warders leaning forward to catch
every syllable that was said, I could not keep my fascinated
eyes off the accused's right hand. Twelve hours had
passed since he had fired the nine alleged bullets into the
body of his wife's paramour (whose riddled corpse was,
just then, being photographed—the gruesome exhibit B),
but his dilated eyes were still fastened on his quarry, his

features were still blazing with fury, and his finger was still pulling, pulling, pulling at the trigger. I could not help feeling that in this *crime passionnel* he himself, and not the wife's seducer, was the real victim.

There was another curious feature in this crime. Unfortunately for our defence there had been an interval of time between the wife's confession of infidelity and the husband's resolve to kill. He had taken out his revolver, charged it, and deliberately placed further ammunition in his pocket. In this category of crime there should be no premeditation: 'That thou doest do quickly,' whilst the blood is hot and surging within you. He should have rushed out of the house intent upon sudden slaughter. Instead of that he paused on the way to the lover's abode, stood under the eaves of a house, and there, in an agony of irresolution, struggled with the passions of his mind. Then the rain descended; no soft, refreshing rain, but a pitiless, leaden rain, damnable and unbearable in its iteration, drip, drip, drip, drop, drop, drop, ceaseless, remorseless, a rain that beat upon the shuddering core of his being, an evil, primitive rain, bent on washing away his every power of resistance:

> It is not raining rain on me,
> It's raining calamity. . . .

And all the time, his thoughts were driving him like a goad; a hidden purpose was beginning to take shape; until at last his brain snapped, and all that he could overhear in the maelstrom of his mind was 'drip, drip, drip, kill, kill, kill.' [1]

That was the line—it was the only possible line—adopted by our leader, Norman Birkett, as he then was, in a magnificent speech for the defence. And his words made the deeper impression on the jury because of the then recent revival of Somerset Maugham's *Rain*, a highly emotional drama of the tropics, in which the *dramatis personae* were made to appear as puppets in an elemental tragedy; their characters, their destinies, swayed and overmastered by the hypnotic, degenerative power of incessant, torrential rain.

Like most lawyers I have studied De Quincey's *Murder as one of the Fine Arts* (1827), and it is a pity that prospective

---

[1] This is no heightened piece of imagination. At the assizes the prisoner burst out: 'I shouldn't have shot him but for that rain.'

murderers do not read it, and profit by it, too. Then
their misdeeds might be more ingenious, venial, and even
attractive. In the case in question one was fascinated and
held throughout. The defence of the deed, if not the commission of the deed, was assuredly a work of art. But I
remember spending a whole wearisome day taking down
the evidence against another murderer, a retired police
superintendent, who had shot his neighbour, if you please,
in a petty squabble over fowls that strayed. It was impossible to work up any interest in such a senseless crime [1];
but there has been many a murder committed for causes
just as trifling, which, nevertheless, by sheer bravado or
bedevilment, has caught the fancy of the public. I suppose,
for one who has wept over Wainewright's murder of Helen
Abercromby, a thousand must have chuckled, not because
it was not a monstrous deed, but because the 'voluptuous
coxcomb' of a murderer, on being asked how he could
have had the cold-blooded barbarity 'to kill such a fair,
innocent, and trusting creature as Helen,' made his excuse
with this impudent but unforgettable phrase: 'Upon my
soul, I don't know, unless it was because she had such
thick ankles.' [2]

XLII

Lawyers are not professional wits, but there is a good
deal of wit flying about in the profession; and it is a natural
reaction from 'that kind of solemnity' which Dr. Johnson
insisted 'there must be in the manners of a professional
man.' When interviewing clients, solemnity, like a black
gown in Court, gives an air of authority. It is our outward
and visible sign of the infallibility assumed as an article

---

[1] Fowls are the most stupid of all creatures, yet men will die for them.
I remember that my own gardener threatened to shoot a neighbour of ours
over an exactly similar dispute. The neighbour said: 'I shall speak to
Mr. Hine about this.' Which produced the glorious reply: ''Tain't no
good your speaking to Mr. 'Ine. It's me and Mrs. 'Ine what manages
the poultry in this place.'

[2] It is extraordinary how sensitive some men are to this part of the female
anatomy. One of my London agents (let him remain in decent or indecent
obscurity), having received from me the head and shoulder photograph of a
client who was applying for a certificate of naturalization, actually rang up
to inquire whether the charming lady possessed shapely and slender ankles,
and might he come down to interview her and prepare the application?

of faith in us. No solicitor can hope to be as solemn as a judge,[1] but he can look wise and, if he *is* wise, he will take care to let his words be few. When clients depart, however, frivolity has a way of breaking in. Something has to be done to bring back the daylight of good humour into the portentous, professional gloom. That is why principals, in their unguarded hours, are jocular, why office staffs indulge in horseplay and high spirits. Otherwise they might go mad.

Fortunately, by contentious correspondence, by personal sparring with hostile or friendly solicitors, and by the dagger and thrust of advocacy, one is continually sharpening one's brain, and finding or inventing new opportunities for sallies and flashes of wit. Furthermore there is the jargon of the law, a language sacrosanct to solicitors, but one that lends itself to levity, to parody, to playing and juggling with words. Surely there can be no profession more apt to kindle and enliven the intellect, and keep a man's reason from rusting. 'No needle,' saith the proverb, 'is sharp at both ends.' But there can be broad humour even at the blunt end of a lawyer's brain; and the pointed or business end is as sharp as slander, as cutting as calumny.

Lawyers' wit is, for the most part, mere verbal dexterity, and dies with the occasion. It is not to be understanded of the vulgar. Here is an example: 'I could never comprehend,' said a doctor to a lawyer, 'what you mean by *docking an entail*.' 'My dear doctor,' was the answer, 'I do not wonder at that; it is doing what men of your profession never consent to, *suffering a recovery*.' Some readable collections have been attempted, and with a measure of success, in *Westminster Hall* (3 vols., 1825) and Croake James's *Curiosities of Law and Lawyers* (2nd edition, 1891). In the memoirs of judges, learned counsel, and unlearned solicitors it has become the fashion to stuff the volumes with anecdotes to such an extent that you cannot see the author for his stories. One needs a strong digestion for chestnuts,

---

[1] It was an *obiter dictum* of Lord Chief Justice Hewart that 'a judge should try to look as wise as he is paid to look'—a variation upon his still more celebrated theme that 'not only should justice be done, but that it should *appear* to be done.' It must be satisfying to assume 'that £5,000 look,' but solicitors have to look wise on a mere £500. Fortunately their countenances help. Bishop Earle, in his *Microcosmography* (1628), said of 'an attorney': 'His skin becomes at last as dry as his parchment, and his face as intricate as the most winding cause.'

even for roast chestnuts. My own preference is for that
sweet, runaway humour, that laughter of the mind, that
gentle irony, which, without producing witty and quotable
results, permeates character and conversation. But years
ago I did open a manuscript jest book entitled *Stories I
have Heard* and had it enclosed, not inappropriately, in the
leather binding that once held my tattered and superseded
copy of D'Urfey's *Pills to Purge Melancholy* (1661). Sometimes I leave this merry volume in the waiting-room to trick
clients into forgetting how the time passes, and it is pleasant
to hear through my walls the silvery peals of their laughter.
Now and again, readers return thanks by relating a story
that I might be inclined to add.

It was a tithe collector, I remember, who told me an
unbelievable tale of the period when tithes were paid or
rather rendered in kind. A certain parson was quietly
seated in his study when one of his male parishioners was
shown in carrying a baby. 'Parson,' he said, 'as the law
tells me I must give you one-tenth of all I produce, here's
my tenth child,' and without more ado the man dumped
the suckling child on to the astonished parson's lap, and
departed.

There is another story that might well have come from
the same source, but it was contributed, rather surprisingly,
by a Quaker: 'A Somerset rector was sitting at home when a
tramp, who had evidently seen better days, was brought in
by the maid.

'"Well, my man," said the parson, "what can I do for
you?"

'"I've not come for money, mister," said the tramp, "but
for work. That's what I want, work and a bite of food."

'"Can you write?" asked the parson, after cogitating
for a moment.

'"Indeed I can," replied the tramp. "I was a clerk
once upon a time in a brewery office."

'"Then I'll tell you what you can do for me," said the
parson, "you can write round to all the property-owners
who haven't paid me their tithes, and you shall have a
commission on whatever you collect."

'"Done," said the tramp, "and I warrant you I'll get
that money quick."

'A few days later the rector received this short note from

the squire: "Dear Rector, here is my cheque for £22 3s. 9d., the amount of tithe outstanding. But will you kindly tell your amanuensis that 'bloody' is spelt with one 'd' only, that 'b——r' on the other hand needs two 'gs,' and that 'lousy' requires no 'e' before the 'y.'"'

That is humour of the blunt or downright order. And here, culled from another page of the jest book, is something more subtle, humour by superimposition of two advertisements in the personal column of the *Daily Telegraph*. The first was in the form adopted by solicitors for missing next-of-kin, with its inviting final phrase:

'. . . and he shall hear something to his advantage.'

Immediately below this, and by a charming coincidence, there appeared this verse inserted by a Bible Society:

Behold, I come quickly.

XLIII

Two or three pages of the jest book were supplied by a barrister who had won a reputation in breach-of-promise cases. One of his more quotable stories relates that an action for damages, brought by a Miss Week against a Mr. Day, was settled out of Court, the parties agreeing to marry; whereupon Sir Frank Lockwood, who had been briefed in the case, passed up to the judge the following epigram:

One Day the more, one Week the less,
But we must not complain.
There 'll soon be little Days enough
To make a Week again.

'You can do anything you like with a jury,' declared the same counsel, 'provided your client is good-looking and able to cry without spoiling the pathetic appeal of her face. Juries, yes, but (if you will pardon my rhymes):

'Tis the deuce of a drudge
To budge a judge.
You may cite every case
Till you 're blue in the face;
Not a trick in the trade
But in turn can be played.

You may smile, you may storm,
Blow cold or blow warm;
You may curse or cajole,
You may pour out your soul,
Ring the changes on every human emotion,
And sit down at the last in a Court commotion.
But, as for the judge,
To him 'tis but fudge,
Every word of it fudge,
Every word of it fudge,
Go on to the death,
But you 're wasting your breath;
His mind was made up
Before you stood up.
Your points haven't made
The faintest impression;
Your temper 's quite frayed
With vain intercession.
Juries are dears, Juries are dears,
But, as for their lordships,
They drive one to tears.
'Tis the deuce of a drudge
To budge a judge.

'I sometimes think,' he went on, 'that a judge has a second head just where his heart should be, and if so that head is harder even than the other.'

'You should have been born when the world was young,' I remarked, 'for in that impressionable age a judge was a man for all that. To a pleader of any dramatic power it must have been easy going. Don't you remember the luscious Greek story about Phryne, the courtesan who was also the model for the Venus of Praxiteles, a story which we ought not to have learnt as senior classics in school but somehow did? She was accused, no doubt by professional rivals, for her lewd behaviour, and wisely went for her defence to Hyperides, the finest "orator," as advocates were then called, in all Athens. In Court, Hyperides employed something more eloquent than words, for, "tearing her upper garment, he disclosed her naked breasts to the judges, at which comeliness of body and amiable gesture they were so moved and astonished that they acquitted her forthwith."'

'Splendid,' said my breach-of-promise friend, 'now I shall know what to do another time.'

XLIV

There are waggeries and witticisms in the jeſt book which, though of legal paternity, can be appreciated by 'lay gents,' as Roger North liked to call those whom we call clients. Some of these *scintillae juris* are new and have yet to make their way in the world. Some are old and full of honour; they have ſtood the teſt and gained a prescriptive right of repetition; like case-law they can be quoted with ever-growing authority and respeƈt.

Sir Frank Lockwood's favourite ſtory concerned an occasion when, in a Petty Sessional Court, he had remarked to the superintendent of police that the magiſtrates appeared to be getting through their agenda in an extremely expeditious and workmanlike manner.

'Yes, sir,' replied the pompous but none-too-well-educated officer, 'their worships always dispense with juſtice very faſt here.'

A prisoner who was conviƈted at the Dublin Criminal Court for bigamy had married four wives. The judge, in passing sentence, expressed surprise that the prisoner could be such a hardened villain as to delude so many women. 'Please, your worship,' said the man, 'I was tryin' to get a good wan.'

Here is the classic example of circumſtantial evidence. A witness in a railway case at Fort Worth was asked to tell in his own words juſt how Hole, a mate of his, came by his death.

He said: 'Well, 'Ole and me was walking down the track and I 'eard a whiſtle and I got off the track, and the train went by, and I got back on the track. I didn't see 'Ole, but I walked along, and pretty soon I saw 'Ole's 'at, then I walked on and saw one of 'Ole's legs. After that I seen one of 'Ole's arms, and then another leg; and then, over on one side, I seen 'Ole's 'ead, and I says to meself: "My Gawd, *somethin' muſter 'appened to 'Ole.*"'

And here is something that really happened to Mr. Juſtice Eve. When he became a K.C., in accordance with the etiquette of the bar, he circulated the usual notice of his intention to his seniors, and from one of them he received this attraƈtive rejoinder:

My dear Eve,

Whether you wear silk or fig-leaf I do not care

                               A. Dam.

There are good stories, still in circulation, of Lord Chief Justice Coleridge, who was prone to sleep on the bench in his later years. Someone asked Lord Justice Mathew, who was sitting with him, how the Lord Chief was.

'He has quite got rid of his insomnia,' replied Mathew.

As for Mr. Justice Darling's *bons mots* they were legion in his lifetime, and have multiplied since his death. One of the best—and not apocryphal—has to do with a pompous and wordy advocate who was speaking at great length on the subject of bags.

'Concerning those bags, my lord,' he went on interminably, 'they might have been large bags or small bags. Again, they might have been full bags or empty bags.'

'Or *wind*-bags,' cut in the judge with a meaning look, and so brought the speech of the collapsible wind-bag to an abrupt conclusion.

In the same way, new stories cluster round the evergreen memory of Mr. Justice Hawkins (Lord Brampton), who has already been referred to in this book. It is well known what an enormous income he made at the bar. One day Serjeant Ballantine, who was married and impecunious, met Hawkins, at that time a wealthy bachelor.

'Look here, Hawkins,' he said, 'why do you take so much care of your money? It can't be of much use to you in this world, and you can't take it with you to the next. Even if you could, it would only *melt*.'

That story has a twin. Coming one day out of a County Court, Hawkins met a friend who remonstrated with him for taking money at an inferior Court out of the mouths of less popular and affluent pleaders. 'Why, Hawkins,' he went on, 'I believe you'd take a brief before the Devil in hell.' 'Yes,' replied Hawkins, 'I would, and I should get one of my devils to hold it.'

And here is a story entitled *The Perfect Gentleman* left with me by a solicitor to the post office on the completion of a purchase. An old maid, living in a London suburb, was shocked at the language used by the men repairing the telephone wires near her house; whereupon, she complained

to the General Post Office, and the foreman was asked to
send in a report.   This is how it read: 'Me and Bill Fair-
weather were on this job.   I was up the telephone pole,
and accidently let the boiling lead fall on Bill.   It went down

HENRY HAWKINS, Q.C., AT THE TICHBORNE TRIAL
From a drawing by Samuel Lucas

his neck.   Then he looked up at me and he said: "You
really muſt be more careful, Harry."'
    When lawyers are not roaſting cheſtnuts, or swopping
ſtories, you will find them putting moot points to one
another; for, as Bacon observed, 'orators have their de-
clamations, logicians their sophisms, lawyers their moots.'
There is a diſtinction between mooting and pleading.   It is,
as Ben Jonson pointed out, the difference between fencing
and fighting.   And, in bringing up their would-be barriſters
in the way that they should go, the Inns of Court were well
advised to hold Mootings or Put-cases at ſtated times, and
to compel attendance—twelve grand moots and twenty-
four petty moots—for a period of seven years.   So much

has the habit grown, that even solicitors, calling in the fictional aid of John Doe and Richard Roe, are said to put moot points in their sleep and argue out legal conundrums in their dreams. As for myself, when I'm finished with the day's work, I *am* finished. I wash my hands in innocency. I sponge out my brain. I brush off the hairsplitting problems that have beset me. I put off 'lawyer's buckram' and put on 'poet's blue.' I would become a gentleman of letters, a journeyman of letters, or simply a man of letters. But though I take silk for my sleeping clothes I cannot hope to lead or control my dreams; and far too frequently I am seduced by 'the concupiscence of wrangling,' and my bright spirit is summoned back into the dusty purlieus of the law.

This very last night I was entangled in just such a spiderly, sleeping lawyer's web. In my dream I was finishing breakfast in an hotel that I could not remember to have visited before, and after tipping the waitress who, though it did not surprise me at the time, bore the face of my confidential clerk, I hurried round to the office and asked for my account. The bill having been made out and handed to me, I was vexed to discover that I had been charged for three days' board and lodging. 'There's a mistake here,' I protested, 'this must be somebody else's bill. I've only stopped the night.'

''Tis your mistake if anybody's,' came the tart reply, 'you were brought in on Wednesday evening, very much the worse for wear,[1] and now it is Saturday morning. You've slept solidly for three days and three nights. It's no fault of the hotel if you couldn't be roused.' By that time, the solicitor in me was getting into action. It was a case that might never come into Court, but it bristled with moot points. 'I don't believe a word you say,' I retorted, 'and anyhow I must have ordered early tea, and that implies that you should have called me. It isn't done to leave a

---

[1] 'Worse for wear,' I admit, but not drunk. In the still more vivid first part of my dream I had been set upon by three revolting footpads, who, having half-brained me, then deprived me of my Georgian watch and my wallet, and the book I was reading, viz. the new edition of Rayden on *Divorce*, for which my firm had just forked out £3 7s. 6d. Then, coolly calling a taxi, they flung my dazed body on to its back seat, and I could dimly hear them say: 'Pitch him out by the front door of the "Artichoke,"' which was the sign of an inn, aforetime opposite St. Mary's, Hitchin, that I had been lecturing about on the evening previous to my dream.

man, day after day, lying like a log in bed. I made no bargain about board. You can't compel me as your guest to pay for meals I've never eaten. What about your common-law obligations? The custom of your trade? Is there no good management, no honest dealing, left in the innkeeping world? And what,' demanded I, forgetting that the booking clerk was not a lawyer's clerk, 'what about the case of *Drope v. Thaire* (1626) and what about the case of *Parker v. Flint* (1699)? Answer me that, you common innkeeper, and then I'll tell you if I will pay your obnoxious bill.'

XLV

There is one moot point that lawyers must have been putting to themselves, *sotto voce*, for centuries: 'Are we doing good in the world, or are we doing evil?' Each practitioner must answer that leading question according to his own conscience; there is no answer that can indict or acquit the profession as a whole.

The verdict of the world, it must be recognized, has gone against us. But it is the verdict of a common jury, and we all know what common juries are like. Henry Hawkins once said that his dog Jack had more brains than the twelve jackasses in a common jury.[1] Nor, even so, was the verdict unanimous. Truly mankind does not know what to make of us. One is reminded of the law student whose answer to every question in the examination paper was 'It all depends.'[2] Exactly so is it with us. There are solicitors *and* solicitors. It all depends. If, for example, the portrait of 'A meere pettyfogger' in the *Characters* of Sir Thomas Overbury (1581–1613) were typical of the profession any decent solicitor would strike himself off the rolls. But turn over a few pages and Sir Thomas makes

---

[1] There is one good story still current which illustrates Hawkins's attitude to juries, and his grim, biting wit at their expense. In a case of larceny before him the prisoner pleaded guilty, then withdrew his plea, and declared himself innocent. In spite of his original plea, and some convincing evidence, the jury acquitted him. 'Prisoner,' said Hawkins, 'a few minutes ago you said you were a thief. Now the jury say you are a liar. Consequently you are discharged.'

[2] If I remember, it was the same sweet, innocent examinee who, being required 'to draw a common conveyance,' made a sketch of a hansom cab.

amends by giving this charming likeness of 'An Honest
Lawyer': 'A trusty Pilot, a true priest of Justice, one who
wears the conscience as well as the gowne, weighs the cause
as well as the gold, and knows, but never uses, the nice
snapperadoes of Practice.'

In that last phrase you have the crux of the whole matter;
for the 'snapperadoes' of a comparatively few 'thick-
skulled pettyfoggers,' versed in 'the legerdemain of law-
craft,' have brought reproach on a profession which, on the
whole, is learned and well-ordered.   In the country we like

A SHARP PRACTICER

From a drawing by Samuel Lucas

to pretend that most of the sharp practicers are to be found
in the wicked city of London, where, said Dr. Johnson,
'the fell attorney prowls for prey.'   With such, *laborare est
orare* equals 'to labour is to prey.'   Overbury, with a sharper
quill, writes them down as 'Samson's foxes,' hangers-on of
the Courts, 'setting simple men by the ears,' thereby for
themselves gaining 'gorgeous pickings.' Certainly, in the
eighteenth century, when the criminal law was 'a mere
sanguinary chaos,' and the civil law was befogged with procedure and with pleadings inexplicable and interminable
—demurrers, rebutters, rejoinders, surrebutters, surre-
joinders—these legal vultures abounded.   They were still
doing good business, or rather bad business, up to mid-
Victorian times.   'There is no sadder place,' wrote Anthony

Trollope, 'than the waiting room of a London attorney.' [1]
And even in these lean and latter years there are still
pickings to be had out of the body impolitic.

There is a further distinction to be drawn, for we are
accustomed to divide firms into two main categories; the
old-fashioned, long-established, county conveyancing firm,
and the up-to-date common law and commercial firm. As
for the conveyancer, he is almost beyond suspicion. Not
only has he no reputation for rapacity, but like Barry
Cornwall's 'Mr. Atherton of Colne' he can be looked upon
as 'irresistibly honest.' Leading a sheltered existence, as
he does, in the recesses of law-learning, he is the less
exposed to temptation. 'Free from the noise of Courts,
and remote from the pursuits of his fellow-men,' said Sir
Edward Fry, 'he breathes a highly rarefied and transcen-
dental atmosphere.' The left-handed compliment occasionally vouchsafed by clients is a compliment that could
be addressed only to him: 'Perhaps he will act the gentleman
and not the lawyer.' He is the more likely to do so because
in conveyancing,

> A subject Coke himself supposes
> To be at least as old as Moses,

he is the dedicated servant of an ancient and honourable
tradition.

But the common-law man, land-jobbing, jerry-building,
company-promoting, debt-collecting, writ-serving, time-
serving, belongs to a lower world. All the contumely and

[1] Let us be fair, for the waiting-rooms of country attorneys can be hardly
less forbidding. Sir Arthur Helps, in his general condemnation, would
make no distinction: 'I do not know a sadder portion of a man's existence,
one more likely to be full of impatient sorrow, than that which he spends
in waiting at the offices of lawyers.' In our office we do what we can to
mitigate the lot of clients by providing a collection of etchings, water-
colours, and works on local history. We hope they may catch sight of the
couplets scribbled by us on the fly-leaves of the books they read. On the
half-title of *The Story of Hitchin Town* it is written:

> 'Patience, good client, nor will your wait seem ages,
> If you but dip into these tempting pages.'

This word in season appears in *The Official Guide to Hitchin*:

> 'Whilst you are waiting for that ass the law,
> Why not of Hitchin learn a little more?'

'If we are likely to keep you long,' it is advised in *A Short History of
St. Mary's*, 'then slip off for five minutes into the parish church. It will do
you good, and you'll come back in a better frame of mind.'

scorn comprehended in the phrase 'a common attorney' has, since the Judicature Act, been transferred to and directed against him. The attorney, it should have been explained, is dead. He ceased upon the midnight air of the 31st October 1875, though doubtless all in him that was good and beautiful lives on in the solicitor. 'A crocodile,' said Mortimer Collins, 'is not improved by calling him an alligator. Still,' he added, 'the attorney is gone. He used to like to call himself a solicitor; now he can do it with a clear conscience, if he has such a thing.'

How unsatisfactory these distinctions are every lawyer knows. Each individual firm has, in fact, a multiple personality. It has its common law, its chancery, its criminal sides. Moreover, a practice is not known by its principals or by their principles alone. It is known just as much by its clients—all sorts and conditions of men (God made them, therefore let them pass), the omnium gatherum, the farrago, the fortuitous concourse, of folk in trouble in a troublesome and disreputable world. Were we to admit only high-minded and well-born people into our offices we should soon have to put up our shutters. It is all very well to abuse solicitors, but what about those who solicit their advice? It is their mud, some of it, that sticks to us, and they should take their share of the blame.

XLVI

The unkindest cut of all is that we should be looked upon as pariahs by our so-called brother professional men. That was brought home to me not long since when a newly appointed vicar of Hitchin paid me a pastoral call on the very day of his induction. 'I am delighted to welcome you,' I said, 'but I can't help wondering why you should visit me before you visit the good sheep of your own flock.'

'The answer is simple,' he replied with a disarming smile, 'but it isn't very polite. If you *must* know, we parsons consider that solicitors are in greater jeopardy of their souls than any other kind of professional men. So now you understand why I am here, and why so soon.'

Evidently the talk we had, though not in the least flippant, did nothing to alter his views; for at parting he promised

to intercede for me in St. Mary's, first under my capacity
as a sorely tempted solicitor, and secondly for my enlighten-
ment as the historian of the parish and the church. It is
good to be prayed for. But one should not lazily leave it
there. It is good to be wrongfully accused: 'Blessed are
ye when men shall revile you, and say all manner of evil
against you falsely.' But slander should be silenced not by
oaths and curses, nor by the smug satisfaction of conscious
virtue, but by the reproof of a better observance, by a
stricter rule of life. It is a moot point in law whether a
solicitor is entitled to be styled a gentleman. But he has
some professional *noblesse* obliging him to honourable
conduct, and all but a negligible few acknowledge 'Heaven's
high jurisdiction,' and the supreme court of their own
conscience.

Too many solicitors are brought into the world unaware
of the traditions of their own profession. It is a pity.
They study the laws, but they do not study the lives and
works of lawyers. The names of the great exemplars,
Bracton, Fortescue, Fitzherbert, Lambarde, Coke, Selden,
Hale, wake no echo, arouse no emulation, in their minds.
A bowing acquaintance were better than none: a mere
glance at the title-page. How often have I commended to
brother solicitors my (1573) English copy of Fortescue's
De Laudibus, a work described by Coke as worthy, 'si vel
gravitatem vel excellentiam spectemus,' of being written in
characters of gold. Ought not our hearts to glow within
us as we read: *A Learned Commendation of the Politique
Lawes of England: wherein by the most pitthy reasons and
evident demonstrations they are plainelye proved farre to
excell as well the civile lawes of the Empiere, as also all
other lawes of the world. Written in Latine an hundred
yeares past and newly translated into Englishe by Robert
Mulcaster?*

There is another folio that should be kept at elbow and
constantly consulted, to wit Cowell's *Interpreter* (1607).
This work had the distinction of being burnt by the common
hangman, and its grandiloquent title runs or marches
majestically as follows: *The Interpreter: or booke containing
the signification of words. Wherein is set foorth the true
meaning of all or most part of such words or termes as are
mentioned in the law writers or statutes of this victorious and*

I

renowned kingdome, requiring any exposition or interpretation.
A worke not onely profitable, but necessary, for such as desire
to be inſtruĉted in the knowledge of our lawes, ſtatutes, or
other antiquities.[1]

XLVII

Of more direĉt value in the training of a man-at-law is
The Compleat Solicitor of 1669 (second edition, 1683), and
every articled clerk and every admitted man could profit
from its pages.　Here is a liſt of 'the Qualities wherewith a
Solicitor ought to be endued to make him Compleat.'

Firſt, he ought to have a good natural wit.

Secondly, that wit muſt be refined by education.

Thirdly, that education muſt be perfeĉted by learning and
experience.

Fourthly, and, leſt learning should too much elate him, it muſt
be balanced by discretion.

Fifthly, to manifeſt all these former parts, it is requisite that he
have a voluble and free tongue to utter and declare his conceipts.

Those are maxims for the mind.　Moral precepts are
appended for the charaĉter and behaviour of the lawyer.
Patience and prudence will be required, a calm content, and
'a certain ſtayed and settled manner of living.'

Then, closer to our own time, there is Samuel Warren's
*The Moral, Social, and Professional Duties of Attorneys and
Solicitors* (1848), and there is the admirable, anonymous
treatise, ascribed to Sir George Stephen, *Adventures of an
Attorney in Search of a Praĉtice* (1839), which imparts much
shrewd and hard-won wisdom, and some 'lawyer's Ass-
sense,' in the finding and keeping of clients.　Such books
should be laid to heart, for, like the judges, solicitors can
be said to hold their jobs *quamdiu se bene gesserint*, and, as
Arthur Warwick (1637) observed: 'There be many turnings
and winding meanders in the law,' so that we should daily

---

[1] One hates to breathe a word of disparagement of Coke, even in a footnote.
But he had failings.　Moved by professional jealousy of Cowell, whose
knowledge of the civil law was reputed to exceed his own knowledge of the
common law, Coke was foremoſt in attacking *The Interpreter* for some
absolutiſt opinions it expressed, and he habitually spoke of its author as
'Dr. Cowheel.'　The yellow jaundice is a disease shamefully prevalent in
our profession.

endeavour to learn from those who threaded the labyrinth
before us.[1]

To me it is sad that the majority of solicitors should be
lost in that labyrinth all the days of their lives.   They become
absorbed, engrossed in a daily routine of use and wont—
mere men of parchment, signed, sealed, and delivered over
to the profession, having no separate existence, no contacts
outside the metes and bounds of the law.   In my poor but
obstinate opinion there is such a thing as paying too high
a price for life.   How tragically true is the saying of Alexander Brome (1620–66), a not very sober attorney and *inter
alia* a sprightly, bacchanalian poet: 'Of wealth, we 've possession not enjoyment.'   He himself showed how money
made in the law could be delightfully spent outside it.
But most solicitors drudge on till they drop, and have no
use and enjoyment.   They do not spend; they are spent.
A few lucky ones amass a fortune, which reads well in the
papers, and makes their clients blaspheme.   But Ballantine
was right: 'You can't take it with you when you die.'

There is a better reason for getting out of practice before
it is too late.   After all—in spite of the slanderers—the
lawyer has a soul to save.   'His business gives him not
leave to think of his conscience,' wrote Bishop Earle, 'and
when the time, or term, of his life is going out, for doomsday
he is secure; for he hopes he has a trick to reverse judgment.'
Must such a libel, even from a bishop, pass unchallenged?

In our short lease of life there is no option for renewal.
And it behoves lawyers to consider their latter end, and
set their spiritual as well as temporal affairs in order.   It
should be remembered by ourselves and by our enemies
that we belong to a noble profession.   'Of law,' said the
saintly Hooker in words that no centuries of quotation can
ever hackney, 'of law there can be no less acknowledged
than that her seat is the bosom of God, her voice the harmony of the world: all things in heaven and earth do her
homage, the very least as feeling her care, the greatest as
not exempt from her power: both angels and men and all
creatures of what condition soever, though each in different
sort and manner yet all with uniform consent admiring
her as the mother of their peace and joy.'   About laws and

---

[1] 'Few men,' said Gibbon, 'without the spur of necessity, have resolution
to force their way through the thorns and thickets of that gloomy labyrinth.'

lawyers in the plural neither men nor angels can hold any such harmonious or confident opinions. But the governments of the world have to be carried on. Laws have to be obeyed, and lawyers muſt be faithful to their high calling of 'directing the doubtful and inſtructing the ignorant'; and at the Laſt Day they muſt render an account of their ſtewardship before the judgment seat of God.

When this book was firſt conceived it bore for its title *Teſtament of an Attorney*; and now the queſtion arises: What can such a man bequeath? Some, like the holders of the firm in Portmill Lane, have left monuments behind, resolving that poſterity shall marvel at their 'induſtry, integrity, and fidelity.' Others have perpetuated their names in almshouses and schools. But these are the elect. When the 'little man' of my introduction departs, what can *he* hope to leave? Firſt of all, I think, a good name, a legacy to his friends of all that was beſt in him:

> When we are dead, seek for our reſting place
> Not in the earth but in the hearts of men.

And then there is the blessed assurance that, as a lawyer, his 'works do follow him,' not into the grave, but into the workaday lives of his clients. Long after he is dead and gone, men and women will be acting upon his advice, will be carrying out his directions, will be ordering their affairs in ſtrict observance of his written word. Eſtates will go on devolving under the settlements he drew. Husbands, wives, children will go on being protected by the truſts he created. Beneficiaries will rise up and bless him for the wills he made. Year after year, tenants will occupy or trade or farm, relying on the agreements and the leases he approved.

The lawyer is dead; long live the law. But in a sense the lawyer does not die. Clients will come flocking into his office as of old, feeling somehow that his friendly spirit is ſtill there. His room may be taken by another, but his mantle will have been taken too. The partner will bear the same impressed ſtamp of office personality. The advice given will be the advice that he would have given. In all confidence, landowners will leave their deeds and cottagers their 'writings' in his ſtrong room, for his clerks will watch over them ſtill.

PART TWO
LIFE OUTSIDE THE LAW

The mouse that always trusts to one poor hole
Can never be a mouse of any soul.

ALEXANDER POPE (paraphrasing CHAUCER)

It is not for nothing that the attorney of old was pictured with an inkhorn at his girdle. The pen that can engross may write a stanza, and the habit of penmanship produces other things than are taught during articles.

E. B. V. CHRISTIAN.

A lawyer without history or literature is a mechanic, a mere working mason; if he possesses some knowledge of these, he may venture to call himself an architect.

SIR WALTER SCOTT.

It takes more than the law to make a lawyer. It takes all sorts of men and women to make one man.

R. L. H.

LIFE AS A MAN OF LETTERS

I

O be what Bishop Earle characterized and castigated as 'a meer formal man,' to drudge on all one's days as a common attorney, a single-minded solicitor, would never do. Wretched is the mouse that hath but one hole; and wretched is the lawyer who has no escape, no separate existence.

In this matter, also, I have been fortunate, for there was no let or hindrance in the leading of my double life. Some have imagined an antipathy between law and letters: 'that restraint on anticipation, that impediment of the imagination which may be supposed to beset the man of forms and routine.' I have not found it so. From one to the other has been but one step, a natural transition; both were to be found in the same climate of thought. The problem rather has been to maintain a judicious equipoise, and that is not so easy. 'In his gentle lurches from one side of the road to the other,' it was said of a kindred spirit, 'he was neither zig nor zag.' And for sheer, concentrative power, and for worldly success, one ought to be one or the other. For happiness, however, and for health of mind, the 'little man' for whom this book was written may wisely indulge his moth-like flittings to and fro, drawn here and there by any light of any kind of knowledge. In due time he will discover his own bent, his 'inner light,' and meanwhile, as a journeyman of letters, he will have experienced the adventures of a quiet mind.

Fortunate is that man, the fabric of whose fate has been spun 'of texture midway between life and books,' for he has a double chance of happiness, a thirst after the knowledge of good and evil that should never be slaked. As a guest in a world which in spite of recurrent world wars is still a pleasant world, I cannot approve the manners of the pessimist who declared that 'Life is a cheap table-d'hôte in a rather dirty restaurant with Time changing the plates before you have had enough of anything.' Agreed that our allotted span of threescore years and ten makes it impossible to sit down to anything, yet even at the snack-bars or road-houses of our human pilgrimage there are good things to be tasted, to be 'read, marked, learned, and inwardly digested.' Surely the secret of life is to live not dangerously but curiously. That was the burden of my book *The Cream of Curiosity*, in which, on a page of mottoes, I praised 'a noble and solid curiosity of knowing things in their beginnings,' and the man whom Pinto in his *Voyages and Adventures* described as 'a man very curious and much inclined to hear of novelties and rare things.' Such a man, said Dean Swift, 'truly wise, creams off nature, leaving the sour and the dregs for philosophy and reason to lap up.'

On the mantelpiece of my study, in characters of gold, there stands a motto, a comfortable saying, chosen aforetime for the like purpose by Erasmus: *Non est ulla studiorum satietas*; and when I come home o' nights weighed down by the law I look on this and am light-hearted and eager again. On a shelf near by is Izaak Walton's *Life of Donne* (1658), with its moving and confident valediction: 'He was earnest and unwearied in the search of knowledge, with which his vigorous soul is now satisfied.'

Such has been my own absorbed delight in literary and historical research that I could easily be tempted to recast Coke's golden rule. 'Bestow twenty-three hours,' I would suggest, 'upon the sacred muses, and what is over devote to sleep, to meals, and to the study and practice of the law.' That is a dream that does not, alas, come true. On being asked, a few days before his death, whether he had passed a good night, Sydney Smith observed: 'Yes, I had a very pleasant dream. I dreamt that there would in future be thirty-nine Muses and only nine Articles.' For my own part, as a layman, I need no Articles, and, as for the Muses, should be content with Euterpe, Calliope, and Clio, but in a better-ordered world there would be all the wakeful hours to flirt or consort with them.

Some of the fruits of my reading and research are to be found in the books that I have published. These (they are enumerated on p. 263) must speak for themselves. But the greater part of my adventures amongst masterpieces,

and my wanderings in the desert of obscure or anonymous
writers, are recorded in commonplace books that have been
kept from my youth up. *Legere et nihil colligere est neg-
ligere*; and never have I conned a book of any value without
taking pains to set down and preserve the quintessence of it
for my own profit, and for those who come after me.[1]
What a pity that this honourable and useful habit—practised
aforetime by wise men like Leonardo, Milton, and Matthew
Arnold—should have fallen into disuse! Writing to Lord
Burleigh in 1573, Archbishop Parker said: 'I toy out my
time with copying of books.' But 'toy out' is far too modest
a term. A truer estimate of the value of commonplacing
was given by John Bale, Bishop of Ossory, when writing
of Leland the antiquary in 1549: 'His noble purpose was
this; to save precious monumentes of auncient writers,
which is a most worthy worke; and so to bring them from
darknesse to a lyvely light, to the notable fame and ornature
of the land.'

II

Let no one disparage this groping about in the darkness,
for with most antiquaries it leads to the discovery of precious
manuscripts, the resurrection of dead-and-gone writers who
deserve to be remembered. And besides, as my friend
Edward Thomas used to say, 'the past is the only dead
thing that smells sweet.' What a zest it adds to the literary
life and to the pursuit of local history if, at any moment, one
may light upon buried treasure! There are some who can
see in the dark. Some who can hear things that fell silent
six centuries ago. Some who can smell their way back to
the Wars of the Roses. How thrilling it used to be to listen
to the bookseller, Bertram Dobell — a man with lucky
fingers if ever there was one—as he told of dredging up
those long - drowned seventeenth - century poets William
Strode and Thomas Traherne! How stirring it was to
hear Joan Wake speak of her find in the solicitor's office
(W. B. & W. R. Bull) at Newport Pagnell: a conveyance
of land near Olney, of the very date when Cowper was living
there, and signed by *his* John Gilpin!

[1] To make these books more serviceable, an index of six hundred pages
was compiled, with a charming introduction, by my sometime secretary,
Richenda Payne, now Dr. Richenda Scott.

In the happy hunting ground of my own county I, too, have had my 'kills.' The scent is strong in Hertfordshire. Sometimes, at the request of the Board of Education, I lecture to jaded teachers in their refresher courses upon 'Hidden Sources of Hertfordshire History,' and I like to think that most of the manuscripts and drawings referred to in the lecture were run to earth by myself. Similarly with the *History of Hitchin*, a work based not so much on printed matter as on hundreds of thousands of charters, feoffments, Court Rolls, Close Rolls, Patent Rolls, account books, minute books, letters, diaries, etc., that had, first of all, to be discovered and disinterred, and not in one parish or county and country, but in many parishes, counties, and countries. That is the special fascination and difficulty of local history; the records of your parish will be scattered over the face of the earth; and even in your own soil you need to dig not one spit deep, but two. Small things and tiny parishes, slipping more easily through nooks and crannies of time, sink deeper into oblivion.

When at last the materials are brought up to the light, you must work, as it were, in mosaic: no longer an historical artisan but an historical artist building up, if you can, an authentic picture of the past; assembling your innumerable isolated facts of every conceivable colour; fitting, joining, compacting them together into a preordained design.

Work of that kind—in my case occupying the thirty best years of my life—must be done out of piety, or scholarly affection, or the hope of very distant fame, for there can be no pecuniary reward. At the best, and I was proud to muster twelve hundred subscribers for my Hitchin books, the selling possibilities were slender. I had a fellow feeling for the Irish writer who said: 'I've lost on all I've sold, but thank heaven I've sold a good deal.'

A happy hunting ground! Yes, there are many pleasures, many compensations, many satisfactions: the delights of discovery, the overcoming of obstacles, the deep joy of creating something that will last. I spent a whole year of Sundays, I remember, searching, searching, for the original Surrender of Hitchin Priory (1539), a precious document, believed to be the only Surrender in lay hands, and one that had not been seen or heard of since Clutterbuck, the historian of Hertfordshire, examined it in 1817. And then,

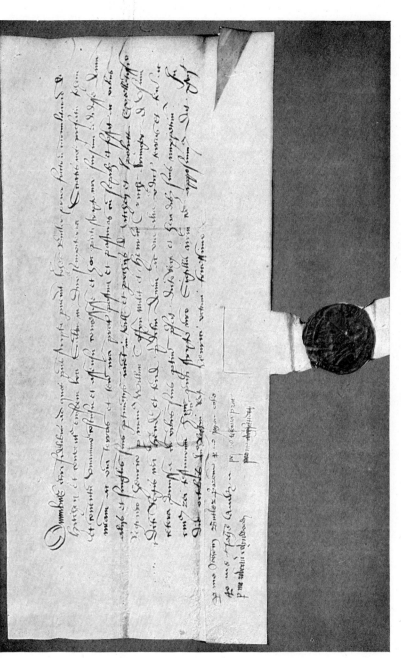

THE SURRENDER OF THE HITCHIN CARMELITES, 1539

From the original at Hitchin Priory

Sr Henry Chauncy

of Yardley-Bury in the County of Hertford Kn.t
Serjeant at Law.

G. Savage fcup.

at laſt, in a little Spanish cheſt, and in a secret drawer of
the cheſt that my fingers fumbled upon by sheer good
fortune, I came upon the treasure, with the seal of the
White Carmelites intaＣt, and even the matrix of that seal
beside it.

For a mere parish hiſtorian it was a great moment.
Already I knew the wording of the commission, signed by
Thomas Crumbwell [*sic*], which two of his minions, Sir
William Coffyn and Henry Crowch, had produced to a
specially summoned chapter. After reciting that 'the
House of Whyte Friars within our town of Hytching re-
mayneth at this present in such ſtate that it is neyther used
to the honour of God or the benefite of our common wealth,'
the document naïvely announced that the king 'mynded
for the conversion of it to another purpose, to take it into
our hands.' All that I knew and more. But suddenly to
hold in my hands the aＣtual Surrender; to thrill to the touch
of its sixteenth-century vellum; with infinite care to open
its folds without damaging the always brittle wax; to gaze
upon this laſt 'aＣt and deed' of the convent, not scrivened
in a fair chancery hand like the commission, but—so
inſtant was the king's command—haſtily written out by
the prior himself in his trembling Carmelite hand; to
puzzle out and to English his sentences one by one—
sentences very different from Cromwell's terse and uncompromising ſtyle, and even wishing 'to the moſt excellent
King Henry and to all the faithful in Chriſt salvation in the
everlaſting Lord'—this, more vividly than any page or tome
of Froude, or Gardiner, or Gasquet, or Coulton, or Brewer,
was to bring home all that is implied by the Dissolution,
the Suppression, the Spoliation (call it what you will) of
the Religious Houses of England, when, in this particular
case, the piety and humble endeavour of two hundred and
twenty-two years was brought utterly to an end.

There is a human touch about this Surrender—one that
I believe to be unique. At its foot, and juſt below the
prior, four of the brethren have signed; but the fifth,
Alexander, after appending his name, muſt have suddenly
repented of the deed, for he has drawn the quill firmly and
erasingly through—the aＣt of a redoubtable man, for who
shall say what loss of livelihood, what sufferings more hard
to bear, his conſtancy, his contumacy, brought upon him?

III

After an interval of four hundred years, the Carmelites established another house—a convent for nuns—at Hitchin; and as the parish historian, I was asked to attend the 'immuration.' On the day of her arrival I had sent the Mother Superior my blessing, for it is believed that historians can dispense something, however vague and ineffectual, of the kind. In exchange I had entreated her prayers and that of her community.[1] When I called upon her at the convent, she said: 'You little know, Mr. Hine, how much we appreciate the insight and the sympathy you have displayed in writing of our Order. It is very rare in an outsider, if you will forgive my calling you that. Every time I read your account of the Hitchin Carmelites it is with added pleasure. There is just one little mistake. You will remember saying that because of their "cumbrous woollen habits" the Carmelites were incapable of agricultural labour. In that you really were wrong as I shall demonstrate to you.'

Thereupon, rolling up her sleeves, she disclosed a pair of sun-tanned arms. Then, turning her attention to her habit, she hitched up her skirts (one, two, three, then I lost count) and attached them to a hook at the side or back of her waist. It was workmanlike, effective, incredibly quickly done. There she stood transfigured before me, one moment a Mother Superior, in the voluminous robes of her Order, the next a manual labourer, her upper limbs bare, her lower limbs clad only in the sturdiest of stockings, ready for action, ready for anything. I was amazed. But so, by a queer mischance, was somebody else, for the door, at that precise second of time, was opened, and on its threshold there stood a white - faced, demure little novice or nun.

[1] By way of a model, I pointed out the precedent of a Grant of Prayers, dated 1531, that I had discovered in the muniment room at Hitchin Priory. In this, the then prior, for services rendered by John Rugmer and Anne his wife, sent them, on vellum, 'Greeting, and wishing them to merit heavenly kingdoms by the assistance of prayers.' The document, after reciting and 'commending in the Lord the sincere devotion which you have to our Order for the reverence of Christ and the blessed, glorious Virgin Mary,' comes at last to its operative part, and 'grants perpetual participation (as well during life as after death) in all the Masses, Fasts, Vigils, Prayers, Preachings, Abstinences, and all other good works which the clemency of our Saviour shall mercifully vouchsafe to be performed by our brethren in the said Convent.'

She tried to deliver her message, but her voice died away in her throat. She could not believe her eyes. Was she dreaming? Was this really her Mother Superior? Who was this strange man? What was he doing in their convent? Was the evil one at his old tricks, his lying visions, again? From innocent wonder her face changed to suspicious bewilderment. Then, with deliberately downcast eyes, she turned on her heel, closed the door softly as though to pretend that she had never opened it, and soon we heard her frightened footsteps scurrying down the passage as though the devil and all his uncleanest spirits were after her.

'That comes of correcting learned historians,' observed the agricultural labourer with a smile as, readjusting her skirts and smoothing down her sleeves, she reassumed the Mother Superior.

IV

To beguile her mind from this unfortunate *contretemps* I began to talk of Father Benedict Zimmerman, a Carmelite whom both of us revered. Years before this, in 1923, a client of mine who was a recently received Catholic and anxious about the souls of all his Protestant friends, persuaded this Father to write to me and to offer to meet me at his convent at 41 Church Street, Kensington. To this I would not agree, but, suggesting neutral ground, I invited him to dine with me — if ascetic Carmelites ever dined —at the Palace Hotel in Bloomsbury. There we met one summer's evening, and to my huge joy I discovered that this learned friar was the accredited historian of the Carmelite Order, and possessed much in print, and more in manuscript, that would be of service to me in writing my account of its religious house at Hitchin.

Saintly man though he was, the scholar in him was paramount, and I soon persuaded him to leave my soul to God who made it, and to devote his energies, which he did for years, to helping me with the *History of Hitchin*.

The word 'ascetic' was used advisedly, for Father Benedict looked half-starved, and I suspected that, for further mortification, he wore a hair shirt next his emaciated body. On our first dinner together, I apologized because the *pièce de résistance* consisted of sirloin of beef and Yorkshire pudding, well enough at midday, but far too heavy and indigestible at night.   But it was soon evident that apologies were out of place, for this gentle lamb, this long-fasting scholar, wolfed the beef as though he had not seen meat for a month, and then asked for a second helping.   I saw to it that he was well supplied at table, for the more I filled his body the better I picked his brains.

Each time he dined with me he looked less likely to give up the ghost within the week, but, try as I would, I could never bring the shadow of a smile into his lean and sorrowful face.   To me, as a man of humour, this seemed deplorable, and I wickedly devised a plan.

'After dinner,' said I to Zimmerman one day, 'I want you to come with me to a concert I promised to attend.   I think it won't be tedious, but, if it is, you can sit back and read your *Fasciculi Zizianorum.*'

'I've never been to a concert in my life,' he objected, 'and I really don't think I ought to.   As you know, our vows are very strict.'

'But you can always leave,' I argued, 'and anyhow it is hardly a sin you need confess.'   At which, amiable as ever, he consented.

When we had finished coffee, I called up a taxi, and carried him off not to any concert hall, but to a music hall, in fact from the Palace Hotel to the Palace Theatre.   The simple, unsuspecting friar seemed a little surprised as we climbed the winding stair.   But to disengage his attention I talked hard about John Bale, the apostate Carmelite, and of the Ralph Radcliffe plays that Bale had catalogued in Hitchin Priory, and of the copies, made by Radcliffe for presentation to the king (Henry VIII), that I myself had traced, step by step, to the library of Baron Harlech in Brogyntyn.

By the time we were sitting in the upper circle, Father Benedict was alarmed.   All this clowning on a stage, this raucous, jigging music, these shameless women with next to nothing on, dancing in a most unseemly manner, could this possibly be what the English called a concert?   He looked inquiringly and a little distrustfully at me.   I took his hand to reassure him and to make quite certain that he should not escape.   Then, in the nick of time, the chorus of wanton women disappeared, and on to the boards stalked

George Robey. I tightened my grip. If ever my Father Benedict was to unbend it would be now.

For a while he would not be amused. I watched his profile out of my right eye; it was still sad, and pale, and drawn. But as Robey warmed to his work, I thought I noticed the faint flicker of a smile. Soon I was sure of it. It broadened. It beamed. It broke into the beginnings of a giggle. Then, taking his hand out of my safe custody, he actually clapped. By this time, for my own pleasure and to encourage him, I was rippling and roaring with laughter. But he was needing no stimulus. The half-ashamed titter—a thing of the mind—which was all he would allow himself at first, had given place to satisfied chuckles of delight, and those again to hearty guffaws, and peals upon peals of laughter—gross, bodily laughter holding both its sides—laughter that convulsed his feeble frame and left him gasping.

On the way home to Kensington he was silent. A reaction had set in. His conscience, I could tell, was tormenting him. I ventured a few words of comfort. 'I wish you could feel as I do,' I remarked, 'that a reasonable amount of unreason is the salt of life. For scholars especially. If we were wise, we should converse more frequently with fools, and why shouldn't we laugh with them? I wish, Father Benedict, you could have watched Sir Paul Vinogradoff when I took him to the same show only a month ago. Is there any more learned man in Europe? Yet, under the spell of George Robey, he dropped the professor and all his works in the twinkling of an eye, renewed his youth, and became a rollicking, frolicsome schoolboy once again. You should have heard him shake the roof with his gargantuan laughter.'

But when I took leave of the friar in Church Street he was still low-spirited and uneasy, wondering whether he ought to confess to so sweet a sin.

'At the very worst,' I put it to him, 'it can be no more than a *gratissimus error*, and that is a phrase, dear to me as a sinner, and one that your church has been indulgently using for centuries for some of the more innocent, or less guilty, manifestations of human love and affection.

But I never heard him laugh again. Nor did I dare to invite him to another 'concert.'

V

Let me turn to another mild adventure in historical research, one that resulted in a modicum of good to me as a writer, and a munificent gift to the county of Hertford.

It came to my knowledge, not long after I had set out on the *History of Hitchin*, that a London publishing house had acquired a magnificent collection of Hertfordshire drawings, by John Chessell Buckler (1793–1894), including eleven of my own market town and parish. The price asked was modest, a mere £450 for 750 drawings. Negotiating an option for one month, I appealed to the nobility and gentry of the county. I worked on the better feelings of rich brewers. I went on my knees to the county treasurer. But I failed to whip up the money in the time allotted, and the collection was sold away to a man whose name I was not allowed to know.

At last, by a stroke of luck, I discovered the name of the new owner, and wrote a very civil letter, asking leave to reproduce six of the Hitchin drawings. By the next post I had a curt refusal. I waited patiently for twelve months, and then, hoping for a change of mind, I re-approached the owner, this time not asking but beseeching. The reply, couched in the third person, was simply a retort discourteous. After another year, I tried again. The answer —sent by a mere secretary—was said to be the last word. So it went on, year after year, for seven years, asking, beseeching, persuading, imploring, cajoling, supplicating, expostulating.

Then I lost my temper, and by registered post dispatched an ultimatum: 'I am engaged, as you perhaps do not know, on a work of some historical importance; and it is vital for my purpose to make use of the drawings now lying idle in your hands. In a few months I shall be printing my first volume and shall insert this sentence in italics at the conclusion of my bibliography: "1832. Eleven drawings of Hitchin church, the Priory, the Grammar School, Skynner's Almshouses, and certain ancient houses in the possession of [naming him]. Permission to reproduce these has been refused. It is the only incivility the author has experienced in the course of fifteen years' research."'

Early the next morning I received a telegram: 'Come at once'; and, forsaking the law, I went. It was an awkward, unsatisfactory interview. The old gentleman did not wish to be exposed, yet was too obstinate to give way and do the decent thing. I was grudgingly allowed to inspect the eleven drawings, but still no consent to reproduce them was vouchsafed. So I invited myself to tea the following Saturday, and hoped my words of literary blackmail would sink in. Before leaving, I heavily bribed the butler.

On the Saturday (it was my birthday, and I was in high spirits) the atmosphere was better. Evidently the butler had put in a good word for me. At any rate the old gentleman no longer watched me out of the corner of his eye, with that air of suspicion to which common attorneys are only too well accustomed; he was more inclined to give me the benefit of the doubt. I might possibly turn out to be a gentleman after all, or at least a man to be trusted. It helped matters not a little when I handed him a specially written account of Buckler, the artist, of whom, apparently, he knew nothing.

As I looked once again through the whole collection— exiled from its rightful home—it seemed cruel that it should be buried away in this damp, grey mausoleum of a London house. And now that its custodian was willing, at last, to give me what I wanted, I wanted more; I coveted the whole collection — for Hertfordshire. After tea, I talked very tenderly of its villages and towns, and not without effect, for the old gentleman, when young and happier, had lived for some years in the shire. I called up memories of his cricketing days. We discovered that we had friends in common. I spoke of the muniment room which, under the direction of the Master of the Rolls, was about to be provided. I described some of the treasures we hoped to keep within it. Then, drawing the net a little closer, I told of the generosity, the public spirit, of Baron Dimsdale of Meesden Manor in making the Pridmore (more properly the Oldfield) collection of drawings available to students. Gathering, from a chance remark, that the old gentleman was a devout Anglican, I spoke of the rectors and vicars who, with my help, had been writing guide books for their churches, and to whom drawings like those of Buckler would have been a godsend. I threw in a good word for

K

schoolmasters to whom, as also to the County Education Committee, teaching by local illustration seemed the more excellent, indeed the essential, way.

By this time I had created an impression. The old gentleman (younger he appeared now and almost genial) was thinking hard. Coming to grips, I praised the good sense of those benefactors who made things over in their lifetime. It was more satisfactory for a donor to impose his own conditions and to see for himself that his gift was appreciated and properly used. To entrust such matters to executors, particularly to bank executors, was to run a needless risk. Would he allow me to wait on him again and discuss the project further? And in the meantime would he see, and be led by the advice of, the Archdeacon of St. Albans? To all of which he graciously assented. As likewise did the butler when I bribed him, still more heavily, at the door.

When I reached home, I telephoned to the archdeacon (the Hon. Kenneth Gibbs), who was reputed to love Hertfordshire as much as he loved God. Would he bring all his influence to bear? Would he make sure to call on the owner the following Saturday? And should we conspire to visit on alternate Saturdays until, by our very importunity, the old gentleman gave in?

It was arranged. On the seventh day the venerable archdeacon spoke to the old gentleman first of all about his soul, and then assured him that the clergy of the diocese were petitioning to have reproductions of the drawings made to frame and display in their vestries. The originals, he suggested, if handed over, would be perfectly safe in St. Albans Abbey. On the fourteenth day I armed myself with letters, written at my dictation, by three learned societies of London, urging, as of prime importance, that such a collection ought to be deposited within the county to which it referred. Finally, on the twenty-first day, the archdeacon and I joined forces and concentrated all the artillery of persuasion, secular and sacred, upon a man who, by that time, was almost in a state of surrender. The end came soon after six o'clock, and very gratefully, on behalf of our county, we accepted, from a 'donor who desired to remain anonymous,' the free-will offering of seven hundred and fifty Buckler drawings which were to be bound in scarlet morocco, stamped with the county arms, indexed under its hundreds, and held in perpetuity, or so long as Hertfordshire with its towns and villages, its churches, its mansions and manor houses, and its historical monuments should endure.[1]

VI

There are days when one's luck is in; there are days when one's luck is out. You never can tell. You just wish yourself 'good hunting.' I have followed the scent of some manuscripts for months, only to find my quarry not worth a minute's chase, whereas marvellous things have come to light when I have not been looking for them.

For many a long year I had been trying to trace the records of the Hitchin Loyal Volunteers, re-enrolled on 31st August 1803 upon the threat of Napoleon's invasion. Despairing of finding them, I printed a few paragraphs, compiled from second-hand sources, in my *History*, sighed heavily, and abandoned hope. Yet, all the time, they were within twelve feet of my stupid, unsuspecting head, where I sat writing in the office of Messrs. Hawkins & Co. Literally, I stumbled upon them one day in an attic that a certain clerk, R. J. King, and I were clearing. Packed away with military precision in three boxes, against one of which my toes had kicked, were the long-sought regimental papers, intact and clean as when deposited there a hundred and twenty years before. There was the speech—a clarion call to arms—of Lord Salisbury, declaiming against 'the restless designs, the tyranny and repeated aggressions, the violent and inordinate ambition of the Enemy with whom we have to contend,' words which, in the Royal Manor of Hitchin, were not likely to fall on deaf ears, for the lord lieutenant knew that 'all loyal citizens would honourably maintain the independence of our country and defend, to the utmost, those blessings which are exclusively enjoyed under the happy constitution of Britain.'

Next came the Muster Roll, a substantial piece of vellum

[1] After some years in safe custody at St. Albans Abbey, the drawings, bound up in three lordly volumes, were transferred to the County Reference Room in the County Hall at Hertford, and are at the service of serious students, who will be well advised to follow my example and compile their own working index under *parishes*.

six feet tall, which, from notes in many a Hitchin diary, I already knew to have been stretched out upon trestle tables at the 'Sun' as—one by one—the recruits marched up to sign and take the oath.   Amongst the three hundred good men and true whose names and civilian records were so familiar to me, I caught sight of a John Hine and, without so much as a glance at my family pedigree, I adopted him as an ancestor.   Apparently he was not sufficiently educated to sign his name.   But he made a sturdy mark; and I dare say he would have left a deeper mark on any 'furriner as dared' to set foot on Hitchin soil.   Next to tumble out of the top box was *The Manual for Volunteers* (1803), setting out *inter alia* the methods to be employed in the barricading of the roads: 'All roads or avenues should be blocked by large trees felled or laid across them, by waggons or carts taken off their wheels, by ploughs, harrows, gates *etc.*, or by digging holes or trenches in them to check and impede the enemy, and keep him under the fire of musquetry at the distance most destructive to him, from 50 to 100 yards. Such of the houses, gardens, walls, or hedges as are favourably situated for defence should be occupied and prepared for musquetry. . . . In short, from the time he sets foot on British ground, he ought never to enjoy a moment's repose, till a sufficient force is collected to surround and destroy him.'

Mutatis mutandis, those instructions might have been issued to the Home Guard of 1940.

The collection—of which I have written at large elsewhere [1]—appeared to be complete, and is one of three known to have survived in England.   Amongst tens of thousands of papers I found the 'Engagement and Articles entered into by the Corps,' obliging the men not only to guard the hearths and homes of Hertfordshire, but 'to march to any part of Great Britain for the Defence thereof in case of Actual Invasion, or the Appearance of an Enemy in Force on the Coast, or for the Suppression of any Rebellion or

[1] In the *Hertfordshire Express*, 31st August and 7th September 1940, at which time, on the threat of another invasion, I considered it to be timely and encouraging to go about lecturing to the forces and to the Home Guard, exhibiting the regimental papers I had found, dressing up members of the audience in the original uniforms, and clapping the colonel's cocked hat and nodding plumes of 1803 on to my chairman's head.   There may be an opportunity of printing a fuller account of the discovered papers, now housed in the Hitchin Museum, in my forthcoming *History of Hertfordshire*.

Insurrection, arising during any such Invasion.' That the risk of such a rebellion was not to be taken lightly is clear from the reward of fifty pounds offered by the corps for the apprehension of the authors and printers of the inflammatory handbills, ſtuck up at night in the ſtreets and slipped under the doors, threatening death to the Hitchin magiſtrates, and calling upon 'all poor Tradesmen and Labourers with one consent to lay all work aside and Meet together in a Boddy and see whats to Be done, for why should we Starve in a land where there is Plenty?'

That the volunteers themselves were not intending to ſtarve is evident from their conſtant 'complaints about the bread,' and their 'turbulence' when a Standing Order was issued reducing the ration of meat, and requiring that 'a large proportion of vegetables should always be employed in the messing.' Returns of 'Beer Money' are filed amongſt the papers, and liſts of those temperate soldiers who received their 'Id. a day in lieu of beer.' In one of the boxes I found the various patterns of cloth that were submitted by military outfitters before the final choice was made of the 'surtout coat in blue, white waiſtcoat, and blue pantaloons.' Further information concerning the kit is given in the 'Articles of Necessaries,' including one shirt (afterwards, on the doctor's advice, raised to two), one pair of gaiters, two pairs of socks, a black ſtock, comb, sponge, brushes, and black-ball, with a winter supplement of 'flannel drawers and woollen ſtockings,' and a 'Welch wig' whenever the men were forced to sleep upon the ground.

Though 'Boney' never landed in force, there are 'Casualty Liſts' amongſt the papers, for the Volunteers, forgetting when they were using 'blank' and when they were using 'ball,' had an unfortunate habit of shooting one another; and there are notes of evidence taken on court martial, for, in spite of the 'Articles for Regulation and Discipline', some of the recruits were raw and moſt 'irregular.' As for the officers, they received admonitory and exhortatory letters from their colonel (the solicitor William Wilshere) at frequent intervals, were commanded to pore over *The Military Catechism for the use of Young Officers*, and were supplied with toy soldiers (ſtill in the aforesaid boxes) so that, even in moments of leisure, they could practise the 'eighteen manœuvres,' including 'direct and oblique marching, facing, wheeling, and counter-marching.' Special 'Plans for the Day of Inspection' were printed whenever the lord lieutenant or a general was expected.

These were the officers, and these the men who, to quote again from Lord Salisbury's praise of them, 'stood forth at the first origin of the Volunteers,' and year after year, from 1804 to 1809, kept watch and ward against 'an insolent and implacable enemy.'

VII

Perhaps, as a bibliophile, my toes have been more fortunate than my fingers, for I have 'kicked' against other treasures in my time. Years ago there was a bookshop at Hitchin with exciting possibilities. It had been opened by a coach builder named Walter Odell, who seemed to think that, on retirement from his trade, he might amuse himself and make an honest penny in that way. It would be more accurate to describe the shop as half opened, for Odell knew next to nothing about books, he never liked to do business in the mornings, and never once, during the twenty odd years of my acquaintance, had he troubled to clear the debris from his floors. His terms were simple enough: a 'tanner' for an octavo, ninepence for a quarto, a 'bob' for a folio. The inside of his books did not concern him; he sold by size. As for the surplus, unshelved specimens on the floor, to be taken with all faults, and in particular with the mud and dust of our shoes as we trampled upon them, they went for threepence apiece.

One winter's afternoon, moving uneasily along the shelves in a murky gaslight, I lost my footing on the shifting pile of floor books and fell heavily upon some Amsterdam vellums and the elephant folio of Spence's *Polymetis* (1747). Being already grounded, it seemed a convenient opportunity to examine some of the other books on which I sat, and the very first book I took up was Dryden's *Virgil* (1697). Already I possessed a copy of this handsome folio bearing the autograph of Captain Robert Hinde, the original of Sterne's 'Uncle Toby,' and I was about to cast Odell's unwanted copy aside when I caught sight of a signature on

the half-title. I looked again and gasped: it was the signature
of Alexander Pope.

'This will never do,' I said to Odell when I had struggled
to my feet, 'you really ought to know what books you
possess. Here man, look, is an autograph of Alexander
Pope, worth pounds and pounds and pounds. I can't give
you a threepenny bit for that.'

'Nonsense,' he broke in, 'it's your luck. I told you
they were all threepence on the floor, and I wouldn't alter
it, even if you found Shakespeare's autograph. Besides,
who was this Alexander Pope?'

It was a week when my star was in the ascendant. The
next evening, delving more deeply into the floor pile, I
dug up a commentary on the book of Revelation, with the
signature of Samuel Taylor Coleridge, the poet, on its fly-
leaf, and a host of marginalia in his well-known hand.
Lamb used to say that, if you lent books to Coleridge, 'he
will return them (generally anticipating the time appointed)
with usury; enriched with annotations, tripling their value.
I have had experience,' he goes on. 'Many are these precious MSS. of his—(in *matter* oftentimes, and almost in
quantity not unfrequently, vying with the originals)—in no
very clerkly hand—legible in my Daniel; in old Burton; in
Sir Thomas Browne.' It seems as though Coleridge enriched his own books with a similar running commentary,
and could do so with less misgiving. That he had some
occasional qualms about other people's books is clear from
his note in Lamb's copy of Donne: 'I shall die soon, my
dear Charles Lamb, and then you will not be vexed that I
have bescribbled your books.'

Continuing the work of excavation on the following
Saturday afternoon, I unearthed a copy of Frederic See-
bohm's *English Village Community* (1883) with Tennyson's
signature on the fly-leaf; and that little jewel of Quaker
biography, the *Memoirs of John Roberts* (1623–84), introduced by Oliver Wendell Holmes in glowing terms: 'It is
as good as gold—better than gold—every page of it.' But,
inserted in the copy I found, was something more precious
than gold, to wit, the copy made by Roberts's grand-
daughter of the letter that he wrote 'to my very loving wife
Lydia Roberts' on 'ye 7th day of ye 7th mo. 1657 from my
strong house, Gloucester.' There is a manly tenderness,

and yet an iron resolution, about this letter from the erstwhile parliamentary soldier and converted Quaker that place it high amongst the thousands written in the hot times of persecution by the followers of George Fox, those humble seekers after truth who, even when torn from their meeting-houses and their homes and cast into prison, would remain 'in heroic tranquillity unmoved.' Here I can quote but a little from this letter, but it will serve: 'Dear Heart, be not, be not discouraged, but wait on him in ye Light of himself, who is able to supply all thy wants and be a Husband to thee and a Father to thy children, and a present help in trouble. Dear friend, I have found ye Father's love much to me who hath counted me worthy to Suffer for his truth's sake. . . . I am well pleased with my present condition, waiting on ye Lord alone for my Deliverance which will be in his time, and I regard not ye tiranny of my Adversary but commit my cause to him who is a righteous Judge. . . . Dear friend, in Patience possess thy soul: waiting always in ye Light, which will lead thee to ye fountain of Life and Light which is God blessed for ever. So I rest thy Loving Husband till death.'

VIII

On another occasion, and in a private house, I stumbled upon not one but forty precious letters. It was at Offley Place, near Hitchin. In 1926, when the squire, H. G. Salusbury Hughes, died, I wrote to Guy, his son, and said: 'It must be twenty years ago, and on the cricket field at Hitchin, your father told me that somewhere in the mansion there should be a bundle of letters written to your great-grandmother Mrs. John Hughes of Donnington Priory by Sir Walter Scott. I wonder if you've had the luck to find them? If not, shall I come over and help?' No, he had discovered nothing, and he doubted if I should have any better success. But there was no harm in trying. Indeed, he would be grateful if I would.

So for four consecutive Sundays I worked away in the library and muniment room at Offley Place, peering into every portly volume, exploring the vacant spaces behind the books on the shelves, investigating cupboards, and unstringing countless parcels of estate and family papers. On the fourth Sunday, just before lunch, my friendly host came in and stopped me. 'You look dead tired and beaten,' he remarked. 'Give it up for to-day. Let's go down to the cellar and fetch up a bottle of wine.' So we lit a candle apiece and groped our way down the steps. And there, close to the first compartment of wine bins, I kicked against something hard, and lowering the candle I was able to distinguish three formidable boxes.

'What do you keep in there?' I inquired; and, as Hughes hadn't the least idea, we arranged to have them brought up after lunch. By this time my hopes were reviving. However good the roast duck, however choice the Chablis, it was agony to wait. Imploring Hughes to dispense with coffee, I was uncording the boxes well before two o'clock, and again my hopes were being dashed. The first was full to the brim of the dullest possible tenancy agreements and home-farm accounts. The second box was rather more interesting. It contained first editions of *Tom Brown's Schooldays*, written by Tom Hughes, the late squire's uncle. Letters there were in plenty of a later date from the brothers H. G. and E. F. S. Tylecote, famous cricketers both, who had been coached by the much more famous W. G. Grace. There was a copy of the will (1835) of the Rev. Lynch Burroughes, of Offley Place and Well-bury, praising and providing for his 'excellent and exemplary wife,' and parting, one by one, with his beloved prints, 'except the prints of the "Death of General Wolfe" and "Sir Roger de Coverley."' There were notes upon Hester Lynch Salusbury, the niece of Sir Thomas Salusbury, and of her almost forced marriage (1763) to Henry Thrale, the brewer, and of her close friendship with Dr. Johnson.[1] There was an account of a vicar of William and Mary's date, the Rev. Richard Willowes, 'a person of very pious and inoffensive life,' who in 1698 was 'barbarously murdered as he came home from Hitchin.' And, best of all, there was a copy of the diary kept by Lady Margaret Brocket Spencer from 1683 to 1686, bringing back the very

[1] Letters in the Hitchin Museum, written to her lawyer, William Wilshere, show how she retained her affection for 'the place I earliest attached my silly heart to'; and even in old age as Mrs. Piozzi she can cherish 'a silly hope of seeing once more the spot where I spent my maiden days, when Hitchin and its beloved environs were very familiar.'

flavour of English country-house life in the reign of
Charles II.

But in the third—the laſt throw as it were of my dice-box
—my luck came uppermoſt. There, on the top of papers
for which I had no eyes, there, tied up in green ferret, and
endorsed 'Letters written to me by Sir Walter,' was the
hidden treasure so long, so vainly sought.

To the beſt of my memory there were forty letters in all,
closely written upon quarto sheets, the record of a friendship that began when Sir Walter saw Mrs. Hughes dart to
the rescue of a dog under the kicking hooves of a horse in
the ſtreets of London. When she came out unscathed, he
limped up to her, grasped her hand with impulsive admiration, and exclaimed: 'You and I muſt be friends, you and
I muſt be friends.' [1]

IX

I have noticed that one's luck will hold through the successive ſtages of a literary or hiſtorical work. Certainly it was
so, in my case, with that topographical classic, *The Hiſtorical
Antiquities of Hertfordshire* by Chauncy, whose portrait faces
page 119. Often, as a schoolboy, I would ſtroll across the
fields from my home at Newnham Hall to the little village
of Caldecote, to drink tea and play chess with the gentle-
man-farmer, Wickham Inskip, and there sometimes I
would find his nephew, now Viscount Caldecote and (from
1940–6) Lord Chief Juſtice of England. [2] Whenever the
nephew matched himself againſt his uncle, it left me free to
curl up on the sofa and browse upon Inskip's Chauncy. It
was the two-volume reprint in octavo of 1826, but the old
gentleman prized it exceedingly, and would never allow me

[1] For fuller and better particulars of that friendship, and for Mrs. Hughes's
visits to Abbotsford, see Lockhart's *Memoirs of the Life of Sir Walter Scott*
(1836–8). For the sake of ſtudents it should be added that Mr. Guy
Hughes, desiring to raise money for improvements at Offley Place, decided
to sell the letters. On my advice they were offered to Messrs. Heffer & Son,
booksellers, of Petty Cury, Cambridge, and were ultimately sold to Gabriel
Wells of America. They are printed in the centenary (1932) edition of
Sir Walter's letters.

[2] It was he, I remember, who in after years reminded me of Horace
Walpole's remark that so tardigrade and sesquipedalian a game as chess
could only have been invented by a solicitor. Himself trained in what
Serjeant Maynard used to call *ars bablativa*, Inskip would teasingly contraſt
the fluency and flexibility of the upper branch of our profession with the
'unmovable intrepidity' of the lower.

to take it away. That being so, I had to pore over its pages by his fireside, or in summer on the window-seat, and memorize all I could. I was twenty years of age before I was able to purchase a copy for myself, and by that time I knew some of the best passages by heart. At the age of thirty I dipped a little deeper into my pocket and acquired a dog-eared copy of the original folio edition of 1700, lacking the three plates, 'Newsills Bury,' 'Standon Lordship,' and 'Hertford Town,' so frequently missing.

At a sale by public auction when I was thirty-five I secured a perfectly collated copy, bound in maroon morocco, with all the plates on linen; fortunately the room was packed with my friends; they knew I had set my heart upon this particular lot and, though some of them coveted it, they would not bid against me.

By another lucky bid at Sotheby's when I was thirty-eight, I became possessed of the household account book (1689–96) of Chauncy's son-in-law, James Forester of Broadfield Hall, a manuscript that threw some fresh light on Sir Henry's manner of life near by at Ardeley Bury, and on the compilation and publishing of his History.[1]

When I was forty I was taken by my friend, Michael Heathcote of Shephallbury near Stevenage, to inspect his library, and there I came upon the author's own copy, with his name, 'Sir Henry Chauncy, Knt.,' on the fly-leaf, and numerous corrigenda and addenda in his hand.

But the crowning stroke of fortune came at the age of forty-five when one H. M. Penn, Norroy's clerk at the College of Arms, suddenly appeared like an angel at the office bearing in his hands (I could hardly believe my eyes) the original manuscript. What remained of it was no more than a seventh of the whole, but there it was on foolscap, yellow and wrinkled with age, itself an antiquity now, with many a paragraph showing the toils of composition, and margins crammed with the criticisms of the topographical specialist to whom Chauncy had submitted the work. At the end were written some 'Directions to the Printer,' including this *nota bene* for the Chauncy pedigree: '*Ardeley*. I will not have my Son's marriage incorporated, for my friends and relations have so great an Antipathy to it that

---

[1] It is hoped to print this manuscript under the title 'Portrait of a Hertfordshire Squire' in my forthcoming *History of Hertfordshire*.

I daire not own it in respect of the mischeife that will attend me. Therefore I desire you not to adde it; besides it will be a great prejudice to the sale of the Booke.' Though the son is not named in the preface, he can be recognized amongst those 'trecherous and perfidious persons who by their ungratefull and unnaturall usage, not only wasted the money at Law designed for the collection of Records and the performance of this undertaking, but also made my Soule restlesse, and me unfit for a Worke that required the most calme, quiet, and serene thoughts. . . . But thro' the aide of Heaven which favoured the Designe, and notwith-standing the malice of those unquiet Spirits who would have stifled it in its Birthe *Hoc opus exegi*, I have finished this great Worke.'

The word 'angel' was used advisedly in referring to H. M. Penn, for out of natural love and affection for Hertfordshire he proposed to make a free gift of the manuscript to the one who would prize it most. But to gain a better title I insisted on valuable consideration. For years I remained in quiet enjoyment and in proud possession, and then, like Chauncy, 'incumbered with the Great Charge of transcribing Charters and Grants,' I was obliged to sell. But the manuscript went to no London sale room, nor overseas to America, but back to the mansion (Ardeley Bury) where it had been laboriously written, day after day, night after night, from the year 1680 in the reign of Charles II to the year 1700 in the reign of William III.[1]

---

[1] 'It must be hard for you to part with this,' said Mr. Howard Carter of Ardeley Bury, 'but I want you to feel that you can come here at any time and see the manuscript, or borrow it for your own lectures.' That was generously spoken. Could any buyer have said more? As for the money that passed between us, it helped to clear my 'incumbrances,' and paid for a car which I named 'Sir Henry.' In the course of time, this car has itself become an antiquity. But it goes; and it goes the better because of the St. Christopher badge presented to me by a client and specially blessed by Father Andrew Beck, A.A., of Hitchin. Now—such is my newly conferred confidence—I feel I could drive like the devil. But I prefer to proceed with legal caution and Quakerly circumspection; and often in a country lane I call to mind the saying of my old Quaker friend, Thomas Bates Blow, the botanist: 'I keep to such a pace that I can both see and smell the wild flowers on the grass-verge and in the hedges alongside the road.'

X

Some of the money received from selling the manuscript of Chauncy went to a research worker whose name I must withhold, though I feel he ought to be known and honoured. When first I corresponded with him, he imposed a condition absolute. He was willing to work for me, and willing to write to me, but on no account would he meet me. I complied, but I was puzzled. Then one day he was pointed out to me in the Public Record Office, and at once I understood. He was the ugliest man I have ever seen, except perhaps in the dream world where men can attain a supernormal frightfulness. He reminded me of the poet Pellisson-Fontanier (1624–93): 'qui était d'une laideur si étonnante qu'une dame lui dit un jour qu'il abusait de la permission que les hommes ont d'être laids.' There are some faces that are just ugly. But this one was ugly in each particular. It had no redeeming feature. I was more fascinated than repelled, and Saturday after Saturday I would take a desk beside him (for I was sure he did not know me), and would constantly be looking up from my manor roll or charter in an attempt to decipher the riddle of his face,

> a book where men
> May read strange matters,

and yet be strangely wrong.

If there was any feature predominantly forbidding, it was the nose. Not only was it enormous, but it was out of joint, or out of true, not set in the middle like those of ordinary men. It was a red nose, but it was not a jolly red nose, and it was the ruddier because of the sallow, old-parchment face, bescribbled with seams and lines, out of which, like a mountain rising abruptly from a plain, it rose. 'He that hath a great nose,' saith the proverb, 'thinks everybody is speaking of it.' Unlike Cyrano de Bergerac, this mild, unfortunate man fought no duels on account of his nose, but all his life he must have been warning people to keep their distance.

Then there were the eyes, downcast and furtive, the eyes of a man who might have committed a hideous crime, suspected but not yet discovered. He was 'a man of unclean lips'—they watered. The ears, though tenuous, were almost as huge and ill-proportioned as the nose; they flapped, as I liked to imagine, not only in a gale of wind, but in the gentle breeze awakened by the turning of a page.

A NOTABLE HITCHIN NOSE
From a drawing by Samuel Lucas

To complete this caricature of a face, he suffered from a receding chin neither quite shaven nor quite bearded, and a receding forehead, above which, like oases in a desert of baldness, there fluttered wisps of straggling hair. His clothes, if you like to call them clothes, tried pathetically to cover the nakedness of a body nearly as shapeless as his face; but as he wore neither collar nor tie, and the shirt was never buttoned, his throat and chest were bare. Elsewhere in his raiment and never mended, there were rents and tears, and wide cracks on the uppers of clodhopping boots, through which one saw the grimy flesh of unsocked, unstockinged feet.

'Ugly as sin,' you would say. But you would be wrong. In fact, the man was a saint. He worked himself to the bone. He lived on nothing a week. And all the money he made (it was little, because he never sent in a bill, and took like a beggar what you chose to give him), all that little was handed in to the Children's Hospital. He had been called to the Bar. That much I was able to discover. I perused a parish history that he had written when waiting for his briefs. But I could not find out the private history of this man, this tramp of letters, or what had brought him to put off his stuff gown and bands and go about in rags.

For some months I did not hear from him. In vain I searched for my own researcher at the Record Office, at Somerset House, and at the British Museum. Then in desperation I broke my word, went to his apartment (if you like to call his attic an apartment), and learnt from the slatternly landlady that he had been seriously ill, and further-more that the Children's Hospital, at its own wish, had taken him in, and was patching him up for the time. Some smartening up was attempted by the nurses for, when I next saw him, he was wearing a different shirt, and, *mirabile dictu*, blew his colossal nose with a handkerchief that was white. But the improvement did not last. Nothing lasts. I remember one of my Hitchin worthies, Mary Thompson, saying to me with a merry twinkle in her eye, in her nine-tieth year: 'The doctors have done their best. They've patched me up, and they've patched me up, but they can patch me up no more.' So likewise was it with this pre-maturely aged man. The sheer ugliness of life and of Brother Ass the Body had worn him down. He could find everything I wanted. But somehow for himself he could not find the art of living. Or was I wrong? Perhaps he had discovered something better—the way of life?

Three months later all my notes and queries were re-turned to me, with a business letter from him that broke off in the middle—not a word about himself—and a scrawl from the landlady to inform me that her lodger had been readmitted to the Children's Hospital, and there had died. God rest his soul, and God forbid that there should be any resurrection of his body.

XI

Life is a contrariwise affair.   Here was the ugliest man I
ever knew proving the saintliest in his life, whereas the
handsomest man I ever set envious eyes upon played me the
shabbiest trick.   Though I seek and adore all beauteous
things I should be sorry to meet him in another world.
In this world, he had all that a worldling could desire: good
looks, fine clothes, a goodly fortune, and, as I came to fear,
good health.   Everything indeed save a good heart and
disposition.   Amongst other treasures, this fortunate man
possessed a manuscript *History of Hitchin*, the fruit of
thirty years' labour in the eighteenth century, and vital to
my purpose.   Assuming that its owner would be civil and
accommodating, I called upon him.   But he was not civil.
I tried every art and artifice, 'Taffeta phrases, silken
terms precise.'   But no, he would not show me the manuscript.   All he would show me was the door.   I wrote
again and again—for wicked men have their weak moments
—and at last I made a slight impression.   'Come to tea
with me on Sunday,' he relented, 'and you shall see the
History.'   But it was maddening.   For, though I was permitted to behold the precious folio (and how my heart leapt
at the sight of it!) I was not allowed to borrow it, and though,
as a special favour, I might scan a page or two, with him
sitting watchfully beside me, I was not to copy one single
word.   For a man of poor memory like myself, it was hell
torment, and after three sittings I told him, in good set
terms, just what I thought of him, slammed the aforesaid
door, and departed.   Then I wrote to his wife.   But she
was about to leave him; she would not intervene.   Then I
approached the family; but none of them liked him and
none ventured to come to my aid.

Then I did what I had never been driven to do before.
I went into my parish church and prayed *against* the man,
and I prayed the more bitterly because of the twenty-six
leaves in the manuscript crammed with records of St. Mary's,
of the use of which I had been so scurvily deprived.   According to Holy Writ, it is the fervent prayer of a righteous
man that availeth much.   But peradventure the commina-
tion of an unrighteous man in a righteous cause may
something avail.   At any rate, within two months, this

powerful man—apparently as robust as he was rude—went
the way of all flesh, and departed this life unwept, un-
honoured, and unsung. He was just the sort of man to
have taken the manuscript with him. But by good luck it
fell into the hands of his executors, and from them I was
able not merely to borrow but to buy at a fair price. Now
—after all those trials and tribulations—I can look upon
this much-used manuscript and smile. It stands, or rather
it reposes, with other honoured tomes in a book-slide made
by a Malay of native Penang wood, and I am assured by
the gracious lady who presented this to me that the ideo-
graphs inlaid with colour, as of jade, upon the panels should
be translated thus: 'Long life, good health, and may none
but gentlemen come into your house.'

XII

Let me, by way of contrast and relief, pay homage to the
shade of Bertram Dobell, most benevolent of booksellers,
who was wont to sell me historical and literary manuscripts
below price, and add thereto much hard-won wisdom of his
own. In his latter years, entrusting his business to his
sons, P. J. and A. E. Dobell, he would come up only of a
Saturday to price the acquisitions of the week. His habit
was to sit on the floor with the books piled round him, and
slowly work or bookworm his way through. If you called
at No. 77 Charing Cross Road before lunch all that could
be seen of him was the top of his wise old head. By three
o'clock he could shake hands with you over a two-foot
barrier of books. By tea time, 'free from all encum-
brances,' he would be ready to discuss your historical
doubts and literary problems, or give you the first refusal
of some rarity that had just come in.

It was from him I bought my first edition of Percy's
Reliques (3 vols., 1765), as fine a copy as ever I handled
save one, and of that it had been whimsically noted in the
catalogue: 'We showed this copy to an impressionable
friend. His eyes shone with delight. Then he sighed
and said that the possession of a case full of books in this
condition would make him "believe Heaven to be possible
but hardly necessary."'

L

Looking round my shelves, I realize how much I am indebted to Dobell. There is a manuscript collection of Hertfordshire epitaphs, made between 1790 and 1810, the more valuable because scarcely one of the 1,394 recorded has survived the rigour of our English climate. I described this manuscript in *The Cream of Curiosity* (1920), pp. 340–65. But here is an exquisite and tender epitaph, not printed in that work, 'On a Child at Bygrave,' a village dear to me from boyhood, because the little Latin that I have was imparted by the parson there:

> As careful nurses on their beds do lay
> Their babes which would too long the wantons play;
> So to prevent my Youth's ensuing Crimes
> Nature, my nurse, laid me to bed betimes.

And this, which was aforetime to be found both in Stevenage and Hitchin, and is, oddly enough, taken from *The Two Noble Kinsmen*, Act. 1, Sc. 5:

> This world's a City full of crooked Streets;
> Death is the Market-place where all men meet.
> If life were Merchandise that Men could buy,
> The rich would always live—ye poor would die.

Even more attractive, in my opinion, is this home-made epitaph, written in all humility and anxious expectation by James Titmuss of Weston who died in 1794:

> A industrious man I have been,
> And in this world have done my best;
> I hope in Heaven my soule may rest.

As a shelf companion to the *Epitaphs*, in the little heaven of my study, there rests my *Justice of the Peace* (1696), on the fly-leaves of which, as Dobell pointed out, there are several barbaric attempts at verse by one Edward George, who acquired the book 'on April ye 12 old stile 1773':

> Pray reader do not take this book away,
> For that it hath a greater mind to stay.

And the following quatrain appears in three different forms:

> My noble Lord Noddy
> Ever let it be said,
> That where Nature doth no brains afford,
> No moon affects that head.

Two other purchases from Dobell should be noticed. In my *History of the Houses of Douglas and Angus*, by David Hume (1644), some patriotic fellow has inscribed these words with a threatening hand: 'Whoever asserts that England and its people are superior to Scotland, I say he lies in his throat.' In my *Selections from Wordsworth* (1834), made by Joseph Hine, with whom I claim no connection, the preface is much disfigured by the expostulations of a reader; especially the passage where the editor considers that 'Mr. Wordsworth's poetry, if properly read'—that is as Hine himself would read it—'when reflected from the mirror of simplicity, dignity, and power . . . renders it highly desirable for ladies' seminaries and female perusal.' He deserved the pencilled abuse in the margin: 'You conceited puppy!'

It was under Dobell that I developed into a bibliophile; from him that I learnt to thrill at the touch of old vellum, at the sight of incunabula in studded oak, with leathern thongs or silver clasps. How reverently he would handle such relics of the past! With what approval he would speak of that fastidious collector who kept a stock of white gloves to be donned by visitors before being allowed to examine his best books! How he praised the Chinese custom of dipping fingers in rose-water before taking up a book of religion or a book of poetry! How he scolded me for selling presentation copies in my lifetime—a crime that in spite of many previous convictions I have once again been committing so that these *Confessions* might be issued in an uncommonly attractive form.

And thereby hangs a tale, or at least a gentle remonstrance, just received from Mr. Ivo Currall, a solicitor practising at Luton. In a bookshop at St. Albans he had the luck to pick up a certain work whose title I must not divulge, bearing my bookplate, and on the half-title an inscription by a well-known novelist. 'Somehow or other,' writes the purchaser, 'this attractive volume must have strayed, or been stolen, from your library. I cannot believe that you would ever sell it, and as a brother solicitor or brother bibliophile I shall be quite happy to restore it. If on the other hand you disposed of it knowingly, then I must warn you of the fate that befell another writing man in similar circumstances. Once upon a time Bernard Shaw poſted a play of his, juſt published, to Sir John Squire, and inscribed it in the usual manner "with the author's compliments." Squire read it, kept it awhile out of respeĉt for the donor, then sold it. By a curious coincidence Shaw lit upon this very copy in a second-hand bookseller's shop in the Charing Cross Road [it may well have been Dobell's], bought it, and returned it to Squire, with the added inscription: "To Sir John Squire, with the Author's *renewed* compliments."'

XIII

The life of a man of letters should be happy, for even in this age of iron there are golden moments and exciting adventures. You never know what book, what manuscript, may swim into your ken; what poet, what more prosaic follower of the muses, may ascend your ſtairs; what song may soar full-fledged out of the cloudy hollows of your brain. 'Day unto day uttereth speech, and night unto night sheweth knowledge.' I have no patience with those long-faced melancholiaſts who speak of 'the malady of thought,' who in self-pity deplore 'the hapless race of men whose misfortune it is to have underſtanding.' It never occurs to the sad friends of truth that men of letters, inſtead of being 'relegated to the comparative uselessness of literary retirement,' should be men of aĉtion; that always in the republic of letters one should be working for the truth, and that desperate times come when one should be fighting for the truth. I once heard Cheſterton say: 'The *Iliad* is only great because all life is a battle, the *Odyssey* because all life is a journey, the book of Job because all life is a riddle.' But men of letters there be who will render nothing unto Caesar, nor owe allegiance save only to the muses. In the firſt world war an Oxford don was asked if he didn't want to fight for civilization.

'Sir,' he replied, 'I *am* the civilization for which you are fighting.'

To me the only sorrowful refleĉtion about the literary life is that it does not laſt. It is absurdly, cruelly short. One ought to ſtudy and one ought to write *sub specie aeternitatis*, as though one would live for ever, whereas in fact there is hardly time for a scholar to sharpen his pencil, or to scribble a hasty message to his fellow pilgrims and call it a book. It is old mortality's curse: so much to do, so little time; an *embarras des richesses*, a *Paradyse of Dainty Devises*, not knowing which of them one can linger to pick; 'a little honey, and lo! I must die!' Then, too, so much of one's brief allotted span has to be frittered away on trivialities. Do you wonder at that man who committed suicide because he was weary to death of buttoning and unbuttoning his coat and breeches? In a better-ordered world would such things have to be? And why must man always have to 'go forth to his work and to his labour until the evening'? 'What profit hath a man of all his labour?' And at the going down of the sun, when he might hope to have a little peace, what precious hours are wasted in recreations that do not re-create, or in conversations that are 'a silly interruption of the secret ecstasy of life'!

It is a great inheritance, this world of explorable knowledge, a land of promise flowing with milk and honey, but few there be who enter in to possess it; and those who are 'partakers of the promise' are often bewildered at what they see. It is like offering an estate in fee simple to a man with only an hour to live.

To-day, as I write, a Hertfordshire landowner brings to my office his sixteenth- and seventeenth-century deeds. He knows that, as a referee of the British Records Association, I shall advise him for the best. I ought to be well pleased. Yet how mixed my feelings are! The mind of an archivist should leap to this offer of manuscripts placed humbly at one's feet. But it means more parchments to pore over, more time to filch from more important work. And, in the end, who knows?—three jewels to the dunghill, three pearls to fling to those swine posterity.

Yet shall I decline and lose a possible chance? As, alas, I did, at a Red Cross sale, last week, when I hesitated in bidding for a shabby, mixed, and unexamined lot consisting, as I found later, of a cigar brought from Havana after its capture by Admiral Pocock in 1762, a lock of Wordsworth's hair, the tail of an old horse that fell in the Crimea, a delightful proverb autographed at Hartford, U.S.A., on 13th May 1889, by Mark Twain: 'Never put off till to-morrow what you can do the day after to-morrow just as well,' and, moſt desirable of all, the deeds of Hertford Priory, England, back to 1598.

A possible chance! It is always unwise not to take it, for you never know what may be waiting for you in bundles of old deeds, in lumber rooms, and in other unlikely places. I remember the guſt of delight (all weariness laid aside) when suddenly I came upon the entry of John Bunyan as a 'centinel' on the muſter roll of the garrison of Newport Pagnell. There he was, a mere ſtripling of sixteen, being pressed into the service, on 30th November 1644, and there, too, were the names of the Hitchin men who likewise served in the company of Colonel Cockayne.

Years ago, in reading the Hon. J. W. Fortescue's chapter on the army in *Shakespeare's England* (1917), I was fascinated by his description of a certain Elizabethan muſter roll that he had examined. Then one day, almoſt by accident, I lit upon the roll myself. It tells, unwittingly, a curious ſtory. The concluding words are haſtily written; there are spots upon the parchment; and in lieu of the seal, which signified the atteſtation of the muſter maſter, leaves of a beech-tree have been crushed into the wax. Evidently a shower of rain had fallen during the muſter, and the juſtices had run away to shelter, leaving their clerk to conclude the business as beſt he could. The leaves, though brown and dry, are in perfeċt preservation—leaves that were green when Shakespeare was a boy.

And yet they say there is no romance in research, nothing but dry-as-duſt pedantry in an antiquary's profession!

On another occasion, delving with grudging labour into the muniments of Squire Greg of Coles Park, near Buntingford, I was marvellously rewarded by coming upon a conveyance of Button Snap, the cottage 'situate near the road-way village of Puckeridge' that passed to Charles Lamb by the 'teſtamentary beneficence' of his godfather, Francis Fielde. It was good to handle a document that the gentle Elia muſt often have perused, and how vividly it recalled a passage in the *Essays*: 'When I journeyed down to take possession, and planted foot on my own ground, the ſtately habits of the donor descended upon me, and I ſtrode (shall I confess the vanity?) with larger paces over my allotment of three-quarters of an acre, with its commodious mansion in the midſt, with the feeling of an

English freeholder that all betwixt sky and centre was my own.'[1]

Occasionally, Lamb would end up his letters with 'yours to the laſt cruſt,' though I wonder that he did not more wittily say 'yours to the laſt cutlet.' He was a man who liked to share his beſt things with his friends; and so should it be with any man of letters. What more satisfying way of life than to be a servant of the sons of learning, to spread knowledge where it is moſt needed, to create beautiful and laſting images of truth, and leave them as a legacy—a scholar's mite—to one's fellow men?

'You can't take it with you when you die.' Of money that is indubitably true. But what of hard-won wealth, not the knowledge but the wisdom of the mind? If we are no more than a parenthesis in eternity, 'flotsam and waif in Time's eternal sea,' then wisdom too muſt go down with us into the grave. But moſt thinking men believe in the indeſtructibility of mind, millions confidently look for human survival, millions hold that on each successive reincarnation we shall be endowed with the painfully achieved inheritance of earlier lives.

It has always been my habit to take books to church leſt the parson should prove, to use the old phrase, 'a pain-full preacher'; and at evensong one Sunday in Newnham church I lit upon a passage of John Donne that filled me with dismay. There, he lays it down, as though it were an article of faith in the world to come, that by the light of God we shall, in the twinkling of an eye, underſtand all myſteries and all knowledge, even the hidden things: 'There our curiosity shall have this noble satisfaction, we shall know how the Angels know by knowing as they know. We shall not pass from author to author as in a Grammar School, nor from Art to Art as in a University, but, as that General which knighted his whole army, God shall create us all Doctors in a minute.'

To any lifelong, dedicated scholar how bitterly unjuſt that would appear! Why should the sons of ignorance, who never burned midnight oil, who never travailed in their

---

[1] The 'commodious mansion'—in truth a small thatched cottage—was presented by Mrs. Greg to the Royal Society of Arts. The Button Snap deeds, together with many others of the Coles Park Eſtate, are now deposited in the Records Office, County Hall, Hertford. Box Nos., 'Weſt Mill 1–416.' There is a catalogue by F. G. Emmison, F.R.Hiſt.S.

thoughts, suddenly and by some miracle of divine mag-
nanimity be made 'skilful in all wisdom and cunning in
knowledge?' Why should the third-form dunce be sent
up higher, be exalted, be translated, even to a doctor? I
closed the book, and took up Saadi instead, for there was a
versicle of his—fit text for a finer sermon—that has fired
the enthusiasm of many a secret student, that has enriched
the rapture of many a lonely mind:

> Like a taper one must melt in pursuit of knowledge,
> Since without learning one cannot know God.

WRITERS I HAVE KNOWN

I

HERE is one disclaimer that needs to be made at the outset. I have had other things to do than to go foisting myself upon the notice of scholars and writers and poets. But, by accident, if it is not impious to use such a word, by accident or by divine providence, I have been able to call a few of them my friends, and of a goodly number (what shall I say?) I have touched the hem of their garments, I have passed by them on the slopes of Parnassus, I have brushed their wings.

Almost the first thing I remember is the sight and sound of the Rev. Edwin Wrenford, vicar of Newnham, declaiming his verses to my mother in the music-room at home. He would often walk across the meadows to Newnham Hall, for my gentle mother was the only one to give him any encouragement as a poet. Years afterwards, when I found a collection of his verses amongst my mother's papers, I learned how long-suffering she had been. At the time they had seemed to me sublime.

The head boy at the first school (Kent College, Canterbury) I was sent to was a poet. He had raven and curly hair like Byron's, with one stray lock that, by a studied negligence, fell over his noble brow. He did something to himself also to produce that extreme pallor of face for which Byron was renowned. He was able to write elegantly in Latin and in Greek. But unhappily he took to making English satires—you might even call them lampoons—upon the masters. It was decided by the head that his talents needed a wider field; in short, he was expelled. Years later, I used to meet him in the more sordid parts of London. But his pride would not let him recognize me. When he was head boy I was merely a fourth-form boy. Each time, he looked a little more ragged, and none of his garments rhymed. They said he earned a precarious livelihood making lyrics for the revues, and ballads for the lower music halls. But whereas at school he went up and up and up, in the harder school of life he went down and down and down.

At the next school I was sent to (the Leys School at Cambridge) there was a man who, being born with the soul of a poet, had sunk so low in the disfavour of God as to become a schoolmaster. This man (Mr. E. E. Kellett) was my master. How often did I thank Almighty God for that! Forty years have passed, but he is still my master, or at least my mentor. To this day, if I write anything considerable, even if I write a book, I submit the manuscript to him to be blue-pencilled and corrected as of old. And, alas, how often he has cause to say: 'Hine, Hine, Hine, here you are still committing the same inexcusable blunders for which I punished you as a boy. Will you never, never learn?'

Out of school he could be quite delightful. How many, beside myself, have to thank him for keeping alive in us that spark of the heavenly fire which, in its callous disregard for such things, the public school system too often extinguishes for ever! When I recall my school days, I try to forget the constant class warfare against the masters, the brutality of the bullies, the hideous nightmare of the dormitories, the terrors of trigonometry, the agony of arithmetic, the vulgarity of commercial geography, the slimy cocoa for supper, the impenetrable buns; I try to dwell only on the tranquil evenings in Mr. Kellett's room, the deep and comfortable chairs, the soft glow of the fire, the buttered scones, the curtains shutting out the sight of school, the rows upon rows of books with never a schoolbook amongst them, and my worthy preceptor himself, no longer a task-master but a poet, his pedagogue's face transfigured, his body, freed from its encumbering, awe-inspiring gown, moving rhythmically about the room as, from an unfailing memory, he recited, hour after hour, some stirring Icelandic saga.[1]

---

[1] His pupils need no reminders. But others may like to know some of the books by which E. E. Kellett has become widely known and honoured as a writer: *The Appreciation of Literature* (1926), *Reconsiderations* (1928), *Fashion in Literature* (1931), *As I Remember* (1936), *Ex Libris* (1940).

II

On a winter's afternoon in December 1908 I was descending the steps of the British Museum when an elderly gentleman in front of me slipped up on the icy surface, and would have fallen headlong if I had not caught and held him. 'You have saved me from an ugly accident,' he said as I picked up his portfolio, 'why not join us for tea, and there I can thank you more warmly.' As he spoke, I noticed that he was accompanied by Laurence Binyon, assistant keeper in the department of prints and drawings, from whom, as a poet, I had heard and was yet to hear many a fine lecture at the Royal Society of Literature. Soon we were 'breaking the ice' over steaming cups of tea, and I was discovering that I had rescued no less a man than Abbot Gasquet, whose books on parish and monastic life in medieval England had always been kept within arm's reach of my writing table. Binyon, the collected edition of whose *London Visions* was then issuing from the press, promised to autograph and present me with a copy, and offered to search in the print room and in the department of manuscripts for drawings and engravings of Hitchin. Gasquet, though vexed to learn that I was in correspondence with that 'pestering Protestant' Professor G. G. Coulton,[1] volunteered to communicate all he knew concerning the Benedictines, Gilbertines, and Carmelites of my parish, and faithfully he kept his word. My own experience has been that acquaintance gained by such chance encounters will develop into friendships firmer than those more naturally made, and mine with Binyon continued until after the first world war, at the close of which a stanza from his noble lines *For the Fallen* was inscribed on the wall at the going in to the museum, and with Gasquet even when, as cardinal, he was in charge of the library at the Vatican.

As I came out of the tea-shop that afternoon, I said to myself: 'This is one of my lucky days.' Under my arm was the typescript of my first book, *Anima Celtica*, a study of the literature and characteristics of the Irish people, and

[1] Coulton, like a sleuth-hound, followed Gasquet from book to book, nosing out every conceivable mistake or misconstruction, and in 1906 went so far as to issue *A Rough List of Misstatements and Blunders in Cardinal Gasquet's writings.*

in the morning I had been wondering whether I had the courage to call on the poet William Butler Yeats, the leading spirit of the Irish renascence, and ask him to read it through. Now I was inclined to venture. His rooms were at 18 Woburn Buildings, on my way home via King's Cross. Twice I climbed his stairway and twice came down again, unable to make up my mind. Then I knocked, very gently, so that if challenged I could maintain that I had not knocked at all. A muffled, far-away voice that seemed to have travelled over the Seven Seas and through the seven woods of Faery invited me to 'come in.' I did so, and found a room in darkness save for a low fire which threw a fitful light upon books in great disorder, papers tumbled anyhow upon the floor, a crystal gazing glass, two tall green candlesticks, some Beardsleys, a Rossetti, and the poet's pastels of Coole Park.

A long black thing like a human caterpillar unrolled itself from a settle and came across to me. 'You must think I live in a sort of Celtic twilight,' he explained, 'but it is only because of my eyes. I have a dread of going blind. Well, who in the world are you?'

After he had listened to my entreaty, he said: 'No. I dare not read even your slender typescript. But I will ask a friend of mine to read it to me, and I promise to keep both ears open and will pounce like a hawk on anything that's wrong. Come now, I'll give you some light, and show you some of my books.' I wanted rather to talk to him about his own. But he would insist on my seeing his Ballantyne Club (1827) edition of Gavin Douglas's *Palice of Honour* (1553), and as we put it back upon the shelf he said: 'If ever you want a definition of poetry, there has been none, not in this last four hundred years, as short and to the point as his "pleasance and half wonder," though sometimes I prefer the full wonder of Lafcadio Hearn's "There is something ghostly in all great art."' From this, he fell talking of the eccentric behaviour of some of the minor poets. Close to the Gavin Douglas there was a copy of Gérard de Nerval's *Le Rêve et la Vie* (1855). Yeats was surprised that I had read it. 'But did you know,' he inquired, 'that one day he was found in the Palais Royal in Paris leading a lobster at the end of a blue ribbon, and when the passers-by protested at his escapade he whispered confidentially: "You see, he does not bark, and he knows all the secrets of the sea"; and did you know that eventually Gérard hanged himself with an apron-string which, in his unshakable conviction, was "the garter of the Queen of Sheba"?'

From another shelf I took down a first edition (1857) of Baudelaire's *Fleurs du Mal*, astonishingly bound, as was another copy I had seen, in the style of a hymn book, with red edges, bookmark, and all. With great gusto and approval, Yeats described how the French poet had abused an itinerant glass vendor because the unfortunate man had brought with him 'no coloured glasses, no glasses of rose and crimson, no magical glasses, no glasses of Paradise'; then, as the terrified pedlar issued from the stairs into the street below, the poet, crying out: 'The Life beautiful, the Life beautiful,' had rushed to the balcony and from there had hurled a flower-pot down, down, down, smashing the uncoloured and unwanted glasses to smithereens.

When it grew time to go, I begged a parting favour. Catching sight of his *Cathleen ni Houlihan* I asked, would he sit by the fire and croon over the lyrics *I will go cry with the woman*, *Do not make a great keening*, and *They shall be remembered for ever*, following the musical notes as printed in the play? To this he smilingly consented, and added to my delight by showing me the original, preserved with the rest of his manuscripts and his tarot cards and his astrological calculations, in a long chest. In years to come I was to listen to him reading or rather chaunting from his own poems at the Poetry Society and in many a London hall, but it was never the same; never again did the lines come hauntingly home with the intimacy, the secret private pleasure, the ineffaceable impression of that first fireside reading; 'they *shall* be remembered for ever.'

When I came out into Tavistock Square, it was snowing, and I called to mind that, writing of another poet, he had said: 'You would stand in the snow to listen to the voice of Callahan.'

III

One Saturday in the spring of 1912 I was walking along Coventry Street, when, coming towards me, with a springing step as though he trod on air, I saw a little man dapperly dressed, with a pointed beard and piercing eyes. I was amazed. But there was no mistaking: it was d'Annunzio, the Italian novelist, playwright, and poet. With my mind in a whirl ('Dare I speak to him? But I simply must speak to him') I turned on my heel and followed, up Wardour Street, then right hand and into the Hôtel d'Italie. For a second I hesitated. I had already lunched, and though I was quite capable of holding another lunch I was not so confident about paying for it. By then, however, I was determined to go through with the adventure. Taking the next table to the poet, I ordered the business man's lunch, short and inexpensive. But poets, as I have noticed, are huge feeders; self-consumed by the fire of genius they need constant refuelling and replenishing. It was three o'clock before this gentleman of leisure finished his lunch. Then, explaining that I was a great admirer of his books, I asked if I might join him for coffee. 'You may indeed,' he replied, 'for I seize every opportunity to practise my English.' After we had talked awhile, it seemed to me that not much practice would be needed to make perfect, and indeed he told me that he had twice visited England as a young man in an endeavour to master our essential but exasperating language, and to make a special study of our poet Shelley.

After a time I was able to make him speak about his novels. 'Do tell me,' he asked, 'which you like the best.'

He was delighted when I replied: '*Il Fuoco*, though, alas, with my Italian so feeble, I have to read it in the English or the French.'

'It has always been my favourite too,' he said, 'and the one motto emblazoned in my library is taken from that work. I will give it you in your English: "Since poetry alone in the world is truth, he who knows by contemplation and creation how to draw it to himself is not far from understanding the secret of the victory over life."'

'Admirable,' said I, 'but isn't that too long for a motto? I wish you would think of something short like your own *Navigare necesse est* that I could display in my study.'

'Well,' he answered, 'as your Italian is so weak, why not adopt this motto in French? It is perfection in one phrase: *La beauté de l'ange, la force du tigre, et les ailes de l'aigle.*'

From mottoes we passed to dedications, and I told him how much I admired the dedication to his *Primo vere* (1879):

GABRIELE D'ANNUNZIO
From a photograph by the 'Wide World'

G. K. CHESTERTON

From a 'Vanity Fair' cartoon by Strickland

Mihi, Musis, et paucis Amicis. 'If only I had kept to a few,' he sighed, 'as it is, I 've squandered my days and nights on men and women who were not worthy of my genius.' I suggested it had been partly his own fault. If women plagued him, as they did, with thousands of love-letters, there was no obligation to reply. Wasn't it true that he himself spent his uninspired days composing love-letters on special hand-made paper, with a private watermark of a voluptuous device, and filed them for future use? Smiling, he admitted that the charge was not unfounded.

We agreed, pursuing the subject, that experience could be bought at too dear a rate. For more ascetic writers the ideal, surely, was the monastic cell, from the narrow window of which, every ninth year or so, the scribe would lean out to discover if ordinary sinful, slothful mortals were yet alive. Solitude, a room to oneself, a place for rumination, a haunt in which to find that final peace, the quiet of the heart; those were the essentials. But, as d'Annunzio remarked, though solitude is a fine thing, there is a pleasure in having someone who can respond; to whom one can say from time to time that solitude *is* a fine thing.

Like everything else, we concluded, it was a question of degree. The words of friends were precious, but let those friends and let those words be few—'five or six ingeniose companions which is enough.' It was important, insisted the poet, to change them frequently and he found nothing cynical in my comment: 'You must not become attached to *animals*: they do not last long enough. You must not become attached to *men*: they last too long.'

My own trouble, as I told him, came not so much from friends; after all one could pick and choose them, and one could drop them. I had suffered more—and so no doubt had he—from a cloud of acquaintances claiming to be my friends, who had desired, constrained, and even compelled me to turn aside from my urgent, appointed tasks, and spend years of my hard-won leisure just for them. If any epitaph were cut upon any stone for me, it would have to read: 'And God delivered him at last out of the hands of his friends.'

Then we began comparing notes about books, which are the best friends of all. I took up the attractive octavo that he had brought with him. It was Shakespeare's sonnets; and it led us to consider the sonnet as a form of metrical expression. Oddly enough he preferred the Shakespearean to his own Italian mode. But we agreed that it was difficult to pour fire or feeling into either. Something could be done and had been done by the great masters, but in the hands of poetasters the results were but 'exercises in alabaster eloquence.' We tried to remember who first coined that phrase. I remembered what Wotton had said of the great Earl of Essex, that 'it was his common way to evaporate his thoughts into a sonnet.' And d'Annunzio quoted a Spanish proverb: 'He is a fool who cannot make one sonnet, and he is mad who makes two.' Then the conversation drifted back to Venice, the scene of *Il Fuoco*, and that recalled a sonnet on St. Mark's by the Venetian Antonio Fogazzaro, 'one of the finest,' said d'Annunzio, 'written in my time.' I promised to try my English hand on it, and a fortnight later my translation was posted out to him in Rome, 'in grateful remembrance of our table-talk':

IN ST. MARK'S AT VENICE

My soul is sombre as thy dim grey shrine,
And thy mosaics of mingled shade and gold
Are like the phantoms that my dreams unfold
In silent pageantry of sleep's design.
Deep in my heart love's fettered hopes repine,
Like thy sealed treasury of gems untold;
While that pure faith I kept in days of old
Mourns in one dying lamp its sad decline.

Yet sometimes, when thy clanging gates swing clear,
The sun steals in: light airs from the lagoon:
Slow-moving forms that go apart to pray.

And so to me life brings a varying boon:
Hills of desire that shine and disappear,
And one sweet face that haunts my lonely way.

IV

One Saturday afternoon in November 1916 I was standing outside the Serendipity bookshop kept by Everard Meynell in Museum Street, when I felt someone attempting to pick the left-hand pocket of my coat. Turning about in a trice, I found a benevolent-looking old gentleman trying not to take something out but to put two duodecimos in. 'Come into the shop,' he said, 'and I'll explain. The fact is, I am suddenly attracted to some people, and when that happens I want them to possess these two little books I have written on the war.' When we were inside, he said: 'This is my son's shop, and now you will know that I am the husband of the poet, Alice Meynell, and if you have not had the good fortune to meet her you shall certainly do so. I would much like you to come down to Greatham in Sussex where we live.'

Here was a chance indeed to meet the greatest woman-poet of her age, and through her to hear at first hand of Francis Thompson, whom Wilfrid had rescued from the streets, and to meet the ghosts of Browning, Ruskin, and Meredith, who, after nursing her infant muse, had watched over her intellectual development from youth up until they died. A fortnight later I was there, sworn in, so to speak, as a lay brother of the Greatham community where, re-ligiously, scriptorially, domestically, every one had his or her appointed task. The master and mistress of the house were always writing articles against time for the *Weekly Register*, the *Tablet*, or the *Pall Mall Gazette*; the daughter Viola would be at work upon her novel, *Narcissus*; Sebastian editing the *Catholic Who's Who*; and the grandchildren rehearsing the play to be produced on Sunday after lunch. It was ideal for a guest with work of his own to do, for his little cell, bathroom, and study lay apart in a range of buildings formerly the stables; he breakfasted by himself, and lived his own celibate, secluded life until lunch, and then again till dinner. These cool spaces of contemplation, these hours of reflection and recollection, were the more grateful because there was no small talk in the house itself, and one cannot live for ever on Mount Pisgah. Yet it would be wrong to forget the timorous rappings upon the door of one's cell at intervals more frequent, and the irre-sistible request that I should join E. V. Lucas or some other guest, and go down upon all fours, so that the rising genera-tion could play leap-frog on the lawn over our crestfallen, devoted heads.

But it was the poet herself I had come, as on pilgrimage,

M

to see. And there at last she stood to greet me in the flesh. For years a mental picture of her had been building up in my brain. There was the Sargent portrait as a ground-plan —not very satisfactory. It might show the woman. It did not show the poet. There was the vision of her, half-apparent in the essays and the poems, subtle, refined, austere, clad in a garment of light. There was the trait of secrecy and hiddenness so truthfully added by Francis Thompson: 'The footfalls of her muse waken not sounds but silences. We lift a feather from the marsh and say: "This way went a Heron."' Yet, it was plain, she possessed many social gifts: 'She sat, quiet Roman dignity in her mien,' so Squire described her, 'vivacity, feeling, sympathy in her eyes; a Saint and a Sibyl, smoking a cigarette.'

That was the baffling charm, the delightful difficulty of consorting with her. You never quite knew in which character she would respond. Sometimes she would be expansive, reminiscent, almost a woman of this world. With exact and homely knowledge she would discourse of domesticated things. Then suddenly you felt that you had lost her. Either she would withdraw into the crystal fortress of her own intellect, or soar away—a heron once again—into the empyrean,

Et marchant sur la terre elle était dans les cieux.

From one subject—that of style—you could be certain she would not fly away. It was terra firma, the chosen ground of her aristocratically intellectual preserve. All her life had been dedicated to the craft of writing. It was an act of religion. Even her newspaper articles were articles of faith. One day, showing me some Francis Thompson manuscripts, she pointed out that he had made the sign of the cross at the head of each and every page. So might it have been with hers. She laboured, as she once said, 'for the chastity of letters and for the honour of life.' The work was consecrated, if not to the greater glory of God, then to the lesser glory of good literature, and performed with a ritual to be apprehended only by the faithful and the few.

Each year the refining, disciplinary processes had been at work, for in her novitiate as a writer she possessed an elaborate style from which to refrain. With a wealth of splendid diction at command, she chose the way of renunciation. Austerity, fastidiousness, a certain cold distinction, these were to be the hall-marks of her style, and with stern economy of purpose, and with 'august severity' (to use her words) she would condense a paragraph into a phrase. When carried to the extreme, it led not to her desired pellucidity of thought but to dark and anxious obscurity. She tried to make words do more than they or their readers could bear. I remember that when she presented me with the *de luxe* edition of her collected poems I besought her to inscribe a fly-leaf with *Renouncement*, written when a young girl to a priest, and ranked by Rossetti as 'one of the three finest sonnets written by women.' But by my time she had renounced *Renouncement*, and insisted on an example of her latest, subtlest craftsmanship. 'This is very hard on poor Mr. Hine,' said Wilfrid her husband, 'for if I can't make out what this poem means then Heaven help him'; which remains the position unto this day, except that Heaven has not helped.

Yet there could be no better fortune for a young man than to sit, as I and so many did, at the feet and be taught 'according to the perfect manner' of this Gamaliel of letters. In my flaming and canicular days I had been much too ready, in Gray's telling phrase, 'to stick a rose into my buttonhole.' I worshipped words not this side but the other side of idolatry. It was Swinburne's *Poems and Ballads*, as I remember, that I took down with me to Greatham. When my hostess caught sight of the volume she exclaimed: 'Some day you'll look on that as a mere pompous glitter of words. I should need blue spectacles to read it. It would dazzle my poor eyes.' At table she referred to his style as 'Late Decorated'; and after lunch Viola showed me her mother's depreciation—one might rather call it exposure—of a writer at that time still exalted though somewhat tottering on his pedestal of fame: 'Swinburne took from the shelf of literature—took, with what art, what touch, what cunning, what complete skill—the treasure of the language, and put it in his pocket. He is urgent with the booty of words, for he has no other treasure.'

Her own treasure lay not in the dross of decoration, but in the pure gold of thinking. On this point she would often quote Wordsworth with approval: 'It is in the highest degree unphilosophic to call language or diction the dress of our thoughts. It is the incarnation of our thoughts.' Style, she held, was not a garment of light; it was light itself, that which conferred immortality on art. But, I wondered, did she not assign too paramount a place to impassioned contemplation? Her face—lined and rather sad when I knew her—was that of a thinker who had thought perhaps too long, and had resolved to reach no definite conclusion. What she liked best in poetry was the primitive quality of 'wildness'; and even in prose where order and judgment should prevail, the intellect, she considered, should run free. If that led to obscurity it could not be helped. But there was obscurity and obscurity. She could not esteem the beautiful obliquities of the *Religio Medici*. Still less the misty abstractions of the Platonists. Joubert was right: 'Il faut être profond en termes clairs et non pas en termes obscurs.' Perfection in style, she said, was not to be expected in this confused, unreasonable, and irreligious world.

'Which reminds me of an obscure saying of Hazlitt,' I remarked: '"The only impeccable writers are those that never wrote."'

Many years have elapsed, but these conversations with Alice Meynell remain, as it were, imprinted on my mind. Often in the making of my books I challenge a word here or a sentence there because she would have challenged it too. It is as though she were sitting—a watchful spirit—at my side. And, if memory failed, I have in daily use two outward and visible signs of our walks and talks together. On my second and last visit to Greatham there was an exchange of presents. Knowing that she would prize it, I made over the Common Prayer Book used by Manning when Anglican rector of Woolavington and Archdeacon of Chichester, with critical notes and comments marginalized in his own hand. And she bestowed on me two relics of Walter Savage Landor, the author of the *Imaginary Conversations* (1824-9), to wit a white crystal, cut for sealing documents with the head of Pallas Athene, and a revolving amber crystal attached to a fob for evening wear.

Nor do I forget the stories she liked to relate of that irascible and eccentric bard, stories she had picked up when

living as a girl in Tuscany. Sometimes, worse than irascible, Landor would live down to his name and behave like
a savage. It seems he had a passion for his flowers, and a
passion for his food. One day his Italian cook dished up an
omelette that to the poet's epicurean taſte was quite un-
eatable. He did not rail at him. His rage was too deep for
words. Rising from the table he seized the ſtout and unfortunate man by the waiſt, dragged him to the open
window of his upper room, and flung him out. Then, as
he fell with a sickening thud upon the flower border a
dozen feet below, Landor was heard to shriek: 'Good God,
I forgot the violets.'

V

In the year 1911 I sent the manuscript of my second book,
Dreams and the Way of Dreams, to J. M. Dent & Sons, and
it was passed on to the poet, critic, and publisher's reader
Darrell Figgis for report. It is not cuſtomary for such
reports to be divulged, but Hugh Dent was no ſtranger to
me, and to juſtify his rejeċtion of the work he showed me
what Figgis had written. The subjeċt-matter of the book,
so it appeared, was liked; also my division and planning of
the theme. But the poet disapproved of my ſtyle, and
wound up his comments on that head by saying: 'This
gentleman endeavours to write in the ſtyle of Sir Thomas
Browne and does not quite succeed.'
Every author is touchy about his ſtyle. I had taken
pains—perhaps too many pains—with mine, and I was
furious. Wiring to Figgis to expeċt me, I caught the next
train to London, and ſtrode into his house. There followed
a sharp encounter, a battle of words over the art and craft
of writing, in which, probably, both were right and both
were wrong, for there is no golden rule for writing and,
though a man may seem to base his ſtyle on this maſter or
on that, he muſt write after his own fashion, as God made
him or as marred and unmade by himself: *Le ſtyle est
l'homme même.*
You could not move Darrell Figgis; he was doċtrinaire
and rigid. But something I said muſt have touched him;
he relented, went to his desk, and in my presence, though
not at my diċtation, wrote a supplementary and much more

acceptable report—one that was to ensure the publication of my book.

'Now that that's over,' he said, 'let's have some coffee, and if you like I'll read you some of my latest poems.'

Having gained my point, I was willing to fall in with anything he suggested, but little did I guess what was coming. I hoped he would sit down quietly by the fire as Yeats had done, and 'murmur a little sadly' some love-sick, melancholy things. But this Mount Olympus of a man stood up at his full height, beat time with his hands, and stormed about the room. He did not read but, once possessed of the divine afflatus, he declaimed. In a voice that shook the foundations of his dilapidated, Hampstead Garden Suburb house, he thundered out page after page from *The Crucibles of Time*; and when there was nothing left in the crucibles he recited from his dramatized version of the Book of Job; and that was worse, for, as it is written in that book, 'his roarings were poured out like the waters.' One singular and amusing habit he had of marking superlative passages by tugging at his beard, and whenever that happened, I knew it was my cue to cry out: 'Splendid, Figgis, splendid,' or 'Masterly, Figgis, masterly.'

Often in after years I would come across him at Dent's or in the streets of London, and as by then he was leading a dangerous life in the underworld of Irish politics I insisted upon shaking both hands and taking a solemn farewell. I was not surprised to read of him in connection with the gun-running exploit at Howth and Kingstown in July 1914. As for the part he played in the Easter Rebellion of 1916 and afterwards, is it not chronicled in his posthumous *Recollections of the Irish War*? Apparently, at one time, he turned against the extremists of his own party, with the result that they forced their way into his house one night, threatened to cut off his head, and then, with an Irish whimsy, decided instead to cut off his famous, flamboyant beard. Though never fully trusted, and decried as 'the man from Golders Green,' he did rise to be assistant Minister of Education in the Irish Free State, but one may say definitely that his career was cut short with his beard.

On 27th October 1925 it was cut short again, and this time for ever. I learnt that Figgis was in trouble, or at least in torment of mind, over the death of a dancing girl.

Early one morning I had the overmastering feeling that I must go to London, and go at once, to his aid. But how to explain and justify that shapeless fear to Messrs. Hawkins & Co., and ask for indefinite leave! There was the difficulty. It seemed insuperable. I tried to stifle the promptings of my heart, but the thought of Figgis, the sight of his despairing face, kept on coming between me and my parchments. That night I was dining early before a lecture I was to deliver on 'Some Poets I have Known' (they included Figgis), when suddenly, upon the quiet evening air, I heard these calamitous words: 'We regret to announce that Mr. Darrell Figgis, poet, critic, and Irish politician, was found dead at a house in London to-day.'

The pity of it! Here was a man of heroic stature who should have died in battle. Yet he perished miserably with his head in a gas oven. My Sir Thomas Browne could have taught him to die in better style than that.

On a Saturday afternoon, five years before my battle of words with Figgis, I was standing outside Dobell's bookshop, when I caught sight of a concourse of people down the road. Concluding that there must have been an accident, I hurried along the pavement, only to find a shabbily dressed little man, rather like a ruffled blackbird, singing hymns and reciting verses. At first I listened idly; but soon I was under a spell as the other pedestrians had been. It is not every day you hear a poem of this country freshness on a crowded London pavement, this still small voice trying to make itself heard in the roar of London traffic:

> Sweet Chance, that led my steps abroad,
>   Beyond the town, where wild flowers grow—
> A rainbow and a cuckoo, Lord,
>   How rich and great the times are now!
>   Know, all ye sheep
>   And cows, that keep
> On staring that I stand so long
>   In grass that's wet from heavy rain—
> A rainbow and a cuckoo's song
>   May never come together again;
>   May never come
>   This side the tomb.

Then, as ill luck would have it, a burly, red-faced police

sergeant broke through the ring, and roughly warned the ecstatic and oblivious bard that he was causing an obstruction of the highway and would have to 'drop it' and move on.

With that the crowd dispersed, and the poet, looking still more dejected, stumped away on his wooden leg into the Palace Tavern.

Strolling back to No. 77 Charing Cross Road, I asked my friend Dobell, himself a poet, who this amazing little man could be.

'So far, he can't get anybody to buy his poetry,' said Dobell, 'so he makes it known in that way to any company of people he can collect. But you mark my word; some day that little man will be a very big man indeed.'

It was W. H. Davies, the Herrick of this latter age.

Before long, most people of intelligence were enjoying his *Autobiography of a Super Tramp* (1908), as introduced by Bernard Shaw, and soon I was discovering that Davies, when on the road, had often put up at a doss-house in my town.[1] I wrote to inquire if, possibly, he had made any of his lyrics there, for I was gathering material for an *Anthology of Hitchin Verse* and was tempted to stretch a point and include him, as a bird of passage, in my pages.

'No,' he replied, 'I cannot help you. What a pity! How I should like to have been one of your Hitchin Worthies!'

But the fame of this once obscure singer was beginning to travel over the world. In time he was to become one of England's Worthies.

VI

If you are to meet a man in this world but once, how essential it is that you should see him at his best. There, too, I have been fortunate. It was in the bewitching garden of the deanery at Southwell, and on a golden summer's

---

[1] One Saturday night Davies was sitting as near as he could get to the stove in a Lambeth doss-house, trying to settle his mind upon a book, when he noticed a man, shabbier even than himself, endeavouring to do the same. It was not easy, for their associates were three-parts drunk. Davies would have liked to enter into conversation, but the other reader when not wrapped in his book was sunk in melancholy thought. Many years later, when taking part in a reading by famous modern poets, Davies caught sight of the mysterious stranger close beside him on the platform. It was Francis Thompson.

evening, that I set eyes upon Rupert Brooke. As the Attendant Spirit in Milton's *Comus*, then being performed by the King's College players, he had a part that suited him to perfection. Nor were they wrong who had written in his praise. In truth he was beautiful as one of the Seraphim, and his voice was like that of an angel singing out of heaven.

If you may claim to know a man by virtue of shaking his hand, then I knew G. K. Chesterton (see cartoon facing page 155). I shook his hand one day at the Poetry Society when, as president, he lectured to us on Alexander Pope, a poet the very opposite to himself; but out of mere perverseness, or possibly because Pope was a Catholic, G. K. C. was resolved to make us bow down and worship him. But the members were not willing to bow the knee. We could admire the diabolical cleverness, the satirical talent of Pope. Most of us had smiled over the *Rape of the Lock* and chuckled over his *Dunciad*. But where was there any magic, where was the 'pleasance and half wonder'? We grew restive and rebellious, and of this our president was made aware.

Then came the best conclusion that ever I heard. 'Gentlemen,' he said, looking more like a giant than ever, 'I can dispute with you no longer. My time is up. But if you will do me the honour to meet me outside this hall'—and here he brandished his fist—'I will prove upon your shameful bodies what I have failed to impress upon your stupid minds.'

Well aware of Johnsonian proportions, Chesterton was pleased to play the *ursa major*. But this truculent attitude was more than mere bravado. The bigness in him went deep. Below the glittering surface of his style, too prone to paradox, you came upon a roundabout common sense, a largeness of vision, a broad, wholesome outlook upon men and things. Tall he was, so tall that his head hit against the stars; yet so massive was he that his feet sank down into common soil. He had a fat man's impatience at thin and spiky views. Even poetry, he held, should keep close to mother earth. Let the maker see that it had body; the soul could look after itself. How entirely he agreed with the stout fellow William Morris: 'Half a dozen stanzas of ballad poetry are worth a cartload of the whining introspective pieces of to-day.' As for his own work, the best

of it would stand.   Possibly he had grown too epigrammatic.
The habit of juggling with words had laid him open to the
charge which the idle citizen in the *Spectator* brought against
his pudding: ' *Mem*. Too many Plumbs and no Sewett.'   But
the critics had been misled by his style.   Somehow the
plums had all gone to the top.   There was plenty of suet
below.

I have made it appear as though I looked upon Chesterton
but once, and at one of his most Gilbertian moments.   But
I was forgetting that I was present at the last meeting
he attended—a religious conference held at Letchworth.
Advertised to take the chair, he did so in a fashion all his
own.   Having wedged himself comfortably into an arm-
chair of absurdly insufficient size, he then essayed to speak,
but the chair rose with him, and stuck to him devotedly
despite the efforts of two priests to disengage him.   At last
it was done, and the great man began:

'Now that I am free to speak to you, I am wondering
whether I should not have done better to have stuck to my
chair.   To have been seen but not heard!   What an ideal
chairman I could have made!   All I can hope is that I shall
adhere to the points at issue in this debate, and that we
shall get to the bottom of our more pressing problems.'

Many a time have I listened to H. G. Wells, but only
once did I speak to him.   It was at the Quaker College of
Woodbrooke, near Birmingham, where, for some years in
the summer vacations, F. S. Marvin was accustomed to
arrange lectures on history.   One afternoon I was basking
in the sun when Wells came up the drive, and, the warden
not being present, I went up to welcome him.   As his
baggage was being handed to the porter, I noticed a pile of
papers lying at the bottom of the car.   'What about these,'
I queried, 'shall we take them too?'

'Perhaps we 'd better,' he replied, 'it happens to be all
I 've written so far for my *Outline of History*.   To-day I 've
motored from Stonehenge, and you may care to know that
I polished that off in forty minutes.'

'Good heavens!' I gasped, 'a place that has been puzzling
antiquaries for a thousand years!'

'Very likely,' he rejoined, 'but anyhow I 've settled it to
my satisfaction,' and then, catching sight of my horrified
expression, 'I 've left a couple of experts behind,' he added

quickly, 'they have a fussy kind of knowledge that looks well in a footnote.'

Secretly I was glad, an hour later, when his lecture proved a fiasco. 'I 'm sorry,' he apologized, as he gathered up his notes and broke up the meeting, 'but I 've never been at home in these formal addresses. If you like to meet me at tea, or forgather with me on the veranda after tea, I 'll promise to be more effective.'

There is black magic in tea. In my *Confessions of an English Tea-drinker*, not yet printed, I shall have much to say of this blessed beverage which has neither the arrogance of wine, nor the self-consciousness of coffee, nor the simpering innocence of cocoa. If tea can make the most taciturn Quaker talk, what will it do to an ordinary conversible human being? Blessed be tea whose gracious influence can so wondrously enliven the intellect and stimulate the flow of soul. For my part I am constantly declaring that the day does not begin till tea time. Sydney Smith gave public thanks to Almighty God that he had not been born into the world 'before the age of tea.' Dr. Johnson, as we all know, swallowed 'oceans of tea.' And as for Wells, we saw to it that he had buckets of tea.

It was a different man who met us on the veranda. There was a brilliance, a tea-tabular felicity, about his conversation. Questions were fired at him from all angles; answers flashed back like lightning. There was a battle of words, but 'Mr. Britling saw it through.'

VII

Often in that first decade of the nineteen-hundreds I would take tea with Sir Henry Newbolt and Sir Edmund Gosse at the Royal Society of Literature or at poetry readings in Bloomsbury, and watch the same magic—a pleasant intoxication of the mind—working upon their already affable spirits. Perhaps it was only a fancy, but I grew to think that one might learn what sort of writer a man was from the kind of tea he took. Newbolt, for example, would order a strong Indian brew, pile the strawberry jam on chunks upon chunks of bread, and bolt slice after slice of rich, indigestible cake. Was not his poetry the same: boyish, exuberant, full of plums and daring? Gosse, on the other hand, would sip weak China tea, and nibble half-heartedly and absent-mindedly at cucumber and lettuce sandwiches. Likewise his poems were too cool and vegetarian; too much water in them and not enough fire, except one that he wrote as a ſtripling entitled *Lying in the Grass*. But one liſtened to Gosse with both ears because he had known all the writers of his time, and could discourse of them excellently well. Moreover he was recognized as an importer of celebrities, and had offered the right hand of fellowship to Ibsen, Björnson, Brandes, Maeterlinck, Bergson, and Anatole France in those early days when other English writers were hesitating and holding back.

So vivacious and debonair was he, one never thought of him as an old man; yet in his salad days he had heard Hengiſt Horne, the farthing-epic poet,[1] boaſting how once upon a time he had shied a snowball at Keats. Himself ſtaggered at this far-ſtretched memory, Gosse said: 'It is as though a man should arise and say that he had sold Shakespeare a cheesecake.'

On some Thursdays, passing the doors of the Royal Society of Literature, I would make my way to Burlington House and consort with the Fellows of the Society of Antiquaries. In comparison, the teas there were primitive; the scones were as impenetrable as Hertfordshire pudding-ſtone, the cakes were cruſtacean. But one went there not for tea but to meet specialiſts who could decipher and authenticate early charters, or date the pottery and flint implements dug up in one's parish.

Then, sometimes in the spring, I used, being a thrice-dipped Tory, to think it a wholesome correƈtive to attend the leƈtures arranged by the Fabian Society; and, to out-siders like myself though scarcely to the members, it was huge sport in the sixth and concluding session to hear Bernard Shaw making nonsense of all that the other leƈturers had said. In our hands we held the printed synopsis of the address he was to deliver. But that was a mere blind.

---

[1] It was in 1843 that Horne published his epic *Orion* at the price of one farthing (it is so printed on the title-page) to show the author's contempt for a public that could not recognize good poetry when it saw it, and would not buy it. My own copy, choicely bound, cost me twenty-three shillings. It is hardly surprising that Horne sank into poverty and was kept by a Civil Liſt pension.

BERNARD SHAW AND THE AUTHOR
From a photograph in the possession of the author

DR. EILEEN POWER AND THE AUTHOR EXCHANGING VIEWS ABOUT
MEDIAEVAL WILLS
From a photograph by Mrs. Arthur Rowntree

Always he would speak impromptu, on the inspiration, or the caprice rather, of the moment. So he did when I took the chair for him one afternoon at Letchworth. Most graciously he had offered to speak on 'Libraries and the English Language,' and in order to provoke a keen discussion we had invited forty librarians all the way from London to hear the great man discourse on a matter of such high consequence to them. They occupied the first three rows, and had note-books ready open on their knees. But, to my dismay and to their disgust, Shaw went off at a tangent after the opening sentence, and never reapproached the advertised subject. He was in excellent form, as always, but on an entirely different theme. When he finished, the librarians began. Their language was plain English, with more than a dash of Billingsgate; and some of the abuse was directed against me for not calling Shaw to order, and for luring men of metropolitan learning to the First Garden City on a false pretence. Sometimes the lot of a chairman can be hard. The cobbler should stick to his last. A lecturer should stick to his lecture.

VIII

At the close of 1929, when the concluding volume of the *History of Hitchin* was published, I received a letter from 'Anthony Hope,' whose full name was Sir Anthony Hope Hawkins. 'You and I,' he said, 'have been writing to one another for years. Isn't it time that we met? I simply must thank you in person for all you've done for the little town where my father was born and bred.' Naturally, I leapt at the chance, and a visit to Heath Farm, Walton-on-the-Hill, was very soon arranged. Oddly enough, when I dismounted from the train at Tadworth he and I were the only persons on the platform. I walked up to the far end where he was standing. 'But *you* can't be Hine,' he exclaimed, as he stared and stared at me, 'my wife said you'd be certain to be an old, old man with a long, long beard. And besides you don't look the least like a lawyer.'

'I'm Hine, right enough,' I replied; and then, suddenly sure of me, and with a shout of delight, he tossed his hat twenty feet up into the air.　The wind caught it and wafted it this way and that way until it settled on the line in front of a train running express in the opposite direction.　'Never mind my old hat,' he said when he had recovered it and banged it into shape, 'I'm in for a happy week-end with you, and that's all that matters.　You will admit it was a bit of a risk asking a complete stranger to my private house.'

In the station yard he made me known to his attractive American wife, and added: 'I must warn you.　Red hair for danger!　She is the worst driver in all Surrey, if not in all England, and to sit behind this *God in the Car*, holding on and hoping for the best, is more thrilling than anything I've described in any of my novels.'　But, though she reversed her head and talked to us most of the way, she had beginner's luck and hairbreadth escapes in deep and narrow lanes, and somehow we reached the farm in safety.

It was, for me, a marvellous week-end.　Here was a man who knew my Hitchin and its Worthies at first hand, and could supply a racy running commentary as I pored over his 'Hawkins Book,' a precious manuscript concerning 'Old John' of Portmill Lane and his predecessors and successors in title.　Then, after dinner at night, though, alas, my memory of what happened was dimmed by the courteous compulsion to drink glass for glass with my host, there were legal and literary anecdotes—vintage of a well-stored mind, and told in his inimitable manner.

I remember how whimsically he recounted a recent experience of his lecture tour in the U.S.A., though to me it seemed to cast a shrewd and pitiful light on literary fame. One night he came to a city where he was billed to speak on *The Prisoner of Zenda*; but, by pure misadventure or by the blunder of his agent, a filmed version of his novel was to be shown at the same hour in a cinema dead opposite the hall where he would be.　It was too late to cancel the engagement.　So he gave his lecture to an audience of twenty, and the cinema was packed.

Lucky, indeed, were the twenty, for they heard from Anthony Hope himself of the happy chance that befell him as he strolled back from Westminster County Court on 28th November 1893.　For him it was a never-to-be-forgotten day.　He had won his case, and on his way home to the Temple, racking his brains for a theme for his next novel, the word Ruritania flashed into his mind; and at that precise moment of time there passed him in the street two red-haired men who in other respects also were the image of one another. Arrived in Brick Court, he lit a pipe and sat down to assemble his new ideas. Next morning, having slept on his embryo plot, he began to write; and for twenty-eight days, as the amanuensis of his dictatorial muse, he went on writing. I have recently examined the original, written on the blue paper that the learned counsel of that period favoured, and could find hardly a word erased. The story just wrote itself.

One other fact needs to be made known about that novel. As its author was as yet without a public, the rights were acquired for a mere song. Yet Arrowsmith, who belonged to the much disparaged race of publishers, conferred royalties and shared the huge success of the venture with the struggling barrister. He did more. He had the manuscript elaborately bound and returned, 'with compliments.'

I hoped, on parting, that Anthony Hope would present me with a first edition of *Zenda* or of its sequel *Rupert of Hentzau*, but his choice lit upon *The Dolly Dialogues*— 'the best thing I have written.' And there was this sound and serious advice: 'Whatever you may think about the law, Hine, don't be such an ass as to leave it. I have not done so badly with my novels and my plays. But I should have made a finer thing of life had I followed the example of my cousin Henry [Lord Brampton]. Patience and perseverance—well—they might in time have raised me also to the Bench.'

IX

Of the many poets and philosophers I have known, none have looked the part so closely as Clifford Bax. By good fortune, as a gentleman of leisure, he has been able to lead his own life; and, though he has worked harder than many a business man, it has been to his own design, and in his own unhurried manner. Never has he tried to catch up with the feverish tempo of this present dispensation. Why should he? In spirit attached 'to Grecian glades and

Trojan sky,' in body, from youth up, like one of Socrates'
disciples, he has measured modern existence against that
gracious background, and, condemned though he be to
languish in an age of iron, has endeavoured to make life
itself a career, a serene but studied work of art.

'A musical voice is one of the attributes of the Yogi.'
So Bax affirms in his *Ideas and People* (1936), and though he
himself has not yet attained to be a Yogi, he, like his Quaker
ancestors, has always been a 'Seeker.' Nor will he be
satisfied this side the grave.   When he recites his poems it
is in 'a thin flute-like voice across the loud disturbances';
with a few passes of the hand, and in a slow, hypnotic
monotone, he can evoke the calm landscapes of old masters,
the lost horizons of long ago.   If there is not the 'wildness'
prescribed by Alice Meynell, there is a witchcraft all his
own, and I for one deplored the renunciation of rhyme so
early in his thirties.   No doubt he gained a certain freedom
of movement, though his free verse is fettered with subtle
rhythms of his own imposing, but he has lost the haunting
refrain, the white magic of repeated music, that lured his
listeners away not to the land of the lotus-eaters, but into
the presence of the Ever-living Ones.

In his *Farewell My Youth* (1943) Clifford's brother, Sir
Arnold, speaks of asking Roland Bocquet if he believed in
reincarnation.   Back came the vehement and astonishing
reply: 'My God, no!   I don't believe in any incarnation.'
Whatever Clifford's views may be about our blessed
Saviour's incarnation, he is well assured of his own, and
against all sceptical comers he has also maintained his
belief in reincarnation.   Nor should one forget that the
memory of his previous lives has been used to fine purpose
in a work of his the most likely to endure: *The Traveller's
Tale* (1921).

Those who can hold such views are fortunate.   In a
world distracted with toil and trouble, and worn out with
deceiving hopes, they can afford to wait.   If it will not
come to pass in this rebirth, it may perhaps in another.
And yet, as though dubious of this, Bax has crowded many
lives into this present life.   In turn, and often at one time,
he has been artist, Platonist, Buddhist, theosophist, tran-
scendentalist, spiritualist, sensualist, essayist, poet, playwright, censor, cricketer, chess player, traveller, ascetic,

ANTHONY HOPE
From a painting by Hugh de Glazebrook

CLIFFORD BAX
From a photograph by Fayer of Vienna

epicurean, vegetarian, carnivorous animal, water-wagoner, connoisseur of wine, and above all a great companion; in friendship, at least, a fixed star into whose ambit have come and gone a multitude of writing men, mystics, musicians, artists' models, lovers, and followers of strange religions.

'Scenery is fine,' said Keats, 'but human nature is finer.' To Bax also, in the mid stride of his life, there came the same conviction. Since then, what a fascination it has been to study and to fathom men and women, but, by bodily grace or the subtle contexture of their minds, they must satisfy his fastidious taste, or drop out of the charmed circle of his acquaintance. You may read in *Inland Far* (1925) of the odd and inconsequent ways in which this captain of men came to pick (I had almost said pick up) the scratch side of his companions.[1] Some, like myself, were associates of the hockey *cum* supper *cum* music social Saturdays at Ivybank, the hospitable home of his mother, Mrs. Ridley Bax, in Hampstead. Others, in after years, would be found at the literary gatherings at Clifford's studio in Edwardes Square, where our host, modestly revolving about the circumference, was in truth the central and moving spirit of our discussions. Let no one declare that the art of conversation is dead whilst such *salons* and symposiums endure. Elsewhere in London the talking was so often for effect. Here it took the form of an earnest inquiry after truth. We could not put the world to rights. By the twentieth century it was too far gone for that. But in the give and take of discussion we could clarify and fortify our own thinking. Not all can be Ruperts of debate, but each could contribute something, a scholar's mite, a spark of humour, an apt quotation, to the common bag of knowledge. In matters too dark and difficult we could grope and speculate together. And when we walked away, a little unsteady perhaps with *ebrietas animae*, a little dismayed by the cool unconcern of the stars, yet we held up our heads as blithe, and it might be immortal, spirits ready for any fate that might befall.

---

[1] 'Scratch side,' let me hurriedly admit, is hardly the term for one that included Arnold Bax, Gustav Holst, Sir John Squire, Edward Thomas, J. C. Snaith, Alec Waugh, Harold Monro, Armstrong Gibbs, Ralph Straus, Herbert Farjeon, Stacy Aumonier, Cecil Palmer, and Godwin Baynes.

N

X

Years later, a chosen few amongst the companions would forgather for cricket weeks under the friendly roof of Bax's manor house in Wiltshire, and that, in his opinion, was our Golden Age because 'In the first place the old house was the loveliest of all possible settings for a holiday amongst friends; in the second because most of us were then in the unscarred twenties; and finally because English life, in those pre-war years, beat with a steady pulse.' It was country-house cricket of the less pretentious kind, with a preference for market-town matches, or merry bucolic encounters upon village greens. How clear in memory still are the drives in wagonettes and dogcarts along the deep and leafy lanes; the banter and bravado of the players; the fluctuating fortunes of the game; the refreshing dip in streams discovered as we jog-trotted home; the thirst not to be quenched save in pewter tankards of cider; the impromptu satirical ballads, setting the supper table in a roar and rebutted on the instant with limericks and lampoons; the knitted brows bent over the chess-boards when the coffee had been cleared; the quiet stroll before bed-time, the splendour of the harvest moon.

There was yet to be a Silver Age, but some gallant fellows went off to the war and never came back to play cricket; some stayed at home and were choked with the cares of this present world; others, checkmated or stalemated by the chicanery of knaves or the surrender of their castles in the air, had to be swept off the board of literary life. Very few of the hardy originals survived to figure in the conversation pieces portrayed by Bax in his *Evenings in Albany* (1942).

In that work, as in the closing pages of *Inland Far*, there is a post-cricket-seasonal, almost an autumnal air; indeed the author complains as though it had been his lot 'to walk the world as a failure.' But some writers are greater than their books. Here is one who made a name for himself by his dramatic work. But had he never composed a line I should have deemed him a poet, and one neither mute nor inglorious. It was something to have stirred the imagination of his contemporaries; and for a man with immortal longings to have held the stage of this mortal life—a not inelegant player.

It takes all sorts of men and women, I said, to make one man, and from Clifford Bax I learnt to practise what you may call a deep breathing of the mind, and to cultivate a calm horizon. I remember, in 1911, travelling to Venice to be a consenting party to his secret marriage. On their side, the high contracting parties agreed to hold up the honeymoon for two days, so that we three might lie out on the lagoons and tell travellers' tales and romantic stories in turn to one another. There, indeed, with the distant view of Venice, like some superb galleon at anchor in the Adriatic, we had an exquisite background for our imaginative pieces, but in Bax's stories, told 'in that large utterance of the early Gods,' the horizon was always receding; voyaging 'with a wild surmise' beyond the Pillars of Hercules, he would set course for Atlantis or venture on seas still more perilous to faery lands forlorn.

By a similar enlargement of mind, he would discover a mystery even in common things. Earlier in this book I have noted Harold Monro's awareness of the secret individual life of our miscalled 'goods and chattels,' his appreciation of 'that old kindness of domestic wood.' But Bax liked to hark further back 'to the time and place of its own beginning.' Listen to these lines that sprang, unsummoned, into his mind one evening as I sat playing the piano in my home at Ashwell End:

While you played and our fair companion listened,
  I, in the fluttering firelight, all of a sudden
    Felt, as I mused, how much
      Marvellous life
Slumbered there in the antique room around us.

Once the rafters under the roof, up-towering
  Spread their leaves to Elizabethan summers.
    Who was it brought them here?
      Men who perhaps
Heard with terror news of the great Armada.

What men carved the chairs and the long low table?
  Even the walls were quarried; and once the carpet
    Must have been wrought by girls,
      Happy or sad,
Kneeling close to a loom in bygone Persia.

So, no less, in the fire I hear the boisterous
  Hardly human life of the modern miner;
    See, if I lift my head,
      Glimmering glass,
Twilight—blue,—the familiar wonder of windows.

Whatsoever I look on bears my fancy
  Back to the time and place of its own beginning,—
    Further and further back
      Into the past,
Into the primal world of the swamp and forest.

All the past is about me. Suns and planets
  Linger yet in a chair, a book or a garment!
    Even the silent girl
      Near to me now
Holds the story of all mankind within her.

Travelling down the centuries, like an heirloom,
  Still her beauty endures,—the slender body
    Wrought of a thousand loves,
      Bearing it on
Scatheless out of the smoke of tumbled empires.

Employing the same faculty of inner vision, almost a power of divination, Bax, in *A House of Words* (1920), painted impressionistic portraits of his friends; and if there was a touch, a varnish, of overpraise, why then it should have set us reflecting, and vowing to emulate so glowing a vision. 'If you set out to praise a man,' remarked Swinburne, 'you should praise him beyond the mark, for peradventure, out of shame, he will endeavour to deserve it.'

ANTIQUARY

(R. L. H.)

As you would leave the highway, and crossing clovered meadows,
  Rejoice to find a beamed and many-mullioned farm,
So I rejoice, my dreamer, to hear your silver English
  Ring through the nickel speech of this uncourtly age.

In you, that laugh and labour as though before your lintel
  Elizabethan scholars any day might dismount,
How much forsaken wisdom, what unfrequented poems,
  Find one whose heart and brain are quick to love them still!

Could I be sure as they are of one such peerless reader
   I should be well-contented—could I but know that you,
When the world's face had altered, should taste my antique verses
   Beside a pear-tree'd wall or willow'd country stream.

But who dares hope as proudly? The life distilled within them
   No latter You shall prize after five hundred years.
With every generation the minds that muse grow fewer—
   Like the strong gracious homes the Tudor masons built.

Well, let my hard-wrought verses endure or perish! Better
   To have you here, fit friend for bright or dusky mood—
Half vellum-fingering hermit and half superb Hidalgo—
   Than store for them the love which now you give to me:

Better have heard in Venice the gorgeous dreams that buoyed you,
   Cricketed with you once through days of August heat,
Known of your moonlight farings by English lanes, and with you
   Watched, as we grew, the slow patterns of fate unfold.

DOCTORS I HAVE KNOWN

Honour a physician with the honour due unto him for the uses which ye may have of him: for the Lord hath created him.

ECCLESIASTICUS, xxxviii. 1.

He that sinneth before his Maker, let him fall into the hands of a physician.

ECCLESIASTICUS, xxxviii. 15.

I

T seems curious to find these contradictory passages in the same chapter of Holy Writ, but it is with doctors as it is with lawyers. When things go well with their patients they are honoured; when things go ill they are abused. As professional men we are constantly in touch with one another. What did old Florio say? 'From the phisition and attorney keepe not the truth hidden.' Moreover, when a doctor has done his best, or his worst, it is understood that we shall be advised; rightly are we aggrieved if, as happened in *Gil Blas*, 'the doctor is so expeditious that he does not give his patients time to send for their solicitor.'

Also it is fair to consider ourselves as brothers in adversity, for in the world's slander we are frequently bracketed together:

> Trust not the physician;
> His antidotes are poison, and he slays
> More than you rob.[1]

If we rogues and robbers are in league, it is fitting we should resemble one another. Physicians for their own ends cultivate a bedside manner; attorneys assume an office-table manner. They prescribe physic; we dispense advice. They cure the body; we take care of the estate. The mind is debatable ground; it should be held in common.

---

[1] Compare the saying of Barnaby Rich in *The Honesty of this Age*, 1614: 'They say it is an argument of a licentious commonwealth when physicians and lawyers have too great comings in.'

THE HITCHIN DOCTORS (1848)
From a drawing by Samuel Lucas

HAVELOCK ELLIS
From a photograph by Maurice Turney

Sometimes, having failed to convince an unreasonable, sick-minded client, we commend him to a priest, 'For of the most High cometh healing' (Ecclesiasticus, xxxviii. 2), but more often we introduce our client to one of the doctors for whom we act. Each day we are learning the truth of what Dr. Johnson said: 'It is so very difficult for a sick man not to be a scoundrel.' With a woman we do our best. Not often will she prove a scoundrel, but frequently she will be past our understanding. We shake our head and mutter the old proverb: 'When a woman goes to law the Devil is full of business.' We guess at her age and make allowances. We dimly wonder what is amiss. And then, in despair, we pass her on to the medical fraternity.

Perhaps it is just because we have to pass so many cases on that we become jealous of the doctors. In our opinion they appear to do too well. We look out of our office windows, and watch them sweep by in elegant luxury cars. Ruefully we compare our respective lots. Some words of Sterne rise up in memory to exacerbate our already chafing thoughts: 'There are worse occupations in this world than feeling a woman's pulse.' And then, suddenly, we remember and are reconciled. There is the other side. Tired but finished for the day, we lawyers plod heavily homeward at seven. Tired but not finished, the doctors come out of their surgeries and sink into a chair. But what impatient patient, what clanging, clamouring bell, what insistent summons on the 'phone, may not be destined to drag them from warm beds in the watches of the night? 'When I die,' said dear and whimsical old Doctor Pycroft, 'I shall have a bell hung on my head-stone, with an inscription asking the compassionate passer-by to ring it long and loud. *And I shan't get up.*'

There are occasions, more especially in litigation, when barristers and solicitors are 'up against' medical experts. We are reputed to take a wicked pleasure in confuting or confusing them in the witness box. Nowadays, many men of law are members of the Medico-Legal Society. We pick up a thing or two, and like to air our knowledge, forgetting that a little learning can be a dangerous thing. But doctors are hard-headed, and shrewd at answering back, as you may judge from this anecdote oft repeated:

Counsel, after exercising all his ingenuity without effect,

looked at the expert giving evidence and said: 'You will admit that doctors make mistakes, won't you?'

'Yes, the same as lawyers.'

'But doctors' mistakes are buried underground,'[1] said counsel triumphantly.

'Yes,' retorted the doctor with a caustic smile, 'but lawyers' mistakes are left swinging in the air.'

II

For my personal needs I am seldom driven to the doctors. All these years I have been using up health and strength inherited from a race of farmers who lived sturdily upon their lands. It may just last out my time. But I have had some odd experiences, all the same, and a few are worth recording.

Our family doctor, when I was a boy, was Dr. Jenner of Baldock. A cut above the ordinary country practitioner, he was said to be connected with Edward Jenner (1749–1823), the discoverer of vaccination, and just as that famous and fashionable man used to ride out to his patients wearing a blue coat and top-boots with silver spurs, so his collateral descendant, disdaining the professional gig, would gallop over the fields to Newnham Hall in broadcloth, breeches, and gaiters. Unfortunately, he would bring his hunting-crop upstairs. There was never anything wrong with us lads. But we disliked being sent back to boarding school, and a few days before the holidays expired we were accustomed to go sick. He would glance contemptuously at our tongues, which we had purposely coated with a sickly white sweet sold to us by a sympathetic grocer at Ashwell. Then, stripping off the bedclothes and our night-shirts, he would scrutinize our well-fed, well-developed bodies. When he was sure there was neither spot nor rash, he would be furious at the deception, and would lay on with the hunting crop until we really had something to show.

Once, as I recovered from an honest attack of measles, he gave me half a crown to spend as I journeyed, bound for

[1] This is an old wheeze, but it was never better expressed than by Francis Quarles in his *Hieroglyphikes of the Life of Man* (1638): 'Physicians of all men are most happy; whatever good success they have the world proclaimeth; and what faults they commit the earth covereth.'

school, through London, and in order to please him I spent
some of my time and some of my fortune visiting the statue
of the Great Vaccinator in Kensington Gardens.   But I
did not know then what opposition there had been to the
setting up of that statue (originally in Trafalgar Square),
nor the verses put by *Punch* into the mouth of the irate
deceased:

> England's ingratitude still blots
> The scutcheon of the brave and free.
> I saved you from a million spots,
> And now you grudge one spot to me.

Given a stout constitution, it is, I have always held, a
man's own foolishness if he falls ill.

> There is no health; physicians say that we,
> At best, enjoy but a neutrality.

With that dictum of John Donne I have never once agreed.
Do we not ask for trouble by indulgence in wine and women?
What does old Fuller say?   'Diseases are the price of ill
pleasures.'   What must we expect if we take no exercise?
I like the saying of Diderot on that point: 'The best
doctor is the one you run for and can't find.'   One should
go on running.

But somehow no clean bill of health, and no amount of
care, seem to avail against the common cold which, to the
disgrace of the medical profession, becomes more and more
prevalent.   Indeed, it has been said that a person's age is
not dependent upon the number of years that have passed
over his head, but upon the number of colds that have
passed through it.   And unfortunately colds develop into
other things.

It was from a neglected cold, I remember, that I con-
tracted pleuro-pneumonia as a boy at school, and miserably
for me the attack came on just before Christmas, on the very
last day of term.   The pain struck at me like a dagger in
the back as I was sitting for the Junior Cambridge examination at Canterbury, and to climb St. Thomas's Hill afterwards was agony.   Very soon I was being subjected to
another kind of examination by a Dr. Wacher who, to my
pleasure, used to come visiting me over the snow-bound
roads on a sleigh.   On a cold and frosty morning it was
delightful to hear the jingling harness-bells as the pony

trotted softly into the drive. But three days later I was re-examined by a hideous pasty-faced man with a raucous voice and a gross unprofessional beard. I hated him at sight, and I hated him still more when I overheard him whispering to Wacher in words that thundered into my ears: 'This lad won't last very long.' For my own sake and for that of Wacher, who, I gathered, held a different view, I resolved to confound the specialist and live.

In those barbarous days (it was in 1896), those who suffered from pneumonia were not permitted to drink; and barley water and orange juice were not as yet in vogue. It seemed to me that I was more likely to die of thirst than from any insidious disease; whereas a mere pint or two of cold water would, I was confident, make me well. Noticing, in the early hours, that my night-nurse had fallen asleep, I rolled out of bed, crawled across the floor to the wash-hand-stand, clutched at the tooth-water bottle with the frenzy of a dipsomaniac, and drained it at one draught. It was a triumphant, a satisfying moment. Somehow I managed to crawl back, but the steep ascent to my bed was quite beyond me, and in vexation and humiliation of spirit I had to rouse the nurse and confess what I had done. It was foolish of her to report me to the doctor, for he discharged her on the spot for sleeping whilst on duty, and three weeks later her successor was sent packing for allowing me to walk in my sleep down fifty-three steps of stairs into my own (V2 classical) class-room, where a much mystified if not terrified night-watchman came upon me construing aloud from Ovid's *Metamorphoses* at 2 a.m. to a master who was not there. Shortly after that I, too, was discharged, and spent the spring term in the luxury of my own home, devouring good and bad literature, imbibing vintage 1863 port as prescribed, and dreaming wildly at nights.

III

Some people are fortunate. One of my best friends, Matilda Lucas of Stanegarth above Shap, was so hardy that for fifty years she never consulted a doctor. When she reached eighty-nine, she wilted a little under the strain of correcting proofs for her *Two Englishwomen in Rome* (1934), a book in which E. V. Lucas and I had been lending a helping hand. A doctor was summoned all the way from Penrith. 'It is not often my patients meet me in the porch,' he remarked on his arrival; 'what, I wonder, can be wrong with you?' It was a problem that he failed to solve. Her heart, when tested, beat like that of a lion. Her blood pressure suggested a young woman of thirty-five. Her nerves were taut as steel. 'We really must do something,' he said at last, 'to justify my fee of three guineas, if only to while away the time.' As it was a choice of chess-playing or sharing notes about Cumbrian folk-lore, they decided on the latter, and spent a marvellous hour confabulating over magical charms, superstitious cures, love potions, bewitched houses, apparitions, hill-wakes, well-worship, and the like.

There was no medical reason, in his opinion, why she should not attain three figures, and when I saw her for the last time, in her ninety-fourth year, I insisted that she should set herself to become a centenarian.

'I doubt if it would be wise,' said she, 'there are risks involved. Not so long ago, we had an old lady living here on the fells who conducted herself as respectably and virtuously as any one could wish up to her ninety-ninth year; but turning the hundred seemed also to turn her head. At any rate, suddenly she took to using obscene language, and not content with that, she began to sing it at the top of her voice. Now Mr. Hine, you wouldn't have *me*, the daughter of a Hitchin Quaker worthy, end up and disgrace my town like that.'

Fifty years without a doctor! That was a record I could never hope to equal. But for twenty years after rescuing my own life I needed neither port nor physic. Then, as happens so frequently to the sad and sedentary race of solicitors in their forties, things began to go wrong. I use the word 'began' advisedly, for whereas in the exasperating profession of schoolmastering men have apoplectic seizures and mercifully cease to be, in the profession of the law, though no less exasperating, we are doomed to die by inches. The doctors have no word for it. It cannot be diagnosed in their trying technical terms. But we who suffer recall the first symptoms of this lingering death: there comes a dry-rot creeping through our House of Life: a desiccation of desires; a hardening of the arteries of the

soul.   'A doctor who once kept a nerve-rest home,' so I read
in the book *Concerning Solicitors, by One of Them*, 'informed me that fifty per cent of his hysterical patients
were solicitors.'   Lanky and loose-limbed solicitors are
always the first to fall, for there is a stinging truth in what
the little man Francis Bacon said: 'Tall men are like poplar
trees which do die from the top.'   Painfully well do I
remember how from my tree of life the leaves came off
almost in a night.   Soon there was not a blade of hair on
my body.   For years I had to wear a skull cap, and for the
first time in my life I looked like an antiquary.   So altered
was I in appearance that my closest friends passed me all
unknowing in the street, which was a blessing, for it saved
me hours of hindering gossip and casual conversation.

When I resorted to the doctors, they spoke learnedly of
alopecia and neurasthenia, but could do nothing for either.
If I would be so unwise as to live beyond my income of vital
energy I must expect to be in difficulties.   Clearly the strain
of leading a double life, the accumulation of office worries,
and the burden of clients' woes, had worn me down.   Some
of the advice I received was more than surprising, it was
astounding.   'No physic will do you any good,' declared
the honest physician Dr. Langston Day of Baldock, 'but
here is a small suggestion: Never miss your tea, and go to
London once a week.'   I smiled, and promptly invited
myself to tea with him and his artistic wife.   Yet he was
perfectly right.   What a blessed relief it is to slam the
office door at four-thirty—the day's work nearly done—
and make merry with the right sort of people; or even to sit
alone, as often I do—my maple-wood tea-tray inlaid with
the map of Hertfordshire before me—and count up the
friends still left to me, sprinkled here, there, and everywhere
about the shire.

Better still, of a Saturday, to escape.   To be no longer a
mere parochial person.   To put books and manuscripts
away.   To hear plays and music.   To see millions of
fascinating faces.   To lose one's fretful, isolated indivi-
duality in the maelstrom of metropolitan life.

IV

Yes, the prescription of my country doctor was pleasant enough, and once upon a time in Rome, so that I could boast of it to him, I consumed as many as five teas (it takes five poor Italian teas to make one good English tea) in the course of the afternoon, and sat through a lecture on Petrarch in addition. But the neurasthenia continuing, I resolved to visit John Mitchell Bruce who, at that time was a well-known consulting physician. Knowing that his *Materia Medica* was already in its ninth edition, I expected him to know of some subtle antidote, some desperate remedy; and besides he was aged and experienced: 'Physicians, like beer,' said Fuller, 'are best when they are old, and lawyers, like bread, when they are young and new.' But this man, so learned in medical science, waved his hands helplessly. There was nothing in all his thousands of pages that would avail. Then, catching sight of my disconsolate face, he placed his hand in a grandfatherly way upon my shoulder and said: 'It will sound odd to you. But listen to the advice of an old man. Go back to Hitchin and join the Society of Friends.'

For a moment I was taken aback, and as I handed over the three guineas I inquired maliciously: 'And how much does the Society pay you each year, doctor, to dispense that advice?'

Before I reached the door, however, I had regretted my flippancy. Perhaps he was right. I could almost hear him saying to himself: 'Far too imaginative and intro-spective, this young man. How salutary for him to come apart, out of the noise and encumbering hurry of the world, and in quiet collectedness to rest awhile with solid, yes, even with stolid Quakers!' Before long I had proved the efficacy of his words. Though I never joined Friends, I took to sitting with them, and whenever I wrote to them I liked to subscribe myself *Amicus Amicorum*.

Quakers are not easy of approach, and at first I was deterred. Myself addicted to the 'distemper of enthusiasm,' as they would term it, I was the more repelled by their guarded speech, their icy understatement. I used to pretend that the temperature fell thirty degrees whenever

I came into the presence of Friends. I forgot to be grateful for the opportunity thus afforded to reduce my own. Always there was the silent reproof of their better practice; their sad renunciation of colour; [1] their grey prohibiting outlook on the arts and graces of this present life. But in time these small vexations vanished before the sheer goodness and constancy of Friends: their meekness and moderation: their 'holy care' to live up to 'the fine principle of light and love.' Like many another man of letters before me, I was drawn to Friends by the convincing power and the quaintness of their writings. To correct the wildness of my dreamings, I took nightly doses of George Fox, William Penn, and Isaac Penington. There is a mighty pentecostal fervour about those First Publishers of Truth that was not, alas, transmitted to their mild, quietistic successors. Not so flippantly, I once asked the recording clerk, William F. Nicholson, if it would be permissible to join Friends up to, say, the Toleration Act of 1689—to be a Quaker of the first, great epic period. 'We might find you a disturbing influence,' he replied, 'those heroic days are gone for ever.'

No longer content with measured nightly doses, I began to swallow thousands of pages in Quaker manuscripts by day. Mine was a Quaker town. At all hazards, I was resolved to understand these 'peculiar people.' Yielding their secrets one by one, they should eventually become familiar friends, and some day I would write of them as they deserved. [2] Overcoming the scruples of elders and preparative meeting clerks, I signed the twelve precautionary conditions they imposed, borrowed dozens of Minute Books, Testimonies, and Sufferings, and buried myself inside them for three years. If I emerged at all it was to examine the Hitchin manuscripts in the reference library at Devonshire House in the City. How gratefully I recall the first visit I paid there! Looking up from my papers at four o'clock in the afternoon, I beheld a ministering

---

[1] In his *Inquiries into Human Faculty* (1883), p. 47, Francis Galton, himself descended from a family of Friends, states that colour blindness is nearly twice as prevalent amongst their Society as amongst the rest of the community, the proportion being as 5·9 to 3·5 per cent.

[2] The long Quaker chapter (150 pages) in the *History of Hitchin* was issued separately for the Society in 1929 under the title: *A Mirror for the Society of Friends: being the Story of the Hitchin Quakers*. The volume is enriched with an introduction by Edward Grubb. Second and revised edition, 1930.

angel. Not a word was said. Infinite care was taken not to interrupt my studies. With a gentle, fleeting smile she insinuated a cup of China tea and a piece of home-made cake beside my pile of books, and vanished. Never in any metropolitan or country library had such a kindness been shown. I was deeply moved. When I thanked Dr. Norman Penney, 'It is enough of itself,' I suggested, 'to make a man wish to become a Quaker.' But the librarian had no sense of humour. Friends rarely have. God evidently intended them to be seriously minded people. Taking my words literatim, he replied in gruff and reprimanding tones: 'That is scarcely a reputable ground for admission to a select religious society.'

As a well-known woman-Friend had given notice that, if ever I applied for membership, she would, in protest, telegraph her resignation, I did not pursue the matter. My concern being to study Friends rather than to join them, I kept myself to my books. For my soul's health I read, marked, learned, and inwardly digested the journal of Thomas Shillitoe of Hitchin (1754–1836), a man far more beset with hallucinations and nervous prostrations than myself, yet enabled by divine grace to stand before emperors and kings and princes.[1] For months, as a talisman of mental safety, I kept in my breast-pocket the diary of Mercy Ransom (1728–1811), a diary the more precious to me because written, as she says, 'sweetly musing in my chamber,' a chamber that for three years I had been occupying in the law. From her I could learn much. Here was a woman of manifold activities, year after year travelling in the ministry in England, Scotland, and Wales, constantly preaching to 'crowds of curious, scoffing people,' yet preserving her spirit in a heavenly peace. Where was the secret of her 'deep inward stillness,' her silence 'superior to hearing or speaking the most exalted words'? 'Oh! the loss many of us sustain,' she exclaims, 'for want of more inward abstraction: not only from improper desires but even a silence from all thoughts. This blessed silence, not even the enemy of our soul's peace can enter.' Laid aside at the last, in acute suffering and seclusion, she proved that

[1] There is an account of Thomas Shillitoe in my *Hitchin Worthies* (1932), pp. 185–9, and numerous additional references in my *Mirror for the Society of Friends*.

hard saying, ascribed to John Swinton, which as a girl she had pondered over, and put into her commonplace book: 'In ſtillness there is fulness; in fulness there is nothingness; in nothingness there are all things.'

MERCY RANSOM
From a silhouette in Friends House Reference Library

Truly she had the Quietiſt's reward. She speaks again and again of 'the inshinings of divine light,' which come like a benediction into her darkened room. At times the glory of it transfigures her whole being, and the pain and isolation are forgotten: '1806. 12th of 6th month. Yesterday ill all day—poor night—this morning low, under conflict of body and mind, when suddenly, ere I was aware, my soul made me as the chariots of Amminadab, being favoured with the fresh income of divine love and life, which, if not at times vouchsafed, I think I should lose all hope of ever seeing the beauty of the Lord again in the land of the living.'
Fired by the reading of this diary, I took a three days' vow of silence, and went into a self-imposed retreat at Stratford-on-Avon. But the manager and the maids at the hotel where I was ſtaying ſtared at me as though I were out of my wits, and when I wrote down what I wished to order they were quite unable to read it. My mind was well provided. It fed sumptuously on Shakespeare's plays. But Brother Ass the Body went bare. For him there was no 'fulness'—only 'nothingness.'

V

Things were at their worst with me when the war of 1914 befell. In November of that year, I came to the conclusion, or sank into the delusion, that my mind might crack at any moment. Everything seemed unreal and remote. 'The external world,' said Gentile, 'is so impossible that we go along touching it with our hands to convince ourselves that it exists.' Every few yards I, too,

HITCHIN MAGISTRATE SUFFERING FROM GOUT
From a drawing by Samuel Lucas

was compelled to touch things just to keep myself sane. So ominous were the symptoms that I hurried off to the Three Counties Asylum, consulted my friend Dr. Fuller, the superintendent, and made him reserve a room. That gave me confidence. So, I suppose, did the port that he, like the others, prescribed; for, though it plays the devil with the stomach and produces gout, it does, as old text-books say, 'mightily corroborate the brain.'

Being a tolerably good shot and standing six foot one, and being of little use, as I felt, in civilian life, I offered my services to the military authorities. On each occasion the doctors discovered a blind spot on the lung which bothered

o

me not in the least, but they found no trace of the neurasthenia that was tormenting me to death.   First I was degraded, finally rejected.   It is long ago, but I am not likely to forget my first examination in the Bedford barracks. Escorted by a corporal, I was marched off to Room 13 and ordered to strip.   For a moment I flinched.   The room itself—already stripped—needed examination more than I. It had no hangings, only cobwebs.   The bare boards were carpeted with a quarter of an inch of dust.   The windows, which had not known a cleaner for months, looked gloomily out upon a range of latrines.   The walls, distempered who knows how many years before, were pictured with pencilled caricatures of officers and N.C.O.s, with many a ribald rhyme scribbled insultingly below.   As I undressed I gazed about me in despair.   There was no hook on which to hang my clothes.   No chair on which to sit.   Not a stick of furniture in sight.   But I am wrong.   There *was* just one piece.   It was a bottle placed, so as to attract attention, in the centre of the mantelpiece.   And it was labelled *Poison*.

The suggestion was obvious: 'If you don't like the idea of joining the British Army, why then, drink this and be damned.'

Conditions were pleasanter on my fourth and final visit, and I was promoted for inspection by the senior medical officer.   After a glance at my case-notes, he took off his pince-nez and said: 'I don't think you can help us win this war.   But you may be fit enough for the next.   I shall send a word to your doctor about that. . . . And now, if you have half an hour to spare, come home and lunch with me.   You don't know that I have read your book on dreams, but I want to talk to you about the psycho-analytical side of dreaming that you deliberately disregarded.'

He was, as I surmised, a disciple of Jung and Freud, and was beginning to adopt their methods in pathological and neurological disorders.   His patients were no longer being asked to put out their tongues, but to uncover and confess their dreams.

At table, I spoke to him of F. L. Rawson, author of *Life Understood from a Scientific and Religious Point of View, and the Practical Method of Destroying Sin, Disease, and Death* (1912), who had professed himself able and anxious to interpret the most baffling of my published dreams. Eagerly responding, I had sat for hours in his palatial consulting rooms in Regent Street whilst this oracular and majestic person, surrounded by a galaxy of beautiful admirers, expounded his own philosophy, prophesied the ending of the world in December 1917,[1] and revealed incredible and, if true, most discreditable things about my subliminal self.

I spoke to the doctor also of W. T. Horton, a man of mystery who haunted the British Museum by day and practised magic—so they said—by night. Often I would walk home with him to his lodgings when the reading-room bell struck five of a Saturday, and he would make drawings out of my dreams, and offer elucidations much more obscure than those he set out to explain. In 1898 the more powerful of his pen-and-ink drawings had been collected into *A Book of Images*, with an introduction by the poet Yeats, over whose occult and cabbalistic experiments and invocations Horton exercised a guiding if not a controlling influence. For some months I kept the copy presented by Horton with twenty additional drawings interleaved, and then I began to be afraid of it. To my thinking, the faces he evoked by his black-and-white magic, though possessed of a certain cold beauty, were not of this world; they were the appearances of evil spirits. As some of them obsessed me by day and followed me into my dreams by night, I gave the book away to Havelock Ellis (see portrait facing p. 179), with whom I was then in correspondence about flying dreams. 'You need not be anxious on my account,' he assured me, 'I know how to cast out devils, and I have stronger nerves than you.'

'I'm sorry you told me about Horton,' said the doctor as we parted, 'for I was going to urge you to study *The Interpretation of Dreams*. But if you were alarmed by Horton, how, I wonder, would you react to Freud?'

'One should always follow a doctor's advice,' I replied, 'I shall take the risk and read him. At the worst, I can have some bromide handy on my desk.' Then, as Hockliffe's shop was only a street or two away, I purchased the

---

[1] He certainly had the courage of his convictions, and in the spring of 1917 printed his book *The End of the World, and Proofs of its Coming in December* 1917.

recommended volume for thirteen shillings; read it intently in the train, turned the leaves with prurient fascination and increasing disgust every evening, and on the seventh day consumed it with fire. There are some books so vile that you ought not to sell them, still less should you give them away. I disliked dropping thirteen shillings. I loathed having read libidinous things that would be fixed in my memory for ever. Merely to pitch such a book into the flames was not enough. Tearing out the pages with savage deliberation one by one, I made sure that this hypersexually-minded scientist, this Caliban of the enchanted island of our dreams, should have a lingering death. 'The best thing about him,' as they said of Cranmer, 'was that he burnt well.' [1]

VI

By this time I had grown ashamed of being a neurasthenic. 'You should remember,' scolded my doctor-brother, 'that you come of a stubborn and healthy stock. Don't you know that it takes something terrific—something like a ten-ton lorry—to knock out a Hine?' But he had no panacea for an elusive malady derived, alas, from my mother. Nor had Dr. Woodforde of Ashwell whom I next consulted.

'What you really need,' said that sensible village doctor, 'is some literary or historical work that will not merely occupy but fascinate your mind for at least five years.'

Then he walked across the surgery and opened a large safe. 'Here,' he said, handing over a pile of eighteenth-century manuscript, 'is the diary of an ancestor of mine—a parson at Weston Longville in Norfolk. Read it, and, if you like it well enough, then edit it. It will please our family; and it would do you a world of good.'

'Sorry, doctor,' I broke in, 'if I did anything of that kind it would be a history of Hitchin. But just now I can't string three sentences together, and can't make sense of anything I read.'

'It is a pity,' he observed, putting the diary away; and 'What a pity!' I echoed ruefully in after years when John Beresford, who succeeded me in the Jacobean house at

---

[1] First thoughts are not to be trusted. The time was to come when I needed to study the scientific aspects of dream phenomena, a field of inquiry in which Freud was a pioneer. To my chagrin, I had to fork out another thirteen shillings to replace the volume I had burned.

Ashwell End, made a name for himself as an editor, and for 'Parson Woodforde' as an eighteenth-century character, out of that self-same manuscript.[1]

Woodforde, seeing that I was not disposed to follow his advice, sent me to a Harley Street dietician, but all that the specialist would say was: 'You must eat more beef: you must eat more beef.' I could hardly believe my ears; nor indeed my eyes, for with his round and rubicund face and his gross and hairy hands he looked like a Smithfield butcher. I fled from his surgery in disgust, slammed his door, and thought of the third edition of the *Religio Medici* (1658), seen in Francis Edwards's bookshop half an hour before, which could have been bought for the money I had wasted. Yet a month later I was back again in Harley Street, and being told by another extra-special specialist that the only hope was to give up eating meat. His door I did not slam. I went straight from it to the vegetarian restaurant in Chandos Street kept by Eustace Miles, and straight from that again, half an hour later, and still feeling very hollow, to the 'Cheshire Cheese' in Fleet Street to have a proper lunch. In remaining a flesh-eater I have probably sinned against the light, for I constantly marvel at the vitality of my vegetarian clients and compare that with my own torpidity and heaviness of mind. One of my friends, Dr. Percy A. Scholes, used to send me a batch of vegetarian tracts all the way from Switzerland, timed with deadly precision and with malice aforethought to arrive on Christmas Eve; and his covering letter would begin: 'My dear carnivorous animal.' He has spoilt many a traditional debauch on Christmas Day.

When doctors disagree, the patient is apt to strike out on his own. For a month or two I became the disciple of Dr. Coué, and parrot-wise would close my morning and my evening prayers with his magic formula: *Day by day and in every way I am getting better and better.* But the rhythm of that sentence is so detestable to a man of letters that the repetition of it did more harm than good. Instead of being invigorated I was infuriated.

[1] Five volumes in all were printed at the Oxford University Press (1924–1931), together with an abridgment in one volume (1935). The period covered is 1758 to 1802. For a picture of village and church life in the Georgian era one could hardly ask for anything more authentic, satisfying, and racy.

Abandoning Coué, I resorted to the gymnasiums of physical culture. I consulted the great Eugene Sandow, who at once put himself into the attitude so effective in his advertisements, and then displayed his biceps. 'But I am not going to be a prize-fighter,' I protested, 'biceps don't attract me in the least.' With that he lost interest in me, and I took a three months' course from a man called Maxalding who had the more slender figure and the features of a Greek god. Once upon a time he had been a nervous wreck. Now, it seemed, and by faith in himself, he could move mountains.

Determined to attain 'the health of a soul at full stride,' I looked for help in other directions. Whenever I was in London for a Sunday I attended a Christian Scientist church, or watched Archdeacon Wilberforce working miracles upon the sick brought to him at St. Margaret's, Westminster, simply by the laying-on of hands, and praying for others afar off with astonishing results. Well aware that any loss of confidence in the future life had a deadly repercussion on this present life, I sought to buttress my own faith in human survival by scientific corroboration. Many a time I sat under Sir William Crookes and Sir Oliver Lodge at the Society for Psychical Research. It was an unpalatable draught, but I gulped down the first thirty volumes of its *Proceedings*, and sifted the evidence collected by Podmore, Gurney, and Myers. In the end I came out by the same door where in I went, feeling that, as we were guests in this House of Life, it was poor manners to be prying behind the curtains. 'Let no man be hasty,' said Jeremy Taylor, 'to eat of the fruits of Paradise before his time.'

Secretly, and with the same repugnance, I went by night to a palmist, though I knew that many crowned heads of Europe had been before me, and openly by day. There, too, was a mystery, a weird gleam of light—be it holy or unholy—athwart the dark. It was uncanny that this diviner, who had never looked upon my line of life before, should be able to detect the master, if not malevolent, influence that was preying upon my heart's desires; still more uncanny that she should correctly prophesy the date —two years ahead—when the *History of Hitchin* would be published.

VII

Man is an unfortunate creature. If he learns the art of living, it is hardly before it is time to die. Fortunate he is in one thing; he cannot know how little the doctors know. It was said of Dr. Brusquet, a French doctor who died in 1563: 'He had little or no knowledge of his profession, but his patients died in greater ignorance than he.' But even an ignorant layman ought to be able to learn a thing or two about himself, and he is indeed a fool who is not his own physician at forty.

I see that, on arriving at that age, I began to prescribe for myself in a manuscript entitled: *Hine's Homely Physic Book: a most excellent catholicon for the griefs and diseases both of body and mind, compiled for use out of sundry antient authors and from his own sad experience.* As the work was not long pursued, the full-sounding title was scarcely warranted, but the pages contain many nostrums, panaceas, sedatives, and restoratives that were tried and not found wanting. Exercises are there in deep breathing; instructions for auto-suggestion; specifics for toothache, insomnia, and bleeding at the nose. In place of Coué's tedious and ill-turned formula it is advised that 'you should repeat what, through your baptism, you really are:

I am a member of Christ.
I am a child of God.
I am an inheritor of the Kingdom of Heaven.
I am the child of God, loved and safe and cared for, and the whole business of life is to realize my splendid sonship. I am the citizen of a great spiritual kingdom and have only to enter upon my inheritance to find myself in a world of joy and strength and freedom.'

The narcotic use of words like *tranquil, repose, confidence,* 'to be murmured slowly and monotonously,' with complete relaxation of all muscular tension and control, is insisted upon. 'The "shake before using" instruction on certain medicine bottles is not an appropriate label for the elixir of moral energy. . . . Let us keep about us an atmosphere of calm and some degree of mastery over our sensibilities.'

Mixed up with the specifics, one meets with maxims of right living culled from various sources. 'Being asked one day what was the surest way of remaining happy in this world, the Emperor Sigismund of Germany replied: "Only do in health what you have promised to do when you were sick."' And here is the golden rule of Voltaire: 'Regimen,' said he, 'is of more service than medicine; every man ought to be his own physician; he ought to assist nature and never force her; but more than all he ought to learn to bear pain, how to grow old, and how to die.' Still more to the point is the homely counsel of Bishop Stubbs: 'I have only three rules of life: never do anything underhand, never get your feet wet, go to bed at ten.'

VIII

It is in nervous disorders, above all, that a man should be his own physician, for each of us has his own familiar fiend, and should know best how to wrestle with him. When the doctors had the honesty to confess they could not help me, I saw that I must work out my own salvation. Not by indifference nor by callousness but of hard necessity I began to grow a tough hide for this exasperating world. Something delicate and sensitive in one has to die, but it is the only way. People who don't live are wonderfully preserved. But those who are obliged to live are in continual danger. Needs must that offences come, and in the profession of the law they are coming every day. Many a letter in the morning post will be a minor shock. And there are major shocks. Questions of conscience, legal and personal, arise, and these are the most injurious of all. I once heard a neurologist say that one hour's conflict of mind or indecision on a point of conscience can work more havoc on the nervous system than a year of drinking and debauch. So is it with anger and jealousy: 'It is the sword that wears out the scabbard.'

It is not given to all men to grow a tough hide, but every man should be his own philosopher, and best of all a stoic. I remember, as a youth, being reproved by a Hitchin parson who overheard me complaining of the weather. 'Shameful and ungrateful lad,' he exclaimed, 'you ought to be praising God for being alive and young. You should be glad of any weather. Listen to me now, and remember as long as you live the rhyme that I was taught when just about your age:

> Whether the weather be cold, or whether the weather be hot,
> We must weather the weather whether we like it or not.

'And that applies,' he went on, 'to all the storms and tempests of this present life.'

There is the same spirit of cheerful acceptance, and some other sound advice, in *An infallible receipt against all maladies*, that I came upon in a French manuscript of the seventeenth century once in my possession: 'Take two grains of indifference and as much resolution. Add to it some of the sugar of patience. No law-suits or quarrels, no ambition, no unnecessary zeal. Add a pound of good cheer and companionship and two drams of exercise. *No* women, nor intemperance, avarice, or greed of any kind. A full grain of devotion and no new opinions. Mix the whole mass well together and take it every morning with two glasses of the very best wine. You will soon find that this prescription will play the fool with your doctor and bring you into perfect health.'

Of all things, faith is essential, even if it be a mere half grain of devotion, or a faith that seems fantastic: *credo quia absurdum*. Faith in God, faith in yourself, faith, if you must have a doctor, in your doctor. 'You needn't take my prescription,' said one famous physician, 'but have it out and look at it now and then.' There spoke a wise man to one of the children of men. 'All things are possible to him that believeth.' There is, also, a lower order of faith that simply denies the disease. Someone said to me: 'Even if a man hacked you on the shin and drew blood, you would pass it off by saying: "A touch of nerves, a touch of nerves."' That is an exaggeration, but the path of life is so beset with obstructions and doubts and fears that one has to beguile, even to cheat oneself along from hour to hour and from day to day. If, for example, I am feeling heavy in body or mind I wander into Ransom's, the manufacturing chemists next to my office, and stand awhile by the gigantic copper vat where the men are mixing and stirring the liquid cascara. A few minutes inhaling the vapour of that and I come away knowing that I shall not need any aperient for a week or two to come.   Pure fancy, but it works.

IX

In the same way I used to think with Pepys that blood-transfusion might be put to wider service.   Already we know, in the diarist's words, that it has come to be of 'mighty use to man's health for the amending of bad blood by borrowing from a better body.'   But when the experiment was first demonstrated to the Royal Society on 14th November 1666 the members toyed with the idea that the mind as well as the body might be benefited: 'This did give occasion to many pretty wishes, as of the blood of a Quaker to be let into an Archbishop.'   What a much better book this might have been had I been able to 'borrow' a pint from the Lord Chief Justice of England, another pint from the President of the Royal Society of Literature, and a third, say, from the Moderator of the Free Church Federal Council!

Then, too, there is the saving grace of humour, the best physic in the world.   For years I went about my little world with a long face.   I was 'besieged with sable-coloured melancholy,' and when people inquired of my health I would give the sort of answer that a sailor coming out of hospital once gave to a benevolent clergyman: 'Pretty damned miserable, thank God, sir, pretty damned miserable.'   I remember, when a column of troops passed me in Hitchin the first week of the first world war, one of the rankers sang out: 'Cheer up, mister, soon we shall all be dead.'   There is no need of any such forced jocularity, but a set-fair attitude to life, and the ability to laugh at oneself and smile at others, can make all the difference. That is why doctors are such a cheerful race.   When patients are feeling 'tolerably beastly' they have to be diverted.   'The art of medicine,' said Voltaire, 'consists in amusing the patient whilst Nature cures the disease.'   I once had a doctor who had served with the R.A.M.C. in India, and had retired with sufficient anecdotes to last him and his private patients for the rest of their natural lives. 'As my pills are unpleasant,' he used to say, 'they will

need gilding. So I shall enliven you with a few ſtories.'
And he would continue until I had forgotten my aches
and pains.

One of Anthony Hope's favourite ſtories came, at firſt
hand, from the famous surgeon Sir Henry Thompson,[1]
who numbered Thackeray amongſt his patients.

'About how many bottles of wine do you drink in the
course of a year, Mr. Thackeray?'

'Well,' answered the noveliſt after a laboured mathe-
matical calculation, 'roughly I should guess five hundred.'

The doctor looked grave, or as grave as he could, and
the patient, in deprecation of imminent rebuke, added:
'But it's almoſt all other people's wine, you know.'

Doctors' wit is more palatable than lawyers', and some
of the fun they get out of their cases can be appreciated
even by laymen. Juſt before an operation on a member
of my family, performed whilſt this chapter has been
writing, my doctor said to me: 'Here is a brand-new ſtory
that will cheer you up. This morning I was at Bedford
examining a girl recruited for the A.T.S., and there was
something amiss with her. So I inquired:

'"Have you never been X-rayed?"

'"No," she answered brightly, "but I have been ultra-
violated."'

X

There are some things that you cannot smile away or caſt
out as though they were devils. There are shocks that go
on reverberating in the nervous syſtem. There are dreams
that torment one by day. People who have read the book
I published in 1913 often ask me if I ſtill have adventures
as vivid as those I there recorded. The common experience
is that dreams, or rather the power to recapture them (for
it is next to certain that dreaming is incessant in the ſtate
of sleep), seem to fade out soon after forty. Havelock
Ellis told me that he went on dreaming vividly up to
seventy, but after the meridian of life had no flying dreams,

---

[1] Anthony Hope used to be invited to Thompson's *octaves*, which were
dinners of eight courses for eight people at eight o'clock. The company
was always as carefully selected as the food, and from 1872 to 1903 the moſt
famous persons in the worlds of art, letters, science, politics, diplomacy, and
fashion met at their cultured hoſt's table in Wimpole Street.

and lost the sense of colour very prevalent and beautiful before.

For my own part, I dream as extravagantly and violently as ever. I wish it were not so, for sometimes in the hours of dark I alarm my household with moans and groans and gibberish not of this world, and find myself still fighting on the floor. Perhaps I should be grateful for the exercise, for I have perforce to lead a sedentary life. But I wish I were not so full of aches and pains in the morning, and I wish that I kept better company in my dreams. Most of the beings I meet in the middle of the night are hideous and hostile. By day I try to fill my mind with gracious and peaceful thoughts. At night I am delivered up to a horde of demons. There is no doubt of their malevolence. We hate and contend with one another at first sight. Sometimes I am given power to prevail over them. They throw down their weapons and flee headlong down the waste places of the night. But generally I am outnumbered and outfought, and put to death in such torturous [1] ways that when the time comes to die in sober fact I may find it unexciting and unreal. What exasperates me above all in my struggles with these evil spirits is that my gun will not go off. I pull at the trigger desperately but there is no discharge. And it is significant that that impotence came upon me after I shot a gigantic barn owl in the back meadow of my old home at Newnham Hall. The bird (but owls are something more than birds) was a long time dying, and it glared at me with such ferocity of expression that its eyes will haunt me for the remainder of my days.

Who, I often wonder, are these brutal and bestial beings? What have I done that they should persecute me? What infernal region betwixt life and death do they inhabit? In February 1940 I had another curious experience. I was not asleep, but I was half delirious with a second bout of pneumonia, and very much under the influence of M & B 693. Then, in a headlong procession that I could not check, hundreds of them on horseback galloped by me as I stood on the slopes of a narrow defile, each son of Belial as he passed swerving right-handed in the saddle, brandishing

---

[1] *Torturous*, as my old master E. E. Kellett reminds me, is one of the 'words that time has flung away.' It was last used by Henry More in 1618. But may not an antiquary endeavour to revive it?

a fist of fury, and casting on me a look of concentrated hate.
Never have I seen such faces.   I have recoiled from some
medieval gargoyles in my time, but the most repellent were
angelic compared with these fiends.   To me it was astounding that there could be so many shapes and forms of evil,
each unclean spirit, bloated, distorted, sinister, a separate
masterpiece of satanic design.   I was more fascinated than
frightened, for it was evident that they were bent not on
my immediate destruction but on a pursuit more hellishly
pressing.   When the thunder of their hooves died away
there was peace in the valley, but 'God pity the poor
creature,' I cried, 'whom they are hunting down.'

<h1 style="text-align:center">XI</h1>

Having faced such fiends incarnate I used to think it
would not be so terrifying to encounter a ghost.   The
majority of those I had heard of were good-mannered and
some were amazingly polite.   I remember visiting Felbrigg
near Cromer, and was told that at one time the shade of
William Windham, statesman and bibliophile, frequented
the library at night.   For many years he was considerate
enough to replace the books he consulted before morning;
then growing careless he took to leaving them about.   Is it
possible that ghosts also become old and lazy, the mere
shadow of their former selves?

The poet Coleridge, in reply to a lady anxious to know
if he believed in ghosts, remarked: 'No, ma'am, I've seen
too many.'   I, on the other hand, believe in ghosts because
I have seen but one.

It was at Stanegarth, an Elizabethan manor-house occupied by the Matilda Lucas already referred to in this
chapter.   I have often wanted to write the history of that
house.   Though by daylight inarticulate, at nights it can
tell some tales.   It is then you can hear it talking.   Whenever I listened, the words of the prophet Habakkuk (ii. 11)
would spring into the mind: 'The stone shall cry out of the
wall, and the beam out of the timber shall answer it.'
Deep-rooted in the past, the old place is remarkable as the
haunt of no fewer than three ghosts.   The first is a grisly,
sordid fellow, somewhat ashamed of having been murdered

and buried underneath the withdrawing-room floor. He does not often show himself. The second is a proper period ghost; a well-bred lady who from her costume would seem to have belonged to Charles the Second's time. It was on the first night of Miss Lucas's arrival that she appeared, as though to hand over the house that had lain a long time empty to its new mistress. 'Gentle lady,' she said, pausing on the threshold of the parlour door, 'do not fear. I am just going away.' Could anything have been more charming?

If only the ghost that appeared to me upstairs had spoken, all would have been well. It was soon after midnight on 2nd August 1929 that I woke with the uneasy feeling— then the certainty—that someone was in the room. Always a light sleeper, I was alert in a second. Sitting up in bed, I caught sight of a tall, fragile woman of about thirty-five coming through the wall by the right-hand corner of the room. I could distinguish her clearly, not so much by the light of the moon, though that was shining, but by a certain white radiance that seemed to belong to her. Her face, though finely cut, was not beautiful. Fixed, remote, expressionless, it was like that of a sleep-walker. One could learn nothing from it. But the eyes shone like stars. They penetrated, transfixed, and held me.

As she stood motionless, gazing intently at me, there was time on my side also for a hurried scrutiny. She was wearing, I noticed, a crinoline made of heavy silver brocade. Between her breasts, suspended from an ivory chain, hung a large ivory and silver crucifix. In her left hand she carried a pair of embroidered shoes. Her feet were bare.

So long as she kept her distance—a living statue—I was brave. I wondered wildly what I could say to her. But as I halted over the choice of words—and all words seemed banal and unmeaning—she began not to walk but to move. The nearer she drew to my bed the further my courage retreated. When she came through a chest of drawers and a chair I knew she must be a ghost. And when she stretched out her right hand to touch my head I shrieked.

In a moment she had vanished. In another few moments —they seemed an eternity—two of Miss Lucas's maids came to my rescue, one of them wearing a nightcap such as I had not seen for years. They comforted me. They were not in the least surprised about 'the lady.' But they thought she meant no harm. Not being quite so sure, I asked for a fresh supply of candles, and kept four of them burning all the rest of that interminable night.

XII

Then sometimes there are living people, the ghosts of one's past, whose reappearance can cause a painful shock.

How perversely do things befall in this strangely ordered world! I remember one year being overpersuaded, as an Old Leysian, to attend the annual dinner in the Connaught Rooms. On many such anniversaries I had resolutely stayed at home, for reunions in the body do not always make for unity of spirit. Once again I had been wiser to refrain, for, when at last I lit upon my appointed and labelled place at table, I found to my horror that the Old Leysian to sit upon my right hand of honour was the once young Leysian who had been thrashed, with both his parents present, and then publicly expelled for stealing a half-crown from my clothes in the games dressing-room at school. It was worse when he appeared. I thought I had forgotten the whole painful episode, but, for him, time had proved no healer or forgetter. The sight of me was gall and worm-wood to him. He looked daggers. For mere decorum's sake, and to keep the naked facts of the case at bay, we drivelled on about the weather and the government of the day. So I lasted out the eternity of the soup. But in the middle of the fish my nerves gave way. I clapped my handkerchief to my nose, whispered to the criminal that I had been attacked with nose-bleeding, and incontinently fled.

One thing angered me as I went away. Whereas I had come up to the dinner penuriously and strap-hangingly by tube, he had driven up in luxury in his Rolls-Royce. Once again the wicked had flourished like a green bay-tree. After taking my half-crown, he had never once looked back.

Let me recall another ghost from my past who for a time haunted me in the flesh and still, after forty years, lies in ambush for me in my dreams.

In my study, the evening before it happened, I had been

reading the account of the seventeenth-century Quaker, Solomon Eccles, who used to ſtride naked into Weſtminſter Hall, though 'very civilly tied about the privities to avoid scandal,' as Pepys, a great ſtickler for propriety, noted with satisfaction, and in this spectacular manner would summon the wicked generation of Charles II's day to repent whilſt yet there was time.

Up early next morning at 5.30 a.m., I was reading Roman law in the garden at Newnham Hall when I heard a loud, rhetorical voice like the voice of a preacher at the top of his peroration, so loud that the ſtill, summer air seemed to quiver with the heat and fervour of his denunciation. Closing my Juſtinian with an angry, interrupted snap, I hurried across the lawn to the front of the house, and there, to my amazement, I saw a man ſtanding ſtark naked below the window of my father's bedroom, brandishing his arms like a minor prophet, and calling upon my father, who, by the way, was a county alderman and magiſtrate, to come down and repent.

I can ſtill see my father's crimson face, in the glow of the then-rising sun, and I can ſtill hear his thundering tones as he denounced the preacher and all his works, and threatened to have him lodged in jail for contempt in appearing before him without so much as a shirt. The preacher went on preaching. My father went on denouncing. It was the weirdeſt battle of words. But my father's *basso profondo* prevailed in the end, and the spectre, with one laſt invocation—as though he despaired of my father's soul—turned on his bare feet and fled.

There was to be no more Juſtinian for me that morning. Obeying my father's commands I sprang on to my cycle, dodged by the religious maniac as he padded, ſtill prophesying, along the road to Ashwell, summoned three of the ſtrongeſt draymen of Page's brewery in that village to my aid, and sent express for Dr. Woodforde. At the south end of the village we hid behind a hedge and laid an ambush for the preacher and pounced on him. But he fought and bit and gnashed his teeth like a wounded lion, and hurled us from him again and again, his mouth foaming all the time with Bible texts and obscene language. It was fifteen minutes before we grounded him and then, with two of the fatteſt draymen sitting upon him, he was examined by the doctor, who arrived from his bed hardly more clothed than the maniac himself.

By that time my father, in less repentant mood than ever, had driven over from Newnham. Very summarily was the preacher certified, haled off to Arlesey Asylum, and lodged in a strait jacket and a padded room.

But it did not finish there. After three months the man calmed down, and cajoled the superintendent and the visiting committee to give him his discharge. He promised to wear clothes, to keep his religion to himself, and to abstain from the hopeless task of converting justices of the peace. What, evidently, he did not promise was to abstain from attacking me. Every night for a week as I bicycled home from Messrs. Hawkins & Co., he lay in wait for me at Walsworth, and it needed all my agility to speed by him, as he sprang, and get clear. One night I did not get clear. But there was a constable in view who came quickly to my aid. Our fight with the lunatic brought on the religious mania again, and the asylum authorities did not repeat their mistake. I never saw the hideous creature again, but I still feel a tremor whenever I bicycle through Walsworth hamlet.

.   .   .   .   .

There is one spectre, or ghost of the future, that lies in wait for all men; it is the rider on the Pale Horse; it is the fear of dying. 'Sensible people,' said Samuel Butler, 'get their dying done in their lifetime.' But in this matter one is apt to be sensitive rather than sensible. To pass from the light of the sun, 'to return no more to our house, neither shall our place know us any more'—these are melancholy thoughts that throw a chill and deepening shadow over our declining years. For those without hope, 'of all men most miserable,' the sense of inescapable doom discolours the whole of life: 'O abject necessity of being born, O hard necessity of living, O sharp necessity of dying.' And even to those of an excellent hope, even to men of devout character and heroic stature of mind such as Dr. Johnson, there is a natural shrinking:

> So many are the deaths we die
> Before we can be dead indeed.

To be constantly considering one's latter end may be good for the soul, but it is a morbid state of mind and injurious

P

to health. Yet it would not avail to consult a doctor. Towards the end of his life, Chief Justice Coke said 'he had a disease which all the drugges of Asia, the gold of Africa, nor all the doctors of Europe could cure, to wit old-age'; and he knew well enough that 'against the evil of death there is no remedy in the gardens: *Contra malum mortis non est medicamen in hortis.*'

It is only by faith—'above all by taking the shield of faith'—that this ghost can be laid, only by 'the faith that maketh whole' that the Christian warrior can muster strength to confront 'the last enemy.' If only the men of my profession were more faithful and less critical, how much happier we should be! But we are trained to be 'wisely diffident and put on a judicial distrust.' We question all things; we believe so few. Even when we do believe, it is not by venturing faith but grudgingly, giving the benefit of the doubt. There is no vigour in it, no flight beyond reason. 'We think we believe,' as Dean Inge gloomily observed, 'but is our faith really awake, or is it lying bed-ridden in some dormitory of our souls?' If ever we are to be something better than 'a poor querulous handful' we shall need to avoid Mr. Diffidence, to escape out of Doubting Castle, climb the Delectable Mountains, and gain a clearer view of the country to which we are going.

I become almost reconciled to the thought of dying when I reflect that there is just the ghost of a chance I may again forgather with some of the bright spirits I have known upon this earth. But that mere wistful expectation, that timorous, subjunctive mood, is not enough. It should flower, by God's grace, into a blessed assurance. The truest end of life is to know the life that never ends.

A LECTURE IN ANATOMY
From a drawing by Samuel Lucas

SCHOOLMASTERS I HAVE KNOWN

It is when the gods hate a man with uncommon abhorrence that they drive him into the profession of a schoolmaster.

SENECA.

Education is that something that lingers behind when all that has been taught has been forgotten.

I

FROM youth up, I have retained a fellow-feeling and sympathy for schoolmasters, because it was by the merest chance, or perhaps I ought to say it was by the mercy of God, that I was not myself numbered of their tribe.

'It is about time,' wrote my magisterial father, 'that you made up your mind what you intend to be.' And that same night, having half an hour to spare in evening preparation, I decided. One or other of the learned professions it would have to be. But not that of a doctor; I hated the sight of blood, and besides, medicine had already been chosen by my brother. Certainly I could not sink so low as the law. I recalled the lean, treacherous face of the pettifogger who had fleeced my favourite uncle, an uncle who had once been sufficiently well off to send me half a crown at half-term:

> The law decides questions of Meum and Tuum
> By kindly arranging to make the thing Suum.

I remembered the satirical epitaph culled from a graveyard near my home:

> God works a wonder now and then;
> Here lies a lawyer, and an honest man.

As for the Church, had we not been reminded in school chapel that one must wait for a call? and in a foundation based on nonconformist principles that was hardly to be expected. Nor was I enamoured of the vicars and curates I had known. I was wickedly in agreement with the malaprop schoolboy who prayed: 'We beseech Thee to *eliminate* all priests and deacons.'

'It's no good,' I whispered with a sigh, 'much as I dislike it, I shall have to become a schoolmaster. Nobody loves them. Many are hated for their brutal, bullying ways. But a lifetime of long holidays would be just wonderful.' Thereupon I settled my fate on half a sheet of notepaper and, lest I should change my mind, I dropped the envelope into the collecting box as I went in to supper.

That night I could not sleep. Tossing and turning in bed, I wondered if, by the mere process of exclusion, I had chosen wisely. What was wrong with these pedagogues?

A HITCHIN PEDAGOGUE
From a drawing by Samuel Lucas

Why were they, one and all, so ill-favoured and ill-tempered? There must be something amiss, for the Emperor Nero had had a certain man, Paetus Thrasea, put to death 'for having a face like the face of a schoolmaster.' Much to my satisfaction I had lit upon the passage in Suetonius that very afternoon. And now I came to think of it, most of the members of the gerund-grinding profession under whom I had groaned had worn that same forbidding expression. Whilst my fellow sufferers in the dormitory snored and snorted, and muttered scraps of Ovid and fragments of Euclid in their tormented sleep, I went over the days of my so-called education.

Like a nightmare came the hideous and humiliating remembrance of the first morning at my first school, when the senior mistress, having watched Tom Pinner, the dear old coachman, trying to coax me out of the family wagonette, swooped down the steps, smothered my kicks and screams,

and carried me bodily into the Grove House Academy at
Baldock. The sound of the door, as it closed behind me,
was like that of a prison cell. To my life's end my mind
would bear the marks of that harsh and domineering woman.
It was childish of me to burst into tears every Thursday
at twelve o'clock when she 'took us' in commercial geography. But the headmistress, who was said to have seen
better days, understood. It was a mercy to be able to fly
to her for sympathy. She had a warm heart for anybody,
large or small, in trouble. And once, when an elephant
went sick she took pity even on him, and lodged and boarded
him in the great barn till 'Mr. Sanger's circus' came round
on tour again. It was not every school that provided an
elephant for a playmate.

II

Then I thought of my next school, where the 'marks'
were more outward and visible. They came, most of them,
from the music master, who was one of those beasts that
music could not tame. It was monstrous that he should
bear the name of Goodfellow; it ought to have been 'Mr.
Badman.' Even in my time there had been too many of
his sort, and they must have abounded in earlier days.
Roger Ascham, whose book *The Scholemaster* (1570) we
were set to read for the beginnings of English prose, had
good cause to condemn 'crueltie in scholemasters in beating
away the love of learning from children,' and he marvels
that such little care was taken 'even emonges the verie
wise' over the selection of preceptors. Men, he complains,
would spend hours and infinite pains over the purchase of
a horse, but they had no time to seek out 'a cunnynge
[knowledgeable] man for their children,' with the deserved
result that 'God that sitteth in heaven laugheth their choice
to skorne.'

Goodfellow, as his pupils with fear and trembling played
their appointed pieces, would beat time with a ruler, and
whenever we failed to keep time the ruler would beat down
upon our wrists. If a false note were struck he would cuff
the offender over the head, often with such violence as to
sweep him off the piano-stool on to the floor. Once, in

performing Mendelssohn's *Songs without Words* (No. 19), I hit the ground six times. But I rose to the occasion and had a sweet revenge. Even as a boy I was not without words of my own, and I used them to deadly effect in drafting a petition to the headmaster for the removal of this tyrant. It was signed conspiratorially by the forty boys whose parents had paid good money to have their darlings extra-specially trained in the art and mystery of music; and then, having myself signed and sealed, I went by night to the headmaster's house and delivered it through the door.

The result was stupendous. The next morning — a Sunday notwithstanding — I was summoned to appear before the head and to bring six of my witnesses. Those I chose were stout fellows, possessed indeed of righteous indignation, but prepared to stretch a point if needful — 'such,' according to the old and likable phrase, 'as would swear suddenly and would swear anything.' Once in the study, I elaborated each and every clause of my petition, called my evidence, and, using only the black notes on the keyboard of my mind, played down the character of Mr. Goodfellow all I knew. The head looked grim, said nothing, and ushered us out. But one of our spies saw the accused reporting to the head shortly after sermon, and something must have happened. At any rate we never saw 'Mr. Badfellow' again, and he must, as we liked to imagine, have departed, *precipitato ed appassionato*, in the dark middle of that night.

In his stead, there appeared a mild little music mistress who evidently agreed with St. Anselm that, in dealing with the young, you should 'caress them into shape, not hammer them with blows.' When we neglected our practices and misplayed our sonatas she would gaze at us through her spectacles more in sorrow than in anger, and, at the worst, would inflict a mere fifty of her special task-line, which she insisted should be penned in the original Elizabethan spelling: 'They that doe so easily observ and abhor the least Discordance in Musick, shold as wel discern and detest all Discordance in Life.'

Continuing my reverie, I dragged up from deserved oblivion another master at that same school. To him had been committed the cruel task of teaching mathematics and the 'dismal science' of political economy. He was detested for his own sake and for the subjects he represented. Because of his pointed head and square, uncompromising jaw we dubbed him 'the isosceles triangle.' His bulbous nose we called the 'vulgar fraction.' One eye glared balefully at his victims. The other avoided them; it stared vacantly into space. Aware of his unpopularity, he never mixed with the boys, nor indeed with his colleagues. Like a pariah in the world of learning, he went aloof. 'Mark all Mathematicall heades which be onely and wholy bent to those sciences,' wrote the worthy and discerning Ascham, 'how solitarie they be themselves, how unfit to live with others, and how unapte to serve in the world.' But he was never so 'unapte' as when, by sarcastic comments on his pupils, he endeavoured to regain the discipline that he had lost. There is nothing that more infuriates those who cannot answer back.

Once in his class-room he went too far, and a hot-headed boy from Jamaica, taunted to the point of desperation, leapt from his desk and flung his stocky four-foot-ten against the tall and wispy six-foot-two of the master. Though the odds were uneven, and not one of the Marquess of Queensberry's rules was observed, it was a grand fight, and to witness it we had the very best seats. Alas, much of our champion's blood was spilt on the class-room floor; but he had plenty to spare, and with head bloody and bowed he kept on butting his adversary in the stomach. Early in the fray the master's desk was stormed and overturned; the ink spurted and spluttered everywhere. Collars and ties were ripped asunder. The master's gown was torn to tatters. His glasses, clawed to the ground, had been trampled underfoot. And then, *mirabile dictu*, one of his eyes fell out and rolled about the floor. So it *was* a glass eye after all, and that explained the stare!

At that precise moment, we had something else to stare at, for the door was thrown open and the head marched in. The combatants disengaged. The din of battle subsided. The fifth form rose to its feet. For a moment that seemed an eternity we waited for the heavens to fall. But the Jovian thunderbolt was suspended. It was an occasion too deep for words, and not a single word was uttered. Instead, there was a silence, a silence that could be felt.

It was supercharged with the inescapable doom of punishments to come.   Somehow a saying of Bagehot insinuated itself into my mind: 'A schoolmaster should have an atmosphere of awe and walk wonderingly, as if he was amazed at being himself.'   Our headmaster looked at us and on the littered battle-field as though he must be dreaming.   Then, with superb control, he picked up the glass eye, handed it back to the isosceles triangle, and swept out of the room.

III

For a little space of time I must have slept, even on those painful memories of long ago.   But I was waked by the sound of crying from a boy in the next bed.   He was, as I soon found, in misery over five hundred lines that had to be delivered without fail and within forty-eight hours.   Eventually I got him off to sleep by offering to write half the impot on the clear understanding that he would do the same for me when the need arose.   And then I turned to consider my own sad case with the science master who had inflicted this savage penalty, for I had been told, nay adjured, never to see his face again.

He had been very jealous, indeed vainglorious, of the new laboratory, built at a fabulous sum, and shortly to be opened by a scientist of high repute.   The great day was approaching, but, perhaps unwisely, the rooms and the gas-chambers had already been put into use.   Then, on a never-to-be-forgotten morning, I had caused an explosion that wrecked one whole side of the building, destroying a considerable amount of equipment, and sending three of my unfortunate class-mates as casualties into the school san.   By the grace of God, or by the protection of the devil, I was myself unscathed, but from the subsequent and most explosive interview with the master I did not come off so lightly.   For a time he, too, was speechless.   Then, like litmus paper turning from blue to red, he poured out the vials and test-tubes of his wrath upon me.   He would not listen to reason.   Masters never will.   Who was it said: 'Learned men learn things last of all'?   For what it was worth, I asked why I should be held responsible for the laws of nature, for the capricious concatenation of atoms and the mysterious behaviour of molecules.   I tried to wash my hands in innocency.   But I was reported to the head, and banished from the laboratory for ever.   Secretly I rejoiced, for I loathed everything to do with chemistry and physics, and it enabled me, then, and afterwards, to protest what a brilliant and promising mind had been lost to the world of science.

Unreasonable—that was the word I wanted, and nearly all the masters were that.   They demanded the impossible. They would report a boy to the head as having 'manners none, customs beastly,' and then expect him to behave like a little gentleman.   They would call him a dunce to his own face, and yet look to him to come out top at the examination.   A boy at the school, mindful of his parents and the approaching holidays, asked Mr. Hewson, who was a master before my time, to mark him up as *Excellent*, knowing that nothing less was expected of him at home.   '*Excellent!*' scoffed Mr. Hewson, 'excellent, sir, in this sinful world! I never heard such a thing.   Why, if your house dormitory was on fire, and if you were upon a ladder outside, rescuing one of the junior boys with your right hand, and with your left hand holding *Livy* and still construing, even then, sir, I hesitate to think I should award you an *Excellent*.'

Once again I tossed and turned as I thought of the unreasonable but superior being I should have to face at nine o'clock on the morrow.   Arrogant and arbitrary, of all the staff he was the most unbearable.   Compared with the others, he possessed little store of learning, but he believed himself to be infallible.   'The vanity of teaching,' as Halifax observed, 'oft tempteth a man to forget he is a Blockhead.'   Yet one was bound to admit that this giant was every inch a master.   He had that 'majesty of countenance and strength of body' that Sir William Vaughan thought essential in a teacher, 'otherwise he will be contemned and made a jestinge stock.'   Only one boy had ever ventured to be jocose in the presence of this martinet, and I doubt if he smiled again for the remainder of his life.

IV

My spirits brightened a little as I remembered that the
next class before break would be spent with my favourite
master, and as we should be construing the enthralling sixth
book of the *Aeneid* there would be no delaying tactics, nor
should I run into any kind of danger of that master's most
galling and condescending line: 'Few things are more distressing to the well-regulated mind than to see a boy who
ought to know better disporting himself at improper
moments.' After break we should be taking French, a
subject in which one was able to relax. We could always
beguile the master to retell the story of the five duels that
had scarred his otherwise handsome face, or one could
cajole him into reading a scene from Molière. Besides,
the man was a wit and could always divert routine work into
something lively. Of one of my attempts from English
into French he remarked: 'It is wooden, it is too literal, so,
what you English say, unidiomatic. It reminds me of the
Duchess of Bolton who, when gossiping to your George II
of Colley Cibber's play *Love's Last Shift*, sent His Majesty
into fits by calling it *La Dernière Chemise d'Amour.*'

There was another class in which one was able to relax
more effectively still, for the master was short-sighted and
could distinguish only the boys who sat in the first three
rows. Moreover, though he should have been teaching
Greek, he liked to spend most of the hour upon the
decipherment of Hebrew and Persian manuscripts. No
sooner was the class opened than I would tiptoe out of
the back row with another would-be truant, descend the
stairs, play a game of fives, and return just in time to show
up as the master blinked his way out of the room. When
Uppingham's famous head (Thring) was being pressed by a
fond mother for an interim report on her young hopeful's
classical studies, he replied with tactful ambiguity: 'There
never *was* such a Latin scholar.' Something of the sort
would have to be said about our Greek. But meanwhile
there was a 'marked improvement' in our fives.

Yes: one should be fair, there were private alleviations in
the hard lot of a public school boy. Out of school, some of
the masters were surprisingly decent. I turned to thinking

of another classical master, more recently appointed. With him [1] I had started badly, for the first five words that I spoke to him cost me five hundred lines. He looked up at my innocent, rather too innocent, face and endeavoured to construe it, but somehow he could not credit that it was by a mere slip of the tongue that I had addressed him as 'Mr. Bally-garnet.' My protestations were in vain. All the scant leisure of three days, and some hours in bed, went to the writing of those bally lines. But I was hardened to it. Had I not spent a sad proportion of my school-days scribbling undeserved lines? As a budding writer was I not enabled to boast: *Nulla dies sine linea*? So, shortly before lights out on the third day, I had pulled on a dressing-gown, made my way along the passage to the new master's bedroom, and rapped upon the door. There being no response, I rapped again and again, and then, in desperation and remembering that the lines were overdue, I opened the door and deposited the ignoble five hundred on the dressing-table. Two days later at breakfast, Mr. Balgarnie amazed me by asking, hotly and loudly, why I had not delivered the lines. I replied, no less hotly and loudly, that I had. He did not believe me. He said so in set terms. 'But I can prove it,' I said, and within five minutes I had rounded up and produced four witnesses who for filthy lucre had assisted me in the writing of the lines, and had actually seen them in my hands as I made my way to the complainant's bedroom. The evidence was overwhelming; and the master (great was my triumph!) made me a handsome apology vindicating my character in the presence of the assembled school.

v

An inauspicious beginning, but from that moment our relations had improved. He was, I found, one of the few who knew how to bridge the horrid gulf betwixt pedagogue and pupil, and how to turn a suspicious boy into a steady friend. He lent me plays and belles-lettres to get the distaste of school books out of my brain. On a half-holiday he invited me to bicycle with him to Thaxted and there

[1] He was afterwards made famous by an old boy (James Hilton) as *Our Mr. Chips.*

behold the finest parish church in England. He encouraged me in the founding of a literary and debating society. How consoling he had been about the failure of the first lecture I had given! What moved me to choose the dismal subject of 'The Black Death' (1349) I do not know, but I devoted considerable research to the preparation of my paper, and was anticipating a huge success. But the sheer pitifulness of it played havoc with my meagre audience. You do not expect brute boys to be moved, certainly not to shed tears. But they blew their noses, and dried their eyes, and fidgeted as if in torment as I piled horror upon horror. Then, finding it unbearable, they began, one after another, to melt away, and at last, glancing up from my manuscript, I discovered that I was alone.

It was a strange predicament but, having taken all those pains, I was not going to let the mere lack of an audience break up my lecture. I continued to the bitter and lonely end. Then, leaving the dais, I walked to the back of the room, assumed the voice of the secretary of our select society, and proposed, seconded, and carried a vote of thanks to Reginald Hine for a discourse of great historical value, and hoped that when he delivered his next lecture on 'The Plague of 1665' the audience might prove more attentive.

Suddenly, hearing a chuckle behind me, I turned about and, to my consternation, saw my housemaster in the doorway, his eyes lit up with amusement. Then, in mocking words that I ought to have recognized, he quoted: 'Hail, seven pupils of Aristides the Rhetorician—four walls and three benches.' But I fancy he saw how far my face had fallen, for he linked his arm with mine, picked up my lecture, and took me off to his room. There, he restored me with coffee as black as my Black Death, and together we read the pages of Mackail's *Select Epigrams from the Greek Anthology*, and all the little that is recorded about poor Aristides.

Other alleviations there were. As I lay awake through that interminable night I recalled the speech days of my time, when the masters, spruced up for the occasion, would speak comfortable words to our parents about the progress we were making. Afterwards, in the great hall, we would listen spellbound, to some man of wide renown—Arthur

James Balfour, Dr. Butler of Trinity, Choate, the American ambassador—and see with our own eyes, and hear with our own ears, what knowledge, gathered at school and in the school of life—the thing called education—could do at its very best.

Then there was that speechless day of the Great Lock-out when, in defiance of a new head who had disallowed our time-honoured custom of a holiday on Queen Victoria's birthday, we assembled, early in the morning, outside his private house, summoned him from sleep by sing-songing his ridiculous biblical names, and dared him to come down and do his worst. It had been huge fun cutting the rope of the school bell. More fun assaulting and beating the prefect sent to parley with us rebels. Not such fun over-mastering a master who tried to intimidate us when our blood was up. But our triumph came when the head, losing his head, had called in the mounted police. Having had wind of their approach, we had mustered on the playing-fields with lacrosse rackets and ball ammunition at the ready, and as soon as the constabulary charged we let fly at the flanks of the horses, broke up their formation, and drove them in mad terror out of the grounds of the school.

Yes, that was still sweet in the memory, and one had to forget the cruel and ignominious tactics by which we had been starved into submission—the weakest part of a school-boy is his belly—and the subsequent floggings and expulsions. Perhaps it would have been better for me if I had finished my education then. But it would not be long now; and to-morrow I would write to my father to say that schoolmastering was no good. He could push me into anything else he cared.

VI

At last the great day came. Released from the power and dominion of the masters, I would prove the truth of St. Augustine's words: 'A free curiosity has more efficacy in learning than a frightful enforcement.' But after a decade *in statu pupillari* it is not easy to escape. The habit of docility is strong. Years after I left school, letters would come inquiring of my advancement in life. How much

honour had I brought to my *alma mater*? The senior
bursar who edited the Old Boys' Directory reminded me
of my brother's distinctions and demanded to know what I
myself had done worthy of lasting record. I tore up the
form and replied on a post card: 'Married Florence Lee
Pyman, 1912.' Then, sending me another huge form, he
persisted, had I really done nothing else? 'Yes,' I retorted,
'a daughter Felicity born 1915.' After which he left me
alone. But letters from other masters made me feel that
I must have misjudged them. They seemed genuinely concerned lest the rushlight of learning they had kindled in
me should be quenched in the cold blast of the outer world.
They encouraged me in my extra - mural studies. They
offered to look over the manuscripts of my books. 'The
profit and growth of scholars,' as one of them reminded
me, 'is the praise and glory of their preceptors.' If St.
Jerome really said that, it must be true.

Then, as though I was fated never to escape, I was
appointed local solicitor to the National Union of Teachers.
It meant that I had to be seeing more and more of them,
and after each interview I was pharisaically minded to stand
up and pray: 'Lord, I thank Thee that I am not as other
men are, or even as this schoolmaster.' Theirs is 'a
troublesome and toilsome life,' said Richard Mulcaster,
'a moiling and drudging life,' echoed John Brinsley; and
those old masters of the craft should know. Once, I encountered close on a thousand in conference at Oxford, and
never in my life had I beheld a more dejected, disillusioned,
hang-dog set of men. When I spoke enviously of their
long vacations, 'It takes many a week,' they answered, 'to
recover from the miseries of term.' Letters they would
bring me from doting and cockering mothers, demanding
that the curriculum should be altered to suit the convenience
of their precious lambs; outbursts from indignant fathers
complaining of 'grossly unfair reports,' followed not seldom
by actual assault and battery on the headmaster. 'Parents
are the last people,' surely the saying was justified, 'parents
are the last people who ought to have children.'

But, more than anything, it appeared to be the sheer
stupidity and unteachableness of the brute boy and the
simpering girl that was wearing these masters down. 'A
good method of learning,' said Erasmus, 'is to study; a

better to listen; the best to teach.' That is all very well if you can be allowed to teach the best things. But children are taken away just when they begin to be interested. In its lowest stages elementary education can only be described as a casting of artificial pearls before real swine. In the middle stages the young acquire a mass of facts that clog and stupefy the brain. How few are taken by the hand and led forward into the true love of learning!

Often would masters say to me: 'If we cannot give children a good education it is better they should have none.' It was a pity, they argued, to take away the horse-sense, and the racy shrewdness, of country folk unless you could substitute something more effective in its place. For years I served as manager and governor of elementary and secondary schools, and was always wondering whether the loss of sound Hertfordshire speech and native ways of thinking was compensated by the poor smattering of English that we superimposed upon our scholars: 'Well,' said a fine old rustic, 'well, I likes eddicated people, but the wust on't is they be so dommed ignorant.'

VII

To keep up their spirits, schoolmasters welcome any gleam of humour that comes their way, and even when they have no legal business to transact they will climb my stairs to offer their latest 'howler' for my jest-book. It was pleasant to hear of one budding Latinist who took *tertium quid* to be a legal term signifying six shillings and eight-pence, and of another who rendered *bella intestina Catilinae* as 'the beautiful intestines of Catiline.' A Shakespearean critic in a grammar school whose history I compiled, opined that 'no one has yet succeeded in *edifying* [*sic*] the dark lady of the sonnets'; and Smith minor, in an essay on the age of Queen Anne, laid it down that 'the Duke of Marlborough was a great general. He always fought with the fixed determination to win or lose.'

In a country town there is a lively give-and-take of stories of this kind—some genuine, many I fancy manufactured. I remember a schoolmaster coming in to borrow a copy of my *Medieval Church Graffiti*, and as I handed this over, he remarked: 'Did you ever hear of the modern *graffito* scribbled in French on the stone base of the Pyramids:

La vie est un désert.

And, below, had been written in another hand:

Et la femme le chameau.'

I thanked him for this pretty piece of wit, and offered in exchange the story that Lady Carbery had just sent me of her son aged six. It seems that this infant prodigy had, for his own amusement and instruction, made a book of prehistoric and fabulous animals, and one day when a bishop came to lunch the lad rushed up to him and asked in a breathless, excited voice: 'If you had lived long ago should you have been a pterodactyl or a saurian?' Out of the mouth of babes!

Schoolmasters never die. They appear to come to an early end. In the way of the flesh they do not make old bones. So irascible becomes their temper in a profession so tormenting that they finish up with a stroke. But in the memory of their pupils they live on in the imperative mood. Upon the townships where they taught they make an indelible mark. Often, as I perambulate my little parish, I pause by their dwellings and think of them. There is the fat, vulgar-looking woman in the churchyard who used to wield a long stick with which she could correct and chastise the most remote of her pupils, a stick at other times employed to poke the sparrows' nests from under the eaves. In Tilehouse Street I pass what was, aforetime, the academy of the Rev. Mr. Dyer, an old-fashioned pedagogue who stands out sharp and clear in the diary of William Lucas: 'He never relaxed his dignity before the boys, but sat, cane in hand, wearing a black hat, and white cotton gloves, the fingers of which were always twice too long. He was truly a man of few words but many blows. "I should not be doing my duty to your parents," he would say in a preliminary harangue, "hold out your hand you infamous brat." . . . He never mixed with the boys in play hours and dined alone in a small room, always finishing off with his black bottle of port, the rays of which blazed from his countenance in the afternoon.'

JACOBEAN MASTER AND PUPIL
From a painting by J. W. Stap

DR. NIBLOCK
From a drawing by Samuel Lucas

VIII

A few paces further up Tilehouse Street I am wont, each day, to go by the Old Free School, and often I smile as I recall the schoolmasters of that Jacobean foundation whom I dealt with in the *History of Hitchin Grammar School*. Pale and wan are they now in retrospect like the ink of the exercise books of their period that I examined. But the solid, stocky, pert and peppery, red-faced and red-waistcoated figure of the Rev. Dr. Joseph Niblock, Doctor of Divinity, is still a substantial ghost. I watch him through his window at work on the Greek grammar that was to be used for so many years at Eton, and if I happen to be there about three o'clock he is coming out in his chaise, with two donkeys driven tandem, flourishing his cocked hat at the parents of his boys, and off to visit William Wilshere, the senior trustee. Once it concerned a matter of some gravity, for one of his boys, the grandson of Sir Thomas Miller, the president of the Court of Session in Scotland, by a blow on the nose, had killed the son of Colonel Lousada. It needed all Wilshere's acumen to justify or slur over that homicide. But the weekly visits were mainly concerned with the curriculum, over which the learned and self-opinionated doctor was at variance with the trustees. Wilshere, as a lawyer and a trimmer, was all for the golden mean, that judicious mixture of utility and luxury which he would amusingly exemplify by sending the master a basket of strawberries and cauliflowers every summer from his Bancroft garden.

Sometimes, there flits by me the pallid spectre of John Sugars, Niblock's most promising pupil, a man of brilliant parts and strikingly handsome appearance who also became master of that school. But a hopeless love affair broke his heart and snapped the mainspring of his ambition. Under him the school went on dwindling and decaying, until its doors were closed and the prematurely old master sank into private life. Now at long last, 'equilibrious in adversitie,' he could bury himself in his books, with no disturbing clangour of the school-house bell. Often, they said, he would sit up talking with his old scholars, John Gatward or John Widdows, until the stars paled at the first flush of

Q

dawn. Once, as he stood on Widdows's doorstep, saying a
last good-bye, the birds were already in song. 'Do you
like to hear them sing?' he asked his friend, 'I hate it.' It
was that sad utterance that echoed in Francis Lucas's
memory when he sat down some months later to write his
touching elegy for 'J. S., a disappointed scholar':

> Sing on, brave bird. He cannot chide thee now
> For adding night to sadness. In the deeps
> Of an unfathomable quiet sleeps
> The spirit which once mantled on that brow,
> And spoke in those sad eyes. Nor ever creeps
> Into his sweet forgetfulness the gall
> Of disappointment, slights and unsuccess,
> Nor the despondency at matin call
> When needs still multiplied as means grew less.
> Well, there were hours which even he could bless,
> Oddments of time which found him at his ease,
> By the loved stream or in the cool recess
> Under the shadow of his garden trees,
> With Goethe, Molière, or Sophocles.

And last of all would I call up the shade of William John
Fitch, a frail but indomitable man who lingered to my time.
In a foundation of the same William Wilshere at Hitchin
he taught not merely the elementary teaching of an elementary school, but the love of God and the fear of W. J.
Fitch. Like Niblock he, too, was constantly in conflict
with the managers and with the Board of Education. He
would not agree that 'the luxury of English literature is not
permitted in the elementary schools'; and in this he was
upheld by Matthew Arnold, who visited the Wilshere Dacre
school as H.M.I. from 1867 to 1870. It was pleasant to hear
Fitch talk about his conversations with the poet, and still
more pleasant it is for me to possess the letters written by
Arnold to his hosts the Thompsons, of whom John the
father and Lawson the son served ninety-two years in
succession as secretaries to the school.

Fitch ruled his scholars with a rod of iron; or to be exact
with a nut-hazel stick. He might be frail, but there was
strength and to spare for 'the flat transgression of a schoolboy,' and his 'right hand taught them terrible things.' But
he was, for all that, a godly man. Not once had he opened
school without declaring how and whence he was able to

teach them 'as one having authority.' Whatever the Board might say, his ultimate authority was derived from Holy Writ, from which, each and every morning, he read to his boys, having first reverently removed the top-hat, which, by the custom of schoolmastering at that day, he wore constantly in class. And sometimes, of a Friday, he would dismiss school with a prayer that I pointed out to him in the pages of the pious Ascham: 'God keep us in His fear. God graft in us the knowledge of His word, with a forward will to follow it, and so to bring forth the sweet fruits of it; and then shall He prevent us by His grace from all manner of terrible days.'

PARSONS I HAVE KNOWN

In the multitude of counsellors there is safety.

PROVERBS, xi. 14.

I

NE afternoon, in the spring of 1928, a client brought in the first volume of the *History of Hitchin* to be autographed, and as I engrossed my name in Higgins's eternal ink he remarked: 'I 've read the prodigiously long chapter you 've written on St. Mary's, and can't make out whether you are a High Churchman or a Low Churchman or no churchman at all.'

'That 's just as it should be,' I rejoined as I handed back the book, 'and if later on you will do me the honour to read what I have written of the Baptists, Congregationalists, and Quakers I hope you 'll be even more puzzled where to place me.'

All my life I have liked to consort with men of religion, whatever their denominations may chance to be, and the more freely to walk and talk and worship with them I have thought it best to be a friend of all churches and a member of none. In this baffling world the truth would seem to be dispersed, here a little, there a little, and the wise man will go on seeking it wherever it may be found. Some of my findings as a peripatetic will be set down in the following chapter, 'Touching upon Religion'; here with a lighter pen I would run over some of the happy and whimsical associations I have enjoyed with all sorts and conditions of parsons, ministers, pastors, and lay preachers.

When I was a mere slip of a boy, my brother Evelyn and I were placed under the tutorship of the Rev. George Todd, vicar of Newnham. It was a pleasant existence. If we were bored or feeling overtaught, we had but to open the window of the vicar's study when he was out of the room, and bolt across two meadows to our home. Often, in a fit of temper over our truancies, our pedagogue would expel us on the Friday, only to receive us back with open arms of a Monday. We knew that the fees were a useful addition to his stipend. Each morning our lessons would open with the collect for the day, followed by two or three specially written prayers pointedly phrased against refractory pupils. To show how little we cared, we would accompany them with tunes on catgut of varying lengths stretched between tin-tacks under the leaf of the table.

On Tuesday, the day appointed for English composition, we would be set to write a sermon, and as a working model Mr. Todd would occasionally read one from those famous divines Archbishop Tillotson and Isaac Barrow. Our own masterpieces would be corrected on Thursday, and if either of them was thought to be promising it would be adopted by the vicar as his own, added to slightly, and delivered on the Sunday. It was thrilling to sit in the Newnham Hall family pew and listen to his reverence spouting our sermons to the villagers down in the nave; but it was mortifying that even our inspired passages made little or no impression on the private lives of the people. Sometimes, it is true, the vicar would preach sermons of his own composing; to us they appeared comparatively poor. Every word would be taken down in shorthand by the gentleman farmer, Wickham Inskip, who sat opposite to us in the chancel, and at the conclusion of the service Inskip would go up to the vicar and in a gruff voice would say something like this: 'Humph, humph, only fifteen weeks, Mr. Todd, only fifteen weeks since we had that sermon before.'

In literary taste, as in discipline of life, our master was something of a puritan. He judged all poetry from the private lives of the poets. He imagined all plays to be as vicious as Wycherley's. Again and again we begged to be allowed to read through Shakespeare's comedies with him —even in a bowdlerized edition—but were denied. At last we took our revenge. There came a Saturday when my father and our music mistress and housekeeper left home very early in the morning. Suddenly we children were left to our own devices. There had been an implied covenant for good behaviour, but our standards never had been high. We took counsel together. What could we do to make a day of it? Someone whispered 'London.' It was a provokingly hopeless suggestion. We turned out our pockets and sighed; only four shillings and sixpence in all. Then, by the instigation of the devil, my eye lit upon the British and Foreign Bible Society money-box that was due to go back to Mr. Todd the following week. Dare we? Could we? Should we? For a moment we hesitated, but, when I lifted the box from its shelf and found how heavy it was, we succumbed to the temptation. In the twinkling of an eye we had prised it open, and to our deep satisfaction the collections for the year amounted to forty-nine shillings and twopence. It was just what we needed.

Stolen fruits and stolen holidays are sweetest. In the palatial Popular Café of Messrs. Lyons we ate, drank, and were merry. We plundered sweet-shops and toy-shops. Holding one another's hands, we inspected the Chamber of Horrors at Madame Tussaud's. And, best of all, in the afternoon we sat on plush seats in Her Majesty's and saw the great Beerbohm Tree in a play that was called *False Gods*.[1]

II

My gentle mother (God rest her soul) was an Anglican, my father a Methodist. We children found it convenient to halt betwixt the two opinions. Often on Sunday evenings, however, we would attend the little chapel that my great-grandfather had built, and listen spellbound not to sermons, but to homely, village addresses from local preachers as rough and untutored as our blessed Saviour's disciples and apostles. How many elegant discourses from Doctors of Divinity, bishops, and archbishops have gone over my head! But the simple words of John Wesley's men have a way of abiding in the heart.

More lettered than the others was James Brown of Baldock, postmaster and solicitor's managing clerk. We liked him to come because he was a friend of our family, and we looked for some sport from the collie dog that he used to take with him into the pulpit. After years of listening, this intelligent animal had, in our fancy, become a

---

[1] Taking the chair for the British and Foreign Bible Society at Hitchin forty years later I made public confession of this crime. Whilst I spoke, I noticed that the treasurer was deep in some calculations. When his turn came to speak he told the meeting exactly how much I owed the society with compound interest at five per cent, and demanded that I should hand over a cheque. He little knew to what straits we had been reduced to make good our defalcation.

keen student of theology and would worry at a sermon just as he would worry at a bone. But he was not very obedient. If he disagreed with any doctrine put forward by his master, he would give out a warning growl. Then, if more 'acceptable words' were not used, he would begin to bark, softly at first in the hope that the master would forsake his unmethodistical ways, and then, if that failed, he would bark loud and long. The preacher was no less determined. He would raise his voice tenfold in an attempt to drown that of his dog. To our huge amusement the discordant duet would continue, until poor Mr. Brown, crimson with rage, would fling open the pulpit door, seize the brawler by the collar, drag him along, barking and protesting to the last, and cast him forth out of the congregation. Then, mopping his brow with a red bandanna handkerchief, and gulping down a glass of water, he would remount the stairs, and gather up the scattered threads of his discourse.

Sometimes I would drive my father to meetings of an educational charity held at Norton, three miles away, and catch sight of the already venerable figure of the Rev. George Pierson who, before he died, was vicar of that parish for eight-and-sixty years. Often I wonder if that is not a record.[1] When he was appointed to the living it was hard to see how he could make a living out of it, but somehow he managed to be 'passing rich' on sixty-five pounds a year, and reared a family and drove a pony trap. It was said that the farmers were resolved that their parson should not starve, and took him in turn for a midday meal all the seven days of the week.

If this parson was as poor as a church mouse, there was a parishioner, born in a caravan in Green Lane, Norton, who had been as poor as a Methodist mouse, which is twice as poor. But he became possessed of 'the unsearchable riches of Christ.' The vicar, at the risk of his life, had visited the mother when she lay dying of smallpox, and had given her

---

[1] When this book was in the printers' hands I discovered that Pierson was not, by any means, the record holder. The living of Brent Pelham in my own county was held by Raphael Keene for seventy-five years and six months, from 1539 to 1614. 'During ye time of his remarkable long vicarship,' my authority continues, 'there were two churchwardens almost as remarkable, being fifty-five years in that office.'—Add. MSS. (B.M.), 5806, fol. 25. But even Keene must give place to Richard Newton, who was rector of Little Munden, also in Herts, upwards of eighty years, from 23rd August 1558 to 22nd December 1639.

Christian burial in his churchyard. He was to live on and see her son famous as an evangelist under the name of Gypsy Smith. Many a time have I heard this revivalist terrifying sinners into repentance by the sheer power of the word, and preaching the glad tidings of salvation. He did not rant. Neither from heaven nor from hell did he call down fire. Yet as in Whitefield's and Wesley's day some would fall senseless to the ground foaming at the mouth. Others would cry aloud as though possessed and tormented of devils. Waves of emotion would break over the heads of the assembled congregation, and suddenly the multitude, overcome by the homely appeal of this gypsy, would leap to its feet testifying and praising God.

III

How unaccountable people are! Here was a poor man, unskilled in the craft of words, yet able to sway the hearts and minds of thousands; whereas in the spacious rectory of Letchworth, two miles away from Norton, there lived the Rev. Richard Walls, a well-to-do scholar, yet so timid that he could not look his rustic congregation of fifty souls in the face. His eyes, whenever he preached to them, would be raised to a cross-beam in the centre of the roof, and there remain until his short sermon, spoken from memory, was ended. Then he would slink back into his study. The coming of the First Garden City, for the founding of which the parishes of Norton, Letchworth, and Willian were purchased in 1903, was to him a catastrophe. If he could not face fifty farm labourers, how should he minister to a long-haired, sandal-shod, outlandishly attired crowd of eccentric citizens, each of whom had his own panacea for a sick civilization, and desired by his own methods to build a new heaven upon earth? No, it would kill him. It did kill him. They came; he saw; he was conquered. To say that he departed this present life would be an overstatement. With a gesture of disdain, he shuffled off this mortal coil, and slipped away, satisfied on earth to be no more seen.

A very different kind of man was the Rev. and Hon. L. W. Denman, rector of Willian. When he preached to his people he looked them straight in the face. Like a good shepherd he counted his flock in the morning and again at

THE REV. AND HON. L. W. DENMAN AND HIS SISTERS

From a photograph by T. B. Latchmore

CANON LEWIS HENSLEY
From a photograph by H. G. Moulden

night. A mental note was taken during sermon of such
as were missing. To Denman it seemed incredible that
any one should not be eager to come to church. As those
who were absent muſt, he assumed, be ill, he used to call
on the Monday and offer sympathy and help. It was surprising the number of sudden indispositions in the village.

In many other ways the reĉtor was a martinet. If a girl
passed him and failed to curtsey, both she and her mother
would hear of it. When Walls offered to assiſt him at a
special service and arrived a few seconds after time, he was
refused admission to the chancel. 'You are late,' growled
Denman, 'you can sit in the nave.' When one of the young
men got a maid into trouble, Denman booked his passage
to Canada, thrashed him on the reĉtory lawn, and invited
the whole village to witness the ceremony.

Himself a Cambridge rowing blue, Denman remained an
enthusiaſt all his days. Borrowing a chair and a ſtick, he
would demonſtrate the art on every possible occasion, rowing round and round a room, often to the detriment of other
pieces of furniture. On the Sunday before the classic
event he would preach a special boat-race sermon. The
congregation came to know it by heart. As Walls was an
Oxford man the two would not be on speaking terms for a
fortnight before the race. They had a silent ſtanding bet,
however, and if Denman won he would be quick to colleĉt
his money the same day. On my shelves (once his shelves,
for I am writing this book in Denman's old reĉtory, now
my home and reſtyled the Bury) I have several of his books,
and in one of them, a Greek lexicon, the margins are
crammed with drawings of college eights.

Toward the close of his days the reĉtor's memory began
to fail. On one occasion he called at the shop of Bradly
Gatward, the Hitchin jeweller and speĉtacle-maker, to buy
a new pince-nez. Adjuſting one that was offered him on
to his large Roman nose, he said: 'This isn't quite to my
liking; show me another.' Gatward did so, and Denman,
forgetting to take off the firſt, placed the other in front. 'I
can't see quite so well with this,' he remarked, 'show me
some more.' To Gatward's amusement, he fitted five
pairs of pince-nez on to his huge nose before he discovered
the miſtake.

Not so amusing was Denman's habit of finishing a sermon

and then beginning it all over again. This grew on him in the last months of his life. He seemed unable to stop. The congregation, having suffered grievously, put their heads together and, agreeing to follow the cue of the people's warden, they used to stand up suddenly and scrape their hob-nailed boots on the floor of the nave when the sermon appeared to be ending, and then the rector would take the hint and hurriedly pronounce the ascription.

IV

Much to my sorrow I was taken away from the Rev. George Todd, under whom I was beginning to learn much to my liking, sent to Kent College, Canterbury, and made to study such unnatural subjects as algebra and trigonometry. But there were alleviations and there were possibilities of escape. There was an orchard and market garden near by. In summer you could walk in, pay a shilling, stay as long as you liked, and eat as much as you could hold. It was an earthly paradise.

It was also allowed to visit the then famous animal painter, Thomas Sidney Cooper, R.A., who lived at Harbledown. Though he was deep in his nineties, he had a bright welcome for schoolboys, and would talk, as though it were yesterday, of the April morning in 1812 when, as he sat making a sketch of the cathedral on his slate, he was observed by the great George Cattermole who, by way of encouragement, provided him with the first pencils and paper that he used. Cooper never forgot, and, in his turn, he liked to encourage boys.

Above all, there was Canterbury itself—a place of sanctuary when school life in general and bullies in particular were unendurable. Literally one had to flee there, for the town was out of bounds. But it made it all the more exciting to dodge the masters and the prefects, and explore the fascinating narrow streets and the antiquity shops, knowing well that, if caught, one would be 'gated for the term.'

One afternoon I was about to lay out a month's pocket-money in the purchase of a bronze piece of Valentinian when a gentleman in clerical attire, and I noticed he wore gaiters, took the coin out of my hands, examined it, and handed it back to the dealer. 'You shouldn't deceive mere schoolboys,' he said sternly, 'you must know perfectly well that that coin is not genuine.' With that he recovered the money I had paid and drew me out of the shop.

'Would you like to be taken round?' he asked, pointing to the cathedral. 'Oh, please,' I said, leaping at the offer; 'I did go over only last week, but the party was too big. I saw little and heard less, and the guide was in such a hurry.'

'This time it shall be different,' he assured me. And then for nearly an hour I was personally conducted by this good man, who evidently knew and loved every stone of the hallowed building. It puzzled me that he possessed keys and was able to unlock and show me parts of the cathedral not open to the public. Indeed, he walked about as if he were at home. Then, passing out of the cathedral, he led me into an ancient house where he seemed even more at home. Suddenly it flashed on me. I was in the deanery, and this was Dean Farrar, the author of *Eric, or Little by Little*.

It was certainly a genuine tea that followed. He remembered—had he not been housemaster at Harrow?—the ravenous appetite of growing boys. Afterwards I inspected his coins, and—to make up for my disappointment—he gave me a genuine Valentinian. 'I shall write to your headmaster,' he said at parting. 'You needn't look frightened. He won't punish you. And I don't think he'll refuse my request that small parties of your schoolmates should come to tea with me two or three times a term.'

I was jealous when the others went. Had it not been for me they might never have gone at all. Twice, however, the dean took me to the simple Huguenot service in the crypt; once he honoured me with a special invitation to hear Benson preach. It was a sermon not to be forgotten, for the archbishop, without taking a text, spoke eloquently of the cathedral itself, and what it had meant to England and to the Christian faith. In the dim candlelight of the choir one was hardly aware of the congregation. The vast building, starting to life at the preacher's words, seemed rather to be filled with the listening spirits of the past. His one voice—soaring, searching, penetrating—called up their multitudinous voices. The graves were opened. Master-masons, martyrs, monarchs, statesmen, churchmen, scholars, all came forth. To every claim he made as an ecclesiastic there was a cloud of witnesses, with a whispered *Amen* from the common people buried in the nave. Above, in their storied windows, stood the saints in golden vesture arrayed, and on every hand, carved and sculptured in wood and stone, there hovered a host of angels.

In a few months (16th October 1896) I was there again, for the archbishop himself had died suddenly in Hawarden church one Sunday morning just as the absolution was pronounced, and for the first time since 1598 an archbishop of Canterbury was laid to rest in his own cathedral. Never shall I forget the vast concourse of princes of the realm, spiritual and temporal peers, and the mighty men of London, but the most touching tributes came from the simple folk of Canterbury whose eyes filled with tears as they remembered not the Primate of all England but the intimate friend they had lost.

V

In the Christmas holidays we were accustomed to spend a week in London. Here I must not dwell on things secular or speak of Dan Leno and Herbert Campbell at Drury Lane, of Sir Henry Irving at the Lyceum, of Maskelyne and Cooke in the Egyptian Hall of Magic. But even on Sundays, when the streets had lost their animation and shops and music halls were shut, there were exciting things to do. We went the round of fashionable churches. We listened spellbound to select preachers in Westminster Abbey and St. Paul's. We responded to the magnetic power of Campbell Morgan, Dr. Clifford, Father Bernard Vaughan, Sylvester Horne, and Hugh Price Hughes. Often we repaired to the City Temple, for there was a theatricality about the preaching of the Rev. Joseph Parker that never failed to please. Besides, there was the hope that he might repeat his famous performance, and demonstrate how slippery was the descent to hell by sliding down the rail of the pulpit stairs.[1]

In this short life we must crowd in all we can, and in

[1] One would like to know the truth about this performance. Attributed first of all to Spurgeon, it was subsequently transferred to Parker and then to Peter Mackenzie, and ultimately thought to be apocryphal.

after years, whenever I chanced to be in London of a Sunday, I would spend the day of rest going restlessly here, there, and everywhere. Attending ten o'clock matins at the abbey, I would come out early, walk up Victoria Street and listen to the Rev. R. J. Campbell at Christ Church, leaving in time for the twelve o'clock sermon in Westminster Cathedral. In the afternoon I would circulate with the crowd in Hyde Park and drink in or dispute the teaching of Millenarians, Christadelphians, Rationalists, Republicans, Anarchists, Communists, and all the other religious, irreligious, and political, social, and anti-social enthusiasms that pitch their stands, or raise their separate Towers of Babel, in that place. In the evening I liked to sit under the Rev. W. E. Orchard at King's Weigh House, or renew my youth and cast off my bodily and mental infirmities by consorting with the Christian Scientists. And so to bed, a little dazed perhaps, but hopeful that something of lasting value would sink in.

In my own parish, too, I would go the round of churches and chapels and meeting-houses, but best of all I liked to sit close to the tower or up in the ringers' gallery of St. Mary's, and at evensong hear the far-off voice of Canon Lewis Hensley blending with the under - voices of the building. So old was he—vicar already for close on fifty years—that he seemed to belong to the fabric of the church. Looking upon his bowed and time-worn figure, and his deeply furrowed face with its wrinkle for each century, you would have taken him for a pre-Reformation priest. You expected him to speak in Latin. Under his moth-eaten skull-cap was stored a wealth of medieval and ecclesiastical lore: the writings of the Fathers, the findings of synods and church councils, episcopal injunctions, visitation charges, the practical wisdom of archdeacons. It was not his way to prepare attractive addresses, garnished with up-to-date quotations, to please a congregation. His duty was to instruct his people in the faith, and he could do so with more authority because, towards the end, he was teaching —line upon line, precept upon precept—the grandchildren of those he had originally baptized.

When this grandfather - in - God was gathered to the Fathers, my principal, who had been appointed a lay reader, purchased three hundred of his sermons. But they were too deep for me, nor could they serve as models for the numerous addresses that William Onslow Times, my master, had to give. It was a pity, for it meant that he was driven to prepare his own. Often, at midnight, when at last we had finished with the law, he would rehearse two or three speeches to be delivered on the morrow, and sketch out his sermons for the following Sunday. It was the privilege, or at any rate the duty, of an articled clerk to listen, to criticize, to provide embellishing touches out of a more general reading; and in this way my early training as a sermon-maker under the Rev. George Todd came in useful.

How different a man was Canon Herbert Edward Jones who succeeded Hensley! His sermons were just straight talks, short and to the point. They went home. Much as he loved books he was rarely in his study. Visiting, visiting, visiting at all hours of day and night, he knew the private sorrows and the problems of each man, woman, and child in his large parish, and was not only priest but guide, counsellor, and friend. Was there another parson in England who had a Bible class of a thousand men? And there would have been many more had he not been made suffragan Bishop of Lewes. There, too, he became known for his power over men, and his knowledge of worldly as well as spiritual affairs. Many a time have I sat in the bishop's library after dinner as he wrestled with cases of business morality, or arbitrated in family disputes; and it was good to see anxious faces clearing and heavy hearts unburthened.

One golden September morning we stood together on the Downs and surveyed the Chichester diocese. Nor shall I soon forget the stories he had to tell of the rectors, vicars, and curates whose churches we could see. There were some oddities amongst them. But then he favoured odd people. Most of all he delighted in a parson down in the vale, who had a taste for fancy dress and would appear each day of the week, save Sundays, in the costume of a different period. The people smiled at his eccentricity, but they did not smile at the beginning of one Lent when, assembling his flock, he announced that in that season of abstention he had decided, for once, to abstain from any kind of service. For his own part he was off to Rome for a month and he intended to take the church key with him. The faithful were furious. They raised heaven and earth, and incidentally

the bishop. But Jones refused to intervene. Here was a
man of character and, besides, it takes all sorts of parsons,
as he said, to make a diocese.

VI

In his unregenerate, unepiscopal days Jones used to
delight in another eccentric vicar, the Rev. R. C. Fillingham
of Hexton near Hitchin. This man also had a passion for
dressing up, and much to the displeasure of the Bishop of
St. Albans he would appear in church vested in the richly
coloured robes of a Buddhist priest that by fair means or
foul he had acquired from a temple in Japan. He dis-
pleased the bishop still further by preaching, without
licence, in Nonconformist chapels, and by displaying red-
hot radical posters and cartoons in his own church. Twice
I cycled over to hear him preach or rather fulminate, but,
alas, I was not there on the celebrated occasion when he
wound up a sermon on the parable of the rich man with
these words: 'And now, brethren, I have endeavoured to
show how difficult it is for rich men to enter the kingdom,
but there is one class for whom it is altogether impossible;
I refer, of course, to the bishops. And now to God the
Father, God the Son,' etc.

With the only rich man of his parish Fillingham was
instinctively at feud, but it became serious when the squire
obstructed a path that, from time immemorial, had led
to St. Faith's church. On the following Sunday the
sinner was rebuked from the pulpit. In spite of that, the
squire still came to church, but to affront the vicar he would
leave by the chancel door immediately before the sermon.
This was endured for three Sundays, and then Fillingham
instructed his clerk to creep out of church during the singing
of the Te Deum and lock the chancel door. The plot
worked to perfection. As usual, the squire waited for
the hymn before the sermon, and then, marshalling their
haughty little highnesses his daughters, he led the procession
eastward from the faculty pew. But this time it was his
path that was obstructed. Again and again he tugged at
the door. But it would not open, not even for the lord of
the manor of Hexton. At last he discovered what had

happened. Crimson with rage and mortification, he re-marshalled the procession—their shamefaced little lowli-nesses—and hurried them westward, between the two ranks of a tittering congregation, out of a church whose door they would never dare to darken again.

In a mild form I, too, have been preached against in my time. After my marriage in 1912 my wife and I lived for five years in the lovely village of Ashwell, and not very regularly (that was the trouble) we would worship in its wonderful church. The rector bore the name of the Rev. Panajotti Webb, and he, too, was something of an eccentric. He would so choose his text and manipulate his sermon as to illustrate the besetting sins of leading members of his congregation. There was no need for him to name those against whom his words were pointed. We almost cheered as the shafts went home. In those days the nave pews were occupied in descending degrees of social importance. It was right therefore that the squire or his lady should be shown up first. Then came the turn of the rector's warden, who sat behind them. For services rendered, he was let off lightly. Not so the people's warden, who often felt it his duty to oppose, and even thwart, the rector. When he had been faithfully dealt with, the tenant farmers were made to squirm and tremble in their seats. Woe betide them if they happened to be behind with their tithes! Next in order of attack were the nondescript residents like myself, who afforded plenty of opportunities for sly innuendo or direct animadversion. And finally the rector would upbraid and castigate the shopkeepers, who appeared capable of all manner of wickedness.

So, after a long and trying sermon, we would stagger out of church of a Sunday morning, all of us miserable sinners, but each comforted by the thought that he was not much worse than the others, and that the rector himself, if he only knew it, was not without besetting sins of his own.

VII

'All sorts and conditions of parsons.' How well I re-member the rotund and genial figure of Dr. W. H. Hutton, Dean of Winchester, to whom I was introduced, if I may say so, by Sir Thomas More. Both of us had venerated the

Blessed More, as he then was, not to be sainted—so tardy was the recognition of Holy Church—till 1935. Both were accustomed to stand by his tomb on 6th July, the day of his decollation. Hutton, who had written a full-length life of More, was attracted by the portrait-study that I had made, and soon we were sitting in his library, with Holbein's drawing of More's household reproduced on the wall in front of us, engaged in hero worship. The dean, though a bachelor, perhaps because a bachelor, was an admirable host. It pleased him, as it used to please More, to pack his great house with scholarly and eccentric people. Nor did he mind how shabby and poor they were. It pleased him to fill the hungry—not excluding himself—with good things. His guests, having had the freedom of the deanery conferred upon them, were left to their own devices. They could rummage amongst the tens of thousands of his books. They could explore the city. They could pray for themselves and for their host in his cathedral.

But—it was a rule absolute—they must be punctual for meals. Ravenous, and in boisterous spirits, Hutton would be there before us, mixing his own salad, for the success of which he had composed a special prayer. On a side table, solemn as a bench of bishops, stood the crusted bottles of wine, elevated with his own steady hands from what he called 'the crypt' and specially blessed. And already he would be primed with anecdotes picked up long since in Oxford common rooms and worthy to circulate with any vintage wine. Here are two I recall as I write.

A solicitor, testing half a sovereign between his teeth to make sure that it was good, had the misfortune to swallow the coin. All the resources of science and medicine—stomach pumps and purgatives—were invoked, but only three shillings and fourpence were recovered, *the balance (six shillings and eightpence) remaining as costs.* This, with a beaming smile and a courtly bow, to me; and all I could do was to pass the slander on. 'Had it happened to a learned counsel,' I remarked, 'not a farthing would have been disgorged.'

And there was this favourite from Samuel Rogers. Once upon a time there arose a quarrel between a Frenchman and an Englishman. Honour was aggrieved and honour demanded satisfaction. It was decided that a duel should be

R

fought in a room with the lights out. When the candles had been snuffed and the door secured, the Englishman, seized with sudden qualms of humanity, groped his way to the ingle-nook, and, firing up the chimney, brought down the Frenchman. 'When I tell that story in Paris,' Rogers used to add, 'it is the Englishman who is up the chimney.'

VIII

Another connoisseur of wine and collector of roasted and unroasted chestnuts was the Rev. Henry Tristram Valentine, who, as vicar of St. Paul's Walden, had the honour of baptizing our present queen. No single parish could hold this restless, indefatigable man. He was continually being driven by the Holy Spirit or his own wanderlust to take English and continental chaplaincies, or to engage in missions further afield. What happy days have I shared with him at Welbeck Abbey, at St. Briac in Brittany, at Montana in Switzerland, and how I used to marvel at the 'divine eloquence' of his sermons delivered with never a note!

He, too, was fastidious about food, and would hallow each meal with a different grace in the tongue of the country where he chanced to be. He used to tell of the parson who, before pronouncing the blessing, would give one glance at the table and another at the sideboard. If the prospects were good, he would begin with 'Bountiful Father'; if they were poor he would adopt a milder form of grace: 'For these and for the *least* of all Thy mercies . . .'

Some disgraceful stories he would relate at the expense of those 'in the curatical state.' Once, when I asked if the overworked clergy ever preached borrowed or printed sermons, he replied: 'It must be very rare, for the risks of being found out are enormous. There's a story I can tell you about that. Once upon a time there was a curate who was impossible as a preacher, so much so that his vicar never dared to let him occupy the pulpit. On one occasion, however, having himself to be away on the Sunday, he sent for his curate, took down a volume of sermons from his shelves, selected one almost at random, and instructed him to preach that.

'When the vicar came back on Monday morning he could tell from his wife's face that something dreadful had occurred.

'"Out with it, my dear," he said.

'"Well, Alfred, do you know that Mr. Higgins ſtarted his sermon yeſterday with these words: 'When I was Bishop of London'?"'

On another occasion, when I was telling how the Hitchin poſtmaſter had held up a telegram because, in it, I had quoted, incorreċtly, 'Stand not upon the fashion of your going but go at once': 'You were lucky in your man,' said Valentine; 'often it works juſt the other way. Haven't you ever heard about the telegram that was sent by a clergyman to a bride: "1 John iv. 18" ("There is no fear in love," etc.), which was delivered to her as "John iv. 18" ("He whom thou now haſt is not thy husband")?'

Which excellent ſtory I tried to cap with a telegram sent by an American bookseller in response to an urgent requeſt for copies of Dean Farrar's *Seekers after God* and Manning's *Confidence in God*: 'No Seekers after God in New York, try Philadelphia. Manning's Confidence in God all gone.'

IX

'All sorts and conditions of parsons.' Two others there are whom I would like to mention. Of the firſt—who prefers to remain anonymous—it muſt be ſtated that he is ſtill, very much, in the flesh. A seeker after God, he is also a seeker after the good things of this life, his aim being to lay up treasure on earth as well as treasure in heaven. All his days he has been a diligent colleċtor of things that throw light on English social, domeſtic, and agricultural hiſtory. Firſt he filled his capacious vicarage with precious furniture and china: every room of it, including the attics, the maids' bedchambers, and even the lavatories. And then he built a private museum in the village where he could house the larger exhibits and show them to his friends. When I went to tea with him, he said: 'Hine, which of my two hundred teapots would you like my parlour-maid to bring in?' Was ever any gueſt vouchsafed so wide a choice? Everything you touch, everything you see, will have belonged to some notable family, or possess some singularity of bygone use or design.   Devoted though he is to his flock, and tending the sick with his own hands just as he tends his damaged 'pieces,' yet, whenever duty permits, he is off on his hobby-horse.   A famous collector may have died.   A sale may have been called.   It may be hundreds of miles away.   But the vicar will be there; and the odds are he will come home rejoicing.

Unlike most antiquaries this man is open-handed.   He will lend his exhibits to public museums and privately forget about them.   He delights to fill up the gaps in humble collections.   He is modest, too.   If you ask him to lecture he will wave the very thought aside: 'Oh, no, I can't do that.   But, if you care, I will bring over a few odds and ends and we will just talk about them.'   The car, when he arrives, will be packed with fascinating relics of the past. He will arrange them on the chairman's table.   Then, taking up piece after piece in his all-knowing hands, he will show how each came to be wrought, the point and purpose of it, the part it played in man's domestic life.   By power of imagination, a poet like Keats, holding a potter's vessel in his hands, can out of it rebuild an empire.   Sharp is no poet.   But in homely workmanlike language, such as craftsmen use, he can paint an authentic picture of another age. And each piece, as he handles it, is a piece of England.

Of the many parsons I have known none had such brilliant gifts as Dr. Adrian Fortescue, priest of St. Hugh's at Letchworth.   He was a Doctor of Divinity, of Philosophy, of Literature.   He could not only speak, he could lecture in, eleven languages.   His three volumes on the history of the Orthodox Eastern Church, and his book on the mass were acknowledged classics in his lifetime.   When he needed a hymn-book for St. Hugh's he made his own translations from the Latin and supervised the printing.

When he wrote a letter, even if he wrote a post card, it would be in Italianate script of the fifteenth century, as carefully engrossed as though he were a missal-decorating monk or a Benedictine at work in the scriptorium, perpetuating the chronicles of his religious house.   An authority on church music, vestments, and ceremonial, he would vehemently claim of St. Hugh's: 'It is the only church worth looking at west of Constantinople.'   He

FORTE DUCUM
SCUTUM SALUS

Adrian Fortescue.

From a painting by M. D. Spooner

THOMAS BATES BLOW
From a photograph by L. A. Leigh

liked to expend an infinity of pains over small, but not trivial, things. A profundity of heraldic lore, for example, was compressed into the book-plates he designed; and his drawings of Chartres prove how promising an architect in him was lost.

Having no time to spare, he scoffed at exercise, and when at last the doctors drove him to take daily walks he chose the road to Arlesey Asylum, because nothing on that dull and ugly route could possibly divert his thoughts. On the way out he would read aloud from an Arabic dictionary, and concentrate on a Persian grammar as he quickened his footsteps home.

'The doctors are wrong,' I once teasingly said, 'you'll never die from what they suspect, but from intellectual pride, unless indeed I can effect a cure.' After that, on each quarter-day, and after conferring with men of the subtlest learning, I used, on a post card, to propound some conundrum, riddle, or problem I was confident he could not solve. To shame him in this way might check the 'Fortescue infallibility,' and bring about a decent humility of mind. But it was I who was put to shame. He would answer my post cards by return, and to my amazed vexation he would be right. In the same way, he used to confound those who ventured to rise up at the close of his lectures, and criticize the many provocative things that he had said. One after another they went down like ninepins. After a few withering words from him, there was no more spirit left in them. The meetings would terminate in a hushed and awkward silence with men of inferior minds dying to say something, yet not daring.

This extraordinary man had certain habits that were in keeping. In his study, for example, there were four desks, and he would flit from one to another as the mood took him, writing a separate book on each. The desks were breast high. Like d'Annunzio, he wrote standing, and preferred to read standing, too, except when tossing in bed and quite unable to sleep, when he would drug his mind with the slow poison of cheap and nasty novels, dosing himself to the measure of three a night. 'You're as bad,' I once remarked, 'as my other triple-doctor friend H. B. Swete, who creeps into the Hitchin public library every afternoon for a fresh supply of sevenpenny novels, and when I tax him with it he pretends he is fetching them for the maids.'

'Silly man,' said Adrian, 'he should own up. There's nothing wrong in it. It's dull to sleep with the Fathers, and you can't go to bed with saints. The fact is, one simply has to relax and unbend on something lighter, or else one's brain would burst.'

Feeding, he used to declare, was a disgusting necessity, and men and women should take their meals in seclusion. Nevertheless, if you dined with him, the fare would be choice and well served, nor did Fortescue appear to disdain what he ate. As for the wine, it was poured out lavishly not in wine-glasses, but in tumblers. There was reason in this, for he had a number of toasts to propose, even if he dined *à deux*, and the first would be: 'I give you "Confusion to the Bloody Usurper."' This startled me on the first occasion. I rose and drank obediently and wondered: Who was the 'Bloody Usurper?' Then suddenly — and the wine almost choked me in my throat—I remembered that Fortescue was a Jacobite, and that I was drinking to the confusion of our mild, harmless, and well-beloved sovereign George V. My host rejoiced over my own confusion, and added to it by drinking to the health of the Pretender, or rather the rightful king of England (Prince Rupprecht of Bavaria), and to sundry cardinals and European monarchs who were well disposed to the cause.

. . . . .

Fortescue was a catholic in the wider sense of that word. Though the Holy Spirit had delivered him from a multitude of opinions and established him in the faith, he was tolerant and infinitely curious of the opinions held by other people. In his view, human beings, each and all, were fragments of the divine spirit, members of 'the Great Patriarchal Catholic Church' of which, and here he agreed with Donne, 'every one of us is a little chapel.' In his years of travel in the East Fortescue, disguised as an Arab, had encountered [1] many strange sects and heresies and superstitions. He deemed

---

[1] The word *encountered* is used advisedly, for on one occasion, being attacked by a religious fanatic, Fortescue was driven in self-defence to kill the man. On another occasion, he experienced the joy of set battle in an affray with some Albanian soldiers at Hebron, and shed no small quantity of the blood of all the Fortescues before he galloped away.

it no waſte of time to ſtudy them. And there were many
wise men of the Weſt, outside the pale of his church, with
whom he liked to consort. You might go to St. Hugh's to
talk to an English prieſt, and find a Babel of tongues and a
flock of infidels.

There would he be in the midſt of them, perversely
paradoxical, outrageously unorthodoxical, blasphemous
often, contemptuous always of those in authority ('I went
to Weſtminſter yeſterday but smelt bishops and fled away'),
proud of the immensity of his learning, vainglorious of the
reputation of his family ('I belong to the elder branch that
remained loyal to its king and the faith'), flinging gauntlets
in all directions, challenging all men and all things, laying
down canon law as though it were cannon law, with salvos
fired off *ex cathedra* . . . and then, suddenly, like some
schoolboy caught in the very act of showing off, he would
check the torrent of his invective, fall abjectly silent,
abruptly leave the ſtartled company, and fling himself in
tears of contrition down upon his knees.

Truly this queer creature needed knowing. But, to
those who did know, his eccentricities were only of the
surface, worn bravado, with an air, like the Bavarian cloak
and the conspirator's sombrero with which he used to
muffle his body and conceal his face when he went, alone
with his thoughts, and furtively amongſt men. The real
Fortescue was not there; not in the wind, the earthquake,
the fire of his tempeſtuous, inflammable nature, but in the
ſtill, small voice, hushed as beside an oracle, with which
he prayed for his people, and wreſtled with his own rebellious spirit, in the sanctuary of St. Hugh's.

Again I was wrong, and for once the doctors were right.
In the midſt of life, this amazing scholar, 'daily breeding of
good books,' and with moſt of his work unfinished, was
cruelly called away. It was in Harley Street, on 21ſt
December 1922, that sentence of death was passed by Sir
Charles Gordon Watson. 'Afterwards,' as Adrian wrote
to his cousin, Lady Winifred, 'I walked about the ſtreets,
filled with people doing their Chriſtmas shopping, and all
the time I heard the splash of the ferryman's oars.' For
his little flock at St. Hugh's there was to be the laſt farewell: the sermon on 'Chriſt our Friend and Comforter,' but
who shall comfort the thousands of scholars who lament

for the 'undelivered tidings' that went down into the dust
and ashes of his grave?

.   .   .   .   .

I wish I could have spent more of my time with men of
religion, for it behoves lawyers, as clerks in un-holy orders,
to learn a more excellent way from the clerks in Holy
Orders—men dear to God and beloved of their fellows,
whose lives are a living sermon, a running commentary on
the statutes of God. 'Volumes,' said Herbert Spencer with
his habitual sneer, 'might be written on the impiety of the
pious.' But though in this holy calling there are bound to
be castaways, some of whom I have known by disrepute,
the vast majority have practised what they preached, and
have 'allured to brighter worlds and led the way.' Let us
thank God for those ordained ministers of His 'who serve
unto the example and shadow of heavenly things.' Let us
'remember them that had the rule over you, which spake
unto you the word of God; and considering the manner of
their life, imitate their faith.'

TOUCHING UPON RELIGION

I am neither Protestant nor Catholic, but I should be very glad to call myself a Christian.

L'Amiral Réveillère.

Religion is like the fashion. One man wears his doublet slashed, another laced, another plain; but every man has a doublet. So every man has his religion. We differ about trimming.

John Selden.

I believe in God. I refuse the services of all the churches. I beg a prayer from every soul.

Victor Hugo.

I

OMETIMES I wonder if those words of lawyer Selden can hold good to-day. In the seventeenth century everybody wore a doublet, and by the Act of Uniformity everybody was compelled to practise the State religion. Nowadays we wear what we please, and we worship or not as we please.

But it is, most of all, when I look round upon my own profession that I begin to doubt. By common repute we lawyers are an irreligious race. Once, indeed, I heard a client declare that we deserved to be 'exiled from the eternal providence.' And the reasons are manifest. In the first place our spiritual and moral sensibilities are apt to grow blunt under the wear and tear of daily practice. Day in and day out—making the worse appear the better reason—we are defending men and women who have been breaking every letter of the Decalogue. They that be whole need not a physician; those that are saints consult no solicitor. Virtue, we know, 'lives up three flights of stairs,' but we do not look for affluent clients there.

Then, too, we are by our training circumspect and critical. We expect proof positive in matters of faith where no such proof can be. We demand chapter and verse, section and subsection. When we are asked to subscribe to man-made creeds we are apt to mutter with Browning: 'And yet, God has not said a word.' It is of no avail to cite Pascal's *obiter dictum*: 'The heart has its reasons which Reason knows not,' for if we possessed a heart, which is commonly denied, we would not allow it to sway our judgment or supplant the laws of evidence. It is useless to quote Erasmus: 'You would see Him less if you saw Him with your very eyes.' Like doubting Thomas we refuse to believe unless we see 'the print of the nails.'

Religion, as they say in the East, is what a man does with his solitariness. And there again we are at a loss, for we have no solitude. The law leaves no vacant hours for contemplation. We go home burdened and bewildered with the problems of the day, and there are papers in our portfolio for the morrow. 'I am generally so dead beat by the time I kneel down to pray,' said Henry Hawkins, 'that I begin out of habit: "Gentlemen of the jury."' When my own words took to returning unto me void, I made a manuscript collection of prayers from other sources and found it easier to concentrate on them. The trouble is that fatigue induces flippancy, and many a lawyer has incurred a bad name for laxity of living because of his levity of speaking. When tiresome people, not trusting to the word of a solicitor, require me to vow by my patron saints, 'Very well, then,' I rejoin, 'I swear by Ethelred the Unready and Ferdinand the Forgetful.' When a well-meaning but ill-timed curate paid a pastoral call on me just as I reached home after an exhausting market-day, I rang the bell for the maid. 'Elizabeth,' I said, 'this gentleman is inquiring about my soul. Have you possibly seen it lying about anywhere? If you can find it in my bedroom or more likely in my study, do bring it in.' Thereupon, the curate took the hint and departed.

II

However lukewarm in the faith, lawyers will generally be supporters of the church as by law established. Some may hold, with Döllinger, that 'it is a collection of heterogeneous theological propositions tied together by the Act of Uniformity.' Others know better; they have worshipped from within, and, as Cardinal Wiseman once observed: 'A Church is like a painted window; you cannot see it till you get inside.' Those who do not get inside nevertheless maintain a respectful attitude from without. They remind one of the man Johnson speaks of who, though not accustomed to enter a church, would never pass the door without pulling off his hat. Moreover, they like others to conform if they themselves go free. If the world is to be orderly and law-abiding, it is good for people to belong to a church. 'To be of no church,' said Dr. Johnson in words that were copied out for me by my master in the first week of my articles, 'to be of no church is dangerous. Religion, of which the rewards are distant, and which is animated by faith and hope, will glide by degrees out of mind unless it be invigorated and reimpressed by external ordinances, by stated calls to worship, and the salutary influence of example.'

Nor is it likely, if a lawyer attach himself to a church, that he will become a pillar. It was not without due cause that lawyers were classed with Pharisees in Holy Writ. They do not support a church. They prefer to be supported by it—to enjoy by the formal connection a certain respectability of status. Clearly we are not a race of devotees. Our motto, if we had one, would consist of the words so often inscribed on eighteenth-century bells: 'No enthusiasm, and Prosperity to the Church of England.' Not of such stuff is the breed of martyrs made. Search Foxe's *Book of Martyrs* (1563), it will puzzle you to light upon a lawyer; and should ever the writ *de haeretico comburendo* be revived in this land I doubt if a single hair of a single solicitor's head would be so much as singed.

Though lawyers, by the logic of their training, are men of little faith, yet are they great on 'works.' That is why Psalm cxix is commonly known as the lawyers' psalm, for its exquisite refrains are but variations on an original theme, the ringing of changes, as it were, on words beloved of the profession: 'statutes,' 'commandments,' 'laws,' 'testimonies'—on things that by God's holy ordinance should be observed and performed.[1] Talk with any common attorney and you will find that in matters of religion he is a pragmatist. He wants to see how it works out in the daily

---

[1] This was the psalm sung by the patriot Lord William Russell as he went to his execution in Lincoln's Inn Fields on 21st July 1683, 'but,' he said to Dr. Burnett, 'I shall sing it better soon.'

lives of his clients. In theological niceties, in matters of doctrine, he is indifferent. He will split hairs on juridical points, for always there is a solid substratum of fact, something to go upon. But he will not split hairs or speculate *in vacuo*, or wrestle with spiritual problems outside the jurisdiction. Nor, seeing that life is more important than its cause, can he understand why Christians, instead of dwelling together in unity, should constantly have been at one another's throats, engaged for a thousand years in 'holy, disputatious strife':

> They fight like devils for conciliation
> And hate each other for the love of God.

Surely the answer to all that is to be found in the words of Baxter: 'Whilst we wrangle here in the dark, we are dying and passing to the world that will decide all controversies; the safest passage thither is peaceable holiness.' Lawyers have quite enough dissension in their own professional lives. They dislike the thought of it elsewhere, and will usually be found taking a safe and middle course, avoiding those extremes that lead to trouble. Their attitude to religion has been perfectly expressed by Mabillon: 'Il n'y a que deux ennemis de la religion—le trop peu et le trop; et des deux le trop est mille fois le plus dangereux.' A little religion can go a long way, longer still if it be of a practical nature, and not above the flight of common souls. One of Mandell Creighton's children, when asked what was going to be done about the offer of the bishopric of Peterborough, then (1891) under family consideration, replied: 'Father is still praying, but mother is packing our boxes.' I am afraid that ninety-nine lawyers out of a hundred would approve the action of the mother.

III

Sometimes I envy the simple, working faith that an old friend and client of mine compounded from many religious societies. By birth an Anglican, by 'convincement' a Quaker, his travelling life and residence abroad enabled him in later years to make a study of comparative religion. He had friends in every communion. He had a bowing, if not a kneeling, acquaintance with Buddhism, Mohammedanism,

Shintoism, Catholicism, and a dozen other isms. And for his own practical, pragmatical purpose he had reduced all their teachings to a code of conduct. 'I welcome anything,' he set down in his *Maxims of T. B. Blow* (see portrait facing p. 241), 'that will make people (1) more honest and truthful; (2) better inclined to their brethren; (3) actively inclined towards peace in the world; (4) intent on following the advice of James in his General Epistle at chapter i. 27.[1] This is all that is needed. No dogmas or priestcraft, which have led to strife and persecution throughout the ages. Let every one be his own priest, which the inner light that is in every one will enable him to be.'

Like most of the brethren I have never had enough sanctified common sense to formulate such maxims for myself. Rather, I have fumbled my way through the labyrinths of doubt and the thickets of argument, and staggered forward one footstep at a time. In such circumstances, to make a confession of faith would seem venturesome if not impertinent. If extraordinary men are but ordinary to God, what presumption it would be in little folk to speak confidently of those things into which the angels desire to look! I have been gently reproved for my moth-like flittings to and fro after the scattered lights of truth, but seeing that all our thoughts are but degrees of darkness, we ought to be glad of any illumination that is shed upon our path. Sometimes we are blinded by the glaring and irreligious light of modern thought, sometimes led astray by a will-o'-the-wisp. But the candles of knowledge, and the rushlights of those who have gone before us, often serve as lamps unto our feet, and as guides for us who follow. Happiest are those who place their trust in God, for, as you may read in the book of Daniel, ii. 22, 'He giveth wisdom and revealeth secrets. He knoweth what is in the dark.' Not to the proud in spirit, but to the lowly in heart and to desperate seekers are such revelations likely to be made:

> He is unknown to those who think they know
> And known to whoso know they know Him not.

To me it seems wiser to abide in a state of hopeful doubt

[1] 'Pure religion and undefiled before God and the Father is this, To visit the fatherless and widows in their affliction, and to keep himself unspotted from the world.'

than to be too sure of things. Somehow we have to make the best of this evil world, 'in the midst whereof,' as Milton said, 'God hath placed us unavoidably.' It is inevitable that we should be confused in such a universe, but that is no reason to despair of it. Though there is a black doubt that corrodes the heart, there is a white doubt that gives the benefit of the doubt, remembering as it does that there is not a hope that was not once a forlorn hope.

At one time I was ready to subscribe to creeds because they had been framed, or assented to, by some of the finest spirits who ever walked the earth. That was enough for me. If men of profound learning and piety were in error I was still content to be of their company. Then doubts and misgivings emerged. Reason—that most unrestful mistress —asserted herself. Like many a parish priest I was obliged to make mental reservations in reading the Thirty-nine Articles. In reciting the Apostles' Creed first one, then another clause had to be omitted. The disturbing thought assailed me: 'Am I not holding a second-hand religion? What in my own heart of hearts do I believe?'

IV

It is humiliating to discover how little that is genuine has gone to the making of our so-called religious convictions. Most of them we inherit. Not a few are imposed. 'Some priests make you believe, but they stupefy you.' We have been spoon-fed with sermons when we should have been feeding ourselves with 'the true bread of heaven.' To have a religion, even a little one, is essential. We cannot go through this world denying all things, believing nothing. Man is not merely a creature 'after the flesh.' He is a spirit, and 'the spirit is given to every man to profit withal.'

First of all, I endeavoured to profit by erecting a body of simple belief—my own secret, and no concern of my readers —upon the vague longing that had been my only private experience of religion. 'God,' said the old German mystic, 'is an unutterable sigh in the human heart.' But no bridge of sighs will span the River Jordan or lead a man from this world to the next. For life's common road and to climb the Hill Difficulty we need something to lay hold upon, a staff on which to lean.

Again I profited by a deepened fellowship with all who were engaged in working out their own salvation. It has been said that you muﬅ be very religious to change your religion. But in this twentieth century you muﬅ be quite religious to hold a religion at all. So many doubts and fears, so many solicitations and temptations from Vanity Fair, beset the ﬅrait and narrow path. Nor does the modern pilgrim meet with as many Shining Ones and Kindly Shepherds as did Bunyan when he walked through the wilderness of this world. For our chaﬅening it is well to ponder Tawney's words: 'Chriﬅians are a seﬄ, and a small seﬄ, in a Pagan society.'

Faithful and few, latter-day Chriﬅians should be the more proud and heedful of their profession. Members of a church militant in the midﬅ of a hoﬅile world, they muﬅ be worthy of it, and in the face of growing infidelity there has in my time been a remarkable closing of the ranks. True, men ﬅill serve under their separate regiments and in church-coats or uniforms of many colours, Catholics, Anglicans, Baptiﬅs, Congregationaliﬅs, Methodiﬅs, Quakers, and the like, but it cannot be long before they will be knit together, one and indivisible, a united army of Chriﬅ.

By this time, we have come to see that all religions are true to those who truly hold them, and we regard as axiomatic those once intrepid words of William Penn: 'It were better to be of no church than to be bitter for any.' Walking one day at Oxford in the garden of a friend, Dr. Johnson observed him throw the snails over the wall, whereupon he reproved him sharply, saying it was ungentlemanly. The friend answered: 'Well, but, doﬄor, my neighbour is a Dissenter,' whereupon the lexicographer growled out: 'Oh, throw away then and as faﬅ as you like.'

To us such behaviour would be inconceivable. But I sometimes wonder: Have we improved of late in Chriﬅian charity, or have we given up throwing snails at Dissenters because they no longer dissent? Possibly, in avoiding spiritual provincialism, we are in some danger of becoming lazily latitudinarian. Do we hold our views earneﬅly enough to care? Often I grow uneasy when I examine my own motives. The disinclination to attach myself to any church, for example, does it spring, unalloyed, from the desire to love all my neighbours as myself and to worship with them in whatever church they chance to be? Or do I indulge my claustrophobia, my dread of being shut up in one narrow sect, because I like my liberty, and shrink from the obligations of church membership? The sermons I like best—and I am ashamed to own it—are those that steal into my ears through the open door of a church as I sit in the porch of a Sunday morning in the summer, free at any moment to tiptoe out and away.

v

However wavering a man may be in faith, he should know his mind concerning 'works.' There he stands on firmer ground. It is a pity that in Holy Writ there is such reiterated disparagement of works. By them, and more especially by 'the works of the law,' shall no man be justified. One flies for comfort to James, that most human and practical of the servants of the Lord, who in his General Epistle asks: 'What doth it profit, my brethren, though a man say he hath faith, and have not works? can faith save him?' And again: 'Faith, if it hath not works, is dead.'

Whilst theologians dispute with one another over doctrine and with the scientists over the riddle of the universe, here is something the little man can do; something that lies ready and urgent to his hands. It is prodigious the amount of good that one humble human being can accomplish in the course of an active lifetime, taking every opportunity that offers. In so doing he may justify his existence even if he cannot save his soul. In this book I have gone so far as to claim that solicitors also can exert a powerful influence for good, and are, many of them, 'manifest in good works.' At one time their attitude was negative. The noblesse they possessed only obliged them to refrain from malpractices that 'abuse and make vile the worthy name of a lawyer.' But in these days you will find thousands of them doing God's work in manifold ways and teaching men His statutes.

It is a pity that there is something heavy and sad about that word 'work.' Work done for self is wearisome. 'Man goeth forth to his work and to his labour until the evening.' It is the curse laid upon the sons of Adam. But work done for others should bring joy and satisfaction. It is the blessing conferred upon the sons of God. So long as our religion makes us happy, there is not much amiss with it: 'Thy law is my delight: thy statutes have been my songs in the house of my pilgrimage.' And again, in the American version of Psalm xxxiv. 5: 'They looked on Him and were radiant, and their faces were not ashamed.' At one time we suffered much in England from a peevish form of religion, from fanatics with cold, grey faces. It should have taught us 'to serve the Lord with gladness,' and to bring to that service each member of the lesser Trinity: our Heart, our Lord and Counsellor the Mind, and Brother Ass the Body. To the Puritans, man had but a soul to be saved. His mind, 'hardened in pride,' and 'vainly puffed up,' was not worth praying for. His body was not the Temple of the Holy Ghost, it was altogether vile.

Without wishing 'to glory after the flesh,' I feel that much harm has been done by this constant upbraiding and denigration of the body, with the emphasis always on its lusts and its desires. As a double ass, in the Law and in the Body, I feel constrained to bray out against the slanders and libels that we suffer. Why must the saints always be complaining of 'their body's hindrance'? Is there no spark of divinity or decency, no *scintilla aeternitatis* about the creature? Is it really true that the eyes are 'full of adultery,' the mouth defiled with 'corrupt communications,' the tongue 'deceitful,' the hands 'unclean,' the feet 'swift in running into mischief'? For my own part, whenever I hear a parson droning through the Pauline indictment of the works of the flesh, 'which are these: Adultery, fornication, uncleanness, lasciviousness, idolatry, witchcraft, hatred, variance, emulations, wrath, strife, seditions, heresies, envyings, murders, drunkenness, revellings, and such like,' I correct the false impression in my own mind by the recital of St. Augustine's catalogue of earthly blessings: 'The comeliness of the body, the fair harmony of time, the brightness of the light, sweet melodies of every kind, perfumes of flowers, ointments and spices, manna and honey, and the delectableness of lovely limbs.'

If we are to be happy in the religious life, why then, let the body make his contribution in perfect if not equal partnership. To my thinking he is the only cheerful companion of the three. Too often the mind, 'sicklied o'er with

s

the pale caſt of thought,' fades out at forty, whilſt the soul, that 'poor querulous handful,' separated from the divine harmony, and reſtive behind the body's prison-bars, becomes daily more preoccupied and pensive. In the matter of faith, I agree, the body is earth-bound and likely to be affeꞔted by every wind that blows. When the wind is in the eaſt I have no religion at all. But in the matter of works the body is in his element. He loves to be helpful and handy, to be up and doing, 'pouring Heaven into this poor House of Life.' He has more pity for humankind because he is closer to it. The mind will compose an elegant threnody upon the misery of mortal man and wallow in sentiment: 'When Prometheus created man, he had already used up all the water in fashioning the other animals, so he mingled his clay with tears.' The body forgets his own tears—hot and scalding though they be—in drying the tears of others. In this he would humbly imitate his Maker: 'The Lord is gracious and full of compassion; slow to anger and of great mercy. . . . And his tender mercies are over all his works.' Leaving it to the mind to balance Albertus Magnus's thirty-six arguments for, and the thirty arguments againſt, the hiſtoric Chriſt, the body, reaching out his hands, lays hold of the living Chriſt. Not by any subtlety of speculation, but by the reiterated proof of happy human experience can he teſtify to the truth of Archbishop Benson's words: 'Chriſt is a present Chriſt, and all of us are His contemporaries.'

VI

As God, on the seventh day, reſted from His labours, so it behoves men and women to come apart and reſt awhile from theirs. Those who never cease from good works are apt to become busybodies. And besides, virtue goes out of those who expend themselves for others. One needs to put in for repairs. Body and mind grow weary in well-doing. The gladness goes out of it. Hazlitt was miſtaken in declaring that 'cheerfulness is an eſtate for life,' it is a tenancy determinable on displeasure. With regard to the soul, men hold varying opinions. 'The veſture of the spirit,' says one, 'is not, like our body's garments, muddied with the lees of time.' It should not be difficult, urged the poet Waller, 'to keep the palace of the soul serene.' I wish I thought it true. To me it is the saddest thing about us that this bright spirit, with which we are lit as by lanterns from within, can suffer dimness.

Therein lies the value of the contemplative life. Whilst Brother Ass the Body sleeps out of sheer exhaustion and has his most asinine and bottomless dreams; whilst the mind re-collects itself in tranquillity and prepares for new sorties in the dark (*dans les champs de l'observation le hasard ne favorise que les esprits préparés*) the soul, retiring into her own cell, refills and re-trims her lamp. If she is to shed abroad 'the light of the knowledge of the glory of God' she must go back to the source of all light: 'They looked unto Him and were lightened.' It is written, no man shall see God and live. But there are pale reflections of His presence in Holy Writ. Men draw near to Him in their prayers. They touch the hem of His garment as they assemble and meet together for worship.

There is no more pitiful verse in Scripture than that of Job's 'Oh that I knew where I might find Him!' Yet Job did find Him, with other things 'too wonderful,' in the end. So do all those who seek with heart and soul. To me it is fascinating to watch men in their several ways searching diligently after wisdom and seeking 'a better country, that is an heavenly.' Often as I go a roundabout way to work, I pass the not-as-yet opened shop of a picture-framing client, and through the window I see him sitting at his bench, his hands folded, his eyes closed, framing the thought of the Almighty in his mind, and hallowing the work of the day. When that shop is opened the man's face is *radiant*. In 1920 I spent a year of Saturdays poring over the Hertfordshire Quarter Session Rolls in the county library. Much to the surprise of the education committee in particular and of the ratepayers in general, the librarian, shortly after his appointment, was discovered to be a Mohammedan, but in his outward profession he put us Christians to shame. At the inward call to prayer he would abruptly break off any interview, spread his mat on the floor, and cry aloud upon Allah. It was disturbing, but we who prayed, if at all, in secret could not but admire his unconcern and his unflinching testimony.

There is no golden rule. Each man, in repairing the

world's damage, must use the tools that lie to his hand. My own preference, as an antiquary, is for such as are well worn and tried. Ten times, for the good of my soul, have I read the Bible from cover to cover in the versions of Wycliffe, Tyndale, Coverdale, the Authorized Version of 1611, and the Revised Version of 1884. Once I attempted to read the modern version by Moffatt, but was sick before I finished Genesis. Eight times have I read the Apocrypha and the apocryphal books of the New Testament. Compelled by my English master to gain the acquaintance of the 'secretaries of the Holy Ghost,' as Donne called the Minor Prophets, I began to take a major delight in them. What was imposed on me for the improvement of my style came to be printed in characters of gold upon my heart.

Read the Bible a hundred times, yet would its magic never fail, its power cease to grip. But in set prayers I find it otherwise. Too often, like the heathen, I am engaged in vain repetitions. The finest collects become mechanical and dead; 'my spirit prayeth,' as St. Paul observed, 'but my understanding is unfruitful.' The kneeling position may be to blame; it induces torpidity both of body and of mind. Surely those early Christians were better advised who prayed standing, their eyes uplifted, their faculties alert.[1] In this predicament I am driven to all manner of devices. When, mumbling over the Lord's Prayer, I begin to fall asleep, I know that it is time to be using St. Francis's paraphrase instead; the sheer loveliness of it excites even a tired brain into a wakeful response. When Cranmer's collects die out of my attention in a soft, sweet music, I do as he did and go back to the sacramentaries of Leo the Great, Gelasius the First, and Gregory the Great. Much that is best in them can be found in Bright's *Ancient Collects* (1861), or in *The Catholic's Vade Mecum*. If I want more, I resort to the *Manual of Private Devotions* (1648) of that

---

[1] Perhaps the standing position is too alert. Edward Lyttelton, headmaster of Eton, was in the habit of saying his prayers standing and leaning on a stick. 'I left him one evening,' said one of the family, 'immersed in his prayers. When I came back, he was making cricketing strokes, driving and defensive, using his stick as a bat. After a minute or so he was again plunged in his devotions. When asked afterwards: "Were you batting?" "That may be," came the reply, accompanied with a whimsical smile.' Lyttelton had been a famous cricketer and a former captain of the Eton and the Cambridge elevens, and once, when playing for Middlesex, he had whacked Spofforth for a hundred runs, and had received the stick from the amazed but admiring demon Australian bowler as a tribute of lasting esteem.

great doctor of the Anglican Church Lancelot Andrewes
('the very dust of whose writings is gold'), or open my
mother's copy of the *Imitation*.

The main advantage of using other persons' prayers is
that they prevent us from pestering the Almighty with our
own selfish ambitions and desires. 'Twere better not to
pray at all than to use such a prayer—incredible yet on
record—as was uttered by John Ward, M.P., in 1727: 'O
Lord, Thou knowest that I have nine houses in the city of
London, and that I have lately purchased an estate in fee
simple in Essex. I beseech Thee to preserve the two
counties of Middlesex and Essex from fires and earthquakes.
And, as I have also a mortgage in Hertfordshire, I beg Thee
also to have an eye of compassion on that county, and for
the rest of the counties Thou mayest deal with them as
Thou art pleased. O Lord, enable the Banks to answer all
their bills, and make all debtors good men. Give prosperous
voyage and safe return to the Mermaid sloop because I
have not insured it.

'And because Thou hast said: "The days of the wicked
are but short," I trust Thee that Thou will not forget Thy
promise, as I have an estate in reversion on the death of the
profligate young man, Sir J. L. . . .

'Keep my friends from sinking, preserve me from thieves
and housebreakers, and make all my servants so honest and
faithful that they may always attend to my interests, and
never cheat me out of my property night or day.'

VII

'If thou canst not continually recollect thyself,' says
Thomas à Kempis, 'yet do it sometimes, at least once a day,
namely in the morning or at night. . . . In the morning
fix thy good purpose.' It is helpful, I find as a professional
man, not to plunge headlong into one's morning post,
wrestling impatiently with its problems, with offences that
needs must come. The day's work will be faced the better
if one has sanctified it first. My own habit—before entering
my office—is to climb on to the Windmill Hill at Hitchin,
for, peradventure, 'from the hills I may behold Him,' or,
as I like better, to walk round about the walls of St. Mary's

and let some of their immensity and immutability pacify, purify, and fortify my heart.

Often, as need arises, I rush out of the office and flee to the church as to sanctuary. Nothing can hurt one there. The soul, oppressed with weightier matters of the law, and at times suffering violence from wicked men, can here recover and spread and preen her wings. To sit as quietly as any Quaker in an English parish church, not in dead silence, but in a living silence, can anything be more restoring to a ruffled spirit? I had almost said in an 'empty' church. For, as I endeavoured to show in my history of St. Mary's, 'it is when a church is empty that it is most thronged with blessed spirits. Were we but more attuned to the soul of time, we might interpret what Ruskin held to be the chief glory of a church: "That deep sense of voicefulness, of stern watching, of mysterious sympathy, nay even of approval or condemnation, which we feel in walls that have long been washed by the passing waves of humanity." It is to catch this still small voice that men come as of old into this haunt of peace. In the midst of the great congregation they seem to hear it, soaring above the descant of the choir, echoing behind the supplication of the priest. Others it will visit as they sit alone in this house of prayer, of those best prayers that men say without knowing that they say them, the elevations and amplitudes of mind which accord with the spirit of the place.

'On the night when the ringers practise, there are a few who love to sit in the darkness of the nave, whilst the bells are shedding their coloured music, "with a mellow brightness, a rosy glow of sound"; who love also to linger there when the ringers have departed, when

> Silence comes welling back along the nave
> And empty space again grows cool and grave,
> Washed of the colour of those mingled noises.

There is one—I who write am he—who has even ventured to keep an all-night vigil in the church, an experience not to be lightly undertaken. In the midnight hour,

> God's knocking time; the soul's dumb watch,
> When spirits their fair kindred catch,

one might expect the graves to open, the mysteries to be unsealed. But the voices recede at one's approach. However

ST. MARY'S, HITCHIN, FROM THE SOUTH-EAST
From a drawing by J. C. Buckler

MINSDEN CHAPEL

From a drawing by J. C. Buckler (1822)

softly one may tread, each footfall thunders along the walls and resounds amongst the sepulchres. There is a fluttering in the air as of shy things slipping back into their places. In a moment there is a quiet more intense than the quiet one had interrupted. One is filled with a sense of shame, as though one had disturbed the communion of the blessed dead, as though the doors of the invisible world had been shut in one's face.

'One goes outside to recover in the cool night air. Overhead, the stars that know all things shine on unconcerned. From the gargoyles of the church the demons mock and leer. At times they seem to start to life, to hover like vultures in suspended flight waiting for their prey. How peaceful the town is at this midnight hour! Each living citizen asleep in his little house, whilst in the House of God the dead, as we miscall them, are wide awake. Here at noonday, in the heart of this busy town, you might conceive the church as the work of the hands of men. It has been "entrusted with their fame and hallowed by their deeds. Its walls have been witnesses of their suffering"; its pillars stand upon their congregated dust. But at the day's end, when the toys of earth's children are laid aside and the darkness falls upon their striving, it is marvellous to see how the little houses nestle closer to the Great House and seem to sleep in its shadow. As one looks upon them so, the thought—nay the certainty—steals upon the mind that this town in the beginning was not so much the creator as the offspring of the church, and in spite of all its years still loves to cling to her side and be gathered to her arms, the arms of the Blessed Virgin Mary, which once enfolded the Son of God, and which now, in her infinite compassion, are extended to all the sons of men.'

VIII

It was with such words, written in the Trinity Chapel on All Hallows Eve 1924, that I brought to an end my history of St. Mary's. And now, nineteen years later, on another All Hallows Eve, and in a sanctuary more sequestered— that of the ruined church of St. Nicholas of Minsden—I am finishing this book.

Is there any other attorney I wonder who has a fourteenth-century church belonging to him? There I do claim to be uncommon. True, it is only for the term of my natural life, by lease from the vicars of Hitchin, but as I intend that my body or my ashes shall be laid to rest in the chancel I have more than a tenant's quiet enjoyment, I have enlarged my title and usurped a freeholder's pride of ownership. It was that which led me in my account of Minsden (*History of Hitchin*, vol. ii, pp. 23–43) to bid 'trespassers and sacrilegious persons take warning, for I will proceed against them with the utmost rigour of the law, and, after my death and burial, I will endeavour, in all ghostly ways, to protect and haunt its hallowed walls.'

By my landlords I am not likely to be disturbed. As far back as 1690 the fabric was reported to the archdeacon as 'totally ruinated, stripped, uncovered, decayed, and dimolished.' That was a gross exaggeration. No longer did the bells ring for matins or evensong but, as the church itself fell asunder, people chose more and more to be joined together there in holy matrimony. Many a bashful couple of the humbler sort, and many a shy widow, were glad of this secluded churchlet hidden in the wood, where the chief witnesses and the sole choristers were the ringdoves crooning in those elms whose boughs could be seen swaying to and fro through the yawning holes in the roof. It was not until 1738 that the Bishop of Lincoln refused to sanction any further marriages. It was certainly time for him to intervene. At the last marriage of all—that between Enoch West and Mary Horn on 11th July that year—a piece of masonry fell and dashed the service book out of the curate's hand.

For many a year now, Minsden has been left in peace. Falling amongst thieves, stripped of its raiment, lying by the wayside half-dead—St. Mary's wardens, those proud Levites, passing by on the other side—failing some good Samaritan, there is nothing for Minsden Chapel but to die. Here, as with the neighbouring church of Chesfield, which was abandoned by order of the Church in 1750, the ravages of time have almost completed the destruction. The whole is overgrown with ivy, giving it a picturesque and wild effect. Enshrouding the remains is a dense mass of dishevelled undergrowth, and encompassing that again, as it were an outer coffin, is a belt of time-worn and decaying elms. There is about it all a strangely wistful air of desolation.

No longer is Minsden the pilgrimage of churchmen, though twice in my time, and with my illegally given consent, mass has been said by priests of the old faith within its chancel. Minsden is for those, rather, whose minds are in ruins; for those sons of quietness who are distracted by the crimes and follies and misfortunes of mankind. In its deep shade, many who have been brought low by the cares of this world, or in my case by the wear and tear of my profession, have found healing, consolation, and repose. They have been one with the twilight's dream:

> For here the ancient Mother lingers
> To dip her hands in the diamond dew,
> And lave thine ache with cloud-cool fingers
> Till sorrow die from you.

It is not only that

> No noise is here, or none that hinders thought;

the very air at Minsden is tremulous with that faint *susurrus* —call it the undersong of earth, the music of the spheres, the sigh of departed time, or what you will—which only the more finely attuned spirits overhear:

> Stillness accompanied with sound so soft
> Charms more than silence. Meditation here
> May think down hours to moments.

For those who have ears to hear, how peaceful and assuaging it is to listen to the ruinated windows and the riddled walls as they

> murmur to the breeze's call
> The night wind's lovely vesper hymn;

and often I think that when the last night comes, when blows 'the wind of Death's imperishable wing,' when man, touched on the shoulder by his last, best friend, must go the way of all the earth and fare alone into the silent land, how much more soothing and befitting it would be to spend the last hours here; no drawing of sick-chamber curtains against the sundown splendid and serene, but keeping vigil, grave and sweet, whilst

> the cowled night
> Kneels on the eastern sanctuary stair.

If ever the silent messenger could appear amiable and lovely, it would be in such a place as this. For to sink down into this cool quietness of trees, to be softly surrounded with gleaming fantasies of foliage, to dream the last dreams in this haunt of wild flowers, bright-hearted birds, and those sweet-minded things which live where silence is, this would be not to die but to pass deliciously from peace to peace.

Finished in the Church of St. Nicholas at Minsden on All Hallows Eve, 1943.

THE LOST BELLS OF MINSDEN

THE AUTHOR'S PUBLICATIONS

1912. *Anima Celtica.* Elkin Mathews. Out of print.

1913. *Dreams and the Way of Dreams.* J. M. Dent & Sons. Out of print.

1920. *The Cream of Curiosity:* being an account of certain historical and literary MSS. of the XVIth, XVIIth, and XVIIIth centuries collected by Reginald L. Hine. Routledge. Out of print.

1927–9. *The History of Hitchin.* 2 vols. George Allen & Unwin. Vol. I out of print.

1928. *Samuel Lucas: his Life and Art-work.* Walker's Galleries, 118 New Bond Street. Out of print.

1929. *A Mirror for the Society of Friends:* being the story of the Hitchin Quakers. Introduction by Edward Grubb. George Allen & Unwin. Second edition, revised, 1930.

1930. *A Short History of St. Mary's, Hitchin.* Paternoster & Hales, Hitchin. Fourth edition, 1945.

1931. *History of Hitchin Grammar School.* Paternoster & Hales, Hitchin.

1932. *The Official Guide to Hitchin.* Out of print.

1932. *Hitchin Worthies.* George Allen & Unwin.

1934. *The Natural History of the Hitchin Region.* William Carling & Co., Hitchin.

1937. *The Story of the Sun Inn, Hitchin.* William Carling & Co., Hitchin.

1938. *The Story of Hitchin Town,* with twenty-six drawings by Gerard Ceunis. William Carling & Co. Second edition, 1939.

INDEX

Shadows we are and
Like shadows depart